Education, Culture and Values

Volume V

The six volumes that comprise the *Education, Culture and Values* series bring together contributions from experts around the world to form, for the first time, a comprehensive treatment of the current concern with values in education. The series seeks to address this concern in the context of cultural and values diversity.

The first three volumes provide a wide-ranging consideration of the diversity of values in education at all levels, and thus represent a framework for the second three volumes which focus more specifically on values education (moral, religious, spiritual and political) *per se*. The six volumes, therefore, bring the fundamental domain of values together with the important issue of pluralism to generate new, fruitful and progressive reflection and exemplars of good practice.

The series will be of huge benefit and interest to educators, policy makers, parents, academics, researchers and student teachers. The six volumes contain:

- diverse and challenging opinions about current educational concerns and reforms in values education
- chapters from more than 120 contributors of international repute from 23 different countries
- conceptual clarification and theoretical analysis
- empirical studies, reports of practical projects and guidance for good practice.

Volumes I–III: Values Diversity in Education

Volume I – Systems of Education: Theories, Policies and Implicit Values is concerned with the theoretical and conceptual framework for reflecting about values, culture and education and thus provides an introduction to the series as a whole. It is concerned with state and policy level analysis across the world.

Volume II – Institutional Issues: Pupils, Schools and Teacher Education considers values and culture at the institutional level. What constitutes a good 'whole school' approach in a particular area? There are discussions of key issues and reports of whole-school initiatives from around the world. Several chapters focus on the vital issue of teacher education.

Volume III – Classroom Issues: Practice, Pedagogy and Curriculum focuses on the classroom: pedagogy, curriculum and pupil experience. Areas of curriculum development include the relatively neglected domains of mathematics and technology, as well as the more familiar literature and drama. There is a useful section on aesthetic education.

Volumes IV–VI: Values Education in Diversity

Volume IV – Moral Education and Pluralism is focused on moral education and development in the context of cultural pluralism. There are highly theoretical discussions of difficult philosophical issues about moral relativism as well as practical ideas about good practice.

Volume V – Spiritual and Religious Education distinguishes religious and spiritual education and takes a multifaith approach to pedagogic, curricular and resource issues. The important issue of collective worship is also addressed.

Volume VI – Politics, Education and Citizenship is concerned with political education and citizenship. Again chapters from several countries lend an international perspective to currently influential concerns and developments, including democratic education, human rights, national identity and education for citizenship.

Education, Culture and Values

Volume V

Spiritual and Religious Education

Edited by
Mal Leicester, Celia Modgil
and Sohan Modgil

London and New York

First published 2000 by Falmer Press
11 New Fetter Lane, London EC4P 4EE

Simultaneously published in the USA and Canada
by Falmer Press, 19 Union Square West, New York, NY 10003

Falmer Press is an imprint of the Taylor & Francis Group

Typeset in Galliard by RefineCatch Limited, Bungay, Suffolk
Printed and bound in Great Britain by
TJ International Ltd, Padstow, Cornwall

British Library Cataloguing in Publication Data
A catalogue record for this book is available from the British
Library

Library of Congress Cataloging in Publication Data
A catalog record for this book has been requested

ISBN 0–7507–1018–7 (6-volume set)
        0–7507–1002–0 (volume I)
        0–7507–1003–9 (volume II)
        0–7507–1004–7 (volume III)
        0–7507–1005–5 (volume IV)
        0–7507–1006–3 (volume V) ✓
        0–7507–1007–1 (volume VI)

Contents

Contributors

David Adshead Senior Lecturer, School of Humanities and Social Sciences, University of Sunderland, UK

Derek Bastide Principal Lecturer, Faculty of Education and Sport, University of Brighton, UK

Vivienne Baumfield Senior Lecturer in Education, Department of Education, University of Newcastle, UK

Stephen Bigger Head of Applied Education Studies, University College, Worcester, UK

Marian Carter Tutor, Adult Theological Education, Centre of Christian Theology and Education, University College of St Mark & St John, Plymouth, UK

Jennifer Chapa Research Associate in Moral Education and Human Resource Development, Bahá'í World Centre, Haifa, Israel

Rhett Diessner Professor of Psychology and Education at Lewis-Clark State College, Lewiston, Idaho, USA

Cynthia K. Dixon Associate Professor in Religious Studies, Edith Cowan University, Western Australia

Toinette M. Eugene Associate Professor, Christian Social Ethics, Farnett-Evangelical Theological Seminary, Illinois, USA

Judith Everington Senior Lecturer in Religious Education, Institute of Education, University of Warwick, UK

Brian E. Gates Professor and Head of Department of Religion and Ethics, St Martin's College, Lancaster, UK

Jeannette Gill Senior Lecturer, Faculty of Arts and Education, University of Plymouth, UK

Andrew Hannan Director of Research and Reader in Education, Faculty of Arts and Education, University of Plymouth, UK

John M. Hull Professor of Religious Education, School of Education, University of Birmingham, UK

Robert Jackson Professor of Education, Institute of Education, University of Warwick, UK

Winifred Wing Han Lamb Post-doctoral Fellow, Department of Philosophy, Australian National University, Australia

Mal Leicester Senior Lecturer in Continuing Education, Warwick University, UK

Nick Mead Senior Lecturer in Religious Education, Westminster College, Oxford, UK

Siebren Miedema Professor in Education, Vrije Universiteit, The Netherlands

Celia Modgil Senior Lecturer in Education, Goldsmiths College, London University, UK

Sohan Modgil Reader in Educational Research and Development, University of Brighton, UK

Yoshiko Nomura Director General, Nomura Centre for Lifelong Integrated Education, Tokyo, Japan

Richard Pearce Associate Fellow, Continuing Education, University of Warwick, UK

Alex Rodger Director, Values Education Project, Dundee, UK

Doret de Ruyter   Associate Professor in Education, Vrije Universiteit, The Netherlands

John Shortt   Head of Research and Development at the Stapleford Centre, Editor of *Journal of Education and Christian Belief* (formerly *Spectrum*) and formerly Director of Charis Project

R. Thompson   Retired Headteacher, The Grange School, Bradford, West Yorkshire, UK

Editors' Foreword

This is one volume in a series of six, each concerned with education, culture and values. Educators have long recognized that 'education' is necessarily value laden and, therefore, that value issues are inescapable and fundamental, both in our conceptions of education and in our practice of it. These issues are particularly complex in the context of cultural pluralism. In a sense the collection is a recognition, writ large, of this complexity and of our belief that since values are necessarily part of education, we should be explicit about what they are, and about why we choose those we do and who the 'we' is in relation to the particular conception and practices in question.

The first three volumes in the series deal with values diversity in education – the broader issues of what values ought to inform education in and for a plural society. The second three focus more narrowly on values education as such – what is the nature and scope of moral education, of religious and political education and of political and citizenship education in and for such a society? Thus collectively they consider both **values diversity in education** and **values education in diversity**. Individually they each have a particular level. Thus volumes 1–3 cover the levels of system, institution and classroom. Volumes 4–6 focus respectively on moral education, religious and spiritual education, politics and citizenship education. This structure is intended to ensure that the six volumes in the series are individually discrete but complementary.

Given the complexity of the value domain and the sheer diversity of values in culturally plural societies it becomes clear why 120 chapters from 23 countries merely begin to address the wealth of issues relating to 'Education, Culture and Values'.

Mal Leicester, Celia Modgil
and Sohan Modgil

Part One

Spiritual Education

1 Moral, Spiritual, Religious – Are they Synonymous?

ALEX RODGER

Introduction

This chapter will explore certain aspects of its title's question in an attempt to clarify some issues which, at the present time, seem hopelessly confused. In part, it will draw on – and emerge from my own acquaintance with – the work of people who have written on the subject on the basis of personal experience, reflection and research, but who come from within different specific convictional communities. It makes no attempt to offer a final word on the matter; rather to contribute to an ongoing discussion in the hope that those of us who share in it may profit from attending to each other at the same time as we attend to the subject in hand.

Well, are they?

My short answer to the question, 'Moral, spiritual, religious – are they synonymous?', is 'No'. Nor are these three always so easily distinguishable, let alone separable, from a wide range of other characteristically human interests and activities, as some people think them to be.

There are clearly important and, in some respects, close relationships among 'moral, spiritual and religious' which will be explored to some extent in what follows. But they are not the same. To regard them as synonymous would be to make a category mistake similar to thinking that the terms 'knives', 'cutlery' and 'forks' could be regarded as referring to three distinct types of entity; whereas the truth is that knives and forks are cases or examples of cutlery. Cutlery embraces the whole range of normal eating implements: knives and forks are classified as cases of cutlery because of

their inclusion within the range of items whose *raison d'être* is to serve this purpose.

The relationships between 'moral', 'spiritual' and 'religious' seem to me to be akin to the relationships between the cluster 'social', 'human' and 'political'. In each of these clusters, only beings of the kind appropriately described by the middle term can engage in activities which could be properly described by the first and third terms. And it is the fact that the first and third terms, in each case, are (albeit usually implicitly) qualified by the second term that makes them authentically what they are. It is a part of my argument that, just as the proper use of the terms 'social' and 'political' refer to groups of human beings (and only by extension and in a derivative and reduced sense to non-human groups), so the proper use of the terms 'moral' and 'religious' applies only to activities which are spiritual activities. It is, of course, possible, and frequently the case in practice, that activities which are described, for example, as 'religious' fall short of being spiritual activities; or that social and political activities can be described as '*in*human'.

There is, as appears from this brief discussion, a fair degree of systematic – or at least systemic – ambiguity in the use of such terms. Our difficulties in speaking clearly on such matters owes something, but by no means everything, to this fact.

To put the matter bluntly, morality and religion can both be *un*spiritual when and to the extent that they lose touch with their spiritual roots or core. This has to do with the intention or, at least, the motivation of the agent. It is unspiritual religion, for example, that draws from Robert Burns the jibe:

> Far rather had I been an atheist clean
> Than under religion hid be for a screen.

And it is unspiritual morality that is addressed in the dictum of St Francis de Sales that:

> Honesty is the best policy, but he is not an honest man who lives by that maxim.

Doing the right thing is not necessarily evidence of a spiritual commitment. It is possible to do right in order to seem to be doing good, or even to avoid doing what is good! Similarly many overtly 'religious' actions are devoid of any spiritual awareness or faith on the part of the doer. Not that 'spiritual' activities are always consciously so; but, when the question of motivation is raised, it is concerned with the spirit in which the deed was done and the considerations which impelled the doer. A human action is not simply the thing done. It includes the internal disposition of the doer and its description is incomplete without some reference to its intended goal.

To call an action 'right' may – or may not – include reference to the disposition of the doer. So the same overt action carried out by two different people – or the same person at different times or in different circumstances – may, in the one case, give expression to a genuinely personal disposition, but not in the other. The rightness of the action is no guarantee of the goodness of the agent. Yet the term 'moral' can be used of either.

A similar argument can be developed to distinguish authentic (spiritual) from inauthentic (unspiritual) religion. The crucial distinction, again, concerns the internal disposition of the doer – the source of the activity – and whether it is a genuine expression of a personal faith commitment in relation to some transcendent reality.

My view, then, is that morality and religion are – or, rather, may be under certain conditions – forms or expressions of spirituality. Equally important is the recognition that spirituality has many other forms. This is attested by many writers on the subject. Sir Alister Hardy (1978), for example, writes about:

> the spiritual nature of man, meaning that side of his [*sic*] make-up which, if not always leading him to have what he might call religious feelings, may at least give him a love of the non-material things of life such as natural beauty, art, music, or moral values.

Again, Constantin Regamey (1959) writes about spirituality being expressed in

> disinterested moral feelings, demands for order, responsibility, freedom, justice, longings for immortality or unity with the whole, intuitions of beauty or truth, mental faculties, such as attention, abstraction, coherent reasoning, and quite generally the notion of non-utilitarian values.

It is clear from this and other evidence that the term 'spirituality' is used to cover a wide range of phenomena. It is also clear that it must offer something more than a 'holdall' for the 'non-material' or 'non-utilitarian' if we are to use it with any precision or any hope of clarifying some common understanding of what we are talking about. Without this, we shall be unable even to disagree intelligibly!

On spirituality

With the foregoing comments as background, it may now be helpful to attempt to articulate somewhat more fully and clearly what is intended by the term 'spiritual'. I have argued elsewhere (for example, Rodger, 1996) that the root of all spirituality is lodged in awareness of a specific kind.

Spirituality is not specifically a religious phenomenon. It is rooted in a fundamentally and characteristically human capacity for being aware of the world through relating to it in a particular way. By extension, the term is used to cover the forms in which this awareness is given expression and the means by which it is fostered. The term 'spiritual' refers also to those aspects of reality which human beings believe themselves to be aware of in spiritual experience.

Awareness of a spiritual kind is typically described as direct or unmediated, and as being characterised by inwardness and participation in the reality of what is experienced in this way. Terms such as 'insight' and 'realisation' are commonly used. The awareness is neither that of a detached observer nor of an emotionally involved participant. It holds together the impartiality for which the 'objective' observer strives and the aspect of encounter which is an element within passionate subjectivity.

The sort of involvement which is sought for with whatever is the focus of awareness avoids both the detachment that separates us from it and the kind of ego-involvement which distorts our perception of it. Yet, in other senses of the words, the person is both involved (in a disinterested way) and detached (in a way which retains respect for and commitment to the integrity of what is encountered).

This kind of awareness of otherness cannot be manipulated or produced to order. It conveys to its recipients a sense of disclosure, a seeing into the depths of what discloses itself in this way; leading many, but not all, of its recipients to describe the experience as revelatory. Spirituality thus has both religious and non-religious forms.

Although this awareness cannot be reliably produced by techniques, there is evidence from many traditions that certain practices may predispose a person to experience it. Central to these practices – and, indeed, expressed in many different ways within them – is the 'active passivity' of attending to otherness (whatever kind of other is in view). The parallels between this and what Iris Murdoch (1992) describes in the following extract are obvious:

> The notion of achieving a pure cognitive state where the object is not disturbed by the subjective ego, but where subject and object simply exist as one is here made comprehensible through a certain experience of art and nature . . . A discipline of meditation wherein the mind is alert but emptied of self enables this form of awareness, and the disciplined practice of various skills may promote a similar unselfing, or 'decreation' to use Simone Weil's vocabulary. Attend 'without thinking about.' This is 'good for us' because it involves respect, because it is an exercise in cleansing the mind of selfish preoccupation, because it is an experience of what truth is *like* . . .
>
> . . . A contemplative observation of contingent 'trivial' detail (insects, leaves, shapes of screwed-up paper, looks and shadows of anything, expressions of faces) is a prevalent and usually, at least in a minimal sense, 'unselfing' activity of consciousness.

Attention of this kind embodies and fosters a respect for the other as it is in itself, letting the other be and making oneself available to its disclosure of what it is on its own terms. Normal learned – or taught – categories for understanding it are suspended and the intrusive ego is left behind in such an act of attending. So the reality to which attention is given is neither reduced to fit into a conventional (say scientific) model, nor distorted to meet the observer's wishes. This kind of attention is referred to by many writers.

Neil Gunn, for example, an important Scottish writer of the twentieth century, came to recognise late in his life that his enduring preoccupation with such awareness in its many forms was mirrored in the teaching of Zen. He fastened on the Zen phrase, 'Look lovingly on some object', in recognition of a shared spiritual search and method. Gunn's friend and biographer, John Pick, comments on this: 'the word "lovingly" means the exact opposite of "sentimentally". It means looking with a precise and affectionate attention so that the object is seen as it is and not as the observer has been accustomed to see it or would wish to see it or feels he is expected to see it, or so on.'

'Knowing', Pick says, 'is an intuitive opening to what is already there.' He asks:

> How do we 'know' it is there, and not an illusion we choose to accept? At the very heart of spiritual development are those moments when you 'know in yourself' something you formerly only guessed or thought or believed. There is nothing mysterious about this. At one time you may read something and it means little or nothing. Weeks or months or years later it comes back to mind and you realise immediately what was intended: 'So that's what it meant!' The words are the same, but your consciousness has changed.   (Pick, 1991)

Such attention, therefore, temporarily suspends – and opens up to the possibility of radical challenge – our articulated, 'received' knowing by putting us in touch with the other, which we have known (in this received way) as object, yet now know no longer merely as object but as subject. For the first time – or, again – we *realise* something that we have known for a long time, or see it with fresh eyes free of the influence of all our previous seeing. It is salutary to be reminded that such commonplace human experiences bring us to the threshold of spirituality and the transforming of lives, which in the Christian and other traditions is focused in the discipline of prayer.

This is why W. H. Auden and Simone Weil (his source for the idea) go so far as to identify such attention, *paid to anything at all*, as being of the essence of prayer. Its distinctive and essential characteristic is its focus on the other, accompanied by complete self-forgetfulness, the eclipse of the ego. The person who so attends to *anything* is open and available to the object of attention as it is in itself, in order to be receptive to its disclosure of itself, undistorted by the ego's needs or desires. This attention offers the other a dis-interested interest, an interest in the other for the sake of the other, rather than for one's own sake or for any other alien purpose. Significantly, Weil (1959) and Auden (1970) see the chief goal of a teacher as being to inculcate such attention as the habitual attitude of the learner to whatever aspect of the world is being studied. This sort of attention is characteristic of adoration in religious worship, of appreciation of works of art and of wonder before the glories of nature, as well as of respect for and empathic openness to other persons. It relates to otherness in an 'I–You' rather than an 'I–It' way (Buber 1970).

What has been said thus far forces the recognition that, even though the door through which we enter the world of spirituality is awareness, the beginning is not the whole thing. The very awareness carries within it a sense of invitation to go further.

I note, without elaborating the point here, that any comprehensive treatment of human spirituality will require to recognise at least three levels: (1) spirituality as awareness, described above, (2) spirituality as response to what is received in awareness leading to increasing awareness; and (3) spirituality as way of life, in which response to awareness is generalised to embrace the whole life as a settled disposition which includes acceptance of the discipline of a way of transformation in the direction of human fulfilment.

A more comprehensive recognition of the range and variety of forms of expression of spirituality is made by John Macquarrie (1972) when he writes:

> Fundamentally spirituality has to do with becoming a person in the fullest sense . . . [and] . . . this dynamic form . . . can be described as a capacity for going out of oneself and beyond oneself; or again, as the capacity for transcending oneself . . . It is this openness, freedom, creativity, this capacity for going beyond any given state in which he [*sic*] finds himself, that makes possible self-consciousness and self-criticism, understanding, responsibility, the pursuit of knowledge, the sense of beauty, the quest of the good, the formation of community, the outreach of love and whatever else belongs to the amazing richness of what we call 'the life of the spirit'.

Of particular significance are two claims he makes. The first is that spirituality is a whole-person affair, in two senses: first, it has to do with human wholeness or fulfilment in the sense of completion; second, it is holistic in its inclusion of the whole of human life. 'The life of the spirit' is not a particular aspect of a person's life, it is the whole of that life seen and lived from a particular perspective.

His second claim describes spirituality 'as a capacity for going out of oneself and beyond oneself . . . the capacity for transcending oneself'. Consideration of the kind of awareness from which spirituality emerges reveals that that awareness is itself already a 'going out' in Macquarrie's sense, a leaving behind of the self as it is at any given point, in openness to the call of otherness. In particular, any intentional attention to an 'other' with a view to becoming aware of the other as it is in itself – independently of one's pre-existing conception of it or any needs or wishes one holds in relation to it – is a significant, and potentially radical, step in the direction of self-transcendence, the leaving behind of narcissism. This is very close to the heart, if it is not indeed the essence, of spirituality.

Spirituality and morality

We turn now in the direction of morality, noting its close relationship to what has already been said, by referring to some words of Iris Murdoch (1970): 'I have used the word "attention", which I borrow from Simone Weil, to express the idea of a just and loving gaze directed upon an individual reality. I believe this to be the characteristic and proper mark of the active moral agent . . .' It serves also, as has been suggested above, to provide a cohering focus for the whole value life. Murdoch holds that 'virtue is the same in the artist as in the good man in that it is a selfless attention to nature: something which is easy to name but very hard to achieve'.

It is for this reason that there is no need to 'apply' spirituality to morality. The inherent tendency of spirituality to transcend narcissism and egocentrism is *already* an essentially moral aspect of spirituality itself. Human fulfilment is inseparable from such opportunity for and obligation towards self-transcendence. A little reflection will show that it is also, therefore, inherently linked with human community – in the sense that recognition of others and transcendence of egocentrism converge on that situation. The spiritual roots of moral community come into view when this is recognised. Community arises in situations where attention to others leads to the kind of mutual awareness which promotes genuinely considerate response and relationships. The pattern of awareness, response, way of living and being applies here also. Respect for persons becomes a transforming moral attitude when it assumes the character of this kind of attention.

If the goal of morality can be expressed in terms

of human flourishing, then being moral requires that attention be paid to what will be conducive to the other person's (or persons') flourishing. The needs, interests and feelings of the other will be taken into account in determining how we should act towards him or her. As well as specific and immediate needs and interests, decisions will give weight to the other person's potential for development (self-transcendence: see, for example, Maslow's (1976) 'hierarchy of human needs'). In other words, morality is not self-contained. Its responsibility to human needs takes account of human possibilities as well as present human circumstance. The direction of this development will be determined in relation to a view of what human beings are and what they may become. Can we identify any general outline of what this will mean for morality?

A morality which is rooted in spiritual awareness of other people already contains a commitment to self-transcendence with specific reference to transcendence of the ego, the narcissistic self which cannot bring 'a just and loving gaze' to bear on another person, but suffers from distorted perception. The person I am determines not only what I am capable of wishing for the other person, but what I perceive the other person to be and to be capable of becoming. To love others means to rejoice in their being, their otherness, to let them be, to attend to what they are, so that we may come to know and be aware of them as they are in themselves – seeing them more in the light of their possibilities, their flourishing, than through the distorting lens of our own needs or wishes.

As we *see*, then, so we judge. Our capacity for genuine consideration of other people will inescapably be limited by our capacity for seeing them as they are. Thus our actions, and what we become, will depend on our ability to see – to have a direct, personal and self-involving awareness of the moral realities of our situation. Also, since our being depends on our seeing, the spiritual and moral goals for our development are at one in calling us to pursue the road along which we may 'see, no longer blinded by our eyes' (Brooke, 1952).

Self-transcendence has specific moral aspects. In crude terms, moral progress is along the continuum which begins in narcissism (obsessive focus on the isolated self) and ends in communion (loving union with other persons), the interpenetration of lives. This could be illustrated, for example, in terms of the multiple interpretations which the principle of reciprocity receives (or 'levels' of understanding the Golden Rule), moving from a merely prudent manipulation of other people to a profound empathic and un-self-regarding pursuit of other people's flourishing in the fullest sense.

I have argued that authentic morality emerges from the sustained and committed effort to understand, articulate and coordinate our living in accordance with what is perceived in moments of spiritual awareness of other people and the obligation under which we are placed by such awareness. Can illustrations be provided of how that awareness makes itself felt and is expressed in practice? I shall sketch four situations: one which illustrates its absence; one which recounts an episodic occurrence of it; one which demonstrates our freedom in and responsibility for how we respond; and one which describes an appearance of the effects of this awareness in disposition and character.

The first relates to a colleague, much respected and well liked; highly regarded by clients for her work; who decided to apply for a position in another institution and was successful in her application. Her immediate superior, an austerely and self-consciously 'moral' woman, when informed, offered no word of congratulation or good wishes, expressed no interest in the person's new position or plans, but soliloquised on the problems she herself would have in ensuring that the department's work was 'covered'.

The second concerns a recent occasion when I was in Aberdeen on business with a later appointment in a town ten miles away. My wife, Joan, was with me and had gone shopping, and there was an arrangement for us to meet outside a certain shop by a given time. Joan has difficulty in walking any distance due to a damaged nerve in her spine. Having arrived at the meeting place five minutes before our agreed time, my anxiety and impatience were both rising when – ten minutes after the time – she had not arrived and a friendly traffic warden had told me to move my car into a side street, with no place available where I could park and leave it. When Joan did arrive very soon after, I was edgy. She was flustered and upset, having waited outside a different shop until, the time for us to meet having passed, she realised she must be in the wrong place. Then, after finding where the correct shop was, she had to rush over a quarter of a mile through a busy shopping area. I leave you to imagine how my feelings changed, and my sense of what mattered and what would be an appropriate response on my part, when I became aware of what that meant for Joan.

My third illustration: Kenneth Clark (1986) writes:

> A curious episode took place. I had a religious experience. It took place in the church of San Lorenzo, but did not seem to me to be connected with the harmonious beauty of the architecture. I can only say that for a few minutes my whole being was irradiated by a kind of heavenly joy, far more intense than anything I had known before. This state of mind lasted for several months, and, wonderful though it was, it posed an awkward problem, in terms of action. My life was far from blameless: I would have to reform. My family would think I was going mad, and perhaps after all it *was* a delusion, for I was in every way unworthy of receiving such a flow of grace. Gradually the effect wore off and I made no effort to retain it. I think I was right; I was too deeply embedded in the world to change course. But that I had 'felt the finger of God' I am quite sure and, although the memory of this experience has faded, it still helps me to understand the joy of the saints.

The final example is best told in the words of Basil Mitchell himself. The background is that he and a young woman, in love with each other but separated for several years by the Second World War, found that changes in them and their circumstances raised questions, particularly for her, about the future of their relationship. He writes:

> It had become apparent that, however intractable the problems we encountered as a man and a woman of only partly overlapping vocations, involved in the complexities of a specific social situation, we had nevertheless been enabled to see each other clearly and to recognize and respond to each other's aspirations with a certain kind of disinterested love. I had found that, above all, I wanted her to resolve her tensions, fulfil her varied capacities and flourish as a human being, if possible with, if necessary without, my own participation. And this flourishing was not a matter simply of some satisfactory accommodation between her conflicting desires, but of her becoming fully what she was meant to be. And it had become abundantly clear that this was also her wish for me, whatever role I might subsequently play in her life. (Mitchell 1993)

This other person has needs and interests and feelings as I have. When the *otherness* of this person is realised – her separateness and distinctness from me – together with the realisation that her needs

and concerns and interests and feelings are as urgently important to her as mine are to me, the situation is changed by that very realisation. I now know with a self-involving immediacy which precludes objectivity while, at the same time, it enables an enhanced accuracy in my perception of the other person. This is so because this passing over into the awareness of the other radically reduces the distortion imported into my perceptions by egoism, the narcissistic self-concern which constrains me to look at others for my own sake, rather than for theirs; and therefore, to see reflections (distorted reflections) of my self rather than the other person as she is. So, it is said, we see things and people, not as they are, but as we are. And this is why our need is to be enabled 'to see no longer blinded by our eyes'.

Morality, transformation and religion

Our capacity to act well towards other people, then, calls not simply for making decisions of a particular kind, not merely for letting a principle of justice guide our actions, but for a change in the person we are, so that we are, to some extent and increasingly, freed from our self-obsessed narcissism and become capable of genuinely seeing the other person

This process of being changed is morally significant, but it is not a merely moral change – nor can it easily be confined within our moral living. It is a spiritual change and will, if it is happening in a healthy way, be affecting the whole range of our perceptions of otherness and, therefore, all the ways in which we relate to aspects of the world in which we live: the physical world, the intellectual world, the aesthetic world, the spiritual world, as well as the world of human relationships.

Within education there is a wide range of elements which contribute to the spiritual education and development of the learner. The root of such learning and development is, in all cases, the sort of outgoing openness to otherness; the attention which seeks awareness; the moving out from enclosedness within one's self; which initiates a continuing going beyond, transcending narcissism and so engaging what Maslow called 'the higher reaches of human nature'.

How close this is to spirituality as it appears in the traditional religions and spiritual ways, I shall not explore here. But I am persuaded that the spiritual roots of moral community are to be found here.

Further, that the fundamentally spiritual character of morality does not permit it, finally, to be self-contained or separable from the wider context which is the focal concern of religions.

A religion according to Patrick Burke (1978), is 'a way of life focussed on salvation'. And, while he allows that salvation may be conceived of as deliverance in a very wide range of ways (including victory against enemies in war, freedom from self-concern, escape from the wheel of existence), there is within his treatment a recognition of the inherent tendency of religions – when they remain responsive to their root inspirations – to transcend the local, temporal and cultural constraints of their origins. In other words, the tendency to self-transcendence is a mark of authentic, living religion. So, for Burke, the deliverance must be of cosmic consequence, congruent in some significant respect to the nature of the cosmos itself.

The foregoing sketch of morality as a spiritual enterprise leads directly to the same frontier and raises the same questions. For, in that view, morality is a way of being-in-relation-to-otherness, which carries the impulse to self-transcendence – not only for the person, but for the notion of morality itself. Morality, in other words, is not self-contained, but has its place within some stance for living which includes – explicitly or implicitly – a view of human nature (what we are and what we may become) and of the place of morality within the total context of human living in the cosmos. This issue can be ignored, but it cannot be excised. It remains as a persistent reminder of the futility of all our efforts to provide an exhaustive account of aspects of experience which are not merely puzzling, but fundamentally mysterious. The 'meddling intellect' has only rarely in the history of humankind been taken as an adequate instrument for understanding the totality of things, that whole of which we are part.

Time and space forbid a similar treatment of religion and spirituality to that given above of morality and spirituality. I believe that such a discussion could establish the fact that religion and morality are closely related to each other because of their shared rootedness in a kind of awareness of, response to and way of being within the world – which is a fundamentally spiritual attitude or disposition of the person towards the world, or aspects of it. What faith is toward the cosmos, goodwill is towards other people. Faith may seek to express itself in statements of belief, and goodwill to express itself in rules or principles. And these articu-

lations have their usefulness. Yet they are ambiguous blessings, since what they express they also distort by a process of reduction of the mystery which can never be comprehensively expressed. It may have been this sort of danger that Uhland had in mind when he wrote: 'So long as we do not try to utter what is unutterable, then nothing is lost. But the unutterable is contained, unutterably, in what has been uttered.'

It would be excessively defeatist, however, to imagine that on this account there is nothing to be said that can help the fumbling intellect to prepare itself for the insights which may depend on its relinquishing its claim to omnicompetence. The next section will make brief reference to one source of possible help for those disposed to pursue it.

Spirituality and human wholeness

To recognise that spirituality is a fundamentally human phenomenon and that it is the vital life of morality and religion is one thing. It is a related, though different, claim to hold that spirituality is crucial to human fulfilment. These three are held together in the work of Donald Evans. He writes about a discovery he made while writing his book *Struggle and Fulfilment*:

> which was supposed to deal with religion and morality. At first I considered beliefs: religious beliefs concerning the attributes of God and moral beliefs concerning how we ought to behave. But as I became convinced that matters of belief are secondary in both religion and morality I began to study the attitudes on which the beliefs depend. These attitudes are pervasive stances of the whole personality which shape our responses to the universe as a whole and to each particular in it. As I investigated some of the most important attitudes, for example, basic trust, I gradually came to realise that they are both religious and moral. They are religious in that they are stances towards whatever unifying reality pervades our total environment. They are moral in that they are virtues which radically influence the way we deal with other people. I also came to realise that they are 'ego-strengths' that are crucial in the process of psychotherapy and that they are constituents of human fulfilment. So it became clear that religion and morality and therapy can converge in stances which are central in human life as such. Openness is one such stance. (Evans, 1993)

In that earlier book he had written:

the theoretical structures of religion and morality . . . need to be understood in relation to certain life-affirming stances such as trust which are the core of both authentic religious faith and genuine moral character. And since our fulfilment as human beings depends on the extent to which these life affirming stances prevail over their opposites, religion and morality and human fulfilment have a common core.   (Evans, 1979)

Evans thus provides a way of conceiving human development which enables us to see the integral nature of religious faith, moral character and personal fulfilment. It is also capable of accommodating the recognition that this does not justify any careless or lazy approach which would claim that religion, morality and spirituality are identical – as they would require to be if 'religious', 'moral' and 'spiritual' were synonymous. The truth is much more interesting, satisfying and true to human experience.

Pedagogical postscript

Religious, moral, personal and social development

It is worth noting that Evans, in addition to offering a working definition of spirituality and its elements, provides a basis for a pedagogical rationale in which moral education, religious education and personal and social development can be held together in one synoptic vision of their overlapping contributions to the development of the pupil. Attention to this point might provide practical guidance to those responsible for ensuring that pupils receive a coherent educational experience in this, as in other areas of the curriculum. A more radical grasping of the point might even suggest different ways of arranging curriculum provision.

A possible approach to a holistic way of learning about and understanding ourselves is suggested by this way of viewing human beings, in which the one value life is recognised as having different aspects which are distinguishable in thought, but not (without pathology) separable in reality.

Evans's list of attitude-virtues emerged over a professional lifetime's engagement with ethical, theological and 'humanistic' psychological attempts to understand human beings. The attitude-virtues which Evans identifies in a preliminary way are:

- Trust
- Humility
- Self-acceptance
- Responsibility
- Self-commitment
- Friendliness or I–Thou openness
- Concern
- Contemplation

These *pervasive stances of the whole personality, which shape our responses to the universe as a whole and to each particular in it*, are regarded by Evans (1993) as the characteristics of healthy spirituality. His list is *not* proposed here as being 'correct' in any final sense, but as one suggestion among others – although there is an interesting degree of general agreement in principle among many who, from different perspectives, have sought to understand people as capable of fulfilling – or of failing to fulfil – some as yet not fully defined human potential. More important than the accuracy of his list is the adequacy of his central identification of attitude-virtues as a cohering focus for the study of the value life of human beings, and as a description of essential aspects of human spirituality. His particular attitude-virtues can be regarded as a working definition to be used in further exploration and modified themselves in the light of what that exploration reveals.

At the present time, educational interest in the 'spiritual, social, moral and cultural' development of pupils is vigorous, even though often profoundly unspiritual in its inspiration. It is also frequently confused. However, if the intention is – and surely in the educational sphere it cannot fall short of being – the advancement of understanding for the sake of improving practice, certain requirements are inescapable. Among these are:

- that we move beyond the merely eclectic – simply including everything that anybody wants to regard as spirituality, without discrimination – and seek to use the means at our disposal for applying appropriate canons of study;
- that we use appropriate methodologies and criteria for evidence;
- that we engage in open and vigorous debate, disciplined (but not dogmatic) discussion and empathic dialogue;
- that we attend to the evidence and use appropriate registers for evaluating what we are studying, rather than imposing crassly distort-

ing measures and alien interpretations on what is universally recognised as elusive;

- that we be prepared to take account of the personal participation without which no worthwhile insight is possible, while taking every necessary means to avoid manipulative or indoctrinative procedures (positive or negative);
- that we allow the dialogue between modern consciousness and the spiritual traditions of the world to teach us what we are dealing with, as we are open to relearning what recent generations have lost touch with, in order to learn a language which provides continuity with the developed tradition(s) of the past while speaking in a modern accent and relating to contemporary experience.

Education as a spiritual activity

It is not difficult to see that, although religious education, moral education and personal and social development have a direct contribution to make to pupils' spiritual development (whether in fact they do so or not), other areas of the curriculum are no less importantly involved. This follows from the fact that each of them can contribute to the development of specific aspects of the learner's being which are aspects of any whole and integrated human life. For example, imagination underlies the empathy which is essential to caring in a morally competent way. Similarly, sensitivity to people, art and nature underlies spiritual awareness. Again, the commitment to truth more than to one's beliefs about what is true – a key spiritual characteristic – is the stock-in-trade of such apparently 'cold' subjects as science and mathematics. There is no subject which is properly regarded as devoid of contribution to the spiritual development of learners of all ages – whatever may in fact be true of the manner in which they are sometimes taught.

The above line of argument urges an examination of the fact that any educational process inescapably conveys a spirituality to those whose minds are formed by it. It is unlikely that this will be a conscious, let alone a coherent, intention on the part of most educators who live in – and have themselves been shaped by – a spiritually illiterate culture. Paradoxically, those who are educational leaders may even have been rendered less capable of providing an education which conveys a sensitively spiritual awareness to their charges, by dint of the fact that they themselves are likely to be in many cases the prime examples of successful products of the educational system to which they were subject. The words which George Bernanos (1937) attributes to his country priest are apt:

> I am still very grateful to our teachers. The real trouble doesn't lie with what they taught so much as with the education they had been given and passed on because they knew no other way of thinking and feeling. That education made us isolated individualists. Really we never escaped from childhood, we were always playing at make-believe; we invented our troubles and joys, we invented life, instead of living it. So before daring to take one step out of our little world, you have to begin all over again from the beginning. It is very hard work and entails much sacrifice of pride; but to be alone is much harder, as you'll realise some day.

The case, however, is neither so uniform nor so hopeless as this might seem to suggest. The current interest in spirituality in education, however uncertain its focus, witnesses to an inescapable fact about human beings: namely, their fundamentally human preoccupation with matters which lie on (and even beyond) the frontiers of all securely established knowledge. These boundary issues, whether concerned with knowledge or identity or power or security or survival (of which, indeed, the others may be specific forms or derivatives) are reminders, when we are willing to acknowledge them, of our limitations within an infinite horizon and of the fact that we are fundamentally mysterious to ourselves. It is these facts which help us to understand the irresistible fascination of the spiritual searchings and striving of human beings. Ought they not to figure more securely within education?

Detailed proposals for such provision could only be the outcome of a much more extensive ground-clearing and foundation-laying process. This is not the place for that to be attempted. Instead, I shall indicate what I consider to be a potentially valuable piece of scaffolding for the activity of constructing appropriate educational experiences for providing young people with a perspective on the nature of learning which accommodates spiritual awareness. Not only so, it promises to help restore the recognition of spirituality as an integral aspect of human awareness of and participation within the world which is known, but only ever obscurely and in part. This reminds us that humility, in the sense of submission to what is the case, is a central educational value. Such a recognition is none the worse for the fact that it belongs to a longstanding tradition in education in which it was (is) common for scholars to 'profess' subjects and to 'dedicate' themselves to the 'disciplines' thereby entailed.

The following suggestion is borrowed, with modification, from Baron Friedrich von Hügel. He suggests that there are three ways of religious 'knowing' which are characteristic of, but not confined to, three stages of religious development. These are:

1 the institutional;
2 the critical;
3 the mystical.

In the institutional stage the child is being inducted into and made a member of the society or culture of which he or she is part. This entails taking on and 'indwelling' (to use Polanyi's term) the form of life of that culture, which includes not only its approved 'knowledge', but also its intellectual frame of reference. The cost of becoming a member is accepting the approved pattern and living and learning within it. The way in which one's life is thereby understood will clearly affect the way(s) in which it is, or can be, lived.

In the critical stage the young person begins to reflect upon the inherited patterns of belief in the light of their internal self-consistency, their consistency with other 'well-accredited truth' and their correspondence with experienced reality. At this stage, it is important to recognise that reality is still experienced within the frame of reference, and judged by the canons, inherited in the institutional stage. The move beyond that entrapment within a given 'socially constructed reality' depends on a successful transition to the third stage.

The mystical stage begins to emerge when, in some way, not only the inherited beliefs of the culture, but its way of arriving at, authenticating, scrutinising and modifying its beliefs, is challenged. The impetus for this transition may arise from the recognition of other frames of reference with their different canons and criteria. However, because it entails criticism of the very framework within which its criticism operates, it entails a radical challenge to the adequacy – and certainly to the finality – of the framework itself. This can lead, in adolescence often does lead, to a mere exchange of one frame of reference for another; for example, the fundamentalist believer becomes a radical positivist (or vice versa). In that case, the critical stage remains dominant. A properly mystical understanding recognises that

neither the culture's preferred articulation of its knowledge nor any alternative to it can claim ultimacy. Any such frame is a provisional and heuristic working (and living) hypothesis, subject to modification in the light of what is discovered by working and living within it. The most effective framework for learning will be one which brings us from time to time to the threshold of its own capacity to interpret the experienced world convincingly. At that point, by subjecting ourselves to the world which eludes such interpretation, we dispose ourselves to the possibility (never with a guarantee) of genuinely fresh insight in which something is realised rather than simply understood. The appropriate response is to live with that insight until what has been realised is also understood, together with its implications for change to the previous way of construing the world.

The mystical insight is that *no* such modification can entitle the person to claim that, whereas he/she previously only thought that what he/she believed was the truth, he/she now knows that what he/she believes is true. By a variety of means, it is possible to keep this recognition alive in the growing young person and, at appropriate stages, to bring it into focal awareness in the educational process. This would mean, in general terms, that both the subject (whichever subject it was) and the teacher (however learned) would be relativised by being made subordinate to the subject-matter. All knowledge would similarly be relativised: not in the sense that it was merely subjective, but in its being held provisionally as always capable of correction in the light of further insight into the subject-matter. This would be better described as the relativity than as the relativism of knowledge: what we know is not simply 'relative', it is 'relative to' what is, always incompletely, known.

Thus far, the discussion may seem relevant, if at all, only to education at its higher levels. To think so would be to confuse the attempt to articulate a complex situation with the effort to live effectively within it. Many cultures remind us that as well as a foolish cleverness there is a wise and profound simplicity, and areas in which the child can lead the adult. Perhaps we shall make little progress in educating for spirituality until we come, as adults, to recognise that the deepest insight does not leave behind but returns to the earliest unmediated awareness of our being in the world, and 'knows the place for the first time'. At that point, too, we may discover the difference between 'childlikeness' and mere immaturity – in our learning and in our lives.

. . . and a parting shot

To the question from which this chapter starts, the answer must, then, be 'No'. The willingness, however, to explore the reasons which require such an answer affords our best opportunity to discover a more adequate, insightful and humanly enriching answer. In order to embark on this exploration, we shall have to attend to matters, to ideas and to experiences which have been unfashionable among us for a long time. That attention will, itself, be the first – and inescapable – step towards an answer. For the non-participant in any sphere can never know personally or at first hand. And in such matters as these, any other kind of knowing is in danger of being merely curious and dilettante. If what is written above corresponds in any way to what is true, it will follow that any such spectator interest will either give way to a more participating engagement with the subject matter, or it will exclude the searcher from the evidence without which no convincing knowledge claims can be made.

This is no mere obscurantist or fundamentalist fiat. It arises from a consideration of what it means to understand anything at all, and of the requirement in any study of the world that the methods adopted be in some kind of synergy with the nature of what is studied. The general and essential point was well expressed by G. F. Woods thirty years ago:

> Conflicts of opinion which arise between those who are seeking to understand the world may be distinguished into two classes. They may be the result of using the same methods and reaching different conclusions, or they may be due to using methods which are different. These methodological differences are deeper than the disagreements between those who are in agreement about the proper method which ought to be used. When people are at variance about the appropriateness of the methods to be employed, the conflict is often accompanied by considerable misunderstanding and bewilderment. Their confusion may be increased through the absence of any agreement about the most appropriate method of discussing their disagreement. Evidence does not have the same weight for all parties when they use different methods of estimating its weight. The act of weighing the evidence is on these conditions inevitably inconclusive . . .

> To use a method implies many implied beliefs about ourselves and our world.
> A serious methodological conflict includes a conflict between two views of the nature of the world. It is a contest between two world-views. The appropriateness of the two methods is being judged in relation to the kind of world which they are designed to explain. These deeper divergences of view about the nature of the world and of the status of human personality within it are always playing an influential part in any controversy about our choice of methods in seeking to make the world plain. (Woods, 1966)

Consideration of Woods's point might help us to get clear of that part of the confusion in our current discussion of spirituality which is attributable to the attempt to understand it through a method and in a language which have been framed – sometimes deliberately – to be impervious to it.

References

Auden, W.H. (1970) *A Certain Way*. London: Viking Press.

Bernanos, G. (1937) *Diary of a Country Priest*. London: Bodley Head.

Brooke, R. (1952) A sonnet: 'Not with vain tears'. In *Poems*, ed. G. Keynes, London: Nelson.

Buber, M. (1970) *I and Thou*. Edinburgh: T. & T. Clark.

Burke, T. (1978) *The Fragile Universe*, London: Macmillan.

Clark, K. (1986) *The Other Half*. London: Collins.

Eliot, T.S. (1935) *Murder in the Cathedral*. London: Faber & Faber.

Evans, D. (1979) *Struggle and Fulfilment*. London: Collins.

Evans, D. (1993) *Spirituality and Human Nature*. New York: Suny.

Hardy, A. (1978) *The Spiritual Nature of Man*. Oxford: Clarendon Press.

Macquarrie, J. (1972) *Paths in Spirituality*. London: Harper.

Maslow, A. (1976) *Religions, Values and Peak Experiences*. Baltimore, MD: Penguin.

Mitchell, B. (1993) War and Friendship. In *Philosophers Who Believe*, ed. K.J. Clark. Downers Grove, IL: InterVarsity Press.

Murdoch, I. (1970) *The Sovereignty of Good*. London: Ark.

Murdoch, I. (1992) *Metaphysics as a Guide to Morals*. London: Chatto & Windus.

Pick, J. (1991) Neil Gunn and the eternal landscape. In *Neil Gunn's Country*, ed. D. Gunn and I. Murray. Edinburgh: Chambers.

Regamey, C. (1959) The meaning and significance of religion. In *Philosophy and Culture East and West*. Report of the Third East–West Philosophers Conference held at the University of Hawaii.

Rodger, A.R. (1996) Human spirituality: towards an educational rationale. In *Education, Spirituality and the Whole Child*, ed. R. Best. London: Cassell.

Uhland. Unable to trace reference. Will be grateful for information.

von Hügel, F. ([1908] 1923) *The Mystical Element of Religion* as studied in St. Catherine of Genoa and her Friends, 2nd edn. London: Dent.

Weil, S. (1959) *Waiting on God*. Glasgow: Fontana.

Woods, G.F. (1966) *A Defence of Theological Ethics*, Cambridge: Cambridge University Press.

2 Religious Education, Spirituality and Anti-racism

STEPHEN BIGGER

Religious education (RE) has struggled with its roots in Christian education. Even today, with multifaith approaches demanded by the Education Reform Act (1988) political misapprehensions keep the waters muddied and some schools still provide Christian nurture under the guise of religious education. Although there are many state-funded church schools, permission has not been granted for public sector Muslim, Sikh or Hindu schools. Although the last two decades appear to show great success in developing a multifaith philosophy for RE, there is much in the current situation which is superficial, tokenistic and methodologically confused. Much work has still to be done if RE is to address in any depth issues such as social justice and spirituality. As a means of building a foundation for global social, political and development issues, RE is not well placed to become a major influence in the twenty-first century.

If we were to construct a model for 'racist RE' which supports and validates the racist construction of reality, it might go as follows. It might depict crude pictures of religions, forming stereotypes that are indiscriminately attached to all adherents of each faith. It might be Eurocentric, giving more weight and importance to European aspects of faiths and devaluing others by implication. It might not, for example, note that in world terms most Christians are black. It might imply that Jews are responsible for the death of Jesus. It might make explicit reference to 'primitive' religious practices and beliefs, referring to them as superstitions. It might imply that one particular faith standpoint is better than others and give authority to the dominant cultural religious ideology. Religions might be compared to the disadvantage of those which are understood least. It might separate religion from life, not recognising connections between beliefs, society, ethics and identity. It might depict negative cultural features and examples of extremism as typical of the religion as a whole. I am not arguing that this list characterises RE in schools today: much current practice is helpful. Nevertheless, multifaith RE has developed in a climate of cultural pluralism (see Mullard, 1982) with different priorities than anti-racist education. Anti-racist and multicultural awareness cannot be assumed, so this list might suggest a helpful diagnostic tool for self-critique.

The quality of RE is very varied (see, for example, SCAA, 1996a). Teachers do not for the most part have substantial qualifications in RE and the subject has not been an in-service priority over the years. There is more likely to be a specialist in secondary schools, but some teaching is done by non-specialists. The kind of RE being taught, and the way it is taught, can make a sound contribution to multicultural and anti-racist strategies, and indeed to the whole school ethos. But it can also be destructive.

This chapter examines policy and curriculum issues in the light of anti-racism. Issues include the need to describe religions equitably and accurately but without stereotyping; and the conflict between accepting religions as they are and the need for educational critique. We examine alongside the explicit study of religion the desirability of religious education addressing implicit issues of human relationships and meaning, including the causes and consequences of racism, prejudice, xenophobia, persecution, harassment, lack of respect, bigotry and the possibility of constructing a curriculum around these issues. The spiritual aspect of the curriculum is seen in the light of this as having implications for the whole curriculum, suggesting a whole school approach to 'spiritual' education defined through anti-racist values. The whole curriculum should address racism in children's lives and in society (Troyna and Hatcher, 1992; Commission for Racial Equality, 1988a and 1988b).

A comparison between agreed syllabuses for religious education produced in the middle of this century up to the 1970s with those emerging in the 1980s and 1990s is startling. Early syllabuses were dominantly and explicitly Christian, 'confessional' in that they advocated Christian beliefs and values (see, for example, Cambridge's Agreed Syllabus of 1948). In the 1960s, there was a growing awareness of the needs of 'immigrants', employing a deficit model which presented them as problems to be solved. A Schools Council working paper (1971) raised a range of issues posed by the multicultural nature of the community and suggested solutions for the religious education curriculum. These took a phenomenological multifaith stance in which the curriculum was largely defined as study of world religions. The first authority to incorporate this approach into their agreed syllabus was the City of Birmingham (1975) which required the study of five religions in primary and secondary schools. This became the norm in urban authorities, with the Inner London Education Authority (ILEA), Manchester and others following suit in the 1980s. More rural counties followed the lead of Hampshire (1978 and 1980) in introducing a more gradual coverage of five religions. To these (Christianity, Hinduism, Islam, Judaism and Sikhism) was added Buddhism in the mid-1980s. These multifaith syllabuses advocated respect and understanding by enabling pupils to be informed about faiths. This is seen in handbook titles: *Living Together* (Birmingham) and *Paths to Understanding* (Hampshire). The SCAA model syllabuses (1994) adopted a six-religion 'phenomenological' model giving RE a 'study of religions' flavour.

These changes in RE's curriculum strategy paralleled changes in social and political perceptions. The Schools Council addressed a wide range of multicultural issues (Little and Willey, 1981; Willey, 1982; Klein 1982; Wood, 1984). Its closure coincided with political pressures against anti-racist education (Modgil *et al.*, 1986). The Rampton and Swann reports focused on educational achievement (DES, 1981 and 1985): the Swann Report saw the way forward for RE in phenomenological methodology (explicitly praising the Schools Council 1971 working paper), to ensure that minority faiths would not be and feel marginalised. RE should

inform children about diversity and *in so doing* 'contribute towards challenging and countering the influence of racism in our society' (DES, 1985, p. 496). On this view, racism is tackled by information; factual learning is itself transformative. Informed racists cannot exist by definition. On the contrary, how RE is taught and how it is received by students is of crucial importance. Empathy and enthusiasm come from the individuals involved and set the tone for the attitudes that children develop.

The 1988 Education Reform Act went some way towards the Swann Report's recommendations by providing that RE should cover Christianity and the other principal faiths practised in Britain. This is the first time in law that the RE curriculum has been specified and that a multifaith approach has been required. Not surprisingly, the debate about the balance between faiths has at times been acrimonious. Political pressures have sometimes focused on the need to teach right and wrong; and some people's desire to ensure that Christianity dominates has been fuelled by the provision that acts of worship in school should wholly or for the most part be of a broadly Christian character except where the nature of the school catchment makes a contrary determination desirable. This, in John Hull's view, gave Christianity 'an embarrassing prominence' (Hull, 1989, p. 119).

In a recent article (Bigger, 1995) I argued for anti-racism to have a higher profile in religious education. Concentrating only on cultural and religious pluralism fails to tackle prejudice, discrimination, racism, equality and power (Bigger, 1995, p. 12; Klein 1993, pp. 65–8). Widening the curriculum to include black lifestyles and stances is seductively simplistic but does not address deeper issues (Troyna and Carrington, 1990, p. 20; Troyna and Williams, 1986, p. 24). Not only is a balanced multifaith perspective important, but students need also to be aware that their attitudes to others (especially to those of a different religion, race or colour) affect the way they approach the study of religion. I argued that RE 'needs to focus in particular on intercultural relationships and build up the awareness and skills necessary for successful inter-faith dialogue' (Bigger, 1995, p. 16) as a preparation for adult life, with a particular focus on justice, openness and respect. Wilkinson (1989) demonstrated practical strategies which can give RE an anti-racist focus.

Accurate description of religious practice and

belief is not easy since there are often wide variations within faiths and it can be hard to generalise without stereotyping. RE should establish and develop a framework for students which is intellectually rigorous, open-minded and yet empathetic to the faiths being studied, so that they learn to appreciate, handle and interpret this variation whenever they meet it. This may include establishing a broad outline 'map' of the faith but needs to avoid the rigidity which turns this into a stereotype. This implies a fair coverage of diversity and controversy within faiths, exploring why individuals and groups differ in view on what points of principle. The SCAA model syllabuses for RE (SCAA, 1994) asked selected members of the six 'principal' faiths in Britain to advise on the content and scope of the RE curriculum. This will not in itself suffice: the question of who approves the representatives can be hotly problematic; it is also unlikely that areas of disagreement within faiths will emerge into the public view, since for the faiths involved the syllabus may to some degree have a public relations function.

There are strengths in strategies which approach insider information with respect, but there are also perils if this inhibits critical judgement. Religious studies require the skill and patience of ethnographers who listen, observe and compile data without substantial interference from their own preconceived mental maps, seeking to illuminate rather than to criticise. In my own small-scale work with the Exclusive Brethren (Bigger, 1990a) I was surprised to find that the study overturned many of my previously learnt prejudices about their faith and practice; and that *on their own terms* their views on acceptable education made sense. Their particular concerns focused on religious education, sex education and information technology. Yet patient ethnography does not sit comfortably with the demand for what is termed 'evaluation' in the British examination system; that is, the need to show critical awareness of the subject matter. This should not become an invitation to reintroduce prejudice by asking 'but what do *you* think?'; yet if assessment is not structured with sound critical methodology this can too easily happen (see, further, Bigger, 1989b and 1991). The treatment of religions in the school curriculum is necessarily superficial. What the student personally thinks at that point in time on the basis of the limited information available is less important than being able to justify theoretical positions against clear and well-articulated criteria. One person's opinion is decidedly not necessarily as good, *per se*, as anyone else's: the skill lies in differentiating between alternative views on sound critical grounds.

I have elsewhere argued therefore (Bigger, 1996) that thinking skills are important to religious education. Education should help pupils to become critically aware of their surroundings and to engage positively with the world in which they live. Education through the whole curriculum (to which RE contributes) needs to address issues such as social justice, prejudice, attitudes to others, racist abuse whether personal, structural or institutional, equality of opportunity, gender inequalities, moral choices and ethical debates. Such an education is rationalistic inasmuch as logic and reason are used as arbiters, but it needs to have a breadth of vision than can encompass religious perceptions. It is an essential part of RE to offer a critical analysis of philosophical and ethical issues; and those which focus on race, justice and equality are particularly significant

Our problem in RE is to know how these two approaches – to study religion with respect; and to develop critical skills – can combine. One approach has been to separate moral (or 'personal and social') education from RE; this unfortunately sets the tone that religious understanding is not properly part of the solution to personal and moral questions. The question 'why be moral?' is not an easy one either. The animal world is in general intent on personal and family survival: animals base choices on personal or group advantage, and not from altruistic motives. Why should humans be different? Clearly, in many cases we are not: but there are examples of altruism and self-sacrifice stemming both from religious belief and from humanistic ideology which humans tend to value as examples of the 'better' side of human nature. People need a belief in social justice if they are to intervene in order to make the world a better, fairer and safer place. Where religious and moral education are separated, moral education is cut off from the variety of ideologies that might strengthen and underpin it; it then has to rely heavily on pragmatic approaches to ethical situations. Situation ethics are important but assume that moral solutions are sought and principles are valued. Joining together religious and moral education can restore the debate about issues so long as dogmatism is avoided and critical analysis and moral debates are allowed to thrive.

Thus, combining the two approaches can offer methodological advantages in educational terms. It attempts to treat religious beliefs with respect whilst encouraging debate. That each faith contains within itself a wide diversity of view needs to be recognised and handled. Students need experience of the issues – theological, institutional, ethical – and the conflict-resolution strategies that are needed for dealing with these. This diversity of view within individual religions is increased when we consider a wider range of faiths. Studying religion requires comprehension at as deep a level as possible; but not comparison between different positions or between faiths, since comparison introduces interference which obscures many fine points of detail and invites inappropriate discussion about 'which is better'. Inexperience or misunderstandings can downgrade points of view not personally favoured and can inhibit further open-minded study. Comprehension through critical analysis will enable students to recognise opinions and prejudices held uncritically and thus make them less vulnerable to biased rhetoric.

The exploration of moral issues can allow personal evaluation to develop incrementally. What stance should we take, and why? To support social justice or injustice? This is starkly put, and is in fact not a simple matter. It is one thing to say you believe in social justice as a 'good thing'; it is quite another to give away wealth, property, land and position as a consequence. A *Guardian* feature (22 July 1996) claimed that 358 wealthy people own as much as half of the world's population put together; to give this wealth away would make a real difference. To the affluent, the consequences of a belief in social justice can be less appealing than the idea itself. Nevertheless, issues such as the global distribution of resources (and consequent patterns of wealth and poverty) will need to occupy the political minds of the next generations and will require creative strategies. Personal ideology and religious belief can play a part in developing the rationale for this. Justice and the essential equality of humans 'in the eyes of God' (that is, as an a *priori* assumption) are ideals found commonly in world religions.

Relationships between the sexes can provide another area of social analysis and interest: the role and status of women; sexual behaviour and personal relationships; marriage and family issues. Issues such as these can interrogate religions and find a variety of points of view. Whatever the faith or philosophy of the student, these issues will be thought-provoking and may be resolved differently. Environmental issues deal both with the treatment of animals (including both wild creatures and 'food animals') and the protection of the environment. Attitudes to nature may be linked to ideology or religious belief and may need to be resolved with their assistance. Conversely, religious viewpoints may inhibit good environmental practice. Issues of industry, work and leisure raise interest in the nature of useful work, the relative value of occupations and the esteem which determines levels of income. Our critique of social and economic systems can give us opportunities to explore attitudes, values and criteria of status: power, wealth and class are part of the nature of the society which humans have chosen to develop and are protected at the expense of a fair deal for the majority.

Issues of human concern are addressed by all religions and will be our next area for analysis. I am not attempting to match aspects of religious practice, organisation, history and teaching to particular key stages: the SCAA model syllabuses have given wide flexibility. I would, however, wish to argue that the issue of confusion of religions (or 'mishmash', as used by politicians and press) has been overrated for political reasons to damage multifaith strategies. I argued, after a primary school research project (Bigger, 1987) in which 8-year-olds studied five religions over a term, that they did not confuse religions since the information they received was clear, accurate and carefully paced. Confusion can occur when teachers are themselves unclear: few primary teachers are, for example, confident in their detailed knowledge and understanding of the six religions because this was not part of their training and is not an in-service priority. The high standards required for accurate description, respectful presentation and the avoidance of stereotyping (Bigger, 1995) requires accessibility to further training.

An important question revolves around whether confused teaching is better than no teaching, or whether it can have a long-term effect on the pupils' understanding. Few, if any of us, can fairly claim total balance and accuracy. If we are to draw a parallel with science teaching, very confused and inaccurate science teaching is likely, unless corrected, to embed error and impair progression. The effect of this is to stimulate demands for high entry qualifications and more strenuous initial teacher training. In multifaith RE also there comes a point when inaccuracy becomes damaging. If the work, say, on festivals is respectful and enjoyable (but wrongly explained), the benefits may outweigh the problems; if the overall result is disrespectful and a chore to pupils, this is likely to create lasting damage.

Social justice

Analysing historical, scriptural and contemporary data on ethical positions is never easy (see Morgan and Lawton, 1996). The Jewish and Christian traditions share the biblical accounts of prophets (such as Amos, Hosea, Micah, Isaiah) who made social justice a key element in their teaching, demanding protection of the weak, widow, orphan, alien, poor and oppressed (Bigger, 1989a). Key concepts are 'righteousness', 'uprightness' and 'loving kindness'. These prophets stood out in their own time against contemporary social and political behaviour, insisting on high standards of religious practice and ethical responsibility. Their contributions and comments were not always welcome. Some laws also show a similar concern for vulnerable underclasses.

Christians retained this Jewish concern for social justice. Jesus interpreted tradition flexibly, stressing that ethical behaviour is a matter of sincere personal intentions stemming from the kind of people we are. Killing is wrong, but angry or jealous thoughts cause it. Wealth can inhibit just behaviour, and the dishonest acquisition of wealth receives a stern rebuke. Jesus had great sympathy with other races, and with those regarded as outcast. Where it exists in Christianity, political radicalism based on belief in social justice can become difficult for governments to handle.

Muslims accord the prophets, and Jesus, the status of messengers of God, 'sealed' by the revelations to Muhammad collected in the Qur'án. Through the ages, Muslims have linked almsgiving (*zakat*) with fasting, which offers a shared experience with the hungry and demonstrates the victory of disciplined devotion over unrestrained appetites. Islam should not be imposed by force, and relationships with other religions can be peaceable. Muslims view all people as God's creatures so even the humblest of animals should be respected. The great diversity and variety of people is a reason for rejoicing; all are equal and welcome and so Islam is naturally multiracial. People are recognised rather through their religious identities, joined through beliefs and attitudes in common. Islam regards men and women as different yet complementary, equal in spiritual terms, so women have full civil rights and cannot be excluded from public life. Social and political developments do not always live up to Islamic ideals: scrutiny, for Muslims, must base itself first and foremost on the Qur'án.

Bahá'ís draw inspiration from the same tradition and seek to interpret it for the modern technological age and global economy. The faith is rooted in the work and writings of two Persian visionaries with a Shi'a Muslim and Sufi background who pressed for democracy, monogamy and equality, the Báb (executed 1850) and Bahá'u'lláh (died 1892 after a lifetime in captivity). Bahá'ís set an international agenda involving social justice on a global scale and inter-faith dialogue, forming an essential part of an ethic reflecting religious responsibilities. This demands the empowerment of the weak and vulnerable through consultation and collaboration in a global setting in which human unity is the supreme global vision (Bigger, 1997). Their planetary strategy sidelines nationalism and ethnocentric attitudes. As a faith practising in Great Britain, it is not yet recognised by SCAA.

India has had a history of social inequalities, of which the system of 'out-castes' or 'untouchables' is best known. Outdated social norms can get confused with religious values. Gandhi condemned inequality and the new Indian government supported this in law. Hinduism is hugely diverse because of the size and languages of India, but there are common threads. The concept of *karma* affirms that actions have consequences which affect both our personal futures and society at large. Hindus therefore seek to perform good deeds. A sense of closeness and solidarity within creation puts people into a close relationship with other creatures. Decisions on acceptable food often reflect an unwillingness to exploit and harm animals; rather, if we live supportively with an animal such as the cow, it will provide for us milk for dairy products and dung for building and burning. Support of nonviolence (*ahimsa*) deeply affects Hindu value systems and is best known through Gandhi's political interpretation of the doctrine. There is a particular stress on the interdependency of people within the social order, from which the West can learn a great deal; all of us have our parts to play and have responsibilities which stem from this. In Indian society, however, there is room for social critique.

Sikhs worship one God and revere ten historic gurus, beginning with Guru Nanak (1469–1539). After the tenth guru, Guru Gobind Singh (1666–1708), the Guru's authority was vested in the sacred book, the Guru Granth Sahib and so the scriptures are the main focus of worship in the gurdwara today. Guru Nanak said, at a transformative moment in his life, 'There is no Hindu, no Muslim. Whose path shall I follow? I will follow God's path.' Sikh scriptures have examples of the poetry of Hindu and Muslim sages alongside that of Nanak and the early Sikh gurus. In a sense there are, Sikhs say, many paths to God and there should be no compulsion to follow any particular one. What is important is the sincerity of worship and the behaviour that stems from this; so Sikhs develop positive and supportive relationships with other faiths without feelings of superiority or exclusivity. Guru Nanak's teaching contained a denial of caste conventions and established the expectation that all be prepared to eat together communally. Nanak led Sikhs to the belief in the essential equality between women and men: both wear the five Ks (religious symbols) and undertake the *amrit* ceremony of initiation and commitment; and women have played a significant role in Sikh history, even in battle. Social and cultural factors may interfere with these ideals, so even Sikh youngsters might find this area of discussion rewarding and challenging.

Buddhists draw inspiration and teaching from Siddhartha Gautama (fifth century BCE), the Buddha ('enlightened one') for this age. Concerned with the truth of how things really are (rather than how our minds perceive them) we all have the potential for enlightenment and are at some point on the path towards it. Everything we do has consequences, in this life or in following lives (the principle of *karma*). Selfish behaviour, greed and hatred are part of our delusion about self which obscures the truth. We have to recognise impermanence (*anicca*) and that life is characterised by unsatisfactoriness and suffering (*dukkha*). Our concept of self is not secure: we construct our self-image for our own purposes and need to cast this aside (the concept of *anatta*, 'not self'). Wealth, ambition and power only hold people back. The issue of equality has to recognise that much on which status depends is impermanent, and ideas of status are based on delusion. Relationships with other people (and creatures) need to be based on the absence of violence or hurt (*ahimsa*). If pacifism is a response to war, simple actions and choices suggest wider strategies: only taking enough for our needs; sexual responsibility including celibacy; being compassionate; and being mindful of the consequences of our actions.

Religious studies have been strongly influenced by the phenomenological approach, and since 1971 this has influenced RE. The essence of this approach is to distance ourselves from our own beliefs and values in order to allow us to understand and appreciate another people's points of view. This was a response to earlier Christian-centred views and it reaffirmed and further developed the academic tradition of treating religions with respect and seeking to understand them from their own perspective. Students were invited to investigate religions *as if insiders* – having no concern for the question 'is it ultimately true or not?' which is deliberately not under investigation, and described as 'bracketed out'. It was a helpful and salutary corrective which put pluralism firmly on the agenda.

This approach is not unrelated to sociology, which stems from patient observation and careful interviewing, seeking to show data as objectively as possible. However, sociology tries also to interpret data in the light of the broader picture and to illuminate what is found through theoretical frameworks. Social and cultural anthropology do similarly, although traditionally their 'subjects' are distant in mileage and culture. The Schools Council (1971) working paper 36 recommended the study of manifestations of faith ('manifestation' is often used as a translation of *phenomenon*). Ninian Smart, who worked closely with the Schools Council project in Lancaster, had defined religious phenomena under six headings or 'dimensions': social, doctrinal, mythic, institutional, experiential and ethical, claiming that these fit all religions. Smart has since added 'artistic' to his list.

There are, however, problems in applying phenomenology as the only interpretative strategy. Its origins, in the writings of Edmund Husserl, lay in a general philosophical grand theory: that 'reality' consisted only of 'that which appeared to be', 'appearances' or 'manifestations' about which our minds make assumptions (Bowker, 1995). Greater understanding only came through 'bracketing' these out to try to see things as they really are. This raises the issue of whether in fact we can see beyond our basic mental frameworks; Husserl felt that beyond the brackets we can glimpse the essence of being, and he called this 'eidetic vision'. In applying the philosophy to religion, there are certain consequences. It assumes that religion has no reality except what 'appears to be', the manifestations. These manifestations can be classified in order to glimpse the essence behind our complex assumptions, beliefs and labels. Although there may well be some essential coherence behind religions, the external manifestations (the beliefs and worship) do not constitute what religion is all about. Although phenomenology seeks to describe religion *as if true* and sees things through the eyes of worshippers, the philosophical purpose is then to deconstruct this knowledge. Knowledge about religion is not knowledge about how things really are, but how worshippers imagine them to be. The underlying assumption therefore is that religion is not true but a form of human expression to be recorded.

In RE there has been great emphasis on the first part, accurate description. The truth claims are accepted as what adherents believe but their truth is not explored and debated. To challenge a truth claim is regarded as inappropriate and disrespectful. If this persists, it removes the possibility of enabling pupils to become critically aware. Equally, it sets up different truth claims in ways which cause confusion and accusations of 'mishmash'. Students ask which view is right, even where teachers feel inhibited from doing so. Members of faith communities have the benefit of not being condemned as 'wrong' but in a way that prevents their being treated as 'right'; but this creates the impression that truth is relative and that interpretations of truth cannot be demonstrated or contested.

Phenomenology therefore is at heart not concerned with what is true but with what people claim to believe. It distances the student from the worshipper by being interested but not personally involved. Children from various faith communities do not learn about their own faith in a way that helps them to grow within their faith. True, this is to some extent the role of the faith communities; but if adherents do not find RE's treatment of their religion personally helpful, it is unlikely to give other students a flavour of the faith's inner conviction. It is thus ultimately disempowering as it does nothing to affirm belief or identity. Thus, although phenomenology has been a most useful approach, it needs balancing with others.

Our task is two-fold: to encourage children to reflect critically upon key issues of human existence and ethics; and to consider how religious teaching (of all faiths simultaneously) can be regarded as

'true' rather than 'as if true'. These two may seem contradictory but are not. The process of critical thought by insiders – members of particular faiths – does not rest content with the superficial but struggles with the nature of deity, of humanity and of ethical responsibility. We should encourage children to ask 'what *really* do you mean'. Whatever the faith, dogma soon disappears and sincere questions remain, of what the essence of faith really is. Divisions between faiths soon begin to disappear, just as in the early Sikh writings, writings of Hindus and Muslims were expressing the same points as the Gurus themselves. A truth claim thus is not for placing on one side and bracketing out, but for wrestling with.

We return now to the question of implicit religious education. The Schools Council working papers viewed implicit developmental work to be as important as explicit study of religions. The implicit focused on 'meaning' – the individual personal quest for understanding which inspired the primary curriculum development series *Seeking Meaning, Conveying Meaning*, and *Celebrating Meaning* (Schools Council, 1979). Personal meaningfulness cuts across our understanding of belief, worship, ethics and public behaviour; without inner conviction, religion is meaningless and empty.

One concept of implicit religion is that many ordinary and secular activities have 'religious' undertones – for example, football, the public house, the state. That is, inner loyalties and convictions are to be found there also; in a sense they govern people's lives. 'Religious' here is used as a metaphor: human behaviour *resembles* religious adherence; but neither the object nor the responsibility of worship is present, so the resemblance is superficial. Religion has always been hard to define and impossible to tie down; but a working definition might look like: *religion is a total way of life based on a world view informed by a set of beliefs and values focused around personal transformation*. It may help our sociological understanding to use religion as a metaphor, but it is confusing to claim that such metaphors are realities; and it is particularly confusing to mix categories in this way within RE for children.

Implicit RE became a reaction to the explicit Christian-dominated syllabuses of the 1950s and 1960s. When unfamiliar explicit elements were introduced, it was comfortable to have 'caring and sharing' and other such developmental themes to replace them. Much implicit RE is best described as moral, or social and personal, education: focusing on our responsibilities to others and to the world at large and promoting awareness of self-worth (these are, for example, the three implicit objectives for primary schools in the Hampshire syllabus of 1978, echoed by later syllabuses). The difference for RE is that personal and social insights are illustrated through examples from and principles of religious traditions. The challenge is to ensure that topics reflecting personal and social growth are not Euro-centric but are promoted by all cultures and faiths.

Titles for RE indicate lack of consensus about its purpose this century. Religious *instruction* summed up the belief that there is a body of know-ledge to learn *and accept*. In practice (although not in law, according to the strict wording of the 1944 Education Act) this knowledge was seen as Christian, a legacy that still survives today in the political sphere. *Scripture* shows the emphasis on the Bible (other scriptures would not normally be included). *Divinity* stresses that learning is about God, as do the modern A level syllabuses focusing on Christian *theology*. Religious *studies* emphasises academic and impartial aims, striking a balance between faiths and points of view but tending not to highlight aspects of personal spiritual develop-ment. Religious *education* is used variously to cover all these things, resulting in a confusion of aims. It is of all subjects the most controversial. Two points today seem agreed: that RE promotes understand-ing of religion and religions broadly; and that it is educational in the twin senses of encouraging im-partial investigation and personal engagement with the material. The SCAA model syllabuses describe this personal engagement as 'learning from religion' (which is distinct from 'learning about religions'). This is best seen not in a confessional sense of accepting what is learnt, but in the developmental sense of thinking through the issues, seeing com-mon ground between faiths, and testing the material in the light of one's own experience and perceptions. This is implicitly RE's chief purpose. The reflection on life is not free-ranging, as it might be in personal and social education, but linked with, and stemming from, their study of religion. Experiential strategies, actively exploring feelings and relationships, become part of implicit RE when they are linked with, and draw their inspiration from, aspects of religion being studied. Even where this is not the case, they can also make a very helpful contribution to personal and social education.

It is helpful to view the personal development of pupils not only intellectually but also socially and emotionally in a way which impacts upon their atti-tudes and values. Strategies for encouraging and enhancing such development need to open up young people to new perspectives in ways which are natural and unforced. This process needs first and foremost to be empowering. Paulo Freire (1972) used education in South America to empower people socially and politically to achieve, aspire and succeed, and this provides a helpful model. Educa-tion is not an elite body of information but relates to real people in actual situations exploring their potential and responses. Such an educational pro-cess is political in the sense that it changes people and ultimately changes society. RE can encourage personal change through discussion, reflection and interaction with people provided that it is based on an empowerment philosophy. For members of a faith community, this demands that their faith be respected and not refuted. Challenging questions will be asked, but the context can be positive and supportive. For those without religious commit-ment, positive encouragement can be given to developing students' own value system in the light of dialogue – we need to respect also where they are coming from. The effects of empowerment might include having identity affirmed; translating religious teaching into ethical principles which stand up to scrutiny in terms of human rights and social justice; and enabling members of faith groups to examine their faith tradition so as to develop their understanding in a critically informed way. An empowering RE will produce stronger, and more ethically engaged, Christians, Jews, Muslims, Sikhs, Hindus, Buddhists, Bahá'ís and Humanists. Race awareness, concerned action for equality and anti-racism can thrive in this climate.

Spirituality has risen considerably in public debate since 1988 as the Education Reform Act (ERA) highlights the need to address the 'spiritual' dimen-sion of education (SCAA, 1995 and 1996b). Spir-itual aspects of the curriculum are broader than religious education (see also Bigger and Brown, 1999). RE focuses on religious beliefs and their implications in terms of worship and ethics; spiritu-ality is concerned with the whole picture and the whole curriculum. There are problems in defin-ition, scope, process and assessment which makes a consensus about 'the spiritual' difficult. The spirit-ual is separated from the intellectual, aesthetic and ethical dimensions in ERA and Office for Standards in Education (OFSTED) documentation. If spirituality is a process of reflection on meaning, it is crucial that all aspects feed into it. Only if it is identified with religion will spirituality come to refer to insights about God and doctrine; then, the spiritual humanist becomes impossible by definition and many Buddhists without a central theistic belief cannot be viewed as spiritual. This is clearly untenable, as spirituality refers to a quality and not to doctrinal orthodoxy. Partly, the problem is that the term was once used of pious contemplation; but pluralism today has caused its scope to be extended. How a humanist reflects on personal meaning is now an issue which cannot be marginalised. A tendency to take an imperialistic view over spirituality, assuming that it is the property of a particular (and dominant) religion or of religion in general, is now rightly resisted. What constitutes a spiritual person (or child) is approached more humbly. We recognise that spiritual people do not necessarily worship formally; and that some forms of worship make spirituality difficult, if conformity inhibits the personal quest.

We need to regard spirituality inclusively as a quest for personal meaning at the highest level, which includes intellectual, ethical, social, political, aesthetic and other such dimensions. It marks a *quality* of reflection which is holistic in scope, transcends material needs and ambitions, and transforms the personality in positive ways. Every subject then can contribute to this, bringing values high on to their agendas. Geography, for example, introduces issues of land use and development, work and leisure, nationality, nationalism, identity and conflict (see Bigger, 1990b). History raises social and political values and explores human motivation. Science raises ethical and environmental issues and pushes forward understanding of origins and cosmology. The arts link aesthetic issues with self-expression. Each has its crucial part to play.

All pupils need this holistic vision as the fundamental educational standard. Other forms of knowledge and competence work within such frameworks. Such a vision is not to be imposed but discovered, constructed and developed: discovered, in that insights break in and overwhelm; constructed, in that it is an intellectual process of informed concept building; developed, in that this is a lifetime process of personal growth. Its scope is world-wide, drawing insights from all cultures,

societies and faiths. But it is essentially concerned with values. Attitudes to other people need to evolve within this personal growth, which assumes that prejudice and discrimination are challenged. This spiritual vision will therefore be anti-racist in that negative images and attitudes will not survive the process. Conversely, anti-racist awareness can provide a useful marker of the quality of spiritual growth.

References

Bigger, S.F. (1987) Multifaith education in the shires: two projects in primary RE, *Westminster Studies in Education* **10**, 37–51.

Bigger, S.F. (ed.) (1989a) *Creating the Old Testament: The Emergence of the Hebrew Bible*. Oxford: Basil Blackwell.

Bigger, S.F. (1989b) Religious education: issues from the 1980s, *Journal of Beliefs and Values* **10**(2), 1–6.

Bigger, S.F. (1990a) The 'Exclusive Brethren': an educational dilemma, *Journal of Beliefs and Values* **11**(1), 13–15.

Bigger, S.F. (1990b), The history and geography NC proposals, *Journal of Beliefs and Values* **11**(2), 9–10.

Bigger, S.F. (1991) Assessment in religious education, *Journal of Beliefs and Values* **12**(1), 1–5.

Bigger, S.F. (1995) Challenging religious education in a multicultural world, *Journal of Beliefs and Values* **16**(2), 11–18.

Bigger, S.F. (1996) Race, religion and reason, *Journal of the Critical Study of Religion, Ethics and Society* **1**(2), 21–33.

Bigger, S.F. (1997) The Bahá'í global vision, *Journal of Belief and Values* **18**(2), 181–91.

Bigger, S.F. and Brown, E. (1999) *Spiritual, Moral, Social and Cultural Education*. London: David Fulton.

Bowker, J. (1995) *The Sense of God: Sociological, Anthropological and Psychological Approaches to the Origin of the Sense of God*. Oxford: Oneworld.

City of Birmingham Education Authority (1975) *Living Together: Agreed Syllabus for Religious Education*. Supplement: 1982.

Commission for Racial Equality (1988a) *Learning in Terror*. London: CRE.

Commission for Racial Equality (1988b) *Living in Terror*. London: CRE.

Department of Education and Science (DES) (1981) *West Indian Children in Our Schools* (The Rampton Report), Cmnd 6869. London: Her Majesty's Stationery Office.

Department of Education and Science (DES) (1985) *Education for All* (The Swann Report: final report of the Committee of Inquiry into the Education of Children from Ethnic Minority Groups), Cmnd 9543. London: Her Majesty's Stationery Office.

Freire, P. (1972) *Pedagogy of the Oppressed*. New York: Seabury Press.

Hampshire Education Authority (1978) *Agreed Syllabus for Religious Education*. Winchester: Hampshire County Council.

Hampshire Education Authority (1980) *Paths to Understanding*. Basingstoke, Hants.: Macmillan/Globe.

Hull, J. (1989) Editorial: School worship and the 1988 Education Reform Act. *British Journal of Religious Education* **11**(3), 119–25.

Klein, G. (1982) *Resources for Multicultural Education: An Introduction*. London: Schools Council/Longman.

Klein, G. (1993) *Education Towards Racial Equality*. London: Cassell.

Little, A. and Willey, R. (1981) *Multicultural Education: The Way Forward*. London: Schools Council/Longman.

Modgil, S., Verma, G., Mallick, K. and Modgil, C. (eds) (1986) *Multicultural Education: The Interminable Debate*. London: Falmer Press.

Morgan, P. and Lawton, C. (eds) (1996) *Ethical Issues in Six Religious Traditions*. Edinburgh: Edinburgh University Press.

Mullard, C. (1982) Multiracial education in Britain: from assimilation to cultural pluralism. In J. Tierney (ed.), *Race, Migration and Schooling*. London: Holt, Rinehart & Winston.

Office for Standards in Education (OFSTED) (1994) *Spiritual, Moral, Social and Cultural Development*. London: OFSTED.

School Curriculum and Assessment Authority (SCAA) (1994) *Religious Education Model Syllabuses* (4 booklets). London: SCAA.

School Curriculum and Assessment Authority (SCAA) (1995) *Spiritual and Moral Development*. London: SCAA.

School Curriculum and Assessment Authority (SCAA) (1996a) *Analysis of SACRE Reports 1966*. London: SCAA.

School Curriculum and Assessment Authority (SCAA) (1966b) *Education for Adult Life: The Spiritual and Moral Development of Young People*. London: SCAA.

Schools Council (1971) *Religious Education in the Secondary School*, Working Paper 36. London: Evans Methuen Educational.

Schools Council (1972) *Religious Education in the Primary School*, Working Paper 44. London: Evans Methuen Educational.

Schools Council. Project on Religious Education in Primary Schools (1979) *Discovering and Approach in Practice: Religious Education In Primary Schools*, 3 vols: *Seeking Meaning*; *Conveying Meaning*; *Celebrating Meaning*. London: Macmillan for Schools Council.

Troyna, B. and Carrington, B. (1990) *Education, Racism and Reform*. London: Routledge.

Troyna, B. and Hatcher, R. (1992) *Racism in Children's Lives: A Study of Mainly White Primary Schools*. London: Routledge.

Troyna, B. and Williams, J. (1986) *Racism, Education and the State: The Racialisation of Education Policy*. Beckenham, Kent: Croom Helm.

Wilkinson, I. (1989) Religious education and the fight against racism: some guidelines, *Multicultural Teaching* **8**(1), 42–3.

Willey, R. (1982) *Teaching in Multicultural Britain*. London: Schools Council/Longman.

Wood, A. (1984) *Assessment in a Multicultural Society: Religious Studies at 16+*. London: Schools Council.

3 Facilitating Spiritual Development in the Context of Cultural Diversity

DAVID ADSHEAD

Cultural diversity in the classroom

Every classroom is culturally diverse. In the upper set of a selective grammar school, it may be that the diversity is much narrower than in a mixed ability group of the inner-city comprehensive. But there will still be a diversity. Cultural diversity is not ethnic diversity as such, nor is it religious pluralism as such. Cultural diversity is just as much the television programmes that we watch, the newspapers we read, the music we appreciate, the sporting pastimes we follow, the eat-ins or take-aways we do or do not order, even the drinks we buy and the places where we drink them. It is the same at every level of education, from the nursery to the university. We are indivisibly part of a multicultural society, a multicultural world. As Lynch *et al.* (1992, p. 5) say:

> If we consider the overlapping dimensions of cultural diversity which have seized the headlines even in the recent past – racial, religious, linguistic, regional, ethnic, gender, age, social class and more recently caste – we cannot avoid the conclusion that, not only are most nation states culturally diverse, but that the world's population as a whole manifests a rich diversity across a large number of overlapping cultural factors and dimensions, representing a pluralism of pluralisms . . .

Elsewhere, they reflect that 'there is not, and probably never will be, one perception of cultural diversity, even within the same cultural context, social stratum or nation state' (vol. 1, p. 445).

In the context of such diversity, spiritual development must lead to the liberation of the human spirit. In the world as it has become, it is extremely unlikely that this will be satisfactorily achieved by the domination of any one particular religious ideology. Spirituality will inevitably have to be *human* spirituality rather than any *religious* spirituality – be it Christian, Muslim, Buddhist or whatever – if it is to be truly embracing and inclusive. That is not to say that there is no Christian spirituality, or Muslim spirituality, or Buddhist spirituality; simply that in the search for a unity within diversity, it can *only* be human spirituality. The National Curriculum Council (NCC) and the Office for Standards in Education (OFSTED) have clearly grasped this fundamental principle in their approaches.

What is spirituality?

The primary task which current educational legislation lays upon a school is to promote 'the spiritual, moral, cultural, mental and physical development of pupils at the school and of society' and to prepare 'such pupils for the opportunities, responsibilities and experiences of adult life' (ERA, 1988, p. 1). This must therefore also be the aim and purpose of the whole curriculum, regardless of its somewhat arbitrary division into a range of subjects. The need to promote spiritual development has in fact been there since the Education Act of 1944. It has perhaps only recently moved to centre-stage following the publication of a discussion paper by the National Curriculum Council and because of OFSTED's need to develop some criteria for evaluation in their inspections. The key definition of spirituality has therefore not surprisingly become that offered by the National Curriculum Council (1993, p. 2). The italics, which are mine, serve to identify the five defining aspects of spirituality in this particular approach:

> The term needs to be seen as applying to *something fundamental in the human condition* which is not necessarily experienced through the physical senses

and/or expressed through everyday language. It has to do with *relationships with other people* and, for believers, with God. It has to do with the universal *search for individual identity* – with our responses to challenging experiences, such as death, suffering, beauty, and encounters with good and evil. It is to do with the *search for meaning and purpose in life* and for *values by which to live.*

Spirituality then, so far as the NCC is concerned, 'has to do with' relationships, identity, meaning and purpose, and values. Such an approach includes those like Newby (1996), for example, who identifies the meaning of spirituality with 'the development of personal identity' (p. 93) involving 'the development of an ultimate, overriding perspective on life that influences all one's values and decisions' (p. 106) and Lambourn (1996), who suggests that 'nothing . . . remains in the category "spiritual" after the "personal-social" has been distinguished' (p. 157).

Bradford (1995), writing against the background of the Children Act 1989 and of the needs of children in care, distinguishes 'human spirituality', which is 'related to every child's need for love, security, reflection, praise and responsibility'; 'devotional spirituality' which 'builds directly upon human spirituality and is generally to be expressed in the culture and language of a particular religion'; and 'practical spirituality' which 'combines both human and devotional spirituality and is expressed in our day-to-day living, giving shape and direction to our lives' goals and to our social concerns and duties' (p. 72). If the second and third were reversed, there would be no substantial difference and, in any event, there would certainly be complete agreement with his comment that: 'Spiritual development is not a secondary or disposable part of personal development but the essence of it, and no part of it can be arbitrarily excluded without significant loss' (p. 73).

Rodger's (1996, p. 52) suggestion that 'Spirituality . . . is rooted in *awareness*' (his italics, not mine) which then gives rise to an active response and for some leads to a complete way of life, seems quite consistent with the NCC definition. So does Terence Copley (Marjon, 1990), who says that spirituality for him is 'the awareness that there is something more to life than meets the eye, something more than the material, something more than the obvious, something to wonder at, something to respond to'. King (1985, p. 138) regards a non-doctrinaire and non-confessional spiritual educa-

tion as 'a training in sensitivity for spiritual awareness'. She continues:

> If we can develop a deep concern for what is promised as possible at the heart of all religious teaching, namely, the liberation from self-centred desire, anger and greed, practise loving and caring for others, and hope for ultimate goodness and glory, then we are exploring one of the many forms of the spiritual path. Discovering spirituality is like being on a journey; it is the cultivation of a gift and the learning of discernment. Much of education should precisely be about this.

Most objections to the National Curriculum Council's definition are concerned with the way in which God is presented as some sort of optional extra and with the lack of any specific inclusion of the transcendent. Although he stands outside the immediate debate, Sheldrake (1995, p. 59) claims that 'contemporary spirituality is characterized more by an attempt to integrate human and religious values than by an exclusive interest in the component parts of "spiritual" growth such as stages of prayer'. For him, spirituality is essentially Christian:

> While spirituality, in Christian terms, is not about some other *kind* of life but about *the whole of human life at depth*, our understanding of what this might mean cannot avoid questions posed specifically by the Christian tradition of revelation about the nature of God, human nature and the relationship between the two. . . . In other words, contemporary Christian spirituality is explicitly Trinitarian, Christological, and ecclesial. (pp. 60–1)

Thatcher (1996) reserves most of his polemic for the debate on spiritual development but, in relation to the problem of defining spirituality, suggests that, in the present circumstances, it is 'better for Christian theologians to begin with an overt understanding of spirituality rooted in the lives of the saints and the faith of the church'. His definition of spirituality therefore becomes: 'the practice of the human love of God and neighbour' (p. 119).

An important aspect of the debate would be the nature of the experience which is being interpreted in the development of a spirituality. Is it *religious* in the sense in which that would be understood by James (1902), Hardy (1979) and Robinson (1977 and 1984). It is interesting that there is little apparent difference between Dixon's (1984a) definition of 'spiritual experience' and Robinson's (1984) definition of 'religious experience'. The latter speaks of 'an awareness, however momentary or imperfect, of an order of reality both beyond and yet capable of permeating the rest of life', whilst the former suggests that the term 'usually refers to an awareness of divine presence', which it earlier describes as 'the unseen reality which permeates the human scene'. Hardy (1979) says that:

> It seems to me that the main characteristics of man's religious and spiritual experiences are shown in his feelings for a transcendental reality which frequently manifest themselves in early childhood; a feeling that 'Something Other' than the self can actually be sensed; a desire to personalize this presence into a deity and to have a private I–Thou relationship with it, communicating through prayer.

In the same tradition of understanding, Nye and Hay (1996) found that 'a survey of the available definitions of "spirituality" failed to offer a starting point sufficiently convincing to encompass the uncharted area of children's spirituality' and therefore proposed 'a set of three interrelated themes or categories of spiritual sensitivity' (p. 145). These are: awareness sensing (here and now, tuning, flow and focusing); mystery sensing (awe and wonder, imagination); and value sensing (delight and despair, ultimate goodness, meaning). They are critical of a purely cognitive approach because of its 'tendency to ignore what appears to be the experiential basis for the creation of religious meaning', and they suggest that the 'more cognitive signs of spiritual activity are in many cases the secondary products of spiritual stirrings found in awareness-, mystery- and value-sensing' (p. 151).

The relationship between ordinary experience and religious experience in the approaches to religious education in schools has, however, generally had more to do with the theologies of Paul Tillich and Dietrich Bonhoeffer, popularised by Robinson (1963). This fairly liberal and 'implicit' approach is epitomised by Jeffreys (1972, p. 118):

> It is of the greatest importance to understand that religious truth is not a special kind of truth, nor religious experience a queer, unnatural kind of experience belonging to some strange and other world. *Religious experience is normal experience*, and we have religious experience every day, whether or not we recognise it as such. *Religious truth is normal experience understood at full depth*; what makes truth religious is not that it relates to some abnormal field of thought and feeling but that it goes to the roots of the experience which it interprets. (My italics)

In general conciliatory tone, Priestley (1996) identifies 'six aspects of the spiritual as it most affects curriculum matters'. These are: that it is a wider concept than the religious; that it is dynamic; that it dwells on the process of being and becoming; that it is as concerned with other-worldliness as with this world; that it is communal as well as individual; and that it is holistic.

Rose (1996, p. 180) comments, with an irony that was probably quite unintended, that 'the academic debate as to the nature of spirituality is well under way' and Thatcher (1996, p. 119) rightly declares that 'spirituality is now a site of shifting ideological controversy'. On balance, however, it must be said that the NCC and OFSTED approaches offer the only realistic way forward. The alternative would be for schools to continue to provide the battleground for competing theologies. If the view of spirituality which the NCC and OFSTED documents present is post-Christian secular-humanistic (and non-realist) in character, it is really no more than a sign of the times. To that extent, the unwillingness of a theistic (and realist) minority to accept it because it lacks a transcendent dimension is only to be expected. Their inability to recognise that it represents the most – perhaps the only – workable basis is to be regretted. In fact, their attitude may be quite closely related to the 'Christian Religionism' of Hull's (1996) critique, 'the form taken by religion when tribalistic or exclusive forms of personal or collective identity are maintained' (Hull, 1995).

What is spiritual development?

The National Curriculum Council (NCC, 1993) suggests the following as aspects of spiritual development: the development of personal beliefs that may or may not be specifically religious; a sense of awe, wonder and mystery; experiencing feelings of transcendence; a search for meaning and purpose; self-knowledge; recognising the worth of individuals and building relationships with others; expressing one's innermost thoughts through the arts and exercising the imagination; feelings and emotions: a sense of being moved. OFSTED's (1993) description is very similar:

> Spiritual development relates to that aspect of inner life through which pupils acquire insights into their personal existence which are of enduring worth. It

is characterised by reflection, the attribution of meaning to experience, valuing a non-material dimension to life and intimations of an enduring reality. 'Spiritual' is not synonymous with 'religious'; all areas of the curriculum may contribute to pupils' spiritual development.

Kibble (1996), amending Beesley (1993) to delete any unnecessary involvement of transcendence, becomes virtually synonymous:

> a lifelong process of encountering, reflecting on, responding to and developing insight from what, through experience, one perceives to be the transpersonal, transcendent, mystical or numinous. It does not necessarily involve the concept of God.

Newby (1996), as indicated earlier, argues that spiritual development is in fact the development of personal identity in the context of a contemporary non-religious common culture. The desire for knowledge and understanding, for self-understanding, for sensibility, for continuity, coherence and creativity and the need for cultural narratives are all seen as necessary attitudes and abilities in the process of development toward spiritual maturity.

The most trenchant criticism comes from Thatcher (1996), who undertakes an energetic and impassioned rejection of what he regards as an emerging 'secularised spiritual nature' (p. 122). He dislikes the unquestioning use of the word 'development' and rejects the idea that belief in God can be an optional component of a person's spirituality. He is certainly critical of the amount of 'enlightened discourse' which he finds in the documents and with the 'vacuous' connection with 'a particular strand of philosophy', rejecting the use of the phrase 'meaning and purpose' and the idea of our 'searching for values' on the basis that 'like so many other concepts, it (values) remains distressingly empty'. He describes the NCC's (1993) explanation of 'belief' as 'the price to be paid for the wholesale neglect of the question of truth' (Thatcher, 1996, p. 126), commenting that God has been 'displaced by the self in this modernist document'. Pouring scorn on the 'steps to spiritual development', he concludes that there is very little which can be salvaged, particularly when the documents seem, by the nature of their language, to be including behaviours which do not accord with his own particular values (which are not, presumably, 'empty'). Theoretically, he claims, 'anything goes' in terms of beliefs and behaviours, and

even the most anti-social stances can be supported by the evaluation criteria (p. 129). The net effect is that 'children are to be spiritually developed . . . in accordance with deeply secular criteria, some of which are borrowed from religions' (pp. 121–2). It would be interesting to know what alternative constructive proposals he might be able to offer, once he is able to extricate himself from the mire of his own apparently Christian prejudices.

OFSTED (1994) admits that spiritual development is a 'particularly difficult concept'. As we have already seen, the concept of transcendence represents a key difference between human spirituality and any form of religious spirituality. This raises the question of the role of religious education. Clearly, all curriculum subjects, including religious education, have something to contribute to the development of human spirituality. As OFSTED says: 'To move towards a position where subjects see themselves in this way might seem to require a sea-change in attitudes and approaches, but certainly the potential is there' (p. 10). Perhaps the particular role of religious education lies in its capacity to enable students to learn *from* as well as *about* religion. Certainly there is a general recognition that spiritual development is supremely personal and unique to each individual and that what is needed is an open-ended approach which concentrates on the process of a critical exploration of issues, with pupils taking an increasing responsibility for themselves and their work. At the same time, however, 'although spirituality is a unique personal characteristic, its development, for many individuals, depends in part – as does much of education – upon human interaction' (p. 9).

Since spiritual development is to be promoted by schools, its provision will need to be evaluated by OFSTED inspectors, and the basis of their evaluation will have two elements to it. On the one hand will be the range and quality of the provision. This will include such things as the school's values and attitudes; the contribution of the whole curriculum; the role of religious education, acts of collective worship and other assemblies; and the general ethos and climate of the school including its extracurricular activities. At the same time, inspectors will also need to evaluate the extent to which 'pupils may display evidence of having benefited from provision intended to promote spiritual development' (OFSTED, 1994). The question will be to what extent they demonstrate by their personal responses that they have some knowledge and understanding of other people's beliefs and attutudes and that they are developing beliefs and values which are expressed in socially acceptable attitudes and behaviours. Of course, it may not all be the school's doing. Such development will be affected by many other factors including age, personality, gender, family, peer group, ethnicity, cultural background and, more generally, the moral, spiritual and cultural climate of our society and of the communities to which students belong.

None of this seems particularly unreasonable, given the circumstances first of the original clause in the legislation and second, the attempt to establish standards in the educative process. Thatcher (1996), however, sees spiritual development, like the National Curriculum itself, as 'one massive effort at thought control':

> What calls itself a discussion paper offering guidance is massively prescriptive and proscriptive. A major state bureaucracy will attempt to ensure a double compliance. First, schools must comply with the spiritual development policy in the same way as they are to comply with the National Curriculum. But second, they are to comply with the instructions of a secular bureaucracy determined to police the sublime, to redefine and reproduce a view of religion which renders it unrecognisable to religious people, and enlists in its support the language and ideas of secular liberalism.   (p. 131)

> The diversion and redefinition of spirituality is a mirror image of the complacency, consumerism and individualism of the wider society which women and men of spirit must resolutely oppose.   (p. 134)

His recommended response is one of 'holy irony' which, being translated, appears to be not that far removed from 'cussed awkwardness'.

Structured spiritual development?

The National Curriculum Council (1993) suggests that the steps to spiritual development could include: recognising the existence of others as independent from oneself; becoming aware of and reflecting on experience; questioning and exploring the meaning of experience; understanding and evaluating a range of possible responses and interpretations; developing personal views and insights; and applying the insights gained with increasing degrees of perception to one's own life. There is a sufficient amount of common ground here to prompt an examination of the faith-development theory of James Fowler.

The General Synod Board of Education's (1991) booklet, whose editor and main author was Jeff Astley, provides a useful survey and analysis of the current position in the faith-development research which is particularly associated with James Fowler. The claim that lies at the heart of faith-development theory is that 'there is a development through childhood *and* adulthood . . . in our way of being in faith' (GSBE, 1991). But what exactly is 'faith'?

> For Fowler and his colleagues, 'faith' is primarily about *making meaning*. It 'has to do with the making, maintenance, and transformation of human meaning' (Fowler, 1980 p. 53) As such it includes our knowing, valuing, interpreting, understanding, experiencing and feeling. It is about giving positive value to attitudes and ideals, and finding significant patterns and connections within the world and within oneself. What Fowler means by faith is essentially an orientation of the person to life, our 'way-of-being-in-relation' to what we believe to be ultimate (Fowler and Keen, 1978 p. 24). It is a disposition, a stance, 'a way of moving into and giving form and coherence to life' (ibid.). In a fine phrase, Fowler talks about faith in terms of our 'way of moving into the force field of life' (Fowler, 1981). Faith is a 'way of leaning into life, of meeting and shaping our experience' (unpublished lecture handout).   (GSBE, 1991, p. 3)

Fowler identifies seven aspects to this process of faith, or, as he would say, *faithing*. In many ways, what he presents is an amalgam of the various cognitive structural developmentalists against which he then measures his interviewees, rather than an independent and original structure emerging from his research. GSBE (1991) rightly suggests that 'the relationship between these aspects is a topic worthy of further research ... Fowler does not trace all the connections very clearly'. Be that as it may, the following are the 'integral components of the one faith stance' (ibid.):

a)   the way we think;
b)   our ability to adopt another's perspective;
c)   the way we make moral judgements;
d)   how and where we set the limits to our 'community of faith';
e)   how and where we find authorities on which to rely;
f)   our way of 'holding it all together, of forming a single 'world-view'; and
g)   our understanding of and response to symbols.

Fowler's stages of faith are as follows:

Stage 0:   *Age 0–4 approximately*
           'Nursed' or 'Foundation' Faith
           (Primal Faith/The Incorporative Self);
Stage 1:   *Age 3/4–7/8 approximately*
           'Chaotic' or 'Unordered' or
           'Impressionistic' Faith
           (Intuitive-Projective Faith/The
           Impulsive Self);
Stage 2:   *Age 6/7–11/12 approximately*
           'Ordering' Faith
           (Mythic-Literal Faith/The Imperial
           Self);
Stage 3:   *Age 11/12–17/18 approximately, and
           many adults*
           'Conforming' Faith
           (Synthetic-Conventional Faith/The
           Interpersonal Self);
Stage 4:   *Age from 17/18 onwards, or from the 30s
           or 40s onwards*
           'Choosing' or 'Either/Or' Faith
           (Individuative-Reflective Faith/The
           Institutional Self);
Stage 5:   *Age rarely before 30*
           'Balanced' or 'Inclusive' or 'Both/And'
           Faith
           (Conjunctive Faith/The Inter-
           Individual Self)
Stage 6:   *Age usually only in later life, a very rare
           stage*
           'Selfless' Faith
           (Universalizing Faith/The God-
           Grounded Self)

There may be some potential in exploring the extent to which Fowler may offer a structural approach to spiritual development because the 'faith' which he describes is not, on the face of it at any rate, religious faith. Nelson (1992) uses the term 'human faith' to distinguish what Fowler is referring to from 'religious faith'. He suggests that Fowler is trying to do three things simultaneously:

First, he is trying to develop a theory of human faith which matures by stages. He wants this to be true of human beings everywhere – a descriptive account of every person's development – and in the good sense of the word, secular. Second, he is trying to construct an ideal state of affairs for human beings because his research design is an outward and upward process requiring a top stage above common human experience. This ideal state will provide a way to judge religions, philosophies or anything else that claims human allegiance. Third, he is trying to give the Christian religion the best

possible interpretation to fit both the stages and the ideal state.   (pp. 65–6)

Reference has already been made to the fact that Fowler constructed the stages of faith development from a range of other structural theories. Before their interview, people are asked to spend between two and three hours completing the 'Unfolding Tapestry of my Life' worksheet (GSBE, 1991, pp. 97–8). He then interviews adults for between two and two-and-a-half hours (children for less), using 34 questions ranging across: life review, lifeshaping experience, present values and commitments, and religion (Fowler, 1981, pp. 311–12). The interviews are transcribed, and research assistants who have been trained by Fowler decide in which stage the interviewee is to be placed. During the research 359 interviews were undertaken. A table showing the 'distribution of stages of faith by age' (ibid., 1981, p. 318) reveals that 25 were children below the age of 6 years, 29 were aged from 7 to 12 years, and 56 were aged from 13 to 20 years. If we assume that most of the children below 6 years were able to enter into the conversation, the percentage groupings become 15 per cent of the total number interviewed are in the nursery–primary educational phase and 16 per cent are in the secondary–further–higher phase. In terms of the stages, the majority of the 0–6s are in Stage 1, the 7–12s in Stage 2, and the 13–20s in Stage 3. Only three under-20s are in Stage 4. It is tempting to suggest that the exercise reveals the truth of the old adage that 'the older one gets, the wiser one becomes'. Rodger (1996) offers perhaps a more acceptable summary:

It seems unlikely that we shall soon (if ever) have any assured picture of the stages of spiritual development. It might be a very bad thing if we did! This is not to say that we need despair and conclude that we know nothing. The 'faith development' theory of James Fowler is interesting but lacks, as yet, the kind of field-testing that can permit us to use it with confidence. Work continues on it.

That having been said, faith-development may yet contribute some structural assistance to spiritual development in the classroom.

Facilitating learning

What seems to have much more relevance to the spiritual development of students, though not perhaps at first sight, lies in what has by now become the classic statement of person-centred counselling. Rogers (1957) identifies six necessary conditions which, if they exist and if they continue over a period of time, are sufficient to enable the process of constructive personality change to follow. They are as follows:

1 two persons are in psychological contact;
2 the first (the client) is in a state of incongruence, being vulnerable or anxious;
3 the second (the therapist) is congruent or integrated in the relationship;
4 the therapist experiences unconditional positive regard for the client;
5 the therapist experiences an empathic understanding of the client's internal frame of reference and endeavours to communicate this experience to the client; and
6 the communication to the client of the therapist's empathic understanding and unconditional positive regard is to a minimal degree achieved

It is numbers 3, 4 and 5 which particularly concern us. Rogers (1957) defines each one more fully:

> The third condition is that the therapist should be, within the confines of this relationship, a congruent, genuine, integrated person. It means that within the relationship he is freely and deeply himself, with his actual experience accurately represented by his awareness of himself. It is the opposite of presenting a facade, either knowingly or unknowingly. (p. 97)

> To the extent that the therapist finds himself experiencing a warm acceptance of each aspect of the client's experience as being a part of that client, he is experiencing unconditional positive regard . . . It means that there are no *conditions* of acceptance, no feeling of 'I like you only *if* you are thus and so'. (p. 98)

> The fifth condition is that the therapist is experiencing an accurate, empathic understanding of the client's awareness of his own experience. To sense the client's private world as if it were your own, but without ever losing the 'as if' quality – this is empathy, and it seems essential to therapy. (p. 99)

Later, in a chapter which he describes as 'passionate and personal', Rogers seeks to express 'some of my deepest convictions in regard to the process we call *education*' (Rogers, [1969] 1983, p. 119). He argues that education is not about teaching, in the sense of instruction, but about the facilitation of learning. He claims that the evidence shows that 'the facilitation of significant learning rests upon certain attitudinal qualities that exist in the personal *relationship* between the facilitator and the learner' (ibid., p. 121). It is the same qualities as those that exist in the 'intensive relationship between therapist and client . . . that *may* exist in the countless interpersonal interactions between the teacher and pupils' (ibid., p. 121). The qualities can be described as follows:

> First of all is a transparent realness in the facilitator, a willingness to be a person, to be and live the feelings and thoughts of the moment. When this realness includes a prizing, a caring, a trust and respect for the learner, the climate for learning is enhanced. When it includes a sensitive and accurate empathic listening, then indeed a freeing climate, stimulative of self-initiated learning and growth, exists. The student is *trusted* to develop. (Ibid., p. 133)

Five years later, Rogers argues the value of combining experiential with cognitive learning in a paper entitled 'Can learning encompass both ideas and feelings?' (Rogers, 1980, pp. 263–91).[1] One interesting suggestion (p. 279) is that 'it would be entirely possible now to select candidates who showed a high potentiality for realness, prizing, and empathic understanding in their relationships', something on which those responsible for the selection of teachers or lecturers at every level of education might do well to reflect and then act. In a chapter entitled 'Power or persons: two trends in education' (Rogers, 1978, pp. 69–89), he presses the differences between the politics of the traditional school and the fundamental conditions where person-centred learning develops. In the traditional school:

> The teacher is the possessor of knowledge, the student the recipient . . . The lecture, as a means of pouring knowledge into the recipient, and the examination as the measure of the extent to which he [*sic*] has received it, are the central elements of this education . . . The teacher is the possessor of power, the student the one who obeys . . . Authoritarian rule is the accepted policy in the classroom . . . Trust is at a minimum . . . The subjects (the students) are best governed by being kept in an intermittent or constant state of fear . . . Democracy and its values are ignored and scorned in practice . . . There is no place for the whole person in the educational system, only for the intellect. (Ibid., pp. 69–71)

In person-centred learning, provided the 'leader

. . . is sufficiently secure within himself and in his relationships to others that he experiences an essential trust in the capacity of others to think for themselves', to learn for themselves', then:

> The facilitative person shares with the others – students and possibly also parents or community members – the responsibility for the learning process . . . The facilitator provides learning resources – from within himself and his own experience, from books or materials or community experiences . . . The student develops his own program of learning, alone or in cooperation with others . . . A facilitative learning climate is provided . . . The focus is primarily on fostering the continuing process of learning . . . The discipline necessary to reach the student's goals is a self-discipline . . . The evaluation of the extent and significance of the student's learning is made primarily by the learner himself . . . In this growth-promoting climate, the learning is deeper, proceeds at a more rapid rate, and is more pervasive in the life and behavior of the student than learning acquired in the traditional classroom.   (Ibid., pp. 72–4)

Aspy and Roebuck (1983) report a series of studies undertaken by the National Consortium for Humanizing Education (NCHE) over a period of seventeen years in 42 states in the US and seven countries outside the US, involving more than 2000 teachers and 20,000 students. Using a variety of approaches, they 'examined relationships between Rogers' facilitative conditions (empathy, congruence, positive regard) and a variety of factors such as attitudes (toward self, school, others), discipline problems, physical health, attendance, IQ changes, and cognitive growth'. They concluded that 'students learn more and behave better when they receive high levels of understanding, caring, and genuineness, than when they are given low levels of them' (p. 199). These findings were corroborated by Tausch's (1978) work in West Germany.

Conclusion

Whenever and wherever teachers fulfil the three operant conditions which have been described here, spiritual development *will take place* among their students. If teachers are congruent, if they are absolutely open and transparent without any pretentious airs and graces or delusions of power and grandeur, if they are simply themselves, as they are

and not as they might like to be . . . ; if teachers offer an unconditional positive regard to their students, a personal warmth which is as real as the sunshine on a summer's day, an approach which is concerned to value the students' potential for good, not their capacity for evil . . . ; if teachers are actively seeking to achieve an empathic understanding with their students, suspending their own beliefs and values system in order to enter into the lives of their students, however momentarily, in order to be able to see it and understand it and feel it from their point of view . . . ; if, in other words, these three operant conditions are present, students will respect them, relate to them and respond to them in similar ways. They will develop as whole persons, and so will society. Part of that development will be a deepening and growing spirituality. It may be capable of being traced through various stages or assessed in terms of its progress but to a large extent that will be immaterial. For if society itself were to become congruent, full of unconditional positive regard and thoroughly empathic in its understanding, it would surely be a society which was fit to receive the next generation, and the next, and the next . . .

Note

1 Chapter 12 had been published, in slightly different form, in *Education* 95 (2), 1974, pp. 103–14.

References

Askari, H. (1991) *Spiritual Quest: An Inter-religious Dimension*. Leeds: Seven Mirrors.

Aspy, D. and Roebuck, F.N. (1983) Researching person-centered issues in education. In C.R. Rogers (ed.), *Freedom to Learn for the 80s*. Columbus, OH: Charles E. Merrill.

Astley, J. and Francis, L. (eds) (1992) *Christian Perspectives on Faith Development: A Reader*. Leominster, Herefs. Gracewing Fowler Wright Books and Grand Rapids, MI: Wm B. Eerdmans.

Beesley, M. (1990) *Stilling: A Pathway for Spiritual Learning in the National Curriculum*. Salisbury, Wilts. Salisbury Diocesan Board of Education.

Beesley, M. (1993) Spiritual education in schools. *Pastoral Care in Education* 11 (3), pp. 22–8.

Bradford, J. (1995) *Caring for the Whole Child: A Holistic Approach to Spirituality*. London: The Children's Society.

Brown, A. and Kadodwala, D. (1993) Spiritual development in the school curriculum. In *Teaching World Religions*. London: Heinemann, pp. 33–5.

Coles, R. (1992) *The Spiritual Life of Children*. London: Harper and Collins.

Dixon, D.A. (1984a) Spiritual area of experience. In J.M. Sutcliffe (ed.), *A Dictionary of Religious Education*. London: SCM Press.

Dixon, D.A. (1984b) Spiritual development. In J.M. Sutcliffe (ed.) *A Dictionary of Religious Education*. London: SCM Press.

Education Reform Act [ERA] *1988*. London: Her Majesty's Stationery Office.

Fowler, J. (1980) Faith and the structuring of meaning. In J. Fowler and Vergote (eds), *Toward Moral and Religious Maturity*. Morristown. NJ: Silver Burdett.

Fowler, J.W. (1981) *Stages of Faith: The Psychology of Human Development and the Quest for Meaning*. New York: Harper & Row.

Fowler, J. and Keen, S. (1978) *Lift Maps: Conversations on the Journey of Faith*. Word Books.

General Synod Board of Education (GSBE) (1991) *How Faith Grows: Faith Development and Christian Education*. London: National Society/Church House Publishing.

Hammond, J. *et al.* (1990) *New Methods in RE Teaching: An Experiential Approach*. Harlow, Essex: Oliver & Boyd.

Hardy, A. (1979) *The Spiritual Nature of Man: A Study of Contemporary Religious Experience*. Oxford: Clarendon Press.

Hull, J. (1995) *The Holy Trinity and Christian Education in a Pluralist World*. London: National Society/Church House Publishing.

Hull, J. (1996) A critique of Christian religionism in recent British education. In J. Astley and L.J. Francis (eds) *Christian Theology and Religious Education: Connections and Contradictions*. London: SPCK.

James, W. (1902) *The Varieties of Religious Experience: A Study in Human Nature*. London: Longman, Green.

Kibble, D.G. (1996) Spiritual development, spiritual experience and spiritual education. In R. Best (ed.), *Education, Spirituality and the Whole Child*. London: Cassell.

King, U. (1985) Spirituality in a secular society: recovering a lost dimension. *British Journal of Religious Education* 7(3), pp. 135–9, 111.

Lambourn, D. (1996), 'Spiritual' minus 'personal-social' = ?: a critical note on an 'empty' category. In R. Best (ed.), *Education, Spirituality and the Whole Child*. London: Cassell.

Lynch, J., Modgil, C. and Modgil, S. (eds) (1992) *Cultural Diversity and the Schools*, 4 vols. London: Falmer Press.

Macquarrie, J. (1972) *Paths in Spirituality*. London: Harper & Row.

Marjon (College of St Mark and St John) (1990) *Educating for Spiritual Growth*, video material. Plymouth, Devon: College of St Mark and St John.

Mott-Thornton, K. (1996) Experience, critical realism and the schooling of spirituality. In R. Best (ed.), *Education, Spirituality and the Whole Child*. London: Cassell.

National Curriculum Council (NCC) (1993) *Spiritual and Moral Development: A Discussion Paper*. York: NCC.

Nelson, C.E. (1992) Does faith develop? An evaluation of Fowler's position. In J. Astley and L. Francis (eds), *Christian Perspectives on Faith Development: A Reader*. Leominster, Herefs.: Gracewing Fowler Wright Books and Grand Rapids, MI: Wm B. Eerdmans.

Newby, M. (1996) Towards a secular concept of spiritual maturity. In R. Best (ed.), *Education, Spirituality and the Whole Child*. London: Cassell.

Nye, R. and Hay, D. (1996) Identifying children's spirituality: how do you start without a starting point? *British Journal of Religious Education* 18(3), pp. 144–54.

Office for Standards in Education (OFSTED) (1993) *Handbook for the Inspection of Schools*. London: Her Majesty's Stationery Office.

Office for Standards in Education (OFSTED) (1994) *Spiritual, Moral, Social and Cultural Development: An OFSTED Discussion Paper*. London: OFSTED.

Priestley, J.G. (1996) *Spirituality in the Curriculum*. Hockerill Educational Foundation.

Robinson, E. (1977) *The Original Vision: A Study of the Religious Experience of Childhood*. Oxford: Religious Experience Research Unit, Manchester College.

Robinson, E. (1984) Religious experience. In J.M. Sutcliffe (ed.), *A Dictionary of Religious Education*. London: SCM Press.

Robinson, J. (1963) *Honest to God*. London: SCM Press.

Rodger, A. (1996) Human spirituality: towards an educational rationale. In R. Best (ed.), *Education, Spirituality and the Whole Child*. London: Cassell.

Rogers, C.A. (1957) The necessary and sufficient conditions of therapeutic personality change. *Journal of Consulting Psychology* 21(2).

Rogers, C.A. ([1969] 1983) *Freedom to Learn for the 80s*. Columbus, OH: Charles E. Merrill.

Rogers, C.A. (1978) *Carl Rogers on Personal Power: Inner Strength and its Revolutionary Impact*. London: Constable.

Rogers, C.A. (1980) *A Way of Being*. New York: Houghton Mifflin.

Rose, D.W. (1996) Religious education, spirituality and the acceptable face of indoctrination. In R. Best (ed.), *Education, Spirituality and the Whole Child*. London: Cassell.

Rudge, J. (1993) *Religious Education and Spiritual Development*. Birmingham: Westhill College RE Centre.

Sheldrake, P. (1995) *Spirituality and History: Questions of Interpretation and Method*. London: SPCK.

Sutcliffe, J.M. (ed.) (1984) *A Dictionary of Religious Education*. London: SCM Press.

Tausch, R. (1978) Facilitative dimensions in interpersonal relations: verifying the theoretical assumptions of Carl

Rogers in school, family; education, client-centered therapy, and encounter groups. *Coll Stud Journal.* **12**(2).

Thatcher, A. (1996) 'Policing the sublime': a wholly (holy?) ironic approach to the spiritual development of children. In J. Astley and L.J. Francis (eds), *Christian Theology and Religious Education: Connections and Contradictions.* London: SPCK.

4 Moral Education and Lifelong Integrated Education

YOSHIKO NOMURA

Moral decadence: a world-wide phenomenon

Everywhere today a breakdown in moral values is afflicting mankind with many forms of distress, in the East as well as the West. In particular, delinquency among the young, including violent crimes, illegal use of drugs and casual sex, strike developed and developing societies alike. It is a problem of global proportions which demands an urgent solution.

We shall not resolve the problems posed by this unhappy state of the world's youth unless we realise that they are direct reflections of adult society. The budding problems of children sprout from the social soil of our adult values and attitudes and the lives based on them, which are there for the young to emulate. Without changing the soil, pruning a problem bud here and there cannot bring about a true solution.

Corruption, injustice, bribery, sexual licence and a general moral decadence have pervaded all levels of political life, the civil service, teachers and doctors and even the police. The widespread decadence among the leadership, which should be a source of ethical inspiration for the young, is the first problem that must be dealt with. In other words, the priority must be on the reform of the adult society.

Moral education is too often discussed in a framework of how it should be taught within the school system. Before 'teaching' children, ethics and morality must first be considered as educational issues for adults, who should be a model for the young.

It was from this perspective that since the early 1960s I have expounded the need for lifelong integrated education based on self-education of the adult. In so doing, I have involved not just the educational world but the political and business worlds, the mass media and society at large in a movement to promote educational volunteering as a means to reform adult society, and hence its younger members too.

Causes of moral decadence

To what should we ascribe today's rapid moral degeneration? Responsibility for the corruption of human nature and the rampant materialism and worship of money which people are caught up in all over the world can be traced to the ubiquitous influence of science and technological civilisation, the mother of materialism.

Science and the technological civilisation which originated in western Europe have developed dramatically in the second half of this century. But this development is a two-edged sword with both merits and demerits. On the one hand, it has brought about material prosperity and its attendant wealth of goods, comfort, efficiency and convenience. On the other, it has scientifically and rationally treated human beings, who are by nature also irrational. It has measured humans with a numbered yardstick as if they were mere goods, ignoring their innate spiritual qualities as a consequence. The material civilisation has brought about alienation and disruption within human society, polluting the external environment and endangering the very survival of life on the planet.

The enormous distortion in the balance between the world of goods and that of the spirit is intimately linked to the universal moral decadence of our contemporary society.

The social changes brought about by science and technology have cast an ominous shadow on education itself. School education, reduced to the role of providing qualified manpower for economic development and the insatiable demands of industry, tended to focus on scientific instruction at the expense of spiritual development.

The priority thus placed on economic and material values has resulted in the neglect and denial of traditional values, and therefore in the loss of identity and *raison d'être* of the contemporary man.

Moral education and values

Moral education always begs the question of what it will be based on. The question is particularly pertinent in a multiethnic society with different religious and cultural backgrounds and therefore different bases for their respective values.

Furthermore, scientific progress and development is often accompanied by the undermining of traditional religion, in the process of which a basic human dignity which is the foundation for ethics and morality is lost. And as humans are increasingly apt to be measured by quantifying and monetary values, respect and awe for human life is decidedly being lost. Herein lies the need to pursue values which ensure equal human dignity beyond economic values and regardless of traditional religious affiliation.

Moral education found in Japan's traditional education

I wish here to look back to the unofficial education found pervasively in the old Japan with its emphasis on moral instruction. Towards the end of the Edo period there were private places of education throughout Japan, known as temple schools. In fact, education nation-wide had by then caught up to the point where it was second to none, with in addition clan-managed schools and even some directly managed by the government of the shogun.

Aside from these international places of education, human education focusing on spirituality was part of the everyday life, as girls were taught domestic science and good manners, and boys trades and skills so that they could become artisans and fulfil their national best.

Philosophy of *do* (the way): a total education

All forms of traditional culture in Japan, whether the tea ceremony (*sa-do*), flower arrangement (*ka-do*) or calligraphy (*sho-do*) have the Chinese character *do* attached, signifying a way. The names of martial arts such as fencing (*ken-do*) and archery (*kyu-do*) likewise indicate a way. What 'the way' signifies is that all acquisition of cultural and martial skills is a way towards cultivating the human mind.

The late Dr Inazo Nitobe published a book titled *Bushi-do* (The Way of the Samurai) in English in order to explain to the world spiritual aspects of Japanese culture. *Bushi-do*, developed from the Kamakura period and underpinned later during the Edo period with Confucian thought, was the moral system of the warrior class. The way of the *samurai*, which respected loyalty, sacrifice, trust, shame, courtesy, purity, simplicity, frugality, the spirit of militarism (that is, self-discipline), honour and philanthropy, became the ethical norm of the warriors as social leaders. Their conduct had no small effect on the rank and file and the people at large.

Japanese martial arts based on the way of the warrior were not just another way of prevailing over the foe with might but included among other disciplines years of hard spiritual training in order to achieve victory over the self.

Ken-do especially, since the seventeenth century, focused on spiritual uplift along with training in the necessary skills. The influence of Buddhism (particularly Zen) and Confucianism imported a moral aspect to self-improvement.

Thus, the philosophy of the way aspired to educate the whole person through the acquisition of skills which were not an objective in themselves. Therefore, long before moral education first appeared in schools beginning in the Meiji period, there existed an ancient tradition of cultivating the whole person through finding 'the way' in all forms of endeavor.

Educational achievement through traditional culture

The source at the very root of Japan's traditional culture is a unique spirit of animism which has adopted Buddhism, Confucianism and Christianity, and in modern times western scientific thought.

The spirit of animism is present in every aspect of the life of the Japanese, who live with all products of creation. It openly accepts foreign cultures and integrates them to create its unique multilayered culture, which becomes the ever-changing constitution of the Japanese people. It is this spirit which forms the ethical base of the Japanese, who respect *wa* or harmony.

These are the essential attributes which through a myriad of educational channels and influences created Japanese culture and history.

Manyo-shu, a book of poems written by emperors, aristocrats, commoners and farmers from the fourth to the eighth centuries, represents matchlessly the rich fruits of education and the equality of cultural achievement that would be unthinkable in other societies in which educational opportunities were hindered by class distinctions. The rise of arts and culture throughout all classes, I believe, is largely accountable for and symbolic of the peaceful and cultured land of Japan.

Denial of traditional culture since defeat in the Second World War

Most Japanese lost their traditional sense of spirituality as a consequence of their defeat in the Second World War. The defeat was unprecedented. Japan as an independent unified country with two thousand years of history had lost a war and had been placed under the occupation of the victor. Defeat certainly opened up a way to regain a peaceful country. On the other hand, however, the misfortune of defeat lay in the abandonment of our spiritual and moral heritage such as the love of harmony, sincerity and respect for others that had been passed down through the ages.

Postwar Japan, having lost its identity which was closely linked to our history, culture and education, accepted the western scientific rationale and scientific education as mainstream values. These values, first introduced to the country in the Meiji era a century earlier, now swept through a society devoid of any mechanism to make spiritual and value judgements.

Under a policy of growth imperatives, producers agendas and a newly acquired worship of material values, the natural diligence and honest application of this farming race produced dramatic economic development out of the impoverished state of the nation.

But the after-effect of the loss of confidence following defeat in the war lingered. Without direction in life and without principles the adult community was thrust into uncertainty and confusion in the face of the rapid social changes brought about by the scientific revolution of the twentieth century. It was on this social soil of economic pursuit without an identity and spiritual convictions that the young were raised after the war.

Egoism, worship of money, social position and prestige were our catchwords; unprincipled standards and lack of morality characterised our lives. These were the attitudes, values and role models that the children emulated as they grew up. This is what I mean when I say that the young generation of today is a mirror image of adult society.

The challenge of Nomura lifelong integrated education: the revival of Japan's enviable traditional values

If I were to single out the most important motive in initiating voluntary educational activities at the beginning of the 1960s, it was the anguish I felt at the many misfortunes befalling our young people in the midst of the rapid economic growth of those years. As I involved myself with them and their problems, I found behind each case the ugly shadow of adult society. Behind us lay the unprecedented upheavals of our contemporary world, and beyond that I realised we were in fact living at a historic turning point for the human family as a whole.

These were all indivisible factors that affected each other. I saw that the root of the unhappiness of our youth could be traced to their defenceless situation at the apex of a tormented society, the like of which had never been seen before.

However, it was in the traditional culture of Japan which we Japanese had ourselves discarded that I could see unchanging values beyond time and place. I attempted to rediscover and revive these unchanging values and sought to make them universal through education; which to me is the most universal process.

A new morality based on a view of nature

In formulating my thesis on lifelong integrated education I turned to the eastern or Japanese view of nature for a philosophical foundation. How could the unique strength of this view of nature be harnessed as a universal educational principle so as to convince the rational minds of the modern world and make a contribution to much-needed global educational reform? The challenge called for a monumental attempt to carve a place for eastern thought in the world's intellectual history, while at the same time contributing to the creation of a new education for the future.

I could also see a possibility of creating a new ethical system for the planet based on the eastern view of nature, which teaches that all things in creation share this phenomenon of life. In contrast to the western view of nature, which sets people against nature, the eastern view of nature sees them as part of it. This philosophical principle endows us with a universality which can take us beyond differences of history, religion and culture. In other words, it helps us to visualise people as having a purely objective existence in the cosmic world.

Life proceeds from morning to noon, noon to eve, and from yesterday to today, today to tomorrow, indeed from yesteryear to this and then the next. It proceeds from birth to death along the changing sequence we call time, while maintaining its identity. The individual life is a gift passed down from parents and grandparents. This life which has been transmitted through the generations is one link in an eternal continuum of discontinued individual lives. This single fact is a testimony to humankind's existence in the natural world. Likewise, the human family itself lives in a continuum of past, present and future.

Peoples's existence must first be seen as links in the chain of continuity from time immemorial. Their place on the continuum can then be plotted by reference to their location among the endless generations. In this way each individual identity as well as that of the whole human family is confirmed. In fact, this proves that every human being has historical permanence, incorporating within him or her the entire cultural heritage of the past. Each is endowed with a 'resilient strength of restoration'. That every individual possesses this 'mystic mechanism' entitles them to an equal dignity.

An attempt must then be made to capture humans in a special context. The eastern view of nature, as explained earlier, sees us as part of nature. From this it follows that our individual existence is conceived of as sharing the natural world which surrounds us. Our existence is interdependent with all things in creation. Individual people endowed with both mind and body cannot exist in separation from their environment, including nature and the cosmos itself.

Collectively, therefore, humankind travels along a temporal sequence while in a spatial dimension sharing existence with the environment. To put it another way, the human mind and body and the environment are mutually dependent and inseparable.

In relation to nature, it is self-evident that we humans are subjects and possessors of life but at the same time objects given life by nature. Recognition of this should challenge us to change fundamentally our human-centric sense of morality. It should help us to progress from a set of moral presumptions which determine relationships between individuals who are considered independent and separate from their environment to a vision of humans as inseparable from nature within the cosmic harmony – in other words, a shift to principles which render the pursuit of harmony with the environment the eternal norm.

Moral standards drawn from this view of nature can be shared by all, superseding all historical, religious and cultural differences, because it is based on the cosmic order and nature's plan, which goes beyond human wisdom.

Establishing morality based on planetary consciousness

The other important impetus in my pursuit of life-long integrated educational activities was the experience of my first journey around the world in 1969. My last stop was Hawaii, and there in my hotel room I happened to witness on television the crew of Apollo 11 landing on the moon. It was a historic moment when man for the first time set foot on a planet other than the one which had been his alone since the birth of his primitive ancestors.

Until that day we humans could only see other planets from our own. Now for the first time we were able to see our earth suspended in space just like the moon and the stars we had always watched and wondered at. It left an indelible impression on me. I called this moment my Apollo shock. I was suddenly hit by the realisation that we are all members of a human family sharing the earth and its fate.

This experience added another dimension to the

concept of lifelong integrated education: that it should pursue 'solidarity at a global level'. Since then for the past three decades I have given my life to formulating the theoretical basis of this thought and to initiating a social movement.

A completely new sense of ethics provides the theoretical and practical basis which, as I have explained, captures human existence in a 'changing relationship' within the 'cosmic nature' and channels back this 'relationship' into its original state of harmony.

As I stated at the outset, today the very survival of humankind is at risk from every angle, from national and ethnic conflict stemming from lack of harmony in individual human relations, from nuclear threat, from population explosion, from environmental disruption. All these perils have been created by humankind itself. It makes us shudder to think that we live at a time when a simple, fallible human can hold in his hand the fate of humankind and the survival of life on earth.

It follows from the description of humankind I offered earlier that each of us has a limitless past, which means we have both an unlimited capacity for good as well as an unlimited capacity for evil. I am convinced that the mission of education is to develop this innate human capacity for good and to overcome the capacity for evil.

Nomura lifelong integrated education recognises the unique and inexorable place in the endless continuum of existence in the cosmic environment occupied by every individual human being. It challenges every individual to abandon their fixed ideas and find harmony in this important relationship. It encourages us to identify within us factors that create disharmony and to dispel them.

The change in the individual person will without doubt lead to changes in family and society which are the extension of the individual. Eventually, it must lead to greater changes still at the national, world and global society levels. It should contribute to the realisation of peace and well-being to which all people aspire.

The process by which this is achieved is, I believe, the moral education of a global citizen with a planetary perspective, and this is the great role history demands of lifelong integrated education.

5 Newspapers and Spiritual Development: a Perspective on Religious Education

RICHARD PEARCE

The media are often regarded with concern (Wynne Jones, 1992; SCAA, 1996) and as something from which children need to be protected (Wright, 1988). However, this chapter discusses one sector, newspapers, and argues that because of their distinctive nature – a tangible, easily accessible and ubiquitous print source focusing on people and their 'everyday' lives, and both reflecting and shaping the views of contemporary society – they *potentially* contribute towards spiritual development and the formation of personal identity.

The perspective adopted is that of Newspapers in Education (NiE), a world-wide initiative encouraging newspaper readership among young people, with activities in the UK involving some 600 regional newspaper centres to build positive links with schools, colleges, universities, community and parent groups. Newspapers have been used in schools for some time, but the contention here is that the widespread growth of NiE gives teachers even greater, and more systematic, access to a resource which can stimulate reflection upon the self and others. It is argued that through the evaluation and interpretation of newspapers, and exploration of the 'experience' represented in them, insights can be gained which lead to self-knowledge and more differentiated perceptions which can be applied to one's own life.

Before examining this further, I shall outline the stance taken in relation to the role of the media in our multifaith, culturally diverse society and the growth of 'media studies' in education. The emphasis in this chapter is on exploring the concept of 'spiritual development' and how newspapers – with the focus being on the *local* as distinct from the *national* press – might be utilised as a resource in this context. Questions of 'spirituality' and 'personal development' are taken to be of relevance to everyone, where each person is valued as a *unique individual*. They are also assumed to incorporate issues of race, gender, class, age, sexuality and political or religious persuasion, which are among the aspects of *social identity* that help to structure our experience in western industrialised societies; as Dines and Humez (1995, p. xvii) put it, everyone 'has' race, class, gender and so on. Although the handling of these issues by the media is often contentious, newspapers are part of the fabric of society, and their use in the classroom is here cast in a positive light.

Thus there are important negative issues not explicitly addressed, but which are nevertheless salient to any critical appreciation of the media and their role in a multicultural society, not least in terms of representation and negative stereotyping (Davies *et al.*, 1987; Swanson, 1992; Lont, 1995; Hall, 1996). The press (and especially the popular tabloids), for instance, has been seen as exacerbating and inflaming racist sentiment through a 'powerful concoction of stereotyping of black people, sensationalism, scaremongering and scapegoating' (Gordon and Rosenberg, 1989, p. 1). Likewise with gender, it has been demonstrated how women have been both underrepresented and misrepresented (through negative portrayal) in the media (van Zoonen, 1995); indeed, one of the key tasks of feminist media critics has been to make visible the 'patriarchal *domination* of the media industries, in terms of both ownership and *representation*' (Dines and Humez, 1995, p. xix; original emphasis). Representation, in fact, has proved an important battleground for contemporary feminism (van Zoonen, 1994).

While such issues are not here dealt with at length, their importance and complexity should not be overlooked, and they constitute growing fields of study in their own right. The concept of 'femi- nism' alone, for instance, is not easily delineated or defined (ibid.); although there are common con- cepts which distinguish it from, say, other social science perspectives, it is far from being the 'monolithic entity' that the term might imply, and embodies a wide range of quite different, some- times conflicting, perspectives (ibid.).

Bearing such complexities in mind, however, if multiculturalism is regarded not only in terms of recognising – and respecting – the diversity of 'cul- tures' and sub-cultural lifestyles, but also as sup- porting minority cultural expression (Jakubowicz, 1995), then the sensitive use of newspapers in the classroom, it is suggested, can at the very least con- tribute towards a challenging of preconceptions and support active and more positive engagement with ethnic, religious and other cultural diversity. There has been a rapid growth of media and cul- tural studies (Lusted, 1992; Marris and Thornham, 1996) making possible the interpretation of media texts from an increasingly wide range of perspec- tives (Kellner, 1995). This expansion of interest in the media can be perceived as more than simply 'another topic' on the curriculum to be studied in academic isolation: quite the opposite, in fact; for such is the influence of the media on our lives, some have argued, that teachers *cannot afford to ignore it* (Buckingham, 1992, emphasis added). In this con- nection, analysis of newspapers through categories such as, among others, language, narrative, institu- tion, audience, and representation (Lusted, 1992) can stimulate critical awareness. But 'active engagement' can also manifest itself in highly prac- tical terms. Students are often able to create their own media products (with support materials; see Harcourt, 1991). For example, the *Birmingham Post* runs a project enabling students to write, edit, design – and sometimes assemble in paste-up form – their own news page which then appears in special editions of the paper. This project has been taken up in a range of schools and colleges involving stu- dents of all faiths and cultural backgrounds. In another activity, students plan a two-page feature highlighting cultural differences in their locality, and identifying ways in which 'people of all reli- gions can live side by side in a tolerant society' (Kelly, 1995). Use of newspapers as discussed so far, then, is seen not only in terms of potentially *raising awareness* of diversity through content analysis (and critical reflection) – even if this exposes imbalances and distortions – but also of

giving *practical expression* or a *voice* to young people through the development of communica- tion skills and, in some cases, the creation of their own news pages.

Implicit in the above is the assumption that the growth of confidence and acquisition of basic skills, facilitated through reflective thinking combined with practical activities, are integral parts of per- sonal development and the formation of self- identity. The association of such development with the media can be extended, for a number of theor- ists have argued that the products of media culture 'provide materials out of which we forge our very identities, our sense of selfhood' (Kellner, 1995, p. 5; see also Real, 1989; Lusted, 1992; and Jakubowicz, 1995). Furthermore, personal identity itself has been equated with the development of spirituality (Newby, 1996), with 'narrative' or 'story' playing a significant role in the formation of both (ibid.; Erricker and Erricker, 1996).

Here, too, the connection with newspapers can be expanded upon; for newspapers provide access to 'story' which both confirms and integrates, creat- ing a sense of stability and continuity, through a shared language and cultural assumptions. Mass communication systems, of which newspapers form a significant part, 'knit British society together from Land's End to John O'Groats every day' (Hall, 1984, p. 269). Yet the media also undermine and fragment, through a disruption of those assump- tions and expectations, presenting the reader with challenges which strike at the very core of her or his identity. How do we respond to the image of an 80-year-old man or woman, bruised and bleeding after being mugged? Or news of young children massacred in a gymnasium at the start of their school day? While the concept of spirituality might include notions of the transcendent (Holley, 1978) or trans-personal (Kibble, 1996), of something 'more than meets the eye' (Stone, 1995), this chap- ter argues that it is not simply a nebulous, 'other- worldly' state which fails to inform or be informed by the realities of everyday life, but is embedded in and emerges from the experience and expression of that life (Thornecroft, 1978) and those very real- ities. As Rodger (1996, p. 46) remarks, phrases such as 'self-understanding', 'moral consciousness' and 'awe and wonder at the world', which are char- acteristic of spiritual development, are 'redolent of the learner's engagement with a world that is to be *lived* in rather than merely understood; and under- stood *for the sake of* being able to live more fully within it' (ibid., p. 46). Newspapers reflect certain 'everyday' realities of the societies in which they are rooted; sensationalised, perhaps; exaggerated, perhaps; provocative, perhaps; but nevertheless located in immediate, 'lived' reality in a way that other forms of text are not.

Newspapers are also about change. One definition of news is '*how things have changed* since we last took stock of the state of the world' (Hall, 1984, p. 271). In our own personal development, as we seek and establish our own identities, change and the management of that change become unavoidable – and sometimes disconcerting – parts of the process. Despite their ephemerality, newspapers can impact upon our sense of self and our place in the world, in that they can lead us to question and respond at both intellectual and emotional levels. Rodger suggests that spiritual development is concerned with a person's sense of the kind of universe we live in, the nature and relationships of human beings and how human life ought to be lived. By their very nature, speaking directly to an 'audience', it is possible that newspapers raise awareness, not just of the 'world' – or 'external reality' – in which the reader finds him or herself, but also of the 'inner reality', the subjective experience of the 'self', and how that self responds and even 'acts'; in other words, they potentially facilitate the development of spirituality that is necessarily rooted in awareness and calls for expression in action (Rodger, 1996, p. 52). The intricate relationship between the media and personal identity has been clearly expressed by Real (1989), who describes the media as the 'central nervous system' of the modern world, penetrating our lives so completely that they create the environment 'where identities are formed' (ibid., p. 15) – and 'provide much of the stuff of everyday life through which we construct meaning and organize our existence' (ibid., p. 9).

From this point of view, newspapers are potentially a powerful resource in religious education. As an integral component of the society in which they function, they act as a bridge between the social and the individual, the public and the private, the global and the personal, the 'powerful' and the 'powerless' (Hall, 1984, p. 270). This is no passive condition; the interaction, or point of contact, between person and media text 'creates a complex charge that leaps between the two' (Real, 1989, p. 8). Reading newspapers, then, particularly in the focused environment of the classroom, can become a highly active and motivating process. Newspapers are

already used in RE (Windsor and Hughes, 1990a, 1990b, 1990c, 1991) and it is not difficult to identify how they can be incorporated into investigations of *moral* and *social* issues. However, this chapter addresses their possible impact on *spiritual* development. It is a complex and controversial topic. Not only is there difficulty in clarifying exactly what is meant by the 'spiritual', but there is also debate over precisely how its 'development' is to be achieved and measured.

In order to explore the use of newspapers in this context, consideration will first be given to the problem of attempting to 'define' the concept of 'spiritual'. This is approached with caution, for as Watson (1993) points out, the 'spiritual' automatically transcends all possible categories and definitions. Nevertheless, if schools are to be responsible for spiritual development, then some clarification is necessary. This section, therefore, identifies aspects which have been associated with the concept. It also raises questions related to the 'development' of spirituality and the goals aimed for.

Ways in which newspapers can be used to support the RE curriculum are then suggested. It is assumed that, crucially, these depend upon sensitive interpretation and a 'contextual approach' from teachers, integrating newspapers into a supportive and structured, though not overbearing, learning environment. Case-study material will demonstrate how newspapers can be used; this material includes reference to two newspaper publications specifically intended for religious education; a series of books for lower secondary students in which newspapers become a method of investigating issues in RE; ongoing work in a secondary school, including a module on suffering and reconciliation, where newspapers provide a key resource; and finally analysis of a newspaper article to illustrate more clearly the possible practical application of newspapers in fostering spiritual development.

Finally, I argue that RE has a role to play in a world in which some feel strongly that there is, in fact, moral and spiritual decline and that religious belief is 'outmoded and ridiculous' (Atkins, 1996).

Spiritual development: an elusive concept

The Education Reform Act (1988) refers to a dimension of human existence which is termed 'spiritual' and which applies to all students. The potential for spiritual development is regarded as being 'open to everyone' (NCC, 1993, p. 2). Significantly, it is also acknowledged that such development can occur *outside* religious belief or a particular faith. This view is reinforced by OFSTED (1994a, p. 8) which strongly emphasises that spiritual development is *not* another name for religious education. This presents the possibility of 'secular spirituality', although this notion is itself controversial, and will be returned to. That spiritual development arises out of lived experience, and so in this sense is not 'optional' (Mott-Thornton, 1996), implies something fundamental in the 'human condition'; in their everyday reporting, newspapers reflect something of that condition – at its best and worst.

Attempting to relate the use of newspapers to spiritual development, however, is by no means straightforward. The concept of 'spirituality' is elusive, and there are differences of opinion over how its 'development' should be conceived (see Best, 1996). Yet there are characteristics which have been identified as contributing towards a general sense of the 'spiritual'. What follows is an attempt to delineate a notion of the spiritual and the issues involved in its place on the curriculum. (The terms 'pupil' and 'student' are used interchangeably, reflecting the emphasis of the particular sources referred to.)

Beyond the material, beyond the mundane

Spirituality can be regarded as a source of inspiration and connected to those things 'which support and give life to a person's ideals, goals and sense of purpose and identity' (Mott-Thornton, 1996, p. 77). It deals with 'what is supremely personal and unique to each individual' (OFSTED, 1994a). Our beliefs (and how these contribute to personal identity); the development of a sense of awe, wonder and mystery; seeking meaning and purpose in our lives; acquiring self-knowledge; building relationships; nurturing creativity (and self-expression); acknowledging, and coming to terms with, often conflicting feelings and emotions, are all aspects that have been associated with spiritual development (see NCC, 1993, p. 2).

The idea of spirituality being located in the material world, while at the same time concerned with feelings and emotions and of 'being moved' – in terms of something beyond the material – is

reflected in agreed syllabuses. The Warwickshire syllabus (1996, p. 15), for instance, says that the 'spiritual'

> has to do with 'being' and 'feeling' as well as 'doing' or 'knowing'. It is concerned with what a person is or feels as well as what is known or what skills may be acquired.
>
> The spiritual may also be described as referring to something that is beyond the mundane, something beyond the material, something to reflect on, something to wonder at, or something to be moved by.
>
> This awareness of the spiritual can be expressed in terms of values and visions. For some it has the added dimension of a sense of relationship with a divine being. People are aware of the inner mysteries and questions of concern such as 'what will happen to me when I die?' They formulate personal responses to these concerns.

Key elements include *being and feeling* (as well as *knowing*), *beyond the mundane*, or the *material*; something to *reflect upon, wonder at, be moved by*; *values* and *visions*; *inner mysteries*, *questions* concerning matters such as what happens after death. In other words, spirituality here becomes something embedded in the material everyday world (of doing and knowing and the acquisition of skills) while also being 'other' and transcendent (beyond and visionary).

OFSTED (1994b) describes spiritual development as relating to

> that aspect of inner life through which students acquire insights into their personal existence which are of enduring worth. It is characterized by reflection, the attribution of meaning to experience, valuing a non-material dimension to life, and intimations of an enduring reality.

It further states that effective *provision* for such development depends on curriculum and teaching approaches which embody clear values and enable students to gain understanding through reflection on their own and other people's lives and beliefs, their environment and (an additional aspect included in guidance for secondary schools) the human condition (OFSTED 1995a, 1995b).

Some conceptual challenges

Despite the upsurge of interest in spiritual education, the meaning of 'spirituality' remains notoriously hard to pin down (Ungoed-Thomas, 1986) and appears to have been accompanied by 'no greater clarity in our understanding of teaching, learning and development in the spiritual domain' (Carr, 1996, p. 159). It continues to present a major problem for teachers and inspectors (Brown and Furlong, 1996). Indeed, Carr (1996) argues that in the absence of some attempt to identify precisely what the curricular claims of the spiritual, as distinct from the moral or religious, might be, much talk of spiritual education 'is likely to be vacuous'. The problem, as he sees it, is the 'looseness' of ordinary spiritual language, which will 'enshrine instabilities of sense that cannot simply be "tidied up"'. He proposes three ways in which spiritual usage might be construed as offering some theoretical underpinning for spiritual education; namely, (a) the 'reductionist'; (b) the 'psychological' or 'process' oriented; and (c) the 'knowledge' or 'content' oriented. Carr raises some interesting, significant and challenging issues and, because of his broad overview of the difficulties in conceptualising spiritual education, provides a useful framework against which to place further discussion. What follows is not an exhaustive critique of Carr's position, but a brief elucidation of the main theoretical categories he identifies as a way of providing entry into the debate and locating it within a broader philosophical perspective.

First, at the *reductionist* level Carr (1996, p. 161) identifies two conceptions of 'spiritual': (a) as the 'sublime'; and (b) as the 'ineffable.' One problem in the *spiritual as sublime* is that at its most nebulous:

> spiritual language is hardly more than a pious way of exalting or celebrating certain familiar aspects of human experience and endeavour – aspects of life, moreover, which may be entirely explicable in rational terms.

A difficulty here lies in distinguishing what might be regarded as the 'truly spiritual' from the 'merely aesthetic'. Carr argues, for instance, that at this level, the idea of spiritual development through moral, religious or aesthetic education may amount to little more than the assertion that young people should be encouraged to seek personal fulfilment through religious participation or artistic creativity or to value such activities highly (ibid.).

In terms of the *spiritual as ineffable*, the idea of spirituality beyond rational articulation or explanation can become associated with areas of the school curriculum with respect to which it otherwise seems out of place. Carr cites maths and science where the 'language of spirituality may be invoked to express human incomprehension of infinity or irresolvable paradox' (p. 162). The problem with this is that attention to such sources of wonderment would seem little more than part and parcel of what might readily be associated with good teaching (ibid.). In brief, Carr believes the reductionist account to be quite 'wrong-headed' and, with its account of spirituality focusing on the 'sublime' or the 'ineffable', not 'particularly strong on coherence' (p. 163).

The *psychological* or *process* conception of spirituality offers explanations of the spiritual significance of experience in terms of spiritual attitude, or 'process' that is, 'a certain relationship between persons and things or between agents and the activities in which they engage – more than by actual reference to actual properties or qualities of objects or persons (p. 164). This gives rise to the problem of clarifying the nature of such processes and how they might be promoted through a systematic, educational programme of spiritual development (ibid.).

In terms of the *knowledge* or *content* based conception of spiritual education, Carr argues that we need some idea of what constitutes the 'matter as well as the form' of distinctly spiritual modes of experience. From this point of view, if talk of spiritual education is to be meaningful, it can be so 'only in the light of some intelligible perspective on the nature of spiritual teaching and learning' (p. 169). For Carr, this means acquaintance with some or other substantial tradition of spiritual aspiration or enquiry.

The increasingly popular *phenomenological* approach, concentrating primarily upon *different* social and cultural expressions of spirituality, rather than induction into substantial spiritual beliefs, has caused unease among a number of religious educationalists (Slee, 1992; Watson, 1993). One concern is that it is predominantly informational, with young people exposed to little more than 'scraps and fragments' of different religious traditions (often, adds Carr (1996, p. 171), taught by teachers 'having themselves little more than a tenuous grasp of these traditions'. OFSTED (1995c) has, in fact, identified the 'insecurity' of non-specialist teachers as a weakness in both primary and secondary schools). The acquisition of spiritual education, it is felt, should be construed as 'more than a simple matter of information gathering about a range of social practices' (Carr, 1996, p. 171).

In summary, Carr feels that no genuine understanding of the religious or spiritual can be had 'except via some substantial initiation into religious and spiritual practices' (ibid., p. 174), a perspective echoed by Nichols (1992, p. 116), who feels that something important may be learned by considering the story of religious education within a particular tradition or faith.

In contrast to Carr's argument are attempts to clarify spiritual development in the non-religious context of secular life today, focusing on the connection between spirituality and self-identity:

> The meaning of spirituality is here identified with the development of personal identity, and is distinguished from moral development by its focus upon the psyche as the developing self. (Newby, 1996, p. 93)

In reflecting the post-traditional cultural milieu of our time, this view essentially presupposes that 'spiritual growth is meaningful as an idea outside of tightly-defined religious and ideological traditions' (ibid., p. 93). Indeed, it is pointed out that religious educators are now subscribing to the view that specific religious practices are to be evaluated in terms of a common core of shared values which transcend the boundaries of faiths (ibid., p. 94; cf. Cole, 1993). Newby (1996, p. 94) sees spiritual development in terms of a 'continuous, coherent and creative life-narrative'. His prerequisites for spiritual maturity include: the *desire for knowledge and understanding*; *self-understanding*; *sensibility* (in terms of a recognition of the autonomy of others and away from a desire to manipulate them for our own ends); *continuity, coherence* and *creativity*; and the *need for 'cultural narratives'* (where 'story forms . . . are fundamental to the development of personal identity').

The variety of concepts subsumed within the term 'spirituality', and the formulations that are tentatively beginning to emerge, illustrate the complexities of attempting to discuss the spiritual in terms that will be meaningful when related to education (see Best, 1996).

Continuing process: maturity and the 'end-state'

It has been suggested that 'a concept of maturity is an important prerequisite to any notion of development' (Newby, 1996, p. 94) and that unless teachers and parents focus upon an end-state which they are seeking to develop as educators, they will be 'in no position to progress towards more effective practice' (ibid.). This presents its own difficulties, especially when considering the relationship between designed activities and spiritual development; as McCreery (1996, p. 197) asks: How do we *know* we are developing the spiritual? The notion of an 'end-state' is itself both compelling and problematic. On the one hand, if we do not have a concept of an 'end-state', in this case 'maturity', to aim for, how can we measure progress towards the goal of spirituality, and how do we implement 'effective practice'? On the other hand, research from adult education suggests that there is no 'end-state' to personal development as such. Adult educators tend, implicitly at least, to see education as an open-ended process, not a 'final state' attainable at a particular point in a person's life at which they become educated (Leicester, 1993); similarly, the influence of continuing education on the evolution of personal identity in adulthood has been identified (Pearce, 1995; Leicester and Pearce, 1997). The spiritual and moral development of young people has also been explicitly related to education for adult life (SCAA, 1996; Brown and Furlong, 1996) and the search for 'spiritual truth' described as a 'life long journey' (Wood, 1996). The process of *moving towards* maturity – that is, it is 'an ideal to be aimed at rather than achieved in full' – is also acknowledged as being associated with adulthood (Rogers, 1989). None of this, of course, negates the need to identify the 'goal' of spiritual education; rather, the very fact that, as with learning itself, it is an open-ended, transforming and life-long process both enriches the concept and serves to underline the difficult task faced by educators attempting to foster an enduring sense of the spiritual.

Case studies: resources for the classroom

So far, attention has been given to the difficulties in establishing what is meant by 'spiritual' and its development. But this chapter argues that newspapers can play an important role in spiritual growth, and so assumes that it is possible to nurture spirituality, although this is something to be actively worked at (Matousek, 1996). This assertion is examined more closely by looking, first, at a publication designed by a newspaper specifically for the purpose of RE; second, by referring to a series of books using newspapers as a practical method of exploring different issues; third, by drawing on a project at a school in Rugby, Warwickshire, where newspapers have become a key resource; and fourth, by analysis of a newspaper article, which is offered to suggest ways in which it might, among other things, stimulate reflection, promote the search for meaning and purpose and raise awareness of others and the 'human condition'.

Looking at religion: special supplements

One way of utilising newspapers in religious education is to examine the representation of different religions and their approach to various social issues. In this sense, newspapers become relevant to discussions *about* religion. This use of newspapers may or may not promote spiritual development. At the very least, however, it raises questions about religion and its role in society today. Examples of publications reflecting these issues are *Religious Education* (Harvey and O'Reilly, 1996), a 20-page tabloid supplement published by the *Belfast Telegraph*, and *Religion, Living Faiths of Leicestershire*, produced by the *Leicester Mercury* (Kadodwala, 1992; see also Cole, 1993). Both have been compiled by educationalists working with the respective newspapers in association with Newspapers in Education.

Religious Education is based on articles selected from the *Belfast Telegraph* and *Sunday Life*. Among the topics covered are teenage pregnancy, drug dependency, mixed marriages, church attendance, and divorce and remarriage; the problems of sectarianism – and attempts to resist it – feature strongly.

Religion, Living Faiths of Leicestershire, a 28-page tabloid 'classroom curriculum resource' was designed to complement Leicestershire's Agreed Syllabus (1992), and is also 'a celebration of the richness of religious and cultural diversity represented in Leicestershire'. As with the Belfast RE supplement, the material is local, comprising reports and pictures drawn from the files of the *Leicester Mercury*. The following remarks relate mainly to the Leicester publication, with its stated emphasis on 'religious and cultural diversity'. The supplement is divided into sections, focusing on different religious groups and subdivided into topics such as festivals or places of worship. The selection of topics relates to the Attainment Statements of the Agreed Syllabus. The purpose 'is to be a local resource, illustrating that the religious

dimension of life in terms of time and place is very much alive and part of Leicestershire life' (Nettleton, 1992, p. 2). The images presented of local people living out and practising their religious traditions 'will have a greater impact than words alone' (Kadodwala, 1992: 2):

> The striking pictures will help to provide insights, especially for those pupils in the County areas who, perhaps, are 'meeting' the diversity of religious and cultural traditions for the first time through these images.   (Ibid.)

At points throughout the supplement (in common with the Belfast paper) are suggested activities which stimulate reflection, where readers are encouraged to consider how the content affects them. One section features pictures of people of different ages, sex and race with a range of expressions: a baby crying, for instance, or two boys enjoying themselves on a fairground ride. Pupils are asked to look at the pictures and put a name to the feelings conveyed. This is related to the attainment statement which extends self-knowledge 'by investigating ways of dealing with positive and negative feelings'.

What the supplement provides, then, is a resource, stimulating insight into the diversity of religious and cultural traditions in the area, and calling for engagement with, and creative response to, the content. Like Belfast's *Religious Education*, it is a publication where understanding is arrived at through the study of actual, non-fictional reports.

Bible stories: hitting the headlines

A different approach is provided by Windsor and Hughes (1990a, 1990b, 1990c, 1991), in their Exploring Christianity series for lower secondary school pupils. Here the newspaper format is used extensively to explore stories from the Bible, which are retold in a newspaper style. One 'news report', for example, appears in a 'Special Census Edition' of *The Bethlehem Star* under the headline: 'Shepherds report strange lights in the sky'. The story begins: 'Duty shepherds in the hills outside Bethlehem left their flocks last night after reporting strange happenings in the fields' (Windsor and Hughes, 1991, p. 6). This reflects a newspaper genre, with the dramatic news 'angle' emphasised and the report written in short, journalistic sentences. Giving different aspects of the same event, there is also a Birth announcement in which Joseph and Mary publicise the arrival of their son, and a

Stop Press, informing readers that 'There are now no free rooms to be found anywhere in Bethlehem'. The fictionalised reports are accompanied by questions referring back to the Bible; for example, which parts of the story are the same as Luke 2: 8-21; which parts are different?

In another activity, pupils are asked to design their own newspaper page about Jesus's noisy followers being drunk after claiming that the recently executed 'Galilean rebel' was still alive (Windsor and Hughes, 1990a, p. 74). In this case, writing news reports and designing news pages involves the pupils in the process of interpreting and creating stories. The newspaper disciplines of having to focus on the important points, write succinctly, put the information into a particular order, and attract (and hold) the reader's attention encourages the pupils themselves to extract the essential information. They become aware of the central issues through a practical creative activity.

School lines: an eye on the news

Yet a third approach is that adopted by Bilton High School, in Rugby, Warwickshire. The school, of 1245 (predominantly Christian) students, runs a Suffering and Reconciliation module in which newspapers play a significant part. The module, originally devised by teachers Crawford Payne and Mary Armstrong in 1991 and further developed by Payne and Janice Butterworth in 1995, was introduced to the Bilton School's year 9 religious education programme in 1995 in conjunction with a twentieth-century history project. All year 9 students – 270 pupils – studied it in 1996. In 1997 the module incorporated work on the Cross of Nails Community in Corrymeela, an ecumenical community in Northern Ireland devoted to promoting reconciliation between different Christian denominations. The addition of the Corrymeela Community will 'broaden the students' experience and enable them to gain a deeper appreciation of the complexity of this topic, with specific reference to the Irish situation and its relevance to all of us, not just to the theists' (Payne, 1996a).

The module forms a comprehensive fifteen-week programme aimed at enabling students 'to understand suffering and reconciliation in the widest sense' and providing 'opportunities for them to identify, categorise and analyse the impact on their society and world' (ibid.). A range of teaching approaches supports individual, group and class activities. Adults other than teachers are involved as

appropriate and video programmes are shown in order to deepen the students' knowledge and understanding. Homework gives students the opportunity to specialise in an 'area of greatest interest'. The climax of the study requires students to mount a display on the classroom noticeboards or produce material in a project folder, in order to share knowledge, findings and feelings with the rest of the school.

Content of the module includes: (a) an introduction, with work on the *Coventry Evening Telegraph*; (b) an examination of Christian suffering, featuring a video of the late entertainer Roy Castle and the dilemma that his death from cancer poses for devout believers: Does God cause suffering? Can God stop suffering? Why does a loving God allow such misery to be an inherent part of human life? Is there a God?; (c) the Rugby community, providing students with the opportunity to interview different people and record their feelings; (d) miracles – fact or fiction? A 'detailed and honest assessment' of biblical accounts allied to modern examples of miracles (metaphorical interpretation versus the literal one); and (e) reconciliation: studying the symbolic role of Coventry Cathedral and Dresden and also incorporating the Cross of Nails Community. Resources include textbook material and video footage taken by Payne while on a visit to the Corrymeela Community.

The newspaper element comprises students working in small groups using copies of the *Coventry Evening Telegraph*. This is a local tabloid with a circulation of around 85,000 in Coventry and Warwickshire. It has local editions for districts including Rugby. Students study papers in detail in order to identify and record what they understand to be examples of suffering. The groups' findings are shared with the class and their examples recorded.

These examples are categorised under a range of headings determined by the students themselves: accidental, natural, physical, mental, social, spiritual and so on. The students are also required to watch a news broadcast and write a report of a current example of suffering that has been featured. They then have to make a newsheet. In this case, the students are not reading *about* religion but are exploring their own responses to the *issues* of the day as reported through the media. This activity combines elements of the *Belfast Telegraph* and *Leicester Mercury* supplements with the newspaper-type activities of Windsor and Hughes. They are being extended, however. The issues dealt with emerge neither from simply the retelling of Bible stories, nor from study of texts on religious themes, but are those that 'ordinary people' are being faced with in society today and, moreover, in the local community, to which the students themselves belong. Thus, through guidance within the classroom, events in the community and the wider world as depicted in the local newspaper come to have personal, 'inner' relevance.

Within the columns: a poignant story

The entry into 'inner' personal worlds through examination of the outside world and 'real-life situations' can be explored more deeply. Open any newspaper and there is an abundance of material relevant to the issues addressed in religious education. One example is an article on identical twins, one of whom had died (Handley, 1996). An analysis here of the article will raise some of the issues relevant to the question of spirituality and the potential response of students to newspapers. The visual presentation of the story itself has immediate impact, filling all but one column of a double-page spread. Two large half-tone pictures dominate, taking up more than a quarter of the left-hand page and half of the right. The left-hand page shows the twins, Katharine and Jacqueline, aged 30. They are sitting together on a garden bench. Elegantly dressed and smiling, they are clearly both relaxed. The right-hand picture shows the twins as babies, neatly – and identically – dressed, sitting close together in an armchair.

The main headline extending across the top of both pictures declares: 'The day my twin died half of me died too'. A strapline in a smaller font size above reads: 'The sisters shared the same hobbies, got identical exam results and even had their own special language . . . until tragedy shattered their unique bond.' It is an emotive piece. The language of the headline alone evokes complex emotions and uncertainties: the idea of a 'unique bond' being shattered, of the 'sharing' that has now been ruptured, and the feeling that the remaining twin has lost, not only someone else, but part of her self, too. Death can undermine our sense of continuity. Newspaper stories remind us that the world is, perhaps, not as predictable, settled and steady as we might like to assume.

The pictures tell their own story. We are faced with images of happy, healthy people at different stages of their life nearly 30 years apart. The photo-graphs freeze a moment. We can imagine our own narrative of what happened before and after each was taken. We can also begin to contemplate the intervening years, with the visual clues of the babies and the grown women to help us. The babies and the women are both the same and continuous, yet different and changed people. As we reflect upon the pictures, the lives of Katharine and Jacqueline impinge upon our own; already, we can begin to think of our own life experiences and development. Using the images alone as a stimulus, students could be asked to reflect upon their own childhood, upon how they got to where they are now, and upon their current relationships. They could, perhaps, speculate on their future lives. They could also try to imagine the experience of the twins, and that of Jacqueline, suffering her loss. In other words, they could begin to construct a narrative for both themselves and others, explore compassion and empathy, and reflect upon issues such as care, consideration and respect for themselves and other people.

If the text is studied, even more possibilities emerge. Jacqueline reports how she has felt since her sister's death: 'The rawness of the pain goes, but I don't think that feeling of not being complete will ever leave me.'

What does the 'rawness of pain' mean? How does 'raw pain' feel? What other impressions do the words suggest? Can we begin to relate to people we have never seen, perhaps in countries we have never visited, and feel compassion for them? And then there is the feeling of 'not being complete':

> I have to accept that the huge emptiness is never going to be completely filled by other things in my life. I have a wonderful husband and a marvellous family. I also have a very close relationship with my younger brother, who is fantastic. But no one can ever take her place.

What must it be like for Jacqueline to endure this 'huge emptiness?' What does it mean to be a 'complete' human being? How does 'completeness' compare or contrast with Jacqueline's experience, graphically recollected: 'It is as if a line was drawn down me that day, splitting me in half.'

Students could explore the concept and 'meaning' of pain (physical, mental, emotional), of coming to terms with loss, of the need for support from others. This in itself addresses issues of personal development, but also leads to consideration of how different religious perspectives would handle these matters, providing new symbolic frameworks within which to interpret the events depicted in the newspaper.

In the article under discussion, there are also more discernibly 'spiritual' elements conveying the sense of transcendence and 'unexplained mystery' characteristic of the sisters' close relationship:

> When Katharine fainted in the road, narrowly avoiding being hit by a car, Jacqueline, who was on holiday hundreds of miles away in Tenerife, blacked out. Jacqueline said: 'That was the moment that underlines we had this very close bond. It was really weird but in a way I wasn't surprised. She was very much a soulmate.'

Later, Jacqueline describes the impact of her sister's illness, leukaemia, and how Katharine had died in her arms:

> I never thought she would die. I like to reminisce, because when you talk about somebody, they are very much alive. I do feel sometimes that she's with me, especially when I'm vulnerable.

Using this article as a starting point, students could be encouraged to reflect upon their own experiences and, perhaps, explore notions such as life after death and how this might be perceived from different religious and cultural perspectives. It would be appropriate for a 'suffering and reconciliation' theme, with Jacqueline's emotional and mental suffering at the death of her sister, and, in a sense, a personal 'reconciliation' in having to come to terms with the loss. As she herself remarks: 'Now it's like a process of relearning, working out how to cope now my soulmate, my best friend, my sister, my everything, is no longer there to support me.'

The newspaper extract discussed above has been included here because it addresses some of the issues that have been associated with spiritual development. It also demonstrates how newspapers, focusing as they do on very human predicaments, can become an invaluable resource, constituting a stimulus for reflection upon the self's response to the world and relationship with others. They lend themselves to the application and promotion of skills, processes and attitudes central to religious education such as investigation, interpretation, reflection, empathy, commitment, respect and self-understanding (SCAA, 1994). Newspapers are not the only resource, of course. But as the examples show, they can have an immediacy and relevance that textbooks often lack.

Religious education: a way of seeing

The contribution towards spiritual development need not be restricted to religious education; indeed, newspapers are utilised across the curriculum. The value of religious education, however, is that it is explicitly concerned with these matters; it provides a 'way of seeing' (Kushner, 1990). The newspaper – as has happened at Bilton High School – can become the vehicle for exploring themes of both current and future importance to the students.

A crucial factor is the role of the teacher in receiving and valuing students' ideas, encouraging communication and developing self-confidence and autonomy. Indeed, at Bilton, the aim is not to impose values:

> I don't think values can be imposed. Values do underpin the running and ethos of the school. We encourage things like honesty, integrity, learning how to empathise and so on, so there is a basic framework. But within that, we are trying to encourage the students to think for themselves, to question, to think about the consequences of their actions and attitudes . . . We will keep challenging them, in order to get them to think. They have got to be able to think for themselves, to believe in themselves . . . empathy is important, because being able to empathise is a key feature of reconciliation. (Payne, 1996b)

This encouragement for the students to 'think for themselves' and reach their own conclusions manifests itself in different – and observable – ways, including the making of news sheets and role-playing recorded on video film. For the newspaper analysis, the students are required to construct their own definition of suffering and reconciliation. This 'generated a lot of discussion. Suffering is not just someone being mugged. It can be conditions they are living in, sacrifices they have to make. It can be psychological, social or physical' (ibid.).

The power of evil: a cautionary note

It is being asserted that newspapers, through stimulating critical reflection in the context of an inclusive approach to RE, can facilitate student learning in that preconceptions are challenged and existing perspectives altered, thus potentially contributing towards spiritual and identity development. However, a note of caution needs to be sounded. A basic assumption underpinning this chapter is that spiritual development follows a positive route, that is, one towards well-being and the 'unfolding of one's most enduring and overriding commitments as a person' (Newby, 1996, p. 97). But it is as well to bear in mind that spiritual development can also take on negative and destructive qualities, a point often overlooked. Donley (1992, p. 184), for instance, argues that:

> So indoctrinated with materialistic secularism has our society become that probably the majority of people instinctively feel that the word 'spiritual' automatically connotes something good and beneficial. How many of those who now use the word 'spirituality' so freely actually believe, one wonders, in the reality of the spiritual world, in the world of spirits both good *and evil?* One gets the impression that, for many, the term simply refers to the inner feelings of a given individual.

And Holley (1978, p. 116) points out that the spiritual dynamism of man (*sic*) can be 'destructive as well as creative', while Vardey (1995, p. 297) argues that to ignore the arresting power of evil in the world 'would be a disservice to the spiritual seeker and to humanity as a whole'.

Likewise, the response to newspaper reports is not always predictable and can reveal a startling, even shocking, dimension. Hate mail was sent to the families involved in the Dunblane shooting tragedy, for example ('Your daughter should have died. We wish she had': *Daily Express,* 18 August 1996). But, as indicated earlier, the values inherent in fostering spiritual development in schools, in so far as they are 'educative', are necessarily positive.

Newspapers in the classroom: a perspective on RE

It is assumed that spirituality can be developed across the curriculum in a multicultural context. However, a key point is that RE has a particular role to play in this. Schools must address spiritual development, and need a range of approaches and resources to do so. Newspapers, it has been suggested, can be one of those resources, providing the means of stimulating reflection upon aspects of society – and, in particular, other people's lives – while being embedded in that society. At the same time, RE introduces students to language and symbolism which enable the content of newspapers to be interpreted at a potentially deeper and more significant level. It can play an especially important part in encouraging students' exploration of values and beliefs (OFSTED, 1994b).

Understandably, there is continuing concern over the pressures exerted on young people by the media and advertising, and especially the 'image-makers', who influence and even create contemporary values (SCAA, 1996). One way of addressing this concern is by helping young people to become better informed about the media. Although, as with other mass media, newspapers will inevitably gravitate towards the cluster of news values including disaster, conflict, controversy, change and dramatic reversals and violence (Hall, 1984, p. 272), there is also much within the columns that is positive, uplifting and can induce a sense of awe, wonder, excitement and curiosity; furthermore, and importantly, the appeal of newspapers in the classroom, and the very evident learning that takes place with their usage, should not be underestimated. RE can offer an interpretative framework for the content of newspapers; the use of newspapers can offer a new perspective on the concerns of RE. Regular reading of their local newspaper can give students 'a better understanding of the issues which affect people's lives' (Harvey and O'Reilly, 1996). Through imaginative and sensitive use of newspapers – which, after all, are a cheap, accessible and up-to-date resource – students can explore their sense of self and their place in the world. Through reflection upon the experience of others, they come to know themselves. As they come to know themselves, so they edge closer to spiritual maturity.

Acknowledgements

I should like to thank Jo Price, senior teacher adviser for RE (primary) in Warwickshire; Jenny Pestridge, teacher adviser for RE in Coventry; and author and teacher Gwyneth Windsor, for their helpful comments. I am especially indebted to Ruth Robinson, Head of RE at Shireland High School, Smethwick, for giving her time and offering constructive observations and encouragement; and to Crawford Payne, Subject Head for RE at Bilton High School, for his support, professional expertise and painstaking personal contribution through long discussions and critical reading of the original manuscript.

References

Atkins, P. (1996) Professor of Chemistry at Oxford, quoted by Bryan Appleyard in the *Independent*, Section 2, 12 September 1996.

Best, R. (ed.) (1996) *Education, Spirituality and the Whole Child*. London: Cassell.

Brown, A. and Furlong, J. (1996) *Spiritual Development in Schools*. London: National Society (Church of England) for Promoting Religious Education.

Buckingham, D. (1992) Teaching about the media. In D. Lusted (ed.), *The Media Studies Book: A Guide for Teachers*. London: Routledge.

Carr, D. (1996) Rival conceptions of spiritual education. *Journal of Philosophy of Education* **30** (2), pp. 159–78.

Cole, D. (1993) Common threads in the matter of faith. *The Faiths: eG [Education Guardian] Religions Source Book*. London: *Education Guardian*.

Davies, K., Dickey, J. and Stratford, T. (eds) (1987) *Out of Focus: Writings on Women and the Media*. London: Women's Press.

Dines, G. and Humez, J. M. (eds) (1995) *Gender, Race and Class in Media*. London: Sage.

Donley, M. (1992) Teaching discernment: an overview of the book as a whole from the perspective of the secondary school. In B. Watson (ed.), *Priorities in Religious Education for the 1990s and Beyond*. London: Falmer Press.

Erriker, C. and Erricker, J. (1996) Where angels fear to tread: discovering children's spirituality. In R. Best (ed.), *Education, Spirituality and the Whole Child*. London: Cassell.

Gordon, P. and Rosenberg, D. (1989) *Daily Racism: The Press and Black People in Britain*. London: Runnymede Trust.

Hall, S. (1984) The structured communication of events. In D. Potter, J. Anderson, J. Clarke, P. Coombes, S. Hall, L. Harris, C. Holloway and T. Walton (eds), *Society and the Social Sciences: An Introduction*. London: Routledge & Kegan Paul in association with The Open University.

Hall, S. (1996) Racist ideologies and the media. In P. Marris, and S. Thornham (eds), *Media Studies: A Reader*. Edinburgh: Edinburgh University Press.

Handley, A. (1996) The day my twin died, half of me died too. *Coventry Evening Telegraph*, 19 August 1996.

Harcourt, K. (ed.) (1991) *The Teacher's Guide to Making a Newspaper*. Tunbridge Wells, Kent: Northcliffe (Newspapers in Education).

Harvey, I. and O'Reilly, J. (collators) (1996) *Religious Education*, newspaper supplement for schools. Belfast: *Belfast Telegraph*.

Holley, R. (1978) *Religious Education and Religious Understanding: An Introduction to the Philosophy of Religious Education*. London: Routledge & Kegan Paul.

Jakubowicz, A. (1995) Media in multicultural nations. In J. Downing, A. Mohammadi and A. Sreberny-Mohammadi (eds), *Questioning the Media: A Critical Introduction*, 2nd edn. London: Sage.

Kadodwala, D. (1992) 'Religion, Living Faiths of Leicestershire.' Leicester: *Leicester Mercury*.

Kellner, D. (1995) Cultural studies, multiculturalism and media culture. In G. Dines and J. M. Humez (eds), *Gender, Race and Class in Media*. London: Sage.

Kelly, G. (1995) *Project Utopia*. London: Newspaper Society.

Kibble, D.G. (1996) Spiritual development, spiritual experience and spiritual education. In R. Best (ed.), *Spirituality, Education and the Whole Child*. London: Cassell.

Kushner, H. (1990) *Who Needs God?* London: Simon & Schuster.

Leicester, M. (1993) *Race for a Change in Continuing and Higher Education*. Bury St Edmunds, Suffolk: Society for Research into Higher Education and Open University Press.

Leicester, M. and Pearce, R. (1997) Cognitive development, self knowledge and moral education, *Journal of Moral Education* **26** (4), 455–72.

Lont, C.M. (ed.) (1995) *Women and Media: Content, Careers and Criticism*. Belmont, CA: Wadsworth.

Lusted, D. (ed.) (1992) *The Media Studies Book: A Guide for Teachers*. London: Routledge.

Marris, P. and Thornham, S. (eds) (1996) *Media Studies: A Reader*. Edinburgh: Edinburgh University Press.

Matousek, M. (1996) *Sex, Death, Enlightenment*. London: Piatkus.

McCreery, E. (1996) Talking to young children about things spiritual. In R. Best (ed.), *Education, Spirituality and the Whole Child*. London: Cassell.

Mott-Thornton, K. (1996) Experience, critical realism and the schooling of spirituality. In R. Best (ed.), *Education, Spirituality and the Whole Child*. London: Cassell.

National Curriculum Council (NCC) (1993) *Spiritual and Moral Development; A Discussion Paper*. York: NCC.

Nettleton, K. (1992) 'Religion, Living Faiths of Leicestershire,' newspaper supplement for schools. Leicester: *Leicester Mercury*.

Newby, M. (1996) Towards a secular concept of spiritual maturity. In R. Best (ed.), *Education, Spirituality and the Whole Child*. London: Cassell.

Nichols, K. (1992) Roots in Religious Education. In B. Watson (ed.), *Priorities in Religious Education for the 1990s and Beyond*. London: Falmer Press.

Office for Standards in Education (OFSTED) (1994a) *Spiritual, Moral, Social and Cultural Development: A Discussion Paper*. London: Her Majesty's Stationery Office.

Office for Standards in Education (OFSTED) (1994b) *Handbook for the Inspection of Schools*. London: Her Majesty's Stationery Office.

Office for Standards in Education (OFSTED) (1995a) *Guidance on the Inspection of Nursery and Primary Schools*. London: Her Majesty's Stationery Office.

Office for Standards in Education (OFSTED) (1995b)

Guidance on the Inspection of Secondary Schools. London: Her Majesty's Stationery Office.

Office for Standards in Education (OFSTED) (1995c) *Religious Education: A Review of Inspection Findings, 1993/94.* London: Her Majesty's Stationery Office.

Payne, C. (1996a) Suffering and reconciliation module: school curriculum notes by Crawford Payne, Subject Manager for Religious Education. Rugby: Bilton High School.

Payne, C. (1996b) Personal communication.

Pearce, E.R. (1995) 'Self and open studies: the impact of open studies on students' sense of identity and the educational implications.' Unpublished Ph.D. thesis, Warwick University.

Real, M.R. (1989) *Super Media: A Cultural Studies Approach.* London: Sage.

Rodger, A. (1996) Human spirituality: towards an educational rationale. In R. Best (ed.), *Education, Spirituality and the whole Child.* London: Cassell.

Rogers, A. (1989) *Teaching Adults.* Milton Keynes: Open University Press.

School Curriculum and Assessment Authority (SCAA) (1994). *Model Syllabuses for Religious Education. Model 2: Questions and Teachings.* London: SCAA.

School Curriculum and Assessment Authority (SCAA) (1996) *Education for Adult Life: The Spiritual and Moral Development of Young People.* London: SCAA.

Slee, N. (1 992) Heaven in ordinaire: the imagination, spirituality and the arts in religious education. In B. Watson (ed.), *Priorities in Religious Education for the 1990s and Beyond.* London: Falmer Press.

Stone, M.K. (1995) *Don't Just Do Something, Sit There: Developing Children's Spiritual Awareness.* St Martin's College, Lancaster: Religious and Moral Education Press.

Swanson, G. (1992) Representation. In D. Lusted (ed.), *The Media Studies Book: A Guide for Teachers.* London: Routledge.

Thornecroft, J.K. (1978) *Religious Education through Experience and Expression.* London: Edward Arnold.

Ungoed-Thomas, J.R. (1986) Personal and social education, religious education and spiritual development. In B. Greenwood (ed.), *Perspectives on Religious Education and Personal and Social Education.* Isleworth, Middlesex: Christian Education Movement.

van Zoonen, L. (1994) *Feminist Media Studies.* London: Sage.

van Zoonen, L. (1995) Gender, representation, and the media. In J. Downing, A. Mohammadi and A. Sreberny-Mohammadi (eds), *Questioning the Media: A Critical Introduction,* 2nd edn. London: Sage.

Vardey, L. (ed.) (1995) *God in All Worlds: An Anthology of Contemporary Spiritual Writing.* London: Chatto & Windus.

Warwickshire County Council (1996) *Warwickshire Agreed Syllabus for Religious Education.* Warwick: Warwickshire Education Services.

Watson, B. (1993) *The Effective Teaching of Religious Education.* London: Longman.

Windsor, G. and Hughes, J. (1990a) *Jesus and the Birth of the Church.* Exploring Christianity Series. Oxford: Heinemann Educational.

Windsor, G. and Hughes, J. (1990b) *The Bible and Christian Belief.* Exploring Christianity Series. Oxford: Heinemann Educational.

Windsor, G. and Hughes, J. (1990c) *Worship and Festivals.* Exploring Christianity Series. Oxford: Heinemann Educational.

Windsor, G. and Hughes, J. (1991) *Christian Life: Personal and Social Issues.* Exploring Christianity Series. Oxford: Heinemann Educational.

Wood, E. (1996) County Education Officer's foreword to *Warwickshire Agreed Syllabus for Religious Education.* Warwick: Warwickshire Education Services.

Wright, F. (1988) Welcome to the obstacle race. *Media Education Initiatives,* issue 9. Society for Education in Film and Television.

Wynne Jones, P. (1992) Children under pressure. From *All God's Children,* a report by the Church of England General Synod Board of Education, cited in *Coming Alive,* the *Dorset Agreed Syllabus Handbooks,* Key Stages 1 and 2.

6 'The Open Heaven':[1] Fostering Dialogue and Understanding in the Context of Religious Diversity

WINIFRED WING HAN LAMB

In the context of cultural diversity, an obvious educational concern is the question not only of how to cultivate tolerance for views, lifestyles and beliefs different from one's own, but also the question of how to enable a better understanding of such views. The latter question takes us beyond the matter of coexistence and tolerance, to the matter of how we may take the further step of creating dialogue with and understanding the other.

How then can we foster dialogue through education, especially through religious education within the context of religious diversity?

Now, it is often assumed that in order properly to respect and understand a religious position different from and in some sense opposed to one's own, one needs to adopt a relativist standpoint, that is, one needs to acknowledge that belief positions, including one's own, are not absolute but are contingent and finite. This, of course, creates immediate problems for religious education because any educator in multicultural communities would want to encourage amongst the students a broad understanding of various religious positions and traditions. Those students who come from and adhere to particular religious traditions in a fundamentalist manner, or even in a non-fundamentalist but fairly absolute manner, would, on this view, not be able to participate in such an education because they would not be able to understand positions different from and opposed to their own religious tradition. Such a conclusion would be limiting indeed for the educator!

However, I would suggest that the situation is not so unreservedly grim, that whereas fundamentalist belief may present insuperable problems for religious education (as understood above), a position of religious conviction could *still* allow room for understanding the other; indeed, I would like to suggest that in such a circumstance, there could even exist the positive desire so to understand. Such is conceivable and possible if we teach according to a model of understanding that I will discuss is fuller than a purely cognitive understanding. According to the purely cognitive notion, coming to understand a religious faith involves the assessment of that position for its coherence and intelligibility with reference to one's own categories. Religious positions are therefore treated as knowledge claims. Such an approach to religion has, for example, characterised traditional philosophy of religion in the Anglo-American analytic tradition.

However, this approach is a misrepresentation both of religious positions as well as of ways in which we come to understand them. To begin with, religious positions should not be understood in terms of claims that are somehow impersonal, like scientific hypotheses. Second, understanding itself should not be conceived in such cognitive and disembodied terms because understanding, like religious beliefs and claims, is situated and 'owned'. It is also dynamic, being fuelled by imagination, energy and desire.

To advance my view of what enables understanding and dialogue across the divide of genuine religious differences, I shall compare and contrast two views that we find in the philosophy of education literature advanced by well-known philosophers, both writing in the 1970s. The chapter falls into three parts: in the first part I shall discuss each of these accounts and their relative merits with respect to understanding difference and the promotion of dialogue. I shall use these accounts to develop a phenomenology of understanding that could be employed for promoting dialogue within religious education. In the second part I shall discuss the applicability of each of the accounts to the reality of religious faith and religious conviction. Using fundamentalist faith as a negative example of the kind of religious conviction that does not encourage understanding, I shall show the possibility of a religious conviction that lends itself to dialogue and to understanding the other.[2] In closing, and in relation to the phenomenology of understanding that I have sketched, I shall briefly discuss some implications for religious education.

R.S. Peters' discussion of the nature of reason and of the development of rationality and R. K. Elliott's view of intellectual eros are both attempts to address the question of how students engage in enquiry in such a way that they come to recognise the claim of truth and of viewpoints different from their own. The differences in their accounts is instructive and will help in the expression of my own position.

The first account that I shall examine is R.S. Peters's (1972a, 1972b) discussion of the education of the emotions and the development of rationality. He addresses the question of how we manage our biases and our inclination to be unfair in consideration of the views of others, and our inclination, in the course of enquiry, to be less than careful and objective. Interpreted as the way we understand difference and the other, Peters's view is consistent with the liberal tradition of how we come to practise tolerance and negotiate difference. I shall call his view the 'liberal/rationalist view of understanding difference'. The second perspective that I shall look at is R.K. Elliott's (1974) view of love of truth, in which he employs the analogy of romantic love to account for why we engage in enquiry and why in the quest to understand we transcend our own point of view to embrace another's.

My view is that, while Peters's account has obvious merit in many ways, it is inadequate in addressing the question of how we may hope to foster in our students the desire, not only to tolerate, but also to understand positions different from and even opposed to their own. Whereas Peters is helpful for situations in which people are fundamentally agreed, his position is inadequate for situations of genuine diversity. I shall further suggest that Elliott's view of understanding and of intellectual eros has more promise for situations where people are genuinely different, such as the situation of students in the multicultural classroom today. I shall

call his the 'eros view of understanding difference'.

The views of Peters and Elliott derive from quite fundamental differences in assumptions not only about how we understand, but also about what sort of knowers we are. The differences in philosophical anthropology in these accounts are relevant to the view of religion which each of these positions might accommodate.

Central to Peters's view is his definition of reason as the transcendence of the particular and of the here and now. Reason is also intimately related to generalisation and dependent therefore on the ability to take the here and now beyond itself and beyond the particular. He writes: 'in the use of reason, particularities of time, place and identity are irrelevant to the determination of what is true, correct or to be done' (Peters, 1972a, p. 210). An important function of reason is the avoidance of conflict, both internally for individuals and also between people. The avoidance of conflict between individuals is effected through recourse to the very important rational principle of no distinctions without relevant differences, since reason is opposed to any form of arbitrariness.

Peters also emphasises the public character of reason for being rational involves the employment of procedures of criticism, of testing and of the production of counter-examples. These public procedures are found in the forms of knowledge or academic disciplines in which are also found distinctive tests for truth. However, important as these public forms of knowledge are, there is a sense in which, according to Peters, the procedures of reasoning go against natural human inclinations since we instinctively want to believe what we want to believe rather than subject these beliefs to testing and to counter-examples. Nevertheless, Peters contends that rationality can be developed through initiation into these academic disciplines, since they will not only show us what the rational procedures are, but will also foster new inclinations that internalise these standards and procedures.

If these are the processes of rational development, what sort of outcome can we hope for? What is the rational person like? What traits does he or she possess that will enable him or her to understand and tolerate others? According to Peters, such a person loves truth and respects the other, is willing to discount his or her own particular biases and predilections in order to look at situations from the point of view of others, to adopt the view of the 'generalised other' (ibid.). However, such a stance of impartiality cannot be sustained without the help of certain emotions that Peters calls 'rational passions'. As the term suggests, these are emotions that serve the practice of rationality. They are internalisations of the procedures mentioned earlier, developed in the course of education when rigour and care in thinking is caught and also taught through the forms of knowledge. As a result of this initiation, the rational man comes to take on certain intellectual virtues such as humility, respect for others, a concern for objectivity and consistency and so on. In the words of Gilbert Ryle, the rational man is one who

> systematically takes precautions against personal bias, tries to improve the orderliness or clarity of his theory, . . . hunts industriously for exceptions to his generalisations, deletes ambiguous, vague or metaphorical expressions from the sinews of his argument . . . , [whose thinking is] controlled in high or low degree, by a wide range of quite specific scruples . . . [and] . . . embodies the element of self-correction. (Peters, 1972a, p. 227)

In other words, such a person displays a wide range of academically produced virtues.

This is an admirable picture of a well-educated individual. But the question that concerns us here is whether such a person is likely to understand others vastly different from himself, or understand another who lives by views and beliefs opposed to his or her own. For this individual, Peters claims impartiality and even self-transcendence. But we must ask whether impartiality and self-transcendence are enough or even appropriate for situations of cultural diversity such as the multicultural classroom.

I have my doubts. The first doubt relates to the place that is given in Peters's account to the emotions, and the second to the way in which such an individual appears to relate to others Both doubts are relevant to my view of what makes for understanding and for dialogue.

To begin with, emotions are treated more or less negatively as being disruptive of reason and of understanding (Peters, 1972b). The development of reason and understanding are prescribed by mainly institutionalised attitudes of mind derived from the conventions of academic enquiry. According to Peters, an important aim in the education of the emotions is development towards self-transcendence, away from self-referential emotions and towards abstraction from the particular. From Peters's (1972a and 1972b) accounts, therefore,

we get a picture of the individual who is admirable in self-control and in the possession of intellectual virtues but lacking in daring and imagination, so important in understanding the other. Also the emphasis on public and objective knowledge is such that there is little in this account that is interrelational. The very definition of reason as transcendence of the here and now does not augur well for dialogue. The requirement that rational individuals adopt the view of 'the generalised other' will mean that genuine conversation and meeting between people who are different will not take place since each is required to deny that part of him or her that conflicts with the other. I called Peters's the 'rational/liberal view' because his insistence on abstracting from the here and now and from the particular corresponds very much to the liberal philosopher John Rawls's recommendation that in the search for social consensus, we move away from the 'thickness' of particular positions. Both Rawls and Peters argue that for the avoidance of conflict, we need to abstract from our particularity (see Rawls, 1972 and 1980). I shall return to the significance of this requirement later.

We now turn to another account of enquiry and of understanding, an account of how we come to love truth sufficiently to want to understand the other. Elliott presents his view of understanding and of educational development as an attempt to 'counter the dispiriting aspects of contemporary philosophy of education' (Elliott, 1975, p. 102). What is 'dispiriting' is, in part, due to the prime place given in this philosophy to the public forms of knowledge. The result is that personal development then becomes largely an academic matter and what is native and intuitive within the individual is belittled. As Elliott says, understanding is, for Peters, 'rather like the invasion and taking over of the individual by a public authority' (ibid.). This tendency to belittle the natural is revealed also in the question of curriculum justification, where Peters dismisses any naturalistic justification, appealing instead to the intrinsic worth of knowledge by means of the well-known transcendental deduction (Peters, 1966, ch. 5). In contrast, Elliott puts forward the view that somehow the powers of the mind are native to human beings and the forms of knowledge themselves depend upon the fact that human beings possess these powers as well as the capacity and inclination to understand. It is on this basis that Elliott puts forward a view of education and of understanding in which 'the element of nature is allowed to assert itself more freely against the element of convention' (Elliott, 1975, p. 45). This point of difference between Peters and Elliott is significant for the possibility of dialogue, as we shall see.

Elliott introduces a notion of understanding that is larger than academic understanding. His characterisation includes both the criteria of truth as well as the criteria of comprehensiveness, whereas Peters's account only emphasises the former. For example, Elliott says that a fully developed understanding will have to include not only the criteria of true, correct and valid understanding, but the features also of profundity, sensitivity, creativity and a synoptic sense of the object of understanding.

Whereas Elliott acknowledges the value of the 'rational passions' that Peters speaks about, that is, quasi-moral traits such as integrity, lucidity and courage which constitute intellectual conscience, he argues that understanding cannot be achieved because of these traits alone. He contends that in the course of achieving understanding, there are many 'psychical powers' that are exercised which are nothing like moral traits but are rather 'a composite of energy and desire which calls them into play for the sake of achieving understanding' (Elliott, 1975, p. 48). The account that Elliott gives of this, which he calls 'intellectual eros', is vastly different from that of Peters. One obvious contrast is the picture of the enquirer. Whereas Peters's enquirer is admirable in the practice of care and concern for objectivity and fairness regarding the opinion of others, Elliott's enquirer is driven more by desire and imagination. Whereas Peters emphasises intellectual conscience and self-transcendence, Elliott presents us with a picture of the enquirer who is enjoying him- or herself, at least most of the time, and who, if anything, is self-regarding. That person's primary motivation is the search for understanding, and the restrictions of conventional procedures and partisanship do not seem to limit him or her for, as Elliott says, the lover of truth experiences an intellectual power, 'the successful putting forward of which in great endeavour is a kind of victory, an expression of vitality which is no doubt as satisfying as victory in battle, or at the Games' (ibid. p. 49). The virtues that are characteristic of this domain are eros itself – involvement, ambition, adventurousness, tenacity, endurance, hope and faith. Indeed, the metaphors that Elliott uses to describe the experience convey this sense of vitality.

In contrast to the public nature of understanding in Peters's account, Elliott introduces the importance also of the experience of inwardness in which the enquirer develops not only an understanding of the object of enquiry but also a care for that object as well. This occurs when the clutter of expert opinion is removed from enquiry and when the process is not hurried along. Only then can the enquirer experience a quality of knowing that Elliott calls 'contemplation'. It is a kind of knowing that has the character of resting in the object to which the mind was directed from the beginning of the enquiry and it has the capacity to nurture the contemplator, giving a relationship towards the object that is appropriately called 'friendship'.

'Friendship' is that quality of relationship in which the enquirer allows the object to 'be itself as it is, the revelation to be received without any turning against the object; rather as a friend is willing for one to "be oneself" in his [*sic*] company' (Elliott, 1974, p. 144). Friendship has the character of an unconditional relationship, for Elliott describes the opposite of intellectual friendship as the situation in which one is concerned with the object

> only is so far as it exhibits or can be made to exhibit aspects which conform to a certain pre-given system of concepts and other conventions, with the implicit intention of acquiring knowledge which has the same style as and fits in with knowledge already obtained, and leads on to further knowledge of the same kind. Aspects which cannot be properly described by the accepted vocabulary are nevertheless assimilated to its standard patterns or, if in a particular case this is too obviously an act of violence, the thinker turns away from that aspect, assigning it to some class (e.g. the aesthetic) which justifies his ignoring it. This manner of knowing is like catching prey in a net, for the sake of what one can go on to do with it when it is caught, or for the sake of the hunting. (Ibid. pp. 143–4)

In the experience of 'friendship' and 'contemplation', the enquirer is psychologically nourished, for contemplative knowing bring the reward of insight and a sense of wholeness, even of awe and joy and deep profundity. The enquirer, desirous of understanding becomes someone with 'something to lose', that is, the sense of intellectual integrity, called into play in the quest to understand.

Unlike Peters's account of enquiry, which emphasised the importance of public procedures and the quest for objectivity, Elliott's account is intensely subjective, yet one could also say that the achievement of objectivity is just as realisable, if not more so. In his discussion of this notion, Elliott introduces the idea of 'private objectivity' which he says is largely forgotten in Peters's account (Elliott, 1982). The latter is a notion that Elliott wishes to revive from the Kierkegaardian and Socratic tradition, which stresses, not the consensus of the group, that is, public criteria of verification; rather, it stresses that the enquirer should be 'in a right relation towards that which he transcends' (Elliott, 1982, p. 52).

The notion of private objectivity is along the lines of the metaphor of friendship described earlier, the spirit of unconditionality that is brought into being in the search for understanding. Whereas, for Peters, objectivity relates to transcendence of particularities, of the here and now, to the position of 'the generalised other', in short to the position of neutrality, Elliott is keen to distinguish the lover of truth from the neutral thinker. But the lover of truth is not the partisan either; rather, he or she is called the 'double-minded thinker' and may, in fact, be partisan in the sense of having strong conviction about his or her own position, but the desire to seek understanding and an enlarged understanding will cause him or her to go beyond partisanship. The motivation within intellectual eros is therefore not self-transcending but in some ways, self-regarding. As Elliott (1974, p. 149) writes:

> unlike the neutral thinker, the double-minded thinker lacks neither the sense of urgency nor the inventiveness of the partisan, and (s)he is not tempted to trivialise the issue by underestimating the difference between the two positions. (S)he knows why such importance is attached to matters which seem minor to the neutral.

I made the point earlier that Elliott's model of intellectual eros and his notion of understanding is one that goes well with religious belief. In the case of the double-minded thinker, we can see how it is possible to reconcile a belief position with the ability to be fair to the other, and with the urgent desire to understand the other. Elliott's notion of understanding as comprehensiveness, attained by feats of the imagination, fed by energy and desire, makes this achievable. The account is made convincing by its emphasis, not on self-transcendence but on the stake that one has in one's own enlarged understanding. A well-known writer on interreligious dialogue echoes this point with reference to the

coming together of the Christian and the Buddhist in dialogue. Such dialogue, says DiNoia, has the potential to enlarge understanding and, from the point of view of the Christian, there is great potential to stimulate 'the desired recovery of forgotten or neglected elements in one's own Christian tradition' (DiNoia, 1993, p. 65). Echoing Elliott's point that the lover of truth seeks to be fair and not sell any position short, DiNoia says that enlarged understanding can only take place when the distinctiveness of a religious tradition is taken seriously and as a 'live option', in its uniqueness and distinctiveness. As DiNoia (1993, p. 65) writes: 'interreligious dialogue promises a mutual enhancement of understanding for the dialogue partners when they are prepared to recognise the other as other'.[3]

In this part of the discussion, I will look at the applicability of each of these models to religious education and to dialogue. To begin with, I will consider on a discussion of how the eros account of understanding is consonant with both the nature and spirit of religious belief. To do this, I shall briefly discuss the nature of fundamentalism and of fundamentalist faith, using it as a negative example to throw light on the question of understanding and dialogue.

Recent work on religious fundamentalism has been helpful in making important distinctions between fundamentalism and orthodoxy, as well as between fundamentalism and pre-modern faith (Pelikan, 1990; Marty and Appleby Scott, 1992; Lamb, 1998, 1999). I advanced the claim earlier that it is possible for individuals to understand another religious position different from and perhaps even contrary to their own position. I am less optimistic where the fundamentalist religious believer is concerned (although I would not even want to rule this out) because fundamentalist belief is generally marked by literalism and submission to particular authoritative interpretations of faith and of the world. There is little room to move both in terms of the fundamentalist's psychological make-up and his or her view of truth. Scholars have given helpful explanations of fundamentalist psychology (Ostow, 1990). In her account of 'Southside Gospel Church' (pseudonym for a New England congregation whose members she interviewed), Nancy Ammerman (1987) describes the world of the fundamentalist as dualistic in the sense that there is an 'inside' and an 'outside'. 'Inside' is the faith community which is a sheltering canopy and within which is order and salvation, but outside of that is immorality and chaos. The source of truth for the Protestant fundamentalist is the Bible, which is read 'literally' as the source of all truth and in the expectation that all can become clear since, within this framework, there is no expectation of ambiguity and mystery. The fundamentalist world, says Ammerman, is one in which God is in control and life is no longer a puzzle.

Now it is not overly pessimistic to describe such a position as being closed to dialogue since from the fundamentalists' point of view, they do not only possess the truth once delivered but will lose out if they enquire elsewhere. If, to fundamentalists, there is one truth and they possess it, the other will necessarily be in error and could therefore be the source of their downfall. Any relationship fostered with those outside the faith will ultimately be for the purpose of mission and proselytising. Fundamentalists have, therefore, a naive correspondence view of truth. They believe that their sacred text is the truth and their interpretation, or that of their faith community, is reliable and true. They have no notion of hermeneutics, nor of their own historical and social contingency.

Scholars have shown how the ahistoricity that is the mark of the fundamentalist position is distinguishable from religious orthodoxy which allows more hermeneutical pluralism (Pelikan, 1990; Lamb, 1998). It may be argued that at the heart of orthodox pluralism, such as that of historical Christianity, is a proper appreciation of the human condition. For the sense of our historicity may be expressed in religious discourse as the sense also of our finitude. It may also be argued that the denial of finitude within modern religious fundamentalism may be the single feature that sets it apart from orthodoxy within religious traditions which give expression to finitude through the notions of faith, mystery and ineffability. The claim to unmediated knowledge in fundamentalism is at the same time an unwillingness to accept human limitations and to think of finitude as a flaw. It could therefore be said that fundamentalism is at odds with the nature of religion, for at the heart of religion is the consciousness of 'limit situations', and therefore of human finitude.

Another way of making this point is that fundamentalist claims to truth are a denial of the part that human beings play in knowing. However, the 'longing for absolute certitude and disdain for the man-made' (Soskice, 1995, p. 47) is not new in

the history of Christianity and the longing for certitude increases the more when what is around seems particularly changing and uncertain. North American Protestant fundamentalism, for example, may be seen as a defensive response to the major intellectual and social changes in American society at the end of the nineteenth century. The same tendencies have been attributed to the rise of fundamentalisms in other parts of the world and in other religious traditions (Marty and Appleby Scott, 1992; Neilsen, 1993). Looking at religious fundamentalism as a psychological reaction in this way, it becomes a very understandable human response, even though it may seem contradictory and defiant to assert absolute epistemological certainty in the face of uncertainty and change, just as it is to occupy a superhuman epistemic standpoint in the face of human finitude. Recent scholarship has shown more clearly the human face of fundamentalism with 'naturalised' accounts of its appeal in the world today (Giddens, 1991; Marty and Appleby Scott, 1992). This contrasts with accounts that represented fundamentalists as atavistic and beyond the pale.[4] Those earlier representations of fundamentalists occurred within liberal intellectual assumptions whereas recent accounts make fundamentalists look more human and more 'like us' (see Lamb, 1996, 1999). In 'naturalising' fundamentalism, these recent accounts draw attention to a side of knowing and of understanding that is denied in fundamentalist claims and forgotten also in purely cognitive accounts of knowing and of understanding.

This is a side of knowing that is reclaimed by J.M. Soskice (1995) in an account of truth and understanding that she calls 'perspectivalism'. She rejects the stark, black and white view of truth that comes out of the longing for certitude. It is the view that we either know clearly or not at all, that claims are either objectively true or completely false, that they come either from God or from man. As I remarked earlier, such a view relies upon a naive correspondence view of truth and in its extreme epistemological form poses the alternative to absolute certainty as total relativism.[5] According to such a view, the knower is assumed to be solitary and free and unaffected by the constraints of language, culture, custom and all such other human limitations.

Soskice says that not only is such a view of knowing impossible to defend, it is also not presupposed in historical Christianity in which another view of truth is commonplace, for 'perspectivalism' is the view that whereas reality is 'objective', 'the objects', that is, our representations of that reality, aren't (ibid., p. 50). Thomas Aquinas expressed this human epistemological predicament when he said: 'There is nothing to stop a thing that is objectively more certain by its nature from being subjectively less certain to us because of the disability of our minds' (quoted in ibid., 1995, p. 45).

At the heart of this religious position is the acknowledgement of the humanity and the finitude of knowers. Such a recognition directs us to the position of perspectivalism, which Soskice describes as 'seeking a unity of truth from a diversity of perspectives' (ibid., p. 51). Whereas she is writing with respect to diversity within Christianity itself, perspectivalism can be usefully applied across religious traditions. Perspectivalism is the view that an adequate understanding of reality (in this case religious reality) relies upon a diversity of perspectives, for no one perspective will be adequate on its own. It relies also upon the idea that a complex description will generally be better than a simple one and a comprehensive understanding will be superior to a merely correct one. As Soskice (ibid.) puts it: 'truth is multiform', rendering the fundamentalist insistence on One truth to be very impoverished indeed.

Soskice's account of perspectivalism, the view that 'the truth looks different from here', gives further support to the eros account of understanding in which the double-minded thinker seeks more comprehensive understanding by performing shifts of perspective to appreciate how others see the world. The lover of truth moves temporarily from her or his own perspective to embrace another for the sake of an enlarged understanding and for the sake of truth; in other words, recognises that she or he needs more than her or his own eyes to see.

In this account of understanding, the other is no longer a threat and a nuisance but the source indeed of my own enlarged understanding. However, such enhanced understanding will not occur unless those involved in dialogue, as DiNoia says, are prepared to recognise the other as other. The eros account of understanding is therefore the essence of dialogue since, according to it, I need the other to better understand my own position and to better understand myself. However, this will not happen if I do not practise 'friendship' in my understanding, that is, if I do not allow the other to be revealed in his or her particularity and uniqueness. At this point, we see how the eros account

departs from the liberal/rationalist view of understanding difference which, as we saw, is based upon the view of reason as transcendence from particularity, from the here and now. By transcending the particularities of time, place and identity, reason is expected to provide a resolution for conflict. In other words, to avoid or resolve conflict, the other must be met as an abstraction, 'thinned' of particularity so that we can be similar and can agree. I called this a rationalist/liberal view because it is consistent with the standard view of liberal consensus put forward by the philosopher John Rawls (1971 and 1980).

Rawls argued that in the just ordering of society, diversity and difference can only coexist and consensus can only be achieved if in the public realm the 'thick' content of various religious, philosophical and moral doctrines are not allowed to play a decisive role in public discussions about what is just and fair. Rawls's insistence that 'thick' accounts of human good must not intrude into the discussion of foundational matters pertaining to public life is part of the liberal conviction that highly textured belief systems, especially those of a religious nature, are 'private' matters. Coexistence and consensus could only then occur if individual religious believers, for example, treated their faith as being true in private, but in the public sphere behave as if their faith were one view among many. There is clearly a tension here, a tension that is particularly hard for fundamentalist believers to resolve. This is probably why we may, on the one hand, sympathise with and support the Rawlsian kind of arrangement and yet be pessimistic that some religious believers would want to buy into it for fear of compromising their position. Our ambivalent feelings towards the Rawlsian kind of arrangement help to explain that point of view expressed at the beginning of my chapter that it is only from a position of relativism that one could possibly want to coexist with and understand those who are different. The corollary of this view is that religious believers who believe theirs to be the true and revealed faith will not be able to understand those of a different faith. In other words, the assumption is that religious conviction inevitably stands in the way of dialogue and understanding.

I have, however, been arguing against this kind of claim and so far have done so with the support of the eros view of understanding and with the articulation of perspectivalism. Both models of understanding, I have argued, sit well with religious belief. My argument so far has been based on a phenomenology of understanding. To further strengthen my contention that the position of religious conviction does not have to stand in the way of dialogue and of understanding difference, I shall take my argument further by reiterating the idea (put forward at the beginning of this chapter), that religious conviction, far from hindering the understanding of religious difference, could actually *enable* the process. To do this, I shall advance three more arguments which could be categorised as psychological, moral and ontological.

First, the psychological argument. The idea that a sense of conviction about one's religious vision can provide psychological resources for tolerating and understanding difference has been advanced by John Cuddily (1978 and 1987). Cuddily recognises the tension of maintaining private convictions in the public sphere and describes it as an 'ordeal' that is part of living in the contemporary world. Conforming to the pressures of civility involves, as we have seen, a 'double-take' on one's beliefs. However, much as this creates tension and discomfort, the ordeal can result in a civility that does not require the sacrificing of conviction. Indeed, on Cuddily's analysis, a primary resource for surviving the ordeal of civility (in the case of Christian and arguably, some other faiths) is the eschatological vision: that is, people of conviction can cultivate civility if they can convince themselves that the 'perfect community' will appear at the end of time. That is, instead of seeing religion as the source of difficulty for tolerance and coexistence, Cuddily is saying that the opposite is the case, which is that the conviction that one's religious hopes will be vindicated could help to create patience and humility. He argues that religious hope of this kind could save believers from 'ostentation' and 'triumphalism' in this life, for triumphalism amounts to the vainglorious attempt to claim glory here and now and this is 'vulgar, empty and in bad theological taste' (Cuddily, 1978, p. 202).

Cuddily is writing from the Christian point of view but what he says obviously applies outside the Christian faith tradition where patience, humility and subtlety are also valued. The posture of public modesty and tolerance that he recommends for Christians is valued and, indeed, self-consciously practised by those of many faiths in the religiously diverse communities. Initiatives for dialogue are also taken by people from many religious traditions who are not relativist about their faith. This can be

explained at least partly by the psychological stance that we have described, that is, it is precisely faith that gives believers the resources to refrain from vanity and trumphalism for arising out of faith is the conviction that the appropriate 'creaturely' response is humble gratitude and respectful openness rather than smug vindication.

This takes us to the moral argument. The public ethic of tolerance and humility is fed not only by eschatological hope that is given by religious faith but also by the moral stance that is encouraged by many faith traditions in promoting the view that we have much to learn from those with whom we disagree, that our own weaknesses can be corrected by encountering the strengths of others, that only such an attitude can keep us appropriately humble. The alternative would be to subscribe to a Manichaean view of reality in which believers see moral goodness as being found only amongst those who embrace the 'true religion' (Mouw and Griffioen, 1993, p. 103). This is a form of totalitarianism that is against the spirit of most faith traditions and which becomes particularly vulnerable to the peculiarly postmodern charge of the oppressiveness of totalising metanarratives.[6]

The moral stance that we have just described is an important response to the postmodern charge for only a spirit of humility and openness towards the other can keep religious believers from establishing their own form of totalitarianism. Those who belong to faith traditions must therefore cultivate their inner respect for those who believe and live differently. But there is a third element within religious faith which functions as a resource for such tolerance and openness and that works against totalising tendencies in religious conviction. This could be categorised as an ontological perspective.

Earlier, we referred to the danger of triumphalism and smugness, the attitude of being closed to learning. Here, the fundamentalist world is a good example. We noted earlier that within the fundamentalist mind-set, the world is read unambiguously as a dualism between 'inside' and 'outside' and truth itself admits of no puzzle or sense of contingency. This leads, as we noted, to a closedness to difference and to the other. If reality is 'sewn up' for the fundamentalist, it does not have to be for other religious believers. For fundamentalists, the appeal to God and to transcendence closes off dialogue. But transcendence can mean something different. It can mean openness and dialogue. Whereas the appeal to heaven and to the transcendent for the fundamentalist can justify for him or her disrespect for those 'outside' and even violence towards them, for other religious believers, their understanding of the transcendent could be the reason for encounter. If heaven and spiritual reality is understood as self-contained, as in the case of believers who have no regard or respect for those of other faiths, then there will be nothing new, either in insights or in relationships 'outside' the faith. In contrast, the Dutch philosopher and theologian Dooyeweerd had the concept of 'an open heaven' to counter the organicist idea of society as an overarching community and to emphasise the freedom of associations and encounter (Dooyeweerd, 1957; see also Mouw and Griffioen, 1993, pp. 170–1 for a discussion of this notion). This is based on a notion of transcendence which is larger than the world of the religious believer and his or her faith tradition and community. It is the view of a transcendent, or God, that addresses believers to enlarge their categories. Dooyeweerd's notion includes the idea of the 'transcendent community of mankind' in which believers find themselves, a community that includes the different and the other. In such an open, transcendent community, they will be addressed, warned and taught in ways that they do not expect and in which they will be surprised by a transcendent, a God, whose categories will always be larger and more generous than their own. Such a view of the transcendent promotes dialogue; indeed, it is fed by such since dialogue will enlarge them towards God and will reward them with the experience of 'those mysterious and surprising inklings of a larger kind of love' (Mouw and Griffioen, 1993, p. 171) than they had previously known. Here trancendence and dialogue are one.

So far, I have tried to show that, far from inhibiting dialogue and understanding of the other, religious conviction amongst our students can be used as a resource for tolerance and understanding. I have shown how the phenomenology of understanding from the 'eros account of understanding' goes well with the faith and conviction of the believer, who, like everyone else, is jealous of her or his position and does not want to sell her- or himself short, yet is impelled for a variety of reasons to dialogue in order to better understand the other. In the remaining paragraphs, I shall briefly discuss some major implications of the foregoing account for religious education.

My first point is a general one that relates to the theoretical stance of the teacher in the context of religious and cultural diversity. In the models of understanding that I have sketched, we noted the naturalistic element in the 'eros account', for implicit in this account is Elliott's contention that the powers of the mind, such as the power to understand, are native to human beings and that the forms of knowledge, so central in the liberal/rational account, themselves depend upon the fact that human beings possess these powers as well as the capacity and desire to understand. The 'eros account' is for this reason promising for religious education for it presents students as people inclined towards not only enlargement of their understanding, but towards dialogue as well. From such a perspective, the other becomes, not a threat to understanding, but necessary to the process of comprehensive insight.

The 'eros account of understanding' as we saw, acknowledges the human side of knowing and for that reason gives place also to the acknowledgement of human finitude, so central in traditional religious understanding of life and of the human condition. The notion of 'myth' in religion is one that accommodates such an understanding of the human condition, an understanding that guards against the fundamentalist literalism that is closed to dialogue and to difference.

The naturalistic element in the 'eros account' is promising for students in yet another way, for Elliott emphasises the fact that understanding has an affective element that 'nourishes the soul': while hard work and effort are necessary, there is the experience in such enquiry of fulfilment and of spontaneous love. This will not occur if the approach to the subject studied is merely instrumental or when the emphasis is purely on objectivity. The experience of desire, of friendship and contemplation that Elliott describes will not occur if we mediate students' understanding with an excess of expert opinion. Space has to be allowed for the individual to engage in 'benevolent disputation' with the objects of study. This has obvious implications for styles of teaching and presentation of materials. If contemplative understanding has the character of resting in the object, then teaching must not be restless and hurried but must allow room for students to develop insight and realisation. Journal writing could be an effective means to encourage the development of care for the subject and to cultivate the inwardness that is so necessary for the development of a sense of 'private objectivity'. Teacher feedback on journals should embody respect and care, taking students' comments seriously. Classroom discussion should likewise encourage respect and consideration of ideas.

Because of the limitations of this chapter, I have made only the beginnings of practical suggestions for religious education in the context of increasing religious diversity. I have argued that such an education need be neither relativist nor threatening to students. Rather, it is based on a full-bodied understanding that seeks to develop love of truth in our students in order to promote dialogue with those who are different. Such an approach to religious education neither undermines students' existent beliefs nor leaves them unchallenged and unenlarged in those convictions.

Notes

1 The phrase, suggesting a view of the transcendent that addresses the believer to enlarge his or her understanding, comes from Mouw and Griffioen (1993), inspired by Dooyeweerd's idea of 'the transcendent community of mankind', (Dooyeweerd, 1957, p. 583). This chapter develops ideas found in an earlier paper, Winifred Wing Han Lamb, Intellectual eros: a model for inter-faith dialogue. *Australian Religion Studies Review* 7(1), 1993, pp. 2–8.

I am grateful to Harry Oldmeadow, Philosophy and Religious Studies, La Trobe University, and Graeme Garrett, School of Theology, St Mark's National Theological Centre, for their helpful comments on this chapter.

2 For the sake of simplicity, I shall be considering one example of fundamentalist belief, that of North American Protestant fundamentalism. I also acknowledge in advance that my references to religion are slanted towards the Christian faith, understood in a broad and traditional sense. It can be argued that the 'problem' of religious pluralism discussed here is one that has grown out of western and Christian attitudes and it is thus appropriately addressed by resources within that same tradition. However, the arguments that I put forward throughout for the promotion of dialogical understanding have application to other main religious traditions.

3 Cf. Cox (1988), who says that dialogue and meeting with the other provokes one to understanding oneself better. He writes: 'To expose one's tradition to dialogue is willynilly to open it to change, ferment and internal debate. One ends up asking very fundamental questions of oneself' (ibid. p. 18).

4 See the discussion in Neilsen (1993, pp. 4–6), for a history of representations of North American fundamentalists.

5 See Boone's description of fundamentalist literalism. She says that according to Protestant fundamentalists, one

proved error in the Bible invalidates the whole text and, by implication, Christian faith. In this way, fundamentalists imagine themselves 'either steadfast in absolute truth or whirling in the vortex of nihilism' (Boone, 1989, p. 24).

6 For an attempt to address this charge, see, for example, Middleton and Walsh (1995).

References

Ammerman, Nancy (1987) *Bible Believers: Fundamentalism in the Modern World*. New Brunswick, NJ: Rutgers University Press.

Boone, Kathleen (1989) *The Bible Tells Them So*. Albany, NY: State University of New York Press.

Brown, S.C. (1975) *Philosophers Discuss Education*. London: Macmillan Press.

Cohen, N. (ed.) (1990) *The Fundamentalist Phenomenon*. Grand Rapids, MI: Eerdmans.

Cox, Harvey (1988) *Many Mansions: a Christian's Encounter with Other Faiths*. Boston, MA: Beacon Press.

Cuddily, John Murray (1978) *No Offence: Civil Religion and Protestant Taste*. New York: Seabury Press.

Cuddily, John Murray (1987) *The Ordeal of Civility: Freud, Marx, Levi-Strauss, and the Jewish Struggle with Modernity*. Boston, MA: Beacon Press.

Dearden, R., Hirst, P. and Peters, R.S. (eds) (1972) *Education and the Development of Reason*. London: Routledge & Kegan Paul.

DiNoia, J. (1993) Teaching differences. *Journal of Education* 73(1), 61–8.

Dooyeweerd, Herman (1957) *A New Critique of Theoretical Thought* vol. 3. Philadelphia: Presbyterian and Reformed.

Elliott, R.K. (1974) Education, love of one's subject and love of truth. *Proceedings of the Philosophy of Education Society of Great Britain* VII, 135–53.

Elliott, R.K. (1975) Education and human being. In S.C. Brown (ed.), *Philosophers Discuss Education*. London: Macmillan Press, pp. 45–72, 99–110.

Elliott, R.K. (1982) Education and objectivity. *Journal of Philosophy of Education* 16(1), 49–62.

Giddens, Anthony (1991) *Modernity and Self Identity in the Late Modern Age*. Stanford, CA: Stanford University Press, esp. Introduction and ch. 6.

Lamb, Winifred Wing Han (1996) Beyond tolerance: on describing the fundamentalist. *St Mark's Review* no. 164, 10–15.

Lamb, Winifred Wing Han (1998) 'Facts that Stay Put' – Protestant fundamentalism, epistemology and orthodoxy. *Sophia* 37(2), 88–110.

Lamb, Winifred Wing Han (1999) 'Human Like Us' – some philosophical reflections of 'naturalising' fundamentalism. *Australian Religion Studies Review* 21(1), 5–17.

Marty, Martin E. and Appleby, Scott (1992) *The Glory and the Power*. Boston, MA: Beacon Press.

Middleton, J.R. and Walsh, B.J. (1995) *Truth is Stranger Than it Used to Be*. Downers Grove, IL: InterVarsity Press.

Mouw, Richard J. and Griffioen, Sander (1993) *Pluralisms and Horizons*. Grand Rapids, MI: Eerdmans.

Neilsen, Neils (1993) *Fundamentalism. Mythos and World Religions*. Albany, NY: State University of New York Press.

Ostow, Mortimer (1990) The fundamentalist phenomenon: a psychological perspective. In N. Cohen (ed.), *The Fundamentalist Phenomemon*. Grand Rapids, MI: Eerdmans, pp. 99–125.

Pelikan, Jaroslav (1990) Fundamentalism and/or orthodoxy? In N. Cohen (ed.), *The Fundamentalist Phenomenon*, Grand Rapids, MI: Eerdmans, pp. 3–21.

Peters, R.S. (1966) *Ethics and Education*. London: Allen & Unwin.

Peters, R.S. (1972a) Reason and passion. In R. Dearden, P. Hirst and R.S. Peters (eds), *Education and the Development of Reason*. London: Routledge & Kegan Paul, pp. 208–29

Peters, R.S. (1972b) Education of the emotions. In R. Dearden, P. Hirst and R.S. Peters (eds), *Education and the Development of Reason*. London: Routledge & Kegan Paul, pp. 466–83.

Rawls, John (1971) *A Theory of Justice*. Cambridge, MA: Harvard University Press.

Rawls, John (1980) Kantian constructivism in moral theory. *Journal of Philosophy* 77(9), 549.

Soskice, Janet Martin (1995) The truth looks different from here. In H. Regan and A. Torrance (eds), *Christ and Context*. Edinburgh: T. & T. Clark, pp. 43–59.

7 "Live by the Word and Keep Walking": Religious Education and Contextualization in a Culture of Disbelief

TOINETTE M. EUGENE

JOURNAL

April 17, 1984

The universe sends me fabulous dreams! Early this morning I dreamed of a two-headed woman. Literally. A wise woman. Stout, graying, caramel-colored, with blue-grey eyes, wearing a blue flowered dress. Who was giving advice to people. Some white people, too, I think. Her knowledge was for everyone and it was all striking. While one head talked, the other seemed to doze. I was so astonished! For what I realized in the dream is that two-headedness was at one time an actual physical condition and that two-headed people were considered wise. Perhaps this accounts for the adage "Two heads are better than one." What I think this means is that two-headed people, like blacks, lesbians, Indians, "witches," have been suppressed, and in their case, suppressed out of existence. Their very appearance had made them "abnormal" and therefore subject to extermination. For surely two-headed people have existed. And it is only among blacks (to my knowledge) that a trace of their existence is left in the language. Rootworkers, healers, wise people with "second sight" are called "two-headed" people.

This two-headed woman was amazing. I asked whether the world would survive, and she said No; and her expression seemed to say, The way it is going there's no need for it to. When I asked her what I/we could/should do, she took up her walking stick and walked expressively and purposefully across the room. Dipping a bit from side to side.

She said: Live by the Word and keep walking.
Alice Walker, *Living by the Word: Selected Writings, 1973–1987*

Prolegomena and introduction

In this brief pericope, a combination of folktale and ethical exegesis, Pulitzer prize-winning author and womanist Alice Walker captures the essence of what "*Religious Education and Contextualization in a Culture of Disbelief*" might mean and contain. For professors and researchers in religious education, such a parable and its concomitant hermeneutic can offer considerable sagacity as well as solidarity for those who are making strong efforts to address issues of contextualization, indigenization, and reciprocity and appropriation in our contemporary religious situation.

This chapter, focusing on the words of Walker, will attempt: (a) to discuss the relevance of Stephen Carter's (1993) ground breaking work, *The Culture of Disbelief: How American Law and Politics Trivialize Religious Devotion*, in relation to the work of religious education; (b) to make the claim that "ways of belonging" can provide a paradigm for understanding how contextualization can function in religious education, (c) to reflect on the concept of "cultural worker" as a category which might be useful to conceptualize the work of religious educators and researchers who would wish to engage more practically in the process of contextualization and reciprocity across cultures of belief which call for and offer transformative apertures in an era of cultural politics that seemingly trivialize authentic religious devotion.

The culture of disbelief and the work of contextualization and religious education

In the ingenuous cultural world and belief system

of Alice Walker (1988, p. 2), we are enjoined to "Live by the Word and keep walking." She incorporates into her culturally contextualized fable a religiously educational – indeed a biblical reply – to the ethically constructed question of "what I/we could/should do" in a world that may only survive with our attention given to social and religious transformation (ibid.). I argue that Walker posits a claim for contextualization as an aspect of religious education in a culture of disbelief in much the same way as does Carter in his text which I have taken as a key point of reference in order to arrive at my own locus of authority and accountability as a social ethicist and researcher of religious education.

I am arguing from a framework of liberation-based religious education which emphasizes its own particular social experiences in order to question universal claims of theology and religious education, and to unmask the oppressive particularities of universal claims. Liberational religious educational discourse is of necessity postmodern. It is critical and deconstructionist. It emerges within a world of oppression, focusing on the need for political change and practicing actions for social change. Theologian Sharon Welch (1985, p. 80) points out that "universal discourse is the discourse of the privileged." Liberation-based religious education challenges dominant Christian political regimes of universal truth with the concrete, lived situation of oppressed or marginated peoples and their liberative practices.

A liberation-based religious education can only be theologically understood contextually: "Contextual theology is a method of theologizing which is aware of the specific historical and cultural contexts in which it is involved, and senses that it is directed to experiences and reflections of others" (Witvliet, 1987, p. 97; 1985). A contextual theology and, by extension, a contextual form of religious education can proceed only from critical analysis of the social context that forms our experience, our struggles, and our emergent, innovative, and transgressive project. Contextual religious educational discursive practice emerges from the painful and often lethal struggle against dominant power positions and relationships. This means that no one who is not involved in and committed to the struggle for justice and liberation can write or participate in contextual liberative religious education.

Thus, my chapter on "Live by the Word and keep walking" (a) assumes this understanding of contextuality; (b) finds common cause with Stephen Carter's *The Culture of Disbelief: How American Law and Politics Trivialize Religious Devotion* because Carter's critical analysis urges at least a kind of emergent, transgressive praxis on the part of liberal people who might verge even on becoming radical; and (c) calls for leaders in religious education to act as prophetic "cultural workers" in order to elicit the kind of transgressive education conjured up by cultural critic, bell hooks. hooks (1994a and 1994b) offers such a perspective in her engaging complementary studies of transformative education: *Teaching to Transgress: Education as the Practice of Freedom* and *Outlaw Culture: Resisting Representation*. Similar perspectives are advocated by Harvard educational theorist Henry Giroux in his ongoing work.

Stephen L. Carter (1993), professor of law at Yale University, has written a widely reviewed and widely admired book arguing that the United States has, in the last twenty years, developed a "culture of disbelief," in which religious devotion is trivialized. He writes:

> in our sensible zeal to keep religion from dominating our politics, we have created a political and legal culture that presses the religiously faithful to be other than themselves, to act publicly, and sometimes privately as well, as though their faith does not matter to them.   (Carter, 1993, p. 3)

He wishes to "[restore] religion to the place of honor" (ibid. p. 68).

It is Carter's view that religion's place of honor in American life was relinquished when, following the Supreme Court's decision in Roe v. Wade (1973), the rhetorical value and the moral force of religion in public discourse was ceded by the political Left to the political Right. The effect of this abdication by the Left, he argues, was that religion itself became suspect. In other words, fear of the resurgent religious Right has led to the devaluing of religion as a serious force in American politics (ibid. 57–8). Carter (ibid. 23) argues that the further result has been pressure on religious people not to take their faith seriously, and to regard "God as a hobby."

Carter offers many, many examples and anecdotes from the popular press and elsewhere as evidence of the failure, mainly of those he styles as "liberals," to take religion seriously and of a corresponding liberal effort to ghettoize religious language – to denude the public square. What he calls a fear-driven dismissal of religion from the public discourse by liberal skeptics is a mistake because, he believes, religion functions in society as an autonomous moral force that challenges ever-increasing government regulation of every aspect of modern life.

Religion, and by extension religious education, provides a location from which to challenge the status quo. Religion, and by extension religious education, provides a moral authority and a moral imagination that has the ethical power to dispel a "culture of disbelief" through a public discourse which offers an explicit value system, an explicit claim to authority emanating from the community of faith's own cultural experience and analysis of what it must be and do in order to survive and to "succeed," and to live in right relation to others who do not share its convictions and commitments. Citing Alexis de Tocqueville and David Tracy, among others, Carter (1993, p. 124) argues that "to be consistent with the Founder's vision and coherent in modern religiously pluralistic America, the religion clauses should be read to help avoid tyranny – that is to sustain and nurture the religions as independent centers of power." He insists that "religion, properly understood, is a very subversive force" (ibid. p. 50). Liberals should embrace rather than fear religious discourse.

Carter is also concerned that as a result of liberal fear the religious Right is being criticized for the wrong reasons. It is being criticized for being religious rather than for being wrong. The religious Right is being told by its critics, in his view, that it has no right to exist because it is religious, rather than being argued with for the positions it takes on public issues. Religious liberals should, moreover, in his view, not only criticize the religious Right for its political positions but acknowledge religion as a source of resistance and empty religious rhetoric themselves, when appropriate, in order to prevent tyranny by the state.

While styled as a critique of American public discourse, generally this is, in fact, a very personal book, full of personal experiences and affirmations of faith, which addresses a fairly narrow experience. The "we" of Carter's discourse, is not we-Americans, but we-liberals,[1] we-religious-liberals. Although he wants to include religious conservatives, it is the liberal skeptics in the media and in government whom he is addressing and scolding for "diss"-ing religion.[2] He wants them to see that one can be both religious and liberal. His model is the religious rhetoric of the civil rights movement,

of Martin Luther King. Stephen Carter speaks for and to those who take that religious model as central to their identity.[3]

I am positing that, in the midst of a "culture of disbelief" as described and attested to by Stephen Carter, religious education holds the potential and the power to transform in liberating and justice-orienting ways and means through the process of contextualization,[4] the stultifying discourse of secularism, and of civil and institutional religion. I argue that, as Alice Walker contends, we are enjoined and empowered as wise persons, as provocative providers and purveyors of religious education, to "live by the Word and keep walking" That is, we are responsible and accountable to publicly articulate the content and cross-cultural "context of the Judeo-Christian traditions on behalf of the institutional and denominational forms of Church as well as for the civic community and for civic religion.

In order to address Carter's concern and diatribe against the "culture of disbelief," I would posit that we must find a means of articulating a space and a specificity for "cultures of belief." I would describe this process as one of examining and embracing the role of cultures in American life which are inextricably bound up in the dynamism of pro-justice and pro-liberation movements which have transformed many of us from privatized Puritans to public prophets who have a dream of equality and mutuality, and who hold up an ethos of agape, inclusivity, and solidarity with those who are most vulnerable, fragile, and powerless. This process, I claim, is best understood as the process of actively introducing and advocating the contextualization and indigenization of religious experience into religious education.

I argue that we are enjoined as religious educators and researchers to embrace and to enable the rhetoric and the rituals of justice-loving, diverse, believing, and life-affirming peoples. We are enjoined to "live by the Word and keep walking" in the face and in the forms of a contrary "culture of disbelief" which has chosen to privatize and to de-politicize the ways in which we as a faithful believing people are called to exercise the inalienable rights, responsibilities, and forms of religious education which ought to extend a transforming praxis of liberation and justice for all. I assert that we are ethically and morally bound to explore the ways and means of really bonding and belonging to communities of faith that speak and act out our faith in the face of powers and principalities that actively engage in suppressing and repressing the value givers and value guardians of public religious devotion and faith development.

Ways of belonging as a means of understanding contextualization in a culture of disbelief

I want to suggest one paradigm by which religious educators and researchers might understand their roles as intermediaries, agents, and discussants in the much-needed public dialogue between the culture of disbelief and those who display an alternative approach to the diminishing role of religion and, by extension, religious education in North American society. In the shaping of identity, multi-cultural theorist James A. Banks (1986) suggests that belonging was one of the three most defining characters of communities (the other two being the sources of moral authority for the community and the frameworks for explaining events for community). Christians often cite believing as the criterion for authentic Christianity and can have a tendency to underestimate the role of ways of belonging.

A clearer emphasis on belonging is the need to combat the culture of disbelief because people find themselves in multiple worlds of reference: they define themselves by a variety of communities to which they belong. These can include the communities of immediate and extended family, work, leisure activities, ethnic/racial origin, charitable activities, education, and so on. Belonging in a culture of disbelief is rarely as simple as having one point of location.

In matters of contextualization and religious education, we see people struggling with multiple belonging in their religious worlds of reference. This phenomenon is sometimes referred to as "double belonging," since it often involves relating to at least two worlds, as Stephen Carter's text alludes. Three worlds are not uncommon in South-East Asia where these are local traditions, Confucian traditions, and Christianity. In many parts of the world multiple belonging does not pose a cognitive or emotional obstacle; Japan is the clearest example of that, where there are almost twice as many religious adherents as there are people in the population. But for Christians this has long posed a vex-

ing and difficult problem in attempting to provide religious education in the face of the culture of disbelief. Multiple belonging can be an integral part of the process of "living by the Word and keep walking" if we are able to utilize this form of contextualization as an integral part of incorporating contextualization into our process and praxis.

Sometimes it is a matter of competing worlds (that is the world-view of many western Christians). For many people in these situations, however, introducing contextualization into religious education may be a matter of incorporating the theory of multiple belonging into an acceptance of complementary worlds or even objective, con-communicating worlds – what cultural psychologist Richard Shweder (1991) has called "multiple objective worlds." An example might help here to suggest how contextualization in religious education can be a way of response to the dominant culture of disbelief which Stephen Carter deplores and to which we as religious educators and researchers must find a way to respond.

Some years ago, a Roman Catholic missionary pastor was visiting the villages in northern Ontario. He paid a pastoral call on a native woman on the first anniversary of the death of one of her two sons; he had been killed in an oil-rig accident. He accompanied her and her surviving son to the cemetery outside the village to pray at the gravesite. As they were coming out of the cemetery, a buck walked slowly out of the woods and stopped, facing them only a few yards away. Both the woman and her son dropped to their knees and began to pray in their indigenous language – she, wailing; he, muttering softly. The buck did not move, but continued to stare at them intently. After a few minutes, the prayers ceased and the buck turned around, walking slowly back into the forest.

When they all returned to the house, the mystified priest asked the young man what had happened. He explained patiently:

> That buck was the guardian spirit of my deceased brother. He came to thank us for remembering my brother on the anniversary of his death. You see, my brother communed closely with his guardian spirit. In fact, the spirit came to warn my brother on his last visit home that he would not return alive. My brother confided that to me before he left for the last time.   (Schreiter, 1992)

This is a direct example of contextualization in the process of religious education engaged in dialogue with the culture of disbelief. Multiple worlds? False worlds? Obviously the mother and son saw no incompatibility in praying traditional Christian prayers for their dead son and brother one moment, and in addressing a guardian spirit immediately thereafter. Do these worlds relate, or are they separate dimensions of time and reality that break into each other's realms (Coulianou, 1991)? How does this kind of experience enter into our consciousness as we seek to speak to the cultural and social contexts out of which we must make our own religiously educational responses within a dominant climate of disrespect for socio-religious expressions and valuations which emerge from our own multiple worlds and communities of faith?

Enlightenment North Atlantic types find difficulty making room for this kind of thing, but peoples elsewhere do it routinely. Yet we find parallel beliefs in the New Testament in Paul and the Letter to the Hebrews. There, too, is the belief that Christ has overcome the Powers and Principalities, but Paul and the Hebrews do not deny their existence.

Not much research has been done to date on multiple belonging, but a few things are beginning that have relevance for professors and researchers of religious education. How to classify the varieties of such belonging has not been resolved satisfactorily. I would suggest that there are at least three types that recur and which are related to our topic of religious education and contextualization which must make an appropriate response to the larger and dominant culture of disbelief:

1 multiple belonging out of protest: such would be the case of people forcibly Christianized who maintain their local ways as an act against the oppressor. These are found frequently among the native peoples of the Americas;
2 multiple belonging out of the inadequacy of Christianity to deal with local spirits and immediate, quotidian issues such as healing. This is common in Africa;
3 multiple belonging out of inevitability is often the case where the religious culture is so strong that one cannot be a member of the culture without participating in some fashion in another world. This is the social and religious reality throughout much of eastern and southern Asia.

People from these racial/ethnic and often oppressed communities of faith who have immigrated to North America bring this understanding of multiple belonging with them, and carry this consciousness into our dialogue on contextualization, on indigenization, and on multicultural religious education. I would submit that to the extent that religious educators, theorists, and researchers from a dominant western culture and class can comprehend, apprehend, and admit the importance of multiple belonging as an aspect framing the parameters of debate and dialogue, collectively we are able to embody the parable of Alice Walker.

We may be able to become like the two-headed woman, a wise person who was able to give advice and admonition to those who inhabit a world and a culture of disbelief. Walker includes "rootworkers, healers, wise people with second sight" in her explanation and exegesis of "two-headed people." Might we not, by extension, append the category of religious educators and researchers who understand and make use of the concept of multiple belonging as additional advocates and practitioners of the adage and exhortation, which is implicitly a motif for our vocation: "Live by the Word and keep walking?"

"Cultural worker" as a category for religious educators disputing a culture of disbelief

This final section of the chapter has as its aim to reflect on the concept of "cultural worker" (Giroux, 1992) as a category which might be useful to conceptualize the work of religious educators and researchers who would wish to engage more practically in the process of contextualization, and religious reciprocity across cultures of belief which call for and offer transformative apertures in an era of cultural politics that seemingly trivialize authentic religious devotion.[5]

Harvard educational theorist Henry Giroux (1993) has published extensively on issues of contextualization and education in recent years (Giroux and Purpel, 1983). His theses strongly support the themes of Stephen Carter's discussion as to what might be our appropriate democratic responses to a culture of disbelief that furthers the finest articulation our discipline has to offer. Giroux attempts to address contextualization by drawing upon a new paradigm in order to rewrite the meaning of pedagogy, education, and their implications for a new politics of cultural difference, radical democracy, and a new generation of cultural workers. I suggest that this category has implications for our self-understanding as religious educators and researchers engaged in contextualization that brings about positive social transformation in church, community, as well as the larger secular/civic society.

The concept of "cultural worker" has traditionally been understood to refer to artists, writers, and media producers. In Giroux's framework, he extends the range of cultural work to people working in professions such as law (thus including Stephen Carter's frame of reference), social work, architecture, medicine, theology, education, and literature. His intention is to rewrite the concept and practice of cultural work by inserting the primacy of the political and the pedagogical (Giroux, 1992, p. 5). Giroux argues that the pedagogical dimension of cultural work refers to the process of creating symbolic representations and the practices within which they are engaged. This includes a particular concern with the analysis of textual, aural, and visual representations and how such representations are organized and regulated within particular institutional arrangements. It also addresses how various people engage such representations in the practice of analysis and comprehension. An example of this would be the use we might make of Alice Walker's parable and hermeneutic as a form of religious education through contextualization.

The political dimension of cultural work informs this process through a project whose intent is to mobilize knowledge and desires that may lead to minimizing the degree of oppression in people's lives. What is at stake for Giroux as well as for Stephen Carter is a political imaginary that extends the possibilities for creating new public spheres in which the principles of equality, liberty, and justice become the primary organizing principles for structuring relationships between the self and others.

What might be at stake for religious educators and researchers who would want to identify themselves as "cultural workers" is the potentiality of expanding the ministry and mission of religious education which profoundly respects the complexity of the relationship between pedagogical theories and the specificity of the cultural and contextual sites in which they might be developed. This means paying acute attention to and honoring multiple worlds of meaning and belonging, as has been previously discussed.

This kind of religious education is a discursive praxis, an unfinished language, replete with possibilities that grows out of particular engagements and dialogues of "living by the Word" while we keep on with the journey of walking toward a future filled with hope. This means arguing that religious education must be a public discourse that should extend the principles and practices of human dignity, liberty, and social justice by engaging in social criticism that acknowledges the serious threats faced by public schools, critical cultural spheres, and the state of democracy itself to refer back to the arguments of Stephen Carter.

Indeed, such a task demands a rethinking and a rewriting of the meaning of religious education itself. It means comprehending this kind of religious pedagogy as a configuration of textual, verbal, and visual practices that seek to engage the processes through which people understand themselves and the ways in which they engage their social and cultural environment. It recognizes that symbolic presentations that take place in various spheres of cultural production in society manifest contested and unequal power relations. As a form of cultural production, religious education is implicated in the construction and organization of knowledge, desires, values, and social practices.

At stake here is developing a notion of religious pedagogy capable of contesting dominant forms of symbolic production. As a cultural practice, pedagogy in Roger Simon's (1992) terms both contests and refigures the construction, presentation, and engagement of various forms of images, text, talk, and action. This results in the production of meaning, which informs cultural workers, teachers, and students in regard to their individual and collective futures.

Related to the issue of contextualization and other cultural spheres as democratic spheres is the issue of illuminating the role that religious educators as cultural workers might play as engaged and transformative critics. This suggests a notion of leadership and pedagogical practice that combines a discourse of hope with forms of self and social criticism that do not require cultural workers to step back from society as a whole, or to lay claim to a specious notion of objectivity or authenticity, but to unlearn and transform those practices of privilege that reproduce conditions of oppression and human suffering. It is to this point that the parable of Alice Walker speaks when she describes those cultural communities which have been driven to the brink of extinction while living by the Word and attempting to keep walking.

I argue that religious educators and researchers who might understand themselves as cultural workers need to reclaim and reassert the importance of discourse and politics of location that recognizes how power, history, and ethics are inextricably intertwined so as to position, enable, and limit their work within shifting locations of power. The radical nature of such discourse points to the roles of cultural workers as public intellectuals who combine a sense of their own partiality with a commitment for justice and an attempt to "keep alive potent traditions of critique and resistance" (West, 1990, p. 108).

Religious educators who see themselves through the metaphor of cultural workers and dedicated to reforming all spheres of religious education as a part of a wider revitalization of public life also need to raise important questions of contextualization and its relationship to knowledge and power, learning and possibility, social criticism and human dignity and how these might be understood in relation to rather than in isolation from those practices of domination, privilege, and resistance at work in many arenas of the religious communities in which we find ourselves identified and implicated.

Of primary importance for religious educators and researchers who seek to utilize the benefits of contextualization, indigenization, and cross-cultural religious education is the need to resurrect traditions and social memories that provide a new way of reading religious and secular history and reclaiming power and identity. Within this view of memory, history, and identity, the possibility occurs to create new languages and social and religious practices that connect rather than separate religious education and cultural work from everyday life.

It is in the reconstruction of social religious memory, and in the role of religious educators as cultural workers and as transformative critics, and in the discourse of radical democracy as a basis for social struggle and cultural work that a religiously educational basis exists. The reconstruction of social religious memory provides for a kind of contextualization that engages cultural difference as a part of a broader discourse of justice, equality, and community. The ways and means of how one morally and religiously educates is not a "random path" but an intentional plan of "coherent understanding" transmitted by those who exercise cultural

appropriation and reciprocity across contextual and cultural differences. I suggest that is in the appropriation of the intentionality and integrity of the religious educator as a "cultural worker" and as one who has a care for contextualization that we might be enabled and empowered to "live by the Word and keep walking."

Acknowledgement

"Journal (April 17, 1984)" from *Living by the Word: Selected Writings 1973–1987*, © 1984 by Alice Walker, reprinted by permission of Harcourt, Inc.

Notes

1 "Liberalism" is a term that Carter (1993, p. 55) uses often. He defines it as follows: "I use the term *liberalism* to denote the philosophical tradition that undergirds the Western ideal of political democracy and individual liberty – a tradition that such conservatives as Robert Bork claim to represent no less than many prominent liberal intellectuals. This usage should not be confused with the polemical use of the term in contemporary American politics to signify possession of a particular bundle of policy positions."

2 "Diss," in American slang, means "to scorn, snub, belittle. The vogue word of the late 1980s entered adolescent speech via the *hip-hop* and *rap* sub-cultures originating in the African American community of the United States. A typical 'clipping', like def, treach, etc., it is based on the verbs dismiss, disapprove, or disrespect . . . (perhaps influenced by *dish*)" (Thorne, 1990).

3 For further insights and reference to this issue of "dissing religion," see Sullivan (1995).

4 See Schreiter (1993) for further development of this theme and a prescriptive definition of contextualization as it relates to theological education and religious education.

5 I draw heavily upon the analogy of "cultural worker" as a concept which describes pedagogues and other proponents of the teaching/learning process. This term is introduced by Harvard educator Henry Giroux and explicated in his work, *Border Crossings: Cultural Workers and the Politics of Education* (1992). With this work Giroux names his desire to meet across boundaries, declaring his political solidarity with postmodern feminist thought, anti-racist theory, and all who think critically about pedagogy. With clarity and insight he writes about the points of connection, expanding the scope of critical pedagogy and inviting us to engage in a broad political project that is fundamentally radical – fundamentally democratic.

References

Banks, J.A. (1986) Multicultural education: development, paradigms and goals. In J.A. Banks and J. Lynch (eds), *Multicultural Education in Western Societies*. New York: Praeger, pp. 2–28.

Carter, S.L. (1993) *The Culture of Disbelief: How American Law and Politics Trivialize Religious Devotion*. New York: Basic Books.

Coulianou, I. (1991) *Out of This World: Otherworldly Journeys from Gilgamesh to Einstein*. Boston, MA: Shambala.

Giroux, H. (1992) *Border Crossings: Cultural Workers and the Politics of Education*. New York: Routledge.

Giroux, H. (1993) *Living Dangerously: Multiculturalism and the Politics of Difference*. New York: Peter Lang.

Giroux, H. and D. Purpel (eds) (1983) *The Hidden Curriculum and Moral Education: Deception or Discovery?* Berkeley, CA: McCutchan.

hooks, b. (1994a) *Outlaw Culture: Resisting Representations*. New York: Routledge.

hooks, b. (1994b) *Teaching to Transgress: Education as the Practice of Freedom*. New York: Routledge:

Roe v. Wade (1993), 410 U.S. 113.

Schreiter, R.J. (1992) Address to the Association of Theological Schools Biennial Meeting.

Schreiter, R.J. (1993) Contextualization from a world perspective. *Theological Education*: **XXX**; (supplement I), 63–86.

Shweder, R.A. (1991) Post-Nietzschean anthropology: the idea of multiple objective worlds. In R.A. Shweder (ed.), *Thinking Through Cultures: Explorations in Cultural Psychology*. Cambridge, MA: Harvard University Press, pp. 27–72.

Simon, R. (1992) *Teaching Against the Grain*. New York: Bergin & Garvey Press.

Sullivan, W.F. (1995) Dissing religion: is religion trivialized in American public discourse? *Journal of Religion* **75** (1), 69–79.

Thorne, T. (1990) *The Dictionary of Contemporary Slang*. New York: Pantheon.

Walker, A. (1988) *Living by the Word*. San Diego, CA: Harcourt Brace Jovanovich.

Welch, S. (1985) *Communities of Resistance and Solidarity: A Feminist Perspective*. Maryknoll: Orbis.

West, C. (1990) The new cultural politics of difference. *October*, **53** (summer).

Witvliet, T. (1985) *A Place in the Sun*. Maryknoll: Orbis.

Witvliet, T. (1987) *The Way of the Black Messiah*. Oak Park, IL: Meyer-Stone Books.

Part Two

Religious Education

8 Religionism and Religious Education*

JOHN M. HULL

I Religionism

We do not appear to have a word in English which describes that kind of religion which involves the identity of the believer in such a way as to support tribalism and nationalistic solidarity through fostering negative attitudes towards other religions. Elsewhere, I have suggested that the word *religionism* should be used in this sense (Hull, 1992a; cf. Thompson, 1993; Cooling, 1994).

Wilfred Cantwell Smith studied this phenomenon nearly 50 years ago as it appeared in the late nineteenth and the first decades of the twentieth centuries in the Indian subcontinent. Smith observed a process of narrowing, in which many Indian Muslims no longer took much interest in Islam as a worldwide movement but became preoccupied with the Muslim community in India:

> Muslim communalists . . . have been highly conscious of the Muslims within India as a supposedly single, cohesive community, to which they devote their loyalty – paying little attention to whether the individuals included are religiously ardent, tepid, or cold; orthodox, liberal, or atheist; righteous or vicious; or to whether they are landlord or peasant, prince or proletarian; also paying little, attention to Muslims outside India. (Smith, 1946, p. 157)

In the Qur'án, men and women are called to respond to God with reverence and obedience. The result of their obedience is Islam (Smith, 1976, p. 68). Smith described how under the particular political, economic and social pressures of Indian life,

the goal of many Muslims became the well-being of the Muslim community. Islam was no longer the result of obedience but the focus of loyalty: 'in today's embattled world, men readily press their religion again into the service not of its highest ideals but of the immediate interests of their own group' (Smith, 1946, p. 158). At the same time, membership of the Muslim community was broadened to include many who had little or no sense of the presence of God but were merely Muslims by descent, language or kinship.

Similar trends were observed within the other religious traditions of the sub-continent. Smith shows how Hinduism was a reified creation of western scholarship, having its origins in the late nineteenth century when European scholars were beginning to conceptualise the special features of religious life in India (Smith, 1976, p. 66; 1981, p. 91). The entity thus created, namely Hinduism, became in turn the object of identification on the part of some of the people who belonged to that group of traditions, who thus distinguished themselves more sharply as Hindus from Muslims and Christians.

Smith described this process and its result as communalism, since he wished to emphasise that religious faith became an instrument serving the aggrandisement of a distinct community. Smith spoke of communal*ism* rather than merely 'community spirit' because he saw this process as encouraging a sectarian and tribal spirit. Religious faith was the instrument for the creation of this sense of particularity, but because it involved a loss of universal vision, a lapse in the sense of the mission of the faith in relation to the ultimate or transcendent God, this kind of religious communalism was sharply criticised by the more sophisticated theologians in all the affected religious traditions (Smith, 1946, p. 182).

* Based on a paper delivered to the International Conference on Religion and Conflict held in Armagh, Northern Ireland, 20–21 May 1994. I am grateful to the St Peters College Saltley Trust in Birmingham whose grant enabled this paper to be revised and prepared for the present publication.

By using the word religionism instead of Cantwell Smith's communalism, I wish to draw attention to the ideological content of tribalism, in so far as tribalism uses religious believing as its vehicle. The word religionism emphasises the religious character of this phenomenon, recognising it nevertheless as a distorted form of religious faith. Rather than becoming less religious, the phenomenon of religionism can be thought of as making people more religious, more zealously committed to their religion and opposed to the religion of others. The communalist movements, both within Hinduism and Islam, which glamorised their religious past and were accompanied by a kind of religio-national mysticism, were not in their early stages specifically anti-Muslim or anti-Hindu. They were just enthusiastically Muslim, enthusiastically Hindu:

> As yet, it did not involve inter-communal antagonism and hatred, but simply distinction. It has slowly developed since then, encouraged by a constant interplay of developing political and economic and religious processes, into the furious rivalry of the present day.   (Smith, 1946, p. 169)

In emphasising the ideological character of religion, the expression religionism also focuses attention upon certain aspects of religious belief or doctrine which are particularly conducive[1] to the formation of such sectarian and tribal solidarities.

Religionism, however, should not be regarded as a consequence of religion. It is, rather, a form of religion, exhibiting the entire structure of religion: worship, ethics, myth, doctrine and so on. We may describe it as a misappropriation of religion, as a religious deviation or distortion, but such expressions are evaluative, not phenomenological.

Religious identity and religionism

The identity which is fostered by religionism depends upon rejection and exclusion.[2] We are better than they. We are orthodox; they are infidels. We are believers; they are unbelievers. We are right; they are wrong. The other is identified as the pagan, the heathen, the alien, the stranger, the invader, the one who threatens us and our way of life, and in contrast to whom we know what we are.

Eric H. Erikson (1964, p. 82; 1968, p. 80) distinguished between the identity of wholeness which is inclusive, and that of totalism which is exclusive.

The identity of totalism says that I am an adult just in so far as I am not a child. I exclude my childhood. I am not a child but an adult. The identity of wholeness claims that my adulthood is all the more mature inasmuch as I acknowledge and affirm the childhood of my past and the child who is still within me. I am an adult in so far as I comprehend my whole life, past and future.

Although total identity formation may occur during the adolescent years as a defensive reaction against identity confusion, it may take a more malignant form if it appears during adulthood. During the crisis of intimacy versus isolation, characteristic of early adulthood, a strong and wholesome identity enables one to risk the vulnerability and fusion of intimacy with the other, whereas totalistic identity tends to reject otherness, finding intimacy only with that which is already similar to the self. Thus the path to generativity, the pouring out of oneself in caring for others, is blocked and the fifth Eriksonian stage (generativity versus stagnation) cannot be successfully encountered (Erikson, 1963a, pp. 255ff.; 1968, pp. 135ff.).

Under certain circumstances human groups affirm a totalistic identity which is dangerous because of the clannish loyalties which it creates. Erikson interpreted this phenomenon in biological terms, speaking of 'pseudo-speciation' (Erikson, 1963b, pp. 1–28; 1975, pp. 176–9). So general are human beings that the human itself is too amorphous to be imagined as a focus for identity. It is as if a species-wide identification demands too much empathy, too much abstraction for most people. Closer and more precise definition of the human is looked for, where characteristics such as mother tongue, skin colour or gender become the point of identification. The group thus created becomes a sort of sub-species. It competes with other sub-species for land and for resources.

Whereas pseudo-speciation reduces plurality by establishing a homogeneous group, recent studies in the theory of identity emphasise the plurality and flexibility of identity. Identity should be thought of not so much as a substance or essence which is of a certain fixed kind but as the product of a narrative, a story or series of stories which are used to interpret my experience and my place with others in the world (Meijer, 1991, 1995). When religion feeds pseudo-speciation, we may call it religionism. Erikson was aware that the symbols and traditions of religion could support and even generate such sub-speciation or tribalism. On the other hand, the great world faiths also contain universal and transcendent elements which may enable human faith to achieve a wider and even a cosmic loyalty (Erikson, 1958, p. 264; 1969, pp. 431–3).

Religionism and religious prejudice

Religionism always involves prejudice against other religions and other religious people. The expression 'religious prejudice' is not, however, sufficient to describe the phenomenon in question, because a prejudice is merely a psychological matter.

There is a distinction between racism and racial prejudice. Racism may exist in institutions where individuals are unaware of personal racial prejudice. Racism may be built up in historical experience, in economic structures and in political life. Thus there is a sociology, a history and a politics of racism as well as a psychology. Racism cannot be understood as a mere attitude, although racist attitudes remain a very important part of racism.

It is much the same with religionism. Religionism may develop slowly over centuries. It may be expressed in institutional form; it may mould the mythology of a people and thus become embedded in the culture of opposing peoples. Religionism falls like a shadow upon the hearts and minds of individuals and it may then be experienced as religious prejudice but its structures go beyond the individual. There may be religionist tendencies in the orthodox structure of theological systems. Believers participating uncritically in these theological systems may have certain beliefs about others and their religions, but it will not occur to them that these beliefs generate and perpetuate prejudice. The beliefs about others will simply be accepted as being true. The identity of the believer is conferred by the religious tradition, and if that identity is total, being sustained by negative perceptions of others and their religions, this may all be received as part of what salvation means.

Origins of religionism

For various complex reasons, it seemed to be difficult for some religions to evolve without taking on religionist tendencies: 'Every major ideological movement, religious and not, has begun with a rejecting of the others. This stage is passing' (Smith, 1981, p. 122).

Christianity had already assumed a religionist atti-

tude towards Judaism before the close of the New Testament period, and this was entrenched by the second century (see Reuther 1975; Dunn, 1991). Islam took on religionist features as it emerged from both Christianity and Judaism. Protestantism gathered religionist features during its early struggles with Roman Catholicism. When reforming movements encounter opposition, they attack in order to defend themselves. It must also be realised that inasmuch as new religious movements often take the form of a reforming reaction against the decadence of the surrounding religious life, there may be an attack upon this decadence. Such attacks are not necessarily to be regarded as religionist unless they feed an exclusive identity on the part of the attacker. They may be thought of as ethical protest. Before long, however, the new community may be struggling to maintain its identity. Caricature and stereotype are soon adopted as techniques in this competition for survival. The hearts and minds of the second generation are nurtured within an identity-protecting cocoon, the outer rim of which is hardened by such stereotypes. So religious reform turns into religionism, and the proclamation of the good news to the poor acquires the features of religionistic evangelism.

Religionistic evangelism is not quite the same as proselytising evangelism. There is a market place of ideas, and where there is choice, there is competition. Describing the missionary activity of the early Christians, Karl Jost (1975, p. 51) speaks of 'the sense of competition which developed as they spread their faith. Knowledge now had a moral competitive cast and numbers converted took on importance.' Such evangelism only becomes religionistic if it includes a polemic against other religions which is calculated not so much to convert the others as to build up the exclusive identity of those already converted. There are good and bad reasons for adopting a religion; the promulgation of these ideas is not *per se* to fall into religionism. At the same time, the identity built up by religionism need not necessarily be of an ethnic kind. Jost shows that the Christian movement, like the other international religions of the Graeco-Roman world was explicitly trans-ethnic (ibid., pp. 50–2; see also Legge, 1964). Often, however, modern religionism is regressive in that it revives the pre-Christian and primal association between individual and collective identity.

As the theological world view of the new movement becomes more articulate, elements of religionism acquire doctrinal significance and are built into the orthodox system. When this point is reached, deconstruction will be resisted in the name of the integrity of the religion itself. When it becomes the ideology of imperialism, such a theology will play a role in justifying the exploitation and enslavement of those who are regarded as pagans, heathens or as being without souls. For example, the doctrine of the metaphysical and exclusive uniqueness of Christian salvation has been used

> to make Christians feel uniquely privileged in contrast to the non-Christian majority of the human race, and accordingly free to patronise them religiously, exploit them economically, and dominate them politically. Thus the dogma of the deity of Christ – in conjunction with the aggressive and predatory aspect of human nature – has contributed historically to the evils of colonialism. (Hick, 1989, pp. 371–2)

It is perhaps an epistemic condition of religious faith that the saving religion should be experienced as uniquely true and precious, but it is not an epistemic condition of saving faith that the saving faith of others should be denied a similar status. The standard techniques of self-deception, namely compartmentalisation, selective reading of the evidence, displacement and projection, are used to maintain religionism in the service of the weakened ego, which appears unable to face the threat of its inclusion within a wider humanity.

Religionism and politics

Cantwell Smith showed how it became part of British policy to maintain and even to encourage communalism in India during the early decades of the twentieth century. It was helpful to the Raj that the subjected peoples should be divided into many separate groups, and then it became possible for the imperial administration to portray itself as the even hand of justice and moderation, mediating between the warring parties:

> The Government's method of encouraging communalism has been to approach all political subjects, and as many other subjects as possible, on a communalist basis; and to encourage, even to insist upon, everyone else's doing likewise. (Smith, 1946, p. 180)

Above all, it was in the British press at home that the strikes and riots which occurred in India were portrayed as being religionist in character. They had nothing to do with economics or with the desire for national liberty; they were sectarian conflicts between Hindu and Muslim (ibid., p. 175).

With the growing ethnic and religious pluralism of Britain since the Second World War, the emergence of domestic religionism has become a reality in the United Kingdom. Significant traces of religionism may be found in the relationships between the Church of England, the Free Churches and the Roman Catholics in Britain from the sixteenth to the nineteenth centuries, but on the whole the first 80 years of the twentieth century may be looked upon as a period when religionism was at a low ebb in Britain, although it was actively promulgated abroad, as we have seen. The rise of the ecumenical movement was one of many factors contributing to the greater degree of understanding and mutual respect between Christian denominations during this period. The agreed syllabus of religious education in England and Wales from the mid-1920s until the end of the 1980s may be considered as a fruit of such mutual understanding. The conservative resurgence of the 1980s and early 1990s brought with it a revival of religionism. In the remainder of this chapter I shall illustrate this unfortunate tendency with respect to religious education and I shall propose an antidote.

II Religionism in Religious Education

The resurgence of religionism in British religious education was accompanied by a rhetoric which made use of three positive concepts and one negative one. The positive concepts were those of integrity, predominance and cultural heritage (Hull, 1993). The negative concept was that of a mishmash.[3] In the rhetorical order, the negative normally came first. The country was warned that instead of receiving a clear instruction about Christianity and other important religions, children were being given a mishmash, that is, a superficial and confusing mixture of ingredients taken from various religions, presented out of context, leading to a trivialisation of faith. Next, the rhetoric proposed to clarify this mess by unmixing religions. At this point the positive concepts and images came into play. The integrity of each religious tradition would be restored and respected. Religions would neither be confused with each other nor contaminated nor diluted by contact but each would be presented separately, one by one. In this way the purity and coherence of each religion would be restored.

Once this separation had been achieved, the third step in the rhetoric was to argue that children could not be expected to assimilate more than a limited number of these religious systems. Christianity would obviously always be one, and thus Christianity would predominate. In order to secure this predominance, the balance between Christianity and other religions would be carefully monitored. This was often expressed in statistical terms (see Brown, 1994, p. 5). A stated percentage of the curriculum should be devoted to Christianity. The recommended percentage varied from 50 per cent to 75 per cent. The remaining time should be devoted to the study of the other religions, on a limited basis. It was claimed that this would be sufficient for one or two other religions at the appropriate key stage to be taught 'properly and at sufficient depth to be treated with the respect and intellectual integrity they require' (ibid.).

Finally, having passed through its denunciatory stage (mishmash) and announced the restoration of religious integrity, the preponderance of Christianity was justified by appeal to the British cultural heritage: 'The legislation governing religious education and worship in such schools is designed in RE to ensure that pupils gain . . . a thorough knowledge of Christianity reflecting the Christian heritage of the country' (DfE, 1994, para. 7). It thus became apparent that the interest was not so much in Christianity as a world-wide mission or movement but in the integrity of the traditional religion of Britain. Britain was to be understood not as a multicultural society but as containing a limited amount of ethnic diversity, mainly confined to the large cities.

A few examples will enable the reader to sense the tone of the rhetoric:

> Many of our children are in schools where they are denied the experience of religious worship at all and where teaching about Christianity has either been diluted to a multi-faith relativism or has become little more than a secularised discussion of social and political issues.   (Cox, 1988, p. 4)

many of the Agreed Syllabuses and the new GCSE Religious Education examinations have failed to enshrine the centrality of Christianity. Indeed, the opposite is often true: Christianity is submerged in a welter of shallow dabblings in a variety of other religions, resulting in a confusing kaleidoscope of images of faiths, doing justice to none.   (Ibid.)

This was described as 'the debasement of Christianity in our schools'.

> Of course, they can and must be given some understanding and knowledge of other major world religions, but this does not mean that we should jettison our responsibility to provide Christian worship and the study of Christianity as the major faith of this land.   (Ibid., p. 5)

John Burn and Colin Hart (1988, p. 5) quoted a speech by Robert Kilroy-Silk in which he referred to 'the fashionable but meaningless multi-race creed . . . an artificially created mongrel' (*The Times* 8 April 1988).

A typical feature of rising religionism is to count how many representatives on a certain committee each religion might have. So Burn and Hart (1988) told us that on the agreed syllabus conference which created the Brent syllabus of 1985 there were fifteen representatives of religions other than Christianity on the 23-person 'other denominations' group. The corresponding committee in Manchester had 23 non-Christians and twenty-two Christians (ibid., p. 16). The implication was that Christians were being submerged, losing control, being overwhelmed. Unless the law was changed, it would 'condemn children living in certain boroughs to learn little of the Christian faith' (ibid., pp. 23f.). Burn and Hart called upon Parliament to 'amend the present Education Reform Bill in such a way that Religious Instruction is defined as being predominantly the study of the Christian religion'. The law should set up 'machinery . . . to ensure the creation of national guidelines for predominantly Christian religious education'. The 'other denominations' committee of the agreed syllabus conference 'should be made up of members of Christian denominations other than the Church of England' (ibid., p. 29). Representatives of the other religions were to be excluded.

A characteristic of the British literature of religionism is that other religions are seldom if ever attacked directly. We might be told, as in the previous example, that on a certain committee there are 22 Christians and 23 non-Christians. We are not told why this matters, or who bothered to do the counting. Everything is by innuendo. The explicit attacks are reserved for humanism, atheism and communism. The other religions are always spoken of with respect, but they must keep their distance and they must know their place. They must be separate from Christianity and from each other, because only in this way can their proper place be estimated. Separation makes it possible to count, and then proportions can be reckoned.[4] Only in this way can a preponderance of Christianity be guaranteed. Although official language towards the other faiths remains courteous at all times, the actual implication of the policy, the meaning behind the words, became clearer each year.

From the point of view of the religionists, the water was muddied rather than clarified by the Education Reform Act (ERA) 1988 s. 8(3). Whereas it had been hoped that the agreed syllabuses would have been predominantly Christian, a compromising form of words was presented to the House of Lords by the then Bishop of London, Dr Graham Leonard, to which the Christian religionists reluctantly agreed (*Hansard*, House of Lords, 21 June 1988, col. 639; Hull, 1991, p. 19). This required new agreed syllabuses not only to 'reflect the fact that the principal religious traditions in Great Britain are in the main Christian' but also to 'take account of the teaching and practices of the other principal religions represented in Great Britain' (Education Reform Act 1988 s. 8(3)).

It had become clear that this form of words was little more than a description and thus a confirmation of the general approach of the agreed syllabuses throughout the preceding two decades, and that the new law could be interpreted as requiring the teaching of a world religions syllabus. The expression 'shall reflect' could be interpreted in many ways and several different kinds of syllabus might be compatible with this requirement.[5]

In spite of this, Christian religionism refused to give up. It was insisted that unless an agreed syllabus was clearly divided between the various religions, system by system, in such a way as to guarantee Christian preponderance at all stages of schooling, the so-called requirements of the Act were not being fully met. Attempts were made to bring the Local Education Authorities, which have the responsibility for syllabuses, into line, but these had little effect.

A fresh attempt was made in 1993 to marginalise the other world faiths but with one or two exceptions these attempts failed. The press sensed the atmosphere with the headline 'Tory Christians lose faith battle' (*The Times Educational Supplement* 14 May 1993). Indeed, the Christian religionists seemed to welcome the military metaphors. Lady Olga Maitland, commenting on the model syllabuses, said: 'Christianity is once again fighting for survival in the school room. This is no novelty; wars have been waged for centuries over religious tolerance. The fight is going on . . . this has become another battle ground . . . A mishmash of multiculturalism has crept into RE' (*Education* 14 January 1994, p. 32).

The DfE Circular 1/94 gave the official government interpretation of the religious education and collective worship legislation. School children were to be given 'a thorough knowledge of Christianity reflecting the Christian heritage of this country' and a less-thorough 'knowledge of the other principal religions represented in Great Britain' (DfE, 1994, para. 7). This distinction between the heritage religion and the represented religions marked a new stage in the development of religionism. The heritage which was of interest to the government was only the predominant one: 'Religious education in schools should seek to develop pupils' knowledge, understanding and awareness of Christianity, as the predominant religion in Great Britain' (ibid., para. 16). Judaism, in spite of its centuries-old tradition in Britain, was not to be part of this country's heritage. Judaism is, presumably, only represented in this country. Represented religions have no real home here.

The distinction between being the heritage and being represented applied not only to the content of what was studied in religious education but also to the children themselves. Collective worship was given a much stronger Christian theological profile such that it became impossible for children from Muslim, Jewish and other traditions to take part in the collective assembly. The expectation was that schools would make applications for part-determinations which would enable Muslim pupils to worship as a single religious group. Similar part-determinations would follow for pupils from other religious groups.[6]

The connection between collective worship, religionism and communalism is particularly striking. Let us take the case of Crowcroft Park Primary School in Manchester. A small group of parents protested about the collective worship offered by the school, on the grounds that it was not distinctively Christian but included some elements from the other spiritual traditions represented in the school (Manchester City Council, 1991, p. 12). The Secretary of State supported the LEA in dismissing the complaint, pointing out that section 7 of ERA 1988 quite clearly permits collective worship to be wholly or *mainly* of a broadly Christian character: that is, non-Christian children could take part and elements from various religions could be included.[7] Thus the attempt to purify collective worship, which would have divided children on religious grounds, failed. It is interesting, however, to realise that the complaint from these parents did not begin with questions of worship and religious education, but with the exposure of their children to foreign food served in the school cafeteria. There were also protests about the children being exposed (a favourite word) to Asian languages (ibid., p. 6). These complaints had already been dismissed by the LEA before being revived under a different guise by the passage of the ERA in 1988. New possibilities were then presented for stirring up ethnocentrism and xenophobia, made all the more powerful by the religious context.

A somewhat similar incident took place in two Birmingham inner-ring primary schools. A group of Muslim enthusiasts protested that although what the schools were actually doing in collective worship was unobjectionable it was nevertheless the case that in law Muslim children were being treated as if they were engaged in Christian worship. This objection was understandable and indicated an important sense in which the 1988 legislation is divisive, since it clearly distinguishes between families on religious grounds. Of course, the legislation makes provision for groups other than Christian. An application can be made on their behalf for a part-determination which, as we have seen, would enable them to worship in a manner which was wholly or mainly of a broadly Islamic character. Instead of seeking a part-determination, however, one of the schools made a successful application for a whole-determination. This had the effect of lifting the requirements for section 7 (that is, Christian worship) entirely, such that no pupil would be treated as belonging to a specific religious tradition, and the natural sensitivity about Muslim children being treated as if they were Christians was removed.

The Muslim enthusiasts were, however, not satisfied with this response. They insisted upon a part-determination and refused to accept a whole-determination. It is natural that Muslims should argue that when Christian children have 'their own act of worship' Muslim children should also have their own. But when no child is being treated as a member of a religious tradition but all children are being treated as children attending the school for the purpose of their education, and all are invited to attend and take part in a ceremony of collective worship which will draw upon all the spiritual traditions represented in the school, the case collapses. This particular group of Muslims did not want Muslim children to take part in the common and ordinary collective spiritual life of the school. Other indications from the area suggested that this was part of a general programme of heightening religious sensitivity, including community and political awareness which was clearly religionist in character. It was significant that in the school in question the Muslim parents who wanted a separate Muslim assembly were drawn from one ethnic group. Other ethnic groups, although equally devout Muslims, were happy with the collective worship of the whole school.[8]

One must be sympathetic towards Muslim religionism in Britain, since to a large extent it is the response of a proud and cultivated people to the indignities and marginalisations which they have experienced. When Christians claim to predominate, Muslims will naturally seek to find at least some ground where they also can predominate. As Cantwell Smith (1946, p. 170) remarked so many years ago, religionism is 'like a habit-forming drug, which, as long as it is administered, is needed in ever increasing doses'. Religionism characteristically creates a spiral of escalating tension. It is easy to whip it up; it is extraordinarily difficult to calm it down.

Draft versions of the model religious education syllabuses prepared by the School Curriculum and Assessment Authority (SCAA) were published for consultation on 25 January 1994. These were consistent with the religionist policy which we have been tracing. It was assumed that the legislation only permits one kind of syllabus: that in which religions are to be taught as coherent entities one by one in complete separation. The separatist claim was quite explicit, since the introductory booklet argued that an approach to understanding religion which drew upon more than one religious tradition was unacceptable (SCAA, 1994, p. 5).[9] It was interesting that the statements (required by the DfE) of percentages to be devoted to Christianity and the other religions were to be withdrawn, following advice from the legal branch that the law did not require or even permit such percentage indications,[10] but when the working party withdrew not only the percentages but the diagrams indicating visually the proportions to be devoted to different religions, this diagram was instantly replaced by direct authority of the Minister involved.[11]

It is not surprising that the representatives of the Hindu, Jewish, Sikh, Muslim and Buddhist traditions were disappointed and offended. They were being marginalised, and they knew it.[12] The sad thing is that for years, for decades, religious education syllabuses had given a prominent position to the Christian faith while allowing for a less prominent place for the other religions, and everyone was more or less happy. That was because the atmosphere in those days was not religionist. Nobody bothered to count how many Buddhists or Sikhs were on a committee. It never occurred to the Muslims and Hindus that Christians were trying to dominate. The thinking was educational, not religionist.

In contrast, the model syllabuses were set up from the beginning in the wrong way. A group of Christians was invited to draw up a Christianity syllabus; a group of Muslims did a similar job for Islam and so on. Right from the start, people involved in an educational project were invited to think of themselves as primarily members of a particular religious community. The result was predictable, and presumably well planned.[13]

An alternative strategy, which would not have yielded a religionist result, would have been for a committee comprising people from various religions and perhaps some of no religion, including teachers and educators, to draw up a syllabus indicating the best possible religious educational experience for children in British schools today. Indeed, several such groups could have been established, and a variety of approaches might have been generated. All this could have been published, and the variety and freedom permitted by the law would thus have been reinforced. The local creators of agreed syllabuses would thus have had plenty of inspiration and various examples. Instead, a separatist approach which insisted upon its own supremacy was created, with clear religionist implications for the future. Fortunately, the model syllabuses only have advisory status. The religionist pressures come mainly from the top, as is to be expected in what is quite clearly a part of the ideological superstructure of British political and social power,[14] but at the local level we may hope that the human realities of making contact will overcome the desire for a purified integrity.

III Anti-religionist education

Just as anti-sexist and anti-racist educational programmes seek to combat sexism and racism, we need to create an anti-religionist education. This should be provided not only in school religious education but as part of the adult education programmes in every church and parish, every mosque and synagogue. Speaking from within the Christian faith, it is clear that Christian education should be evaluated as to its faithfulness not merely to the Christian tradition but to the Christian mission. In other words, what matters is not an exact transmission of the tradition but an encounter with the vision which the tradition represents, the purpose of God in reconciling human beings in Jesus Christ. That purpose was not just reconciliation with God, but reconciliation between human individuals and groups. Christ is our peace, who has broken down the barrier which divides us and is making of all people one new humanity (Ephesians 2: 14f.). Any religionist tendencies which the Christian tradition might possess should be overcome in the name of the Holy Spirit who is still revealing new things through the old things (John 16: 12f.).

The anti-religionist curriculum. Strand 1: deconstruction

This task cannot be accomplished merely through encouraging tolerance of other religions. Even the religionists speak of tolerance and respect towards other religions, although their actions belie their claims. It is necessary to realise that the Christian religion has acquired intolerant elements and that therefore a deconstruction is necessary.

The experience of the early Christians was that they entered into peace with God through the Lord Jesus Christ. In reporting that this experience was to be found only through Jesus Christ, the Christians were not making comments about Buddhism and Hinduism, of which they knew nothing, nor about Islam or Sikhism, which had not as yet entered the world (Smith, 1981, p. 171). As for Judaism, it was clear that the great prophets and law givers of the Hebrew Bible walked in peace with God. The Christians had experienced salvation only through Jesus Christ and this is exactly what they said. We misunderstand their spirit of love and peace in Christ when we apply their insights to our modern pluralist and competitive religious world, turning the grace of God to which they are witnesses into a religious system through which we weak little people find powerful identities.

God has no pets, and as Juan Luis Segundo (1973, pp. 40–4) has shown, it is a great responsibility to be called to participate in the world-wide mission of God through Christ. There are thus responsibilities in being Christian; it is less clear that there are advantages. Such advantages would instantly tribalise humanity. The important distinctions recognised by the Kingdom of God do not lie between one religious system and another but between the rich and the poor. It is God's intention to fill the hungry with good things and to send the rich away empty. We have no warrant within the grace of God for claiming that it is God's intention to fill the Christians with good things and to send the non-Christians away empty. This is not the way of God.

Just as anti-racist education goes beyond the question of racial prejudice, so anti-religionist education must go beyond the mere encouragement of tolerance. Two elements in the syllabus may be expected. First, the systems approach should certainly continue, that is, the presentation of religious traditions one by one. However, critical methods of interpretation will help both children and adults to distinguish the salvific from the religionist elements in the Bible, the history of doctrine and present-day Christian experience.

This may be described as the deconstructionist requirement. Moreover, although deconstruction is in a sense an internal matter for each religious tradition and thus requires a more or less systematic exposition from within that tradition, it cannot be conducted in isolation from other traditions. Recognition of this will restore a good deal of reality to the way the religious traditions are treated. After all, no religion came into the world in isolation. Every religious tradition was born into a world already full of religions and has evolved in a continual dialogue with one or several other religions. This pattern of coexistence and mutual influence has differed in, let us say, China on the one hand and the Middle East on the other, but it has always been in a context of relationships.[15] The result of this interchange is seen not only in the frequent borrowings between traditions (for 1000 years the Buddha had a place in Christian hagiography) (Smith, 1981, pp. 7ff.) but will affect what are sometimes called the core elements. The medieval Christian doctrine of God drew upon the Iberian theological melting-pot where

Jewish, Muslim and Christian theologians were in contact with each other. Christian eschatology evolved under the influence of Zoroastrianism and today hundreds of new Christian denominations are being formed, particularly in Africa and in South America, which draw upon primal religious traditions and folk knowledge. If we were to think not so much in terms of Christianity as an absolute and unqualified essence but of participating in the influence and the inspiration offered by Jesus, we would come closer to the nature of Christian discipleship.

The anti-religionist curriculum. Strand 2: universalising faith

The second strand in an anti-religionist curriculum will consist of the study of the religious experience of men and women in a global perspective. We know today what God, presumably, has always known about us: that our religious history as a species is ultimately one and indivisible. There is a world-wide history of religious consciousness. Each religious tradition is more richly understood within that global context. Thus an important object of religious education is religion itself; not just the religious traditions, but the religious sensitivity which millions of men and women, boys and girls, still possess, whether within a particular so-called tradition or completely outside it. What matters in religious education today is not only what happened in the formation of the religious experience of humanity, that is, the religious past, but what is happening today to the descendants of the men and women who made those traditions: that is, all of us. How are human beings today to respond to that to which the spirituality of all religions bears witness?

This kind of study involves inter-religious and trans-religious topics treated from a dialogical perspective. As the connections between religion and conflict seem in so many ways to be getting stronger today, it is the task of religious educators, whatever their faith background or lack of it, to contribute to this anti-religionist enterprise. In this way religious education can play its part in the liberation of religions and could make a valuable contribution to peace and reconciliation.

Notes

1 Contrary to Barnes (1997), I do not believe that religionism can be inferred directly from a religious doctrine, although religious doctrines may permit or support religionism in varying degrees. I have discussed the relationship between Christian doctrines and religionism in my lecture *The Holy Trinity and Christian Education in a Pluralist World* (Hull, 1995a).

2 I have discussed the characteristics of such an identity in a case study approach in Hull (1996).

3 The same concept, that of a mixture of disgusting or ill-assorted foods, may also appear as hotch potch, mess of pottage and so on. I have discussed this rhetoric in Hull (1991).

4 A typical example of the desire to count so that proportions can be so arranged as to secure the marginalisation of the smaller religious groups is found in the 1993 Education Act: 'The numbers of representatives of each denomination and religion are required to reflect broadly the proportionate strength of that denomination or religion in the local area' (Circular 1/94, para. 111).

5 It is interesting to note that the legal opinion obtained by the Secretary of State for Education dated 12 June 1990 in connection with the complaint received against the recently published agreed syllabuses of the London Boroughs of Ealing and Newham confirms this: 'The fact that the religious traditions in Great Britain are in the main Christian could be reflected by devoting most time to Christian traditions but in my opinion the flexibility inherent in the word "reflect" means that this could be done in other ways eg. by comparison with other religions and discussion as to the differences and similarities between Christian and other traditions' (§ 9.5). Unfortunately this crucial passage was omitted in the letter of guidance which the then DES sent to Chief Education Officers on 18 March 1991, and the government persisted with its policy of a narrow interpretation of the law, contrary to its own legal advice and in spite of the deterioration of relations between religious communities which inevitably followed. Such a policy, in the context of debate which I have described, was clearly a manifestation of religionism.

6 I have discussed the implications of Circular 1/94 regarding collective worship in Hull (1995b; 1995c).

7 Letter from the Secretary of State for Education, 23 June 1992. Mr Justice McCullough in rejecting an appeal for a judicial review against the ruling of the Secretary of State provided a very fine summary of the case and of the law on 26 February 1993.

8 'Religious row at crisis point'. *Metro News* (Birmingham), 5 May 1994.

9 The introductory document urges five educational grounds against syllabuses which draw upon several religions. The authors do not claim that the law would prohibit such syllabuses, since it had been clear ever since the legal advice of 12 June 1990 that this was not the case (note 5 above). The SCAA, following guidance from the government, did not see fit to commend the range of syllabuses which the law permits.

10 Letter from Rosemary D. Pearce, Schools 3 Branch of the DfE, 28 October 1993, to Barbara Wintersgill of SCAA.

11 An account of the events was given in a letter from the Methodist representative on the SCAA Model RE Agreed Syllabuses Monitoring Group, the Reverend Geoff Robson, in his letter of protest to Mr Patten, the Secretary of State for Education, 11 January 1994. The bar chart itself appears on page 6 of the *Introduction*.

12 'RE syllabus attacked for Christian bias', *Guardian*, 25 January 1994, p. 8; 'Call for balance in religious education', *Independent*, 25 January 1994, p. 6; and 'Faiths unite against new emphasis in RE', *The Times*, 25 January 1994, p. 2.

13 The background is provided in SCAA, *Model Syllabuses: Faith Communities' Working Group Reports 1994*, where members of the working groups are also listed (pp. 35–6).

14 I have discussed something of this background in Hull (1992b).

15 See the general approach suggested by the various contributors to Hick and Askari (1985).

References

Barnes, L. Philip (1997) Religion, religionism and religious education: fostering tolerance and truth in schools. *Journal of Education and Christian Belief* **1** (1), 7–23.

Brown, Alan (1994) *Christianity in the Agreed Syllabus*. London: National Society (Church of England) for Promoting Religious Education.

Burn, J. and Hart, C. (1988) *The Crisis in Religious Education*. London: Educational Research Trust.

Cooling, Trevor (1994) *A Christian Vision for State Education*. London: SPCK.

Cox, Caroline (1988) Foreword. In J. Burn and C. Hart, *The Crisis in Religious Education*. London: Educational Research Trust.

Department for Education (DfE) (1994) *Religious Education and Collective Worship*, Circular 1/94, 31 January. London: DfE.

Dunn, J. (1991) *The Parting of the Ways between Christianity and Judaism*. Philadelphia, PA: Trinity Press International.

Erikson, Eric H. (1958) *Young Man Luther*. New York: W.W. Norton.

Erikson, Eric H. (1963a) *Childhood and Society*, 2nd edn. New York: W.W. Norton.

Erikson, Eric H. (ed.) (1963b) *The Challenge of Youth*. New York: Basic Books.

Erikson, Eric H. (1964) *Insight and Responsibility: Lectures on Ethical Implications of Psychoanalytic Insights.* London: Faber & Faber.

Erikson, Eric H. (1968) *Identity, Youth and Crisis.* London: Faber & Faber.

Erikson, Eric H. (1969) *Ghandi's Truth.* New York: W.W. Norton.

Erikson, Eric H. (1975) *Life History and the Historical Moment.* New York: W.W. Norton.

Hick, John (1989) *An Interpretation of Religion.* London: Macmillan.

Hick, John and Askari, Hasan (eds) (1985) *The Experience of Religious Diversity.* Aldershot, Hants.: Gower.

Hull, John (1991) *Mishmash: Religious Education in Multicultural Britain. A Study in Metaphor.* Derby: Christian Education Movement.

Hull, John M. (1992a) The transmission of religious prejudice [editorial]. *British Journal of Religious Education* **14** (2), 69–72.

Hull, John M. (1992b) Curriculum and theology in English religious education. *Panorama: International Journal of Comparative Religious Education and Values* **4** (2), 36–45; reprinted in *Bulletin of the Association of British Theological and Philosophical Libraries* **2** (18), 3–15.

Hull, John M. (1993) *The Place of Christianity in the Curriculum: The Theology of the Department for Education* [Hockerill Lecture]. Frinton-on-Sea, Essex: Hockerill Educational Foundation.

Hull, John M. (1995a) *The Holy Trinity and Christian Education in a Pluralist World.* London: National Society (Church of England) for Promising Religious Education.

Hull, John M. (1995b) Can one speak of God or to God in education? In Francis Young (ed.), *Dare We Speak of God in Public?.* London: Mowbray, pp. 22–34.

Hull, John M. (1995c) Collective worship: the search for spirituality. In *Future Progress in Religious Education* [The Templeton Lectures]. London: Royal Society of Arts, pp. 27–36.

Hull, John M. (1996) A critique of Christian religionism in recent British education. In Jeff Astley and Leslie J. Francis (eds), *Christian Theology and Religious Education: Connections and Contradictions.* London: SPCK, pp. 140–65.

Jost, Karl J. (1975) The missionary: an innovative educational model in western learning. *Learning for Living* **15** (2).

Legge, Francis (1964) *Forerunners and Rivals of Christianity.* New York: University Books.

Manchester City Council. Education Department (1991) *Report of a Formal Investigation under Section 23(1) of the 1988 Education Reform Act … against Crowcroft Park Primary School …* [investigating officer: Mick Molloy]. Manchester: Manchester City Council, 9 July.

Meijer, Wilna (1991) Religious education and personal identity: a problem for the humanities. *British Journal of Religious Education* **13** (2), 89–94.

Meijer, Wilna (1995) The plural self: a hermeneutical view on identity and plurality. *British Journal of Religious Education* **17** (2), 92–9.

Reuther, Rosemary Radford (1975) *Faith and Fratricide: The Theological Roots of Anti-Semitism.* London: Search Press.

School Curriculum and Assessment Authority (SCAA) (1994) *Model Syllabuses for Religious Education: Consultation Document.* London: SCAA.

Segundo, Juan Luis (1973) *The Community Called Church.* Maryknoll, NY: Orbis Books.

Smith, Wilfred Cantwell (1946) *Modern Islam in India: A Social Analysis.* London: Victor Gollancz.

Smith, Wilfred Cantwell (1976) *Religious Diversity: Essays,* ed. Willard G. Oxtoby. New York: Harper & Row.

Smith, Wilfred Cantwell (1981) *Towards a World Theology: Faith and the Comparative History of Religion.* London: Macmillan.

Thompson, Penny (1993) Religionism: a response to John Hull. *British Journal of Religious Education* **16** (1), 47–50.

Law, Politics and Religious Education in England and Wales: Some History, Some Stories and Some Observations

ROBERT JACKSON

Introduction

The British experience of religious education is sometimes held up as a model of intercultural achievement. It is true that RE has changed dramatically in Britain, partly (and in terms of temporal sequence, initially) as a result of responses to secularisation (Cox, 1966), partly under the influence of the newly emergent discipline of religious studies in the late 1960s and early 1970s (Smart, 1967, 1968; Schools Council, 1971; Hinnells, 1970) and partly in acknowledgment of the increasingly multi-faith and multicultural nature of society (see, for example, Cole, 1972). However, the transition has not been easy and, as we shall see, there have been some ideological contests in the background. Since the mid-1980s, when Thatcherism was at its most potent, there has been a right-wing backlash against any form of 'multiculturalism' in education and beyond. There are several educational pressure groups dedicated to preserving what they see as Britain's Christian cultural heritage and what are perceived as the old moral certainties that used to keep society well ordered.[1] Britain's past is portrayed romantically, with a stable and bounded culture. Cultures are portrayed as fixed and closed, and migrant groups and their descendants are usually pictured as of alien culture and religion, a potential threat to the nation's heritage and way of life (see, for example, McIntyre, 1978). Religious educators who have supported multifaith approaches tend to be regarded as 'progressives' with their roots in the trendy 1960s, promoting a relativism that is dismissive of any claims to truth (Burn and Hart, 1988).[2] During the period of Conservative rule, and especially between 1988 and 1994, some of these radical right groups managed occasionally to exert some influence on

government policy and legislation. However, the combined professional voices in religious education prevailed,[3] and they had the support of varied faith groups, including the Church of England Board of Education (see, for example, Brown, 1995). The contest will no doubt go on, though, since May 1997, in a different political climate for the foreseeable future.

As might be expected, religious educators who support multifaith approaches do not hold just one view and they have been falsely represented by their opponents as sharing a single 'phenomenological' stance (for example, Burn and Hart, 1988). Supporters of multifaith religious education include committed believers from a variety of religious backgrounds, as well as agnostics and non-believers who argue for the importance of the study of religions in schools. Moreover, they are not all liberals as far as religion or theology is concerned. There has been some valuable work done by writers and teachers from the evangelical wing of Christianity (for example, Cooling, 1994; King and Helme, 1994; Wilkins, 1991) and from writers influenced by post-liberal theology (Wright, 1996).

The political debates referred to above gained momentum at the time of the drafting of the Education Reform Bill, prior to the publication of the Education Reform Act in 1988. However, some trends – especially the increasing secularisation of the subject (Cox, 1966), influence on it from religious studies in universities (Smart, 1967, 1968) and its response to religious diversity (Hinnells, 1970; Cole, 1972) – were evident under the old legislation of 1944, which was being interpreted flexibly by many local education authorities from the mid-1970s.

The legal changes of 1988 in England and Wales

were principally a reaffirmation of some key principles and structures from 1944, together with an acknowledgement of social change and changes in the religious ecology of England and Wales. Since then there has been something of a shift to the right in terms of the non-statutory guidance sent out to schools in 1994 (DfE, 1994), while the local devolution of RE syllabus making has ensured a variety of RE styles and the maintenance of a variety of multifaith approaches. Meanwhile innovations in research and curriculum development[4] and the national model syllabuses produced by the School Curriculum and Assessment Authority (SCAA, 1994a and 1994b) are making an impact on some of the latest syllabuses. Moreover, having come through a period of being muzzled on the topic of RE (Robson, 1996), the Office for Standards in Education (OFSTED) is helping to effect positive changes through its inspection of the subject, its publication of analyses of inspection reports (OFSTED, 1994, 1995) and its published research (OFSTED, 1997). To tell the story from England and Wales in more detail, we need to take a look at developments in religious education law.[5]

The legal framework

The 1944 legislation

Religious education has been an ingredient of English and Welsh state education since the first Education Act of 1870, which set up the first entirely state-funded Board Schools. School Boards could opt for Bible teaching without denominational instruction, in accordance with the so-called Cowper–Temple clause which stated: 'No religious catechism or religious formulary which is distinctive of any particular denomination shall be taught in the school.' This clause influences the legislation to this day. The Act also included a conscience clause by means of which parents could withdraw their children from religious instruction. The 1902 Education Act confirmed the 1870 settlement on religious instruction (RI), adding a further conscience clause for teachers and establishing the dual system of partnership between the state and the churches ·in providing a national system of education.

The 1944 Act clarified the dual system, by distinguishing different types of maintained (as opposed to privately funded) schools. County schools were entirely publicly funded. Voluntary schools (partly funded by religious bodies) were of three types: Aided, Controlled and Special Agreement. Aided schools (Anglican, Roman Catholic, some other Christian schools and a few Jewish schools) had a majority of governors appointed by the sponsoring religious body and the character of religious instruction was determined by the governors of each school. RI in Special Agreement schools usually followed the pattern of Aided schools. Unless parents opted to have denominational religious instruction taught by 'reserved teachers', RI in Controlled schools was identical to that in County schools.

The 1944 Act made mandatory the use by County Schools (and, normally, Controlled Schools) of agreed syllabuses for religious instruction. Early versions of these – aimed at finding agreement at the local level between Christian denominations over the content of RI – had been in use in some local authorities since the early 1920s. Under the terms of the 1944 Act, English LEAs had to convene a Syllabus Conference consisting of four committees representing:

- the Church of England;
- other denominations;
- the local authority;
- teachers' organisations.

In Wales there were three committees, with Anglican representation confined to the committee made up of religious denominations.[6]

In practice, 'other denominations' meant 'other Protestant Christian denominations', since the Roman Catholics confined their energies to their voluntary (aided and special agreement) schools, and no other religion was envisaged. It was not until the 1970s that some LEAs liberally interpreted the Act as allowing representatives of non-Christian religions on to the 'other denominations' panel.[7] Between the publication of the City of Birmingham Agreed Syllabus in 1975 and the advent of new syllabuses following the 1988 Education Reform Act, many new syllabuses included a significant amount of work on religions other than Christianity in addition to studies of the Christian tradition, reflecting both social changes in Britain resulting partly from immigration, and the rise of a globally orientated religious studies as a secular subject in institutions of higher education.[8]

The 1988 Legislation

Changes to religious education brought about by the 1988 Education Reform Act have to be seen against the background of the government's introduction of a national curriculum, with compulsory core and foundation subjects.[9] Some commentators saw the decision to maintain *local* arrangements for designing syllabuses of religious education as showing the government's lack of concern for the subject. Perhaps there was a view in the government that controversy would be avoided by maintaining the *status quo*. However, the official line was that, given the religious diversity in different parts of the country, it was appropriate to adapt the system already in place since 1944 (Copley, 1997). The term 'basic curriculum' was used in the Act to encompass the national curriculum and religious education, and it is the basic curriculum which is the entitlement of all pupils in maintained schools in England and Wales. In retrospect, it has been observed that many schools concentrated on the core and then the foundation subjects of the national curriculum in the years immediately after 1988, to the detriment of RE, and the argument for having a single national syllabus has been advanced by some writers, including John Hull, in his last editorial of the *British Journal of Religious Education* (1996). A response to this, articulating the key reasons for local determination, appears in a letter from Howard Marratt in the following issue (Marratt, 1996). Even before Marratt's letter was published, John Hull had gone back to supporting the 'local syllabus' argument. No doubt the national/local argument will resurface from time to time.

The 1988 Education Reform Act retained many features of the 1944 Act (provision, withdrawal and agreed syllabuses), but introduced changes which strengthened RE's place in the curriculum and acknowledged some recent developments in the subject. A significant change was the use of 'religious education' to replace the term 'religious instruction' with its suggestion of deliberate transmission of religious beliefs.[10] The subject now had to be fully educational with its aims and processes justifiable on educational grounds. Recognising the need for different interest groups to have a say in the production of syllabuses and for local circumstances to be considered, the arrangements for producing agreed syllabuses were retained in a modified form. For the first time in law, representatives of faiths other than Christianity were 'officially' given a place in agreed syllabus conferences on what used to be the 'other denominations' committee. Also Standing Advisory Councils on Religious Education (SACREs) now *had* to be set up (post–1944 they were optional) with functions that include monitoring the use of agreed syllabuses and the power to *require* an LEA to set up a conference to review the locally agreed syllabus. SACREs have a composition which parallels that of agreed syllabus conferences, and they can coopt extra members.

Because of its position outside the national curriculum, RE stayed out of nationally agreed assessment arrangements and did not become a foundation subject. The Department of Education and Science's non-statutory guidance (DES, 1989), stated that agreed syllabus conferences could decide to include assessment arrangements in syllabuses that paralleled those established in national curriculum subjects. Several projects emerged, most notably from Westhill College, Birmingham, and the University of Exeter, which explored issues concerned with the assessment of RE (FARE, 1991; Westhill, 1989, 1991).

The Reform Act requires that any new agreed syllabus 'shall reflect the fact that religious traditions in Great Britain are in the main Christian, whilst taking account of the teaching and practices of the other principal religions represented in Great Britain' (UK Government, 1988, section 8.3). This says nothing about *instruction* in Christianity, and the Act specifically prohibits indoctrinatory teaching. *New* agreed syllabuses had both to give proper attention to the study of Christianity and, regardless of their location in the country, to give attention to the other major religions represented in Britain; this was no longer an option for local authorities.

The Education Reform Act also sets religious education in the context of the whole curriculum of maintained schools which 'must be balanced and broadly based' and must promote 'the spiritual, moral, cultural, mental and physical development of pupils at the school and of society' (ibid., section 1 (2) para. 2). Religious education then, as well as being broad, balanced and open, should not simply be a study of religions but, like the rest of the curriculum, should relate to the experience of pupils in such a way that it contributes to their personal development.

A disturbing feature of the debate about RE

during the passage of the Education Reform Bill through Parliament was the lack of attention by politicians to the research and thinking about religious education since the early 1960s. The debate in 1988 was often reduced to a crude wrangling over whether the content of RE should be 'Christian' or a multifaith 'mishmash' (Alves, 1991). One effect was to produce a spate of statements from certain politicians supporting a form of religio-cultural exclusiveness, demanding the teaching of confessional Christianity as a means to preserving 'British culture' and ordering society morally (see, for example, Coombs, 1988; replied to in Jackson, 1989).

Quite apart from the dismay felt by RE professionals that a vital area of the curriculum should be used as a theological and political football, the debate obscured the real crisis for religious education in England and Wales, namely the chronic shortage of resources in terms of staffing, training and materials. The Religious Education Council of England and Wales's paper *Religious Education: Supply of Teachers for the 1990s* (1988), through detailed analysis of DES statistics, exposed the chronic shortage of teachers with RE qualifications in primary and secondary schools together with insufficient training opportunities at initial and in-service levels. It also pointed to inadequate time on the timetable and low levels of funding for books and other resources (REC, 1988; see also REC, 1990). This abysmal picture was confirmed by a survey of secondary schools conducted by the Culham College Institute (*Christianity in RE Programme News*, 1989), and reflected in reports of inspections in schools carried out by Her Majesty's Inspectors of Schools (Orchard, 1991), and latterly by inspection teams from the Office for Standards in Education (OFSTED, 1994, 1995). In 1996, the Department for Education and Employment (as it is now called) at last acknowledged that RE was a shortage subject, at least at secondary level, and the government-sponsored Teacher Training Agency allocated an increased number of training places in religious education to higher education institutions. The full effects of this recent shift in policy remain to be seen.

The most positive feature of the 1988 legislation, although a compromise, was that it confirmed the *educational* nature of RE and ensured that all the principal religions in Britain would be studied as part of the programme of all students in state-funded county schools.

Political developments since 1988

Since 1988, RE has been seen by the radical right as potentially a means to regenerate moral values and to promote 'British' cultural identity among the young and Christianity as the religion and moral force of the state. Any notion that some British citizens might learn something about personal and social values from other British citizens who are affiliated to religions other than Christianity is rejected. The supporters of this position sought to put a conservative spin on the 1988 legislation and to promote narrower views in subsequent non-statutory guidance and law. The radical right position is implicit in the views of the Centre for Policy Studies, which was influential on Conservative government policy in education, and has been expressed in general writings on education by members of small but vociferous right-wing pressure groups which have targeted religious education or related fields such as collective worship, the provision of separate religious schools for religious minorities, and spiritual development. Prominent in the debates are the Christian Institute (for example, Burn *et al.* 1991; Hart, 1991), the Campaign for Real Education (Flew and Naylor, 1996) and the Parental Alliance for Choice in Education (PACE).

Specifically in relation to RE, the reaction started with a strong attack on 'multifaith RE' and on the 'multifaith' syllabuses which had originated in the mid-1970s with the City of Birmingham Agreed Syllabus (Birmingham, 1975) and which had grown in number in the 1980s. Burn and Hart's *The Crisis in Religious Education* (1988) combined ideas from the politics of the radical right and evangelical Christian theology. 'Liberal educators' in RE were rather slow off the mark in taking the backlash seriously, especially since the arguments of the right were often poor, relying on political invective rather than scholarship. However, Burn and Hart were politically astute, distributing their literature to members in both Houses of Parliament, and cultivating politicians, such as Baroness Cox in the House of Lords and Lady Olga Maitland and Michael Allison in the Commons.

RE professionals became more politicised. The Professional Religious Education Group (PREG) was formed in 1991, bringing together the chairs of the Religious Education Council of England and Wales, the Professional Council for Religious Education (the national professional association for RE teachers), the National Association of Teachers in Further and Higher Education (NATFHE) Religious Studies Section, the Association of Religious Education Inspectors, Advisers and Consultants and the Conference of University Lecturers in Religious Education[11]. PREG took on a number of roles, including lobbying politicians in both Houses; coordinating responses to consultations on the 1992 White Paper on education and the 1993 Department for Education draft Circular on RE; seeking meetings with the then Minister of State for Education, Baroness Blatch; and replying to the arguments of the Christian Institute lobby (for example, Jackson, 1992).

At the same time others from the world of RE responded to the views of the radical right. Special mention should be made of the work of John Hull, Professor of Religious Education at the University of Birmingham, whose comments were so effective that he was vilified in a House of Lords debate by a right-wing peer. Hull's commentary on the RE and worship clauses of the 1988 Act made a skilful liberal interpretation (an interpretation endorsed in the barrister's opinion requested by Kenneth Clarke in 1990 when he was Secretary of State for Education and discussed below) (Hull, 1989).[12] Hull later wrote a devastating analysis of the language used by right-wing critics of 'multifaith RE', especially their use of disparaging metaphors to attack multifaith religious education (Hull, 1991). Following the publication of Circular 1/94 (DfE, 1994) (which made a strongly reactionary interpretation of the 1988 Act) he regretted not directly attacking the clauses of the Act on collective worship earlier (see various editorials of the *British Journal of Religious Education* during 1994–5 and Copley, 1996). Other critics of the Burn and Hart line include Trevor Cooling, an evangelical Christian writer who takes a very different line on RE from that of the evangelical right (Cooling, 1994).

Mention should be made of spokespersons on education from within the Church of England. The Church (through the unlikely figure of Graham Leonard, then Bishop of London) defended a religiously pluralistic RE against Baroness Cox and others in the House of Lords, resulting in the compromise of the 1988 legislation. Alan Brown, Schools Officer for the Church of England Board of Education, worked hard for a just, multifaith solution, both at the time of the Act and subsequently. The Church of England has thus drawn criticism from the Christian Institute lobby (Hart, 1994). Alan Brown's (1995) reply in the *British Journal of Religious Education* pulls no punches.

There are plenty more sub-plots. One is the placing by Ministers of members of the Christian Institute on influential non-elected quangos (quasi non-governmental organisations). John Burn was appointed a member of the National Curriculum Council (NCC), and subsequently became a member of the School Curriculum and Assessment Authority Council (Robson, 1996). Colin Hart was made a member of the Schools Examinations and Assessment Council (SEAC) Religious Studies Panel (even though he had never taught or examined RE) until the merger of SEAC and National Curriculum Council to form the School Curriculum and Assessment Authority.

To illustrate the politics of religious education between 1988 and the demise of the Conservative government, I have chosen five 'stories' involving clashes between the Christian right and professional religious educators, or which indicate a hardening and narrowing of government policy on RE, especially during 1993–4.

Politicians and professionals: five stories

The Ealing and Newham Agreed Syllabuses

In 1990 a pressure group called Christians and Tyneside Schools, based in the city of Newcastle upon Tyne, helped to orchestrate a complaint to the Secretary of State for Education about new agreed syllabuses in the strongly multicultural London boroughs of Ealing and Newham, on the grounds that the syllabuses were not 'mainly Christian' and therefore did not follow the letter of section 8(3) of the 1988 Act.[13] The Secretary of State, Kenneth Clarke, took legal advice on the interpretation of section 8(3) before responding. The following points are from the report of the Barrister who was consulted. The passages in italics are direct quotations from his report:[14]

- Shorthand terms to describe the character of RE (for example, 'mainly Christian') should not be used.
  Any shorthand is bound to reflect the views of the author as to the meaning of section 8(3) and is likely to introduce elements of degree, as does 'mainly Christian'.

- RE must include information on all the principal religions represented in Great Britain.
  ... information on all principal religions needs to be given. Further in my view a local authority cannot
  (a) take a purely local viewpoint,
  (b) confine itself to religious education based on Christian traditions or
  (c) exclude from its teaching any of the principal religions represented in Great Britain.
- Agreed syllabuses should include sufficient content for teachers to know what should be included in RE schemes of work.

The barrister's opinion was essentially the interpretation of section 8(3) that was being followed by most RE professionals, and could not have been more supportive of a multifaith approach. A letter was sent out by the Secretary of State's office to all Chief Education Officers and included some of the above points.[15] However, press releases from right-wing MPs were issued which misrepresented the DfE letter as affirming a policy of 'Christian RE' even before CEOs had received it. These were used as the basis for radio and newspaper reports, giving a widespread and erroneous impression of a change in policy. The only significant change, indicated in the letter and later embodied in legislation, is about the *detail* required in an agreed syllabus. Syllabuses could not be brief indications of principle plus some examples of curriculum work. They now had to include sufficient content for teachers to know what should be included in RE schemes of work designed within the school.

A second attack on new syllabuses

With Kenneth Clarke's departure from the Department for Education and with the arrival of John Patten as Secretary of State and Baroness Blatch as Minister of State, the voices of the radical right had a more sympathetic hearing with regard to their views on religious education. Following an analysis of new agreed syllabuses by the National Curriculum Council, some LEAs were asked by the DfE, at Baroness Blatch's request, to state what action they intended to take to ensure that their syllabus 'clearly complies with the requirements of the law'. Once again press reports (prompted by press releases) misrepresented the facts, and the erroneous view was spread that some LEAs had broken the law.[16] The syllabuses in question were

written after the 1988 Act, but *before* the DES letter of March 1992 which incorporated points from the barrister's opinion quoted above. Thus, if any of the syllabuses needed redrafting, it was simply to add more detail for teachers, rather than to change the balance of their content.

The White Paper and the 1993 legislation

In preparing to implement its policy of encouraging the formation of grant maintained (GM) schools,[17] the Government published a 'White Paper' called *Choice and Diversity* in July 1992. Though primarily concerned with the Grant Maintained issue, there were some points relating to religious education, particularly a controversial clause proposing that GM schools should be able to choose an agreed syllabus from any part of the country, regardless of whether the GM school was in an urban or a rural area. The proposal left the way open for GM schools in very multifaith localities to select a syllabus from a rural 'monocultural' area. Many professional bodies sent in their objections to this proposal, pointing out the dangers of a possible racist use of the law, but they were ignored, and the proposal reappeared in the 1992 Bill and the subsequent 1993 legislation.

The 1992 Education Bill, based on the White Paper, was debated in Parliament. In the debates in the Lords, Baroness Cox introduced a 'probing' amendment intended to modify the law in order to increase the amount of Christianity studied in schools. Lord Judd, the front-bench spokesman for the Labour opposition, resisted the arguments vigorously, arguing for a 'professional', broadly based RE. The Baroness withdrew her amendment, but, once again, there was plenty of publicity for the Christian 'cultural heritage' view.[18]

The 1993 Education Act included the point about agreed syllabuses, referred to above, and also required LEAs to appoint a representative from grant maintained schools in their area to the local SACRE and to any agreed syllabus conference convened in the future. Additionally, the new law required that there should be a five-yearly review of agreed syllabuses. Two further requirements on LEAs were introduced, both following lobbying from the Christian Institute and its supporters. The first was that SACRE meetings should be open to the public and the second that both SACREs and agreed syllabus conferences should reflect broadly the proportionate strength of local religious groups in committee A, the committee including representatives of other denominations and religions (UK Government, 1993, paras 26–7). Neither of these requirements has had the effect hoped for by the Christian Institute. Members of the public have hardly been queuing up to attend SACRE meetings, and some SACREs and agreed syllabus conferences have used their powers to coopt non-voting members to ensure the contributions of representatives from religious minorities.

The national model syllabuses

A fourth story is the role of the National Curriculum Council (NCC) and subsequently the School Curriculum and Assessment Authority (SCAA), especially through Barbara Wintersgill, the Professional Officer for RE for the NCC, who then did the equivalent job for SCAA until 1996. Wintersgill managed to steer a liberal course through the politics and pulled off a remarkable achievement in bringing together representatives from different faiths to produce national model syllabuses which include material on six religions in Britain (Christianity, Judaism, Islam, Hinduism, Buddhism and Sikhism).[19] These were produced largely as a result of a whim of the then Secretary of State for Education, John Patten, whose ambivalence about the local arrangements for designing RE syllabuses led to the idea that national models might create more uniformity and higher standards. The two models (SCAA, 1994a and 1994b) are non-statutory and are for the use of agreed syllabus conferences, which can choose to ignore them or can edit or borrow from them. The process of producing the syllabuses was dictated by very tight deadlines prescribed by politicians. Thus there were weaknesses in the ways members of faith groups were selected and consulted, and in the limited number of models produced by SCAA – hardly the 'range' of models it was commissioned to produce. The radical right's fierce objection to any 'thematic' model which juxtaposed material from different religions (see Hull, 1991, on their fear of 'pollution') and their wish to have a high percentage of Christian studies specified for each key stage influenced the process. The bid for percentages was defeated, but no 'thematic' syllabus appeared (see Robson, 1996, for further details). Towards the end of the process, there was a considerable amount of lobbying from

the right, resulting in some clear political interference from the DfE. However, there was also some intense political activity by members of the faith groups on the syllabus monitoring group, whose muscle flexing ensured a reasonable, if not fully inspiring, outcome.

A group of higher education lecturers, as a protest against the marginalisation of representatives from higher education in designing the syllabuses and in an attempt to broaden the approaches offered in the SCAA syllabuses, wrote an 'alternative' model syllabus which they published and wrote about (Baumfield *et al.* 1994a, 1994b, 1995). In response, Barbara Wintersgill made a spirited defence of the SCAA approach (1995).

The model syllabuses have had an influence (OFSTED, 1997), with some Local Education Authority Agreed Syllabus Conferences using them sparingly and creatively. For example, the 1996 Warwickshire syllabus uses a modified version of the aims of one of the syllabuses, but then produces an entirely original syllabus, with SCAA's useful glossary of technical terms included as an appendix (Warwickshire, 1996). The key achievement of the exercise was the involvement of different faith groups at national level, but the way in which the traditions are represented in the models tends to the essentialist and raises some serious issues of interpretation (Everington, 1996; Jackson, 1997).[20]

The 1994 Circular

The final story concerns the publication of non-statutory guidance by the Department for Education in 1994. Circulars, which are sent to all schools, are a standard means of communicating current government interpretations of law; but, as the Circulars themselves declare, 'these documents do not constitute an authoritative legal interpretation of the Education Acts; that is a matter for the courts' (DfE, 1994, p. 1). The first guidance, distributed soon after the publication of the 1988 Act (DES, 1989), gave a liberal interpretation. The draft of the next Circular, sent out for comment in autumn 1993, caused great consternation among professionals, and critical comments were sent to the DfE from many bodies. Circular 1/94 was published on 31 January 1994, and there was widespread dismay at the Department's lack of attention to submissions from professional bodies, teacher unions and faith groups. The Circular was in some ways worse than the draft in terms of a shift to the right in the interpretation of the Education Reform Act's clauses on RE and collective worship.

The interpretation of section 8(3) of the 1988 Act given in Circular 1/94 is very different indeed from that given by the barrister who was consulted by the DES when Kenneth Clarke was Secretary of State. A number of expressions are introduced which reflect the language of the Parliamentary supporters of the Christian Insitute. For example, the notion of 'Christian heritage' is introduced, which is not mentioned in the legislation:

> The legislation governing religious education . . . is designed . . . to ensure that pupils gain both a thorough knowledge of Christianity reflecting *the Christian heritage of this country*, and knowledge of the other principal religions represented in Great Britain. (DfE, 1994, para. 7, p. 10; italics added)

More significantly, the terms 'predominant' and 'predominate' are applied to Christianity's place in syllabuses. This terminology, with its connotations of superior power and domination, comes straight out of the Christian Institute literature (for example, Burn and Hart 1988). It will be recalled that the barrister's opinion, quoted by the DES in the letter to Chief Education Officers sent out on 18 March 1991, specifically warned against the misleading use of shorthand phrases such as 'predominantly Christian' in giving interpretations of section 8(3) of the Act. The Circular, however, includes the following passages:

> Religious education in schools should seek: to develop pupils' knowledge, understanding and awareness of Christianity as the *predominant* religion in Great Britain, and the other principal religions represented in the country; to encourage respect for those holding different beliefs; and to promote pupils' spiritual, moral, cultural and mental development. (Ibid., para. 16, p. 12; italics added)

> As a whole *and at each key stage*,[21] the relative content devoted to Christianity in the syllabus *should predominate*. The syllabus *as a whole* must also include all of the principal religions represented in this country. (Ibid., para. 35, p. 16; italics added)

In this second passage, a very narrow interpretation of section 8(3) of the Act is given which is again very different from that of the Department of Education and Science's barrister in 1990, and is so

directive and specific that it appears to be at variance with the plain meaning of the law.

With regard to collective worship, there are some new interpretations and schools are faced with paradoxical pieces of advice. For something to be worship it has to be 'concerned with reverence or veneration paid to a divine being or power' but 'will necessarily be of a different character from worship amongst a group with beliefs in common' (para. 57). Participation in collective worship means more than passive attendance; it should be capable of 'eliciting a response from pupils' (para. 59). Acts of collective worship should aim to provide the opportunity for pupils to worship God (para. 50); they must also contain elements which 'accord a special status to Jesus Christ' (para. 63). Yet acts of collective worship also should not include 'elements that could compromise the religious integrity of pupils from the other principal religious and faith traditions taking part'!

These contradictions were there in the draft Circular which was sent out for consultation and was widely criticised. For example, as part of the consultation, the Board of Deputies of British Jews had pointed out the offensive nature of the section of the document referring to 'Jesus Christ'. Their submission states:

> This paragraph . . . has caused universal dismay amongst the Jewish community. Whilst we could accept that acts of collective worship could have a broad Christian character, in emphasising an acceptable and universal ethical and moral code, the inclusion of specific reference to Jesus of Nazareth is unacceptable to pupils from non-Christian family backgrounds. (Board of Deputies of British Jews, 1993)

The Board of Deputies of British Jews suggested the following rewording in order to remove the offending passage:

> In the light of the Education Reform 1988 Act that the collective worship organised by the school is to be 'wholly or mainly of a broadly Christian character', the main emphasis of the act of worship should be on the broad traditions of Christianity. (Ibid.)

However, the published version of Circular 1/94 retained the original passage unchanged. So much for consultation. Circular 1/94's paragraphs on collective worship have stirred a good deal of anger within the teaching profession, not least because of assumptions made about pupils and teachers from non-religious backgrounds, and there is evidence of widespread non-compliance with them. The debate is set to continue (see ATL, 1995; Dainton, 1995; Hull, 1995).[22]

RE under the new Labour government

Since the landslide victory by Labour in the May 1997 General Election, religious education debates have gone quiet. The radical right are likely to have few friends at court and presently (September 1997), other items than religious education are higher on the agendas of government Education Ministers. However, the School Curriculum and Assessment Authority has a range of projects and studies in progress related to RE (including work on standards in RE, moving from the agreed syllabus to schemes of work, the use of language in RE, links between RE and the world of work and the impact of the model syllabuses on new agreed syllabuses) and to cognate areas such as moral, spiritual and cultural development, while the DfEE (through a sub-group of the Curriculum and Assessment Division of the Schools Directorate) has post-experience provision in religious education and the support of SACREs as priorities. At the same time OFSTED has begun to produce research data that should help trainers to target specific weaknesses in the subject (OFSTED, 1997). As soon as RE is higher on the ministerial agenda, a replacement for Circular 1/94 is urgently needed.

Observations

On the surface, the stories told above might seem discouraging, the occasional battle lost, the periodic heroic victory, and some stalemates. It must be remembered, however, that, despite ongoing conflict, religious education in the county schools of England and Wales has been revolutionised as far as the legislation is concerned. According to law the subject is unequivocally 'educational' and not 'indoctrinatory'. The 'principal religions' have to be covered by every child, regardless of location in the country, and there is an official acknowledgement, in the form of the national model syllabuses, that those religions include at least six major religious traditions.

It is necessary to step back from the immediacy of political activity in order to offer some analysis of what has been happening in England and Wales. The basic issue seems to be one of defining national identity in relation to religions and cultures. The position of the radical right sees a monolithic culture threatened by the influence of foreign cultures and religions. In its more extreme forms, the radical right position is deeply racist. Racism is by no means a new phenomenon in the United Kingdom, and, of course, Britain's particular situation gets its character largely from its colonial past. Most black and Asian British citizens are descendants of colonised peoples, and popular and media attitudes still tend to be conditioned and influenced by memories of a perceived cultural and racial superiority (Said, 1981). I say 'cultural' as well as 'racial' for, during the 1980s, there was a marked increase in what some writers refer to as 'cultural racism' (Modood, 1992) or 'new racism' (Barker, 1981), based on supposed incompatibility of cultural traditions rather than 'biological' superiority. There have been a number of overt cases of this in the debate about religious education, and a good example is the following statement from a member of the House of Lords during a debate in 1988 on the Education Reform Bill. Here there is a close association of religion and 'race' through the use of a powerful metaphor, an explicitly 'closed' view of culture and religion, and an assumption of a tight relationship between citizenship of the state and a particular form of religious faith:

> If we consider religious faith and precept as the spiritual life-blood of the nation and all its citizens, then effective religious instruction can no more be administered by and to persons of different faiths than can a blood transfusion be safely given without first ensuring blood-group compatibility ... Indiscriminate mixing of blood can prove dangerous and so can the mixing of faiths in education. (*Hansard*, House of Lords, 3 May 1988, col. 419; quoted in Hull, 1991, p. 17)

The way to challenge the cultural separatism of the radical right is by falsification. Not only is there abundant empirical evidence that majority and minority cultures are internally diverse, negotiated and contested (see, for example, Said, 1978; Clifford, 1986; Jackson, 1995, 1997), it is also becoming clear that the descendants of migrants are not 'caught between' two cultures, but often become 'skilled cultural navigators' (Ballard, 1994), competent in a range of different cultural spheres (Jackson 1997, ch. 4; Jackson and Nesbitt, 1993).

Components of their social identity will include being English or British or Welsh or whatever (though clearly such ethnic categories are themselves not fixed), as well as being Christian or Humanist or Muslim or Sikh, and there are many other potential ingredients and influences (Baumann, 1996; Gillespie, 1995) which need not threaten a sense of national identity (Jacobson, 1996).

Political struggles are inevitable, but they should not deter the quest for a socially just RE. Theoretical work, empirical research and curriculum development have to go on as well as politics if the subject is to develop. In terms of structures, to be pragmatic, one has to start where one's own system is. If that system is confessional, then there needs to be theological support for a multifaith approach as well as educational,[23] social and moral justifications, and religious minorities need to have their own voices in the developmental process. In the field of publicly funded chaplaincies in prisons and hospitals in the UK, there is research evidence that Church of England structures can facilitate the effective involvement of religious minorities in a chaplaincy role (Beckford and Gilliat, 1996), though the danger of paternalism is always there.

If justice and fairness (as values of a liberal, pluralistic democracy) are to be promoted through publicly funded education, then perhaps the ideal form of religious education in state-funded schools would be 'secular' but not 'secularist'. RE should be secular in the same way that India regards itself as a secular country rather than a country promoting secularism; there should be no implication of a general secular humanist interpretation of religions. India's secularity is intended as a guarantee of religious freedom and state impartiality towards religious and non-religious diversity. Taking this stance with regard to religious education is fundamentally a pragmatic rather than an ideological one. It is perhaps the only way that one can be confident that different religions and philosophies are dealt with fairly in schools.

The paradox is that some participants in religious education will have religious views which challenge the notion of openness and impartiality. An epistemology based on the authority of revelation is in tension with a view of knowledge based on reason and experience. However, there are better and worse ways of coping with the paradox. One pragmatic solution would entail that those claiming the universal truth and application of a particular way of

life would have to acknowledge that there were others who held different beliefs equally sincerely or lived according to different ways of life. There would need to be some body of shared or 'overlapping' values for this approach to work. For example, a basic principle of the open society – freedom to follow a particular religious or secular way of life under the constraints of the law – would have to be accepted as a pragmatic if not a theological or epistemological basis for religious education. The sensitive application of academic methods and standards would also have to be agreed, although those methods would themselves be open to the critical scrutiny of commentators within religious and secular traditions. For example, the debate about the relationship between personal autonomy and varieties of religious upbringing could be informed and enriched by different religious and secular perspectives on individualism, responsibility and authority.

Resources reflecting the understandings of different academic disciplines would need to be balanced by those presenting the perceptions of different kinds of 'insiders' from the religious traditions. For pupils, the development of skills necessary to gain an understanding of different ways of life would be vital, as would the capacity to form judgements consistently from each person's perspective.

Specialist teachers would be required at all levels, to teach, to coordinate contributions from members of religious communities and to arrange in-service training, and they should be recruited for their professional knowledge and skill, without regard to their religious affiliation or secular stance. The school would need to have an agreed policy on recognising the centrality of religious faith and practice in the lives of some of its pupils, and of affirming the worth of all children, regardless of their religious or secular roots.

There would be some who could never take part in such a 'conversational' approach, though I suspect that educators and parents from a wide range of religious positions – particularly some of the conservative ones who currently feel marginalised or excluded from policy making in religious education – might decide to contribute to it.

We have not yet achieved this in Britain. The debates about heritage and culture will go on, and there is still the paradox of a legal requirement for collective worship, together with a law that says that RE should be non-indoctrinary. Nevertheless, section 8(3) of the 1988 Education Reform Act goes a long way, in principle, towards allowing this kind of religious education. Moreover, although the structural arrangements need some reform, the establishment of Local Authority Standing Advisory Councils for Religious Education, representing different religious, educational and community perspectives, provides an opportunity to influence and develop forms of religious education which are genuinely conversational.

Multifaith RE is an emergent field, encompassing some on-going debates, rather than a body of factual information, and each debate is sure to reflect the historical and political situation and values of the society in which it takes place. There will be some common issues, but lines of argument will vary from society to society, as is illustrated by recent debates in Norway (Østberg, 1997; Skeie, 1997), Germany (Weisse, 1997), South Africa (Chidester *et al.*, 1992; Stonier, 1997; Weisse, 1996), Namibia (Kotzé, 1997; Lombard, 1997) and in various Canadian provinces (Johns, 1985; Milot and Ouellet, 1997; Watson, 1990).

However, whether multifaith RE is taught within a tolerant and open 'confessional' system or a secular system, the view that religions and cultures are monolithic and unchanging, and the belief that such monoliths can be taken as an indicator of national identity, need to be challenged. If they are not, religious minorities from varied cultural backgrounds will at best be treated paternalistically while at the same time being kept on the margins of society.

Notes

1   The Christian Institute and its close relative Christians and Tyneside Schools have published a number of pamphlets on religious education (Burn and Hart, 1998; Burn *et al.*, 1991; Hart 1991, 1994), while the Campaign for Real Education has taken an interest in spiritual, moral and cultural development (Flew and Naylor, 1996).

2   See Jackson (1997, ch. 6) for a refutation of the charge that multifaith approaches to RE necessarily promote relativism over claims to truth.

3   For example, members of the Professional Religious Education Group, consisting of the chairs of the Religious Education Council of England and Wales, the Professional Council for Religious Education, the Conference of University Lecturers in Religious Education, the National Association of Teachers in Further and Higher Education Religious Studies Panel and the Association of Religious Education Advisers, Inspectors and Consultants, worked together to present the views of RE professionals to Government Education Ministers and Opposition Shadow Ministers, and were particularly active during the period 1992–4.

4   For example, the methodology of the Warwick RE Project (for example, Jackson *et al.*, 1994) had an influence on the 1996 Warwickshire Agreed Syllabus (Warwickshire, 1996).

5   For the benefit of readers unfamiliar with education in the United Kingdom, it should be made clear that Scotland and Northern Ireland have their own educational systems. England and Wales have the same legal and educational systems, but educational policy in Wales is implemented through the Welsh Office and curriculum matters are dealt with by the Curriculum Council for Wales. Thus Government Circulars and so on have different reference numbers in Wales and consultations over proposed legislation and guidance in Wales are also conducted separately. Strictly speaking, then, this chapter discusses the legal situation in England and Wales, but with examples of political debates from England.

6   This distinction between the English and Welsh systems is maintained in the 1988 legislation.

7   Examples include Birmingham (1975), Dudley (1979) and Redbridge (1987).

8   The 1944 Act also had a requirement for a daily act of collective worship, but it did not specify the object of worship. The paradox of acts of worship (compulsory unless parents withdrew children on the grounds of conscience) alongside an RE that was becoming established as non-confessional caused some professionals to advocate the abolition of the former as a legal requirement (Hull, 1974).

9   The dual system was kept intact in 1988, with no significant differences *for RE* in voluntary aided schools. Here we will concentrate on 'county' schools which are fully state funded.

10 The term 'religious education' was actually used in the 1944 Act to indicate religious instruction and collective worship taken together.

11 There had been an earlier lobbying group with this name involving some of the same professional bodies, but with a different membership. For most of the period under discussion, the re-formed PREG consisted of Gwen Palmer (REC); Jeremy Taylor (PCFRE); Paul Bellingham (later replaced by Angela Wood) (AREIAC); Liz Payne-Ahmadi (NATFHE); Robert Jackson (CULRE).

12 There is no space for a detailed discussion of collective worship. In addition to legislation on religious education, the 1988 Act added some new clauses on collective worship. 'Collective worship' had been a daily requirement in all maintained schools since 1944. By the 1970s, many schools offered 'assemblies', sometimes dealing with religious topics, but often exploring

moral or community issues. Apart from the use of hymns or songs and the occasional prayer, many assemblies could hardly be described as 'worship' in any conventional sense. The 1988 Act changed this, requiring that daily acts of collective worship should be 'wholly or mainly of a broadly Christian character'. The non-statutory guidance following the Act (DES, 1989) allowed a liberal interpretation of the Act's requirements, and secular material and material from religions other than Christianity were held to be appropriate for use in collective worship, provided they were consistent with the 'broad traditions of Christian belief'. John Hull's (1989) commentary on the Act took a similar view. Circular 1/94 (DES, 1994), as will be indicated below, took a much harder line.

13   This body, in effect, became the so-called Christian Institute, with leading figures including Colin Hart and John Burn.

14   Unpublished barrister's opinion dated 12 June 1990.

15   DES letter to Chief Education Officers dated 18 March 1991. The letter includes extracts from the legal advice given to the Secretary of State, Kenneth Clarke.

16   See Robson (1996) for a more detailed account. See also Palmer (1993 and 1994) for more general discussions of the politics of RE during this period.

17   This policy takes away financial control and management from local authorities, devolving it directly to schools.

18   The Professional Religious Education Group (PREG) was effective in informing members of the House of Lords and representatives of various faith groups of the implications of the Cox amendment.

19   Humanism was not included on the grounds that there had been an earlier court ruling (not in the context of RE) that it was not a religion. Humanists have also felt marginalised from Agreed Syllabus Conferences and SACREs, being excluded from the committee representing 'other' Christian denominations and non-Christian religions. Many SACREs and AS conferences have coopted humanist members or have ensured a humanist presence on the committee which includes representatives of teachers.

20   From the academic year 1997–8, the Teacher Training Agency has required all students training to be primary teachers and all secondary specialist religious education students to have a working knowledge of the model syllabuses. This decision was made on the recommendation of SCAA as a means to give students some information that would be more likely to be transferable from one local authority to another than knowledge gained through the study of one or two 'official' locally agreed syllabuses. This policy may result in a wider influence of the model syllabuses.

21   For the benefit of readers outside England and Wales, key stages (ks) were introduced when the National Curriculum was established in 1988. Ks 1 is 5–7 years; ks 2 is 7–11; ks 3 is 11–14; ks 4 is 14–16.

22   More generally on the issue on non-compliance, see Cooper (1995).

23   I would maintain that a fundamental educational aim for RE is to develop an understanding of the grammar – the language and wider symbolic patterns – of religions and the interpretative skills necessary to gain that understanding. However, I would also argue that the achievement of this aim necessitates the development of critical skills which open up issues of representation and interpretation of religions, as well as questions of truth and meaning. Finally, I would assert the inseparability of understanding and reflection in the interpretative process, and suggest that 'edification' should be a further educational goal for the subject (see Jackson, 1997, ch. 6).

References

Alves, C. (1991) Just a matter of words? The religious education debates in the House of Lords. *British Journal of Religious Education* **13**(3), 168–74.

Association of Teachers and Lecturers (ATL) (1995) *Collective Worship: Policy and Practice.* London: Association of Teachers and Lecturers.

Ballard, R. (ed.) (1994) *Desh Pardesh: The South Asian Presence in Britain.* London: Hurst.

Barker, M. (1981) *The New Racism.* London: Junction Books.

Baumann, G. (1996) *Contesting Culture: Discourses Identity in Multi-ethnic London.* Cambridge: Cambridge University Press.

Baumfield, V., Bowness, C., Cush, D. and Miller, J. (1994a) *A Third Perspective.* Plymouth: University College of St Mark and St John.

Baumfield, V., Bowness, C., Cush, D. and Miller, J. (1994b) Model syllabuses: a contribution. *Journal of Beliefs and Values* **15** (1).

Baumfield, V., Bowness, C., Cush, D. and Miller, J. (1995) Model syllabuses: the debate continues. *Resource* **18** (1), 3–6.

Beckford, J. and Gilliat, S. (1996) *The Church of England and Other Faiths in a Multi-faith Society,* 2 vols. Coventry: University of Warwick, Department of Sociology.

Birmingham (1975) *Agreed Syllabus for Religious Instruction.* Birmingham: City of Birmingham Education Authority.

Board of Deputies of British Jews (1993) Unpublished submission to the DfE as part of the consultation on the Draft Circular on Religious Education and Collective Worship. London: Board of Deputies of British Jews.

Brown, A. (1995) Changing the agenda: whose agenda? *British Journal of Religious Education* **17** (3), 148–56.

Burn, J. and Hart, C. (1988) *The Crisis in Religious Education.* London: Educational Research Trust.

Burn, J., Hart, C. and Holloway, D. (1991) *From Acts to Action*. Newcastle upon Tyne: Christian Institute.

Chidester, D., Mitchell, G. *et al.* (1992) *Religion in Public Education: Policy Options for a New South Africa*. Cape Town: Institute for Comparative Religion in Southern Africa.

Clifford, J. (1986) Introduction: partial truths. In J. Clifford and G. Marcus (eds), *Writing Culture: The Poetics and Politics of Ethnography*, Berkeley, CA: University of California Press, pp. 1–26.

Cole, W. O. (ed.) (1972) *Religion in the Multifaith School*, Bradford: Yorkshire Committee for Community Relations.

Cooling, T. (1994) *A Christian Vision for State Education*. London: SPCK.

Coombs, A. (1988) Diluting the faith. *Education* 26 August.

Cooper, D. (1995) Defiance and non-compliance: religious education and the implementation problem. *Current Legal Problems* 253–79.

Copley, T. (1996) A tribute to John Hull: a review of editorials in *Learning for Living* and the *British Journal of Religious Education*, 1971–1996. *British Journal of Religious Education* 19 (1), 5–12.

Copley, T. (1997) *Teaching Religion: Fifty Years of Religious Education in England and Wales*. Exeter: University of Exeter Press.

Cox, E. (1966) *Changing Aims in Religious Education*. London: Routledge.

Dainton, S. (1995) Collective worship: reaching a consensus. *Resource* 18 (1), 11–16.

Department of Education and Science (DES) (1989) *The Education Reform Act 1988: Religious Education and Collective Worship*, Circular 3/89. London: Department of Education and Science.

Department for Education (DfE) (1994) *Religious Education and Collective Worship*, Circular 1/94. London: Department for Education.

Dudley (1979) *The Agreed Syllabus of Religious Education*. Dudley: Dudley Metropolitan Borough Education Service.

Everington, J. (1996) A question of authenticity: the relationship between educators and practitioners in the representation of religious traditions. *British Journal of Religious Education* 18 (2), 69–77.

FARE (1991) *Forms of Assessment in Religious Education*. Exeter: University of Exeter.

Flew, A. and Naylor, F. (1996) *Spiritual Development and All That Jazz*, Paper 25. York: Campaign for Real Education.

Gillespie, M. (1995) *Television, Ethnicity and Cultural Change*. London: Routledge.

Hart, C. (1991) *From Acts to Action*. Newcastle upon Tyne: Christians and Tyneside Schools.

Hart, C. (1994) *RE: Changing the Agenda*. Newcastle upon Tyne: Christian Institute.

Hinnells, J.R. (ed.) (1970) *Comparative Religion in Education*. Newcastle upon Tyne: Oriel Press.

Hull, J.M. (1974) *School Worship: An Obituary*. London: SCM Press.

Hull, J.M. (1989) *The Act Unpacked*. Derby: Christian Education Movement.

Hull, J.M. (1991) *Mish Mash: Religious Education in Multicultural Britain. A Study in Metaphor*, Birmingham Papers in Religious Education. Derby: Christian Education Movement.

Hull, J.M. (1995) Collective worship: the search for spirituality. In *Future Progress in Religious Education* [the Templeton Lectures at the RSA]. London: Royal Society of Arts, pp. 27–38.

Hull, J.M. (1996) Editorial. *British Journal of Religious Education* 18 (3).

Jackson, R. (1989) Fortifying religious education. *Resource* 11 (3), 5–6.

Jackson, R. (1990) Religious studies and developments in religious education in England and Wales. In U. King (ed.), *Turning Points in Religious Studies*. Edinburgh: T. & T. Clark, pp. 102–17.

Jackson, R. (1992) The misrepresentation of religious education. In M. Leicester and M. Taylor (eds), *Ethics, Ethnicity and Education*. London: Kogan Page, pp. 100–13.

Jackson, R. (1995) Religious education's representation of 'religions' and 'cultures'. *British Journal of Educational Studies* 43 (3), 272–89.

Jackson, R. (1997) *Religious Education: An Interpretive Approach*. London: Hodder & Stoughton.

Jackson, R. and Nesbitt, E. (1993) *Hindu Children in Britain*. Stoke-on-Trent, Staffs.: Trentham.

Jackson, R., Barratt, M. and Everington, J. (1994) *Bridges to Religions: Teacher's Resource Book*, The Warwick RE Project. Oxford: Heinemann.

Jacobson, J. (1996) British national identity and young Pakistani Muslims. Unpublished paper for conference on 'Multicultultural competence: a resource for tomorrow', Bergen, August.

Johns, E.L. (ed.) (1985) *Religious Education Belongs in the Public Schools: Theory for a Multi-cultural, Inter-faith Approach*. Toronto: Ecumenical Study Commission on Public Education.

King, J. with Helme, D. (eds) (1994) *Teaching RE in Secondary Schools: Ideas from the Classroom*. Crowborough, Sussex: Monarch.

Kotzé, M. (1997) Looking at the Namibian syllabi. In T. Andree, C. Bakker and P. Schreiner (eds), *Crossing Boundaries: Contributions to Interreligious and Intercultural Education*. Munster: Comenius Institut, pp. 101–10.

Lombard, C. (1997) Contextual and theoretical considerations in the Namibian curricular process. In T. Andree, C. Bakker and P. Schreiner (eds), *Crossing Boundaries: Contributions to Interreligious and Intercultural Education*. Munster: Comenius Institute, pp. 111–23.

Marratt, H. (1996) Letter to the editor. *British Journal of Religious Education*, 19 (1), 32.

McIntyre, J. (1978) *Multi-culture and Multifaith Societies: Some Examinable Assumptions*, Occasional Paper. Oxford: Farmington Institute for Christian Studies.

Milot, Micheline and Ouellet, Fernand (eds) (1997) *Religion, éducation et démocratie: un enseignement culturel de la religion est-il possible?* Montreal: L'Harmattan.

Modood, T. (1992) On not being white in Britain: discrimination, diversity and commonality. In M. Leicester and M. Taylor (eds), *Ethics, Ethnicity and Education*. London: Kogan Page, pp. 72–87.

Office for Standards in Education (OFSTED) (1994) *Religious Education and Collective Worship 1992–3*. London: Her Majesty's Stationery Office.

Office for Standards in Education (OFSTED) (1995) *Religious Education: A Review of Inspection Findings 1993/94*. London: Her Majesty's Stationery Office.

Office for Standards in Education (OFSTED) (1997) *The Impact of New Agreed Syllabuses on the Teaching and Learning of Religious Education*. London: Her Majesty's Stationery Office.

Orchard, S. (1991) What was wrong with religious education? An analysis of HMI reports 1985–1988. *British Journal of Religious Education* 14 (1), 15–21.

Østberg, S. (1997) Religious education in a multicultural society: the quest for identity and dialogue. In T. Andree, C. Bakker and P. Schreiner (eds), *Crossing Boundaries: Contributions to Interreligious and Intercultural Education*. Munster, Comenius Institute, pp. 147–53.

Palmer, G. (1993) Politics and religious education. *Resource* 16 (1), 2–6.

Palmer, G. (1994) Religious education: over to you! *Resource* 17 (1), 2–5.

Redbridge (1987) *Religious Education for Our Children*. Redbridge: London Borough of Redbridge.

Religious Education Council (REC) (1988) *Religious Education: Supply of Teachers for the 1990s*. Lancaster: Religious Education Council of England and Wales.

Religious Education Council (REC) (1990) *What Conspired Against RE Specialist Teacher Supply?* Lancaster: Religious Education Council of England and Wales.

Robson, G. (1996) Religious education, government policy and professional practice, 1988–95. *British Journal of Religious Education* 19 (1), 13–23.

Said, E. (1978) *Orientalism*. London: Routledge & Kegan Paul.

Said, E. (1981) *Covering Islam*. London: Routledge & Kegan Paul.

School Curriculum and Assessment Authority (SCAA) (1994a) *Model Syllabuses for Religious Education. Model 1: Living Faiths Today*. London: School Curriculum and Assessment Authority.

School Curriculum and Assessment Authority (SCAA) (1994b) *Model Syllabuses for Religious Education. Model 2: Questions and Teaching*. London: School Curriculum and Assessment Authority.

Schools Council (1971) *Religious Education in Secondary Schools*, Schools Council Working Paper no. 36. London: Evans/Methuen.

Skeie, G. (1997) Some aspects of RE in Scandinavia and Norway: an outline of a cultural approach to RE. In T. Andree, C. Bakker and P. Schreiner (eds), *Crossing Boundaries: Contributions to Interreligious and Intercultural Education*. Munster: Comenius Institut, pp. 155–60.

Smart, N. (1967) A new look at religious studies: the Lancaster idea. *Learning for Living* 7 (1), 27–9.

Smart, N. (1968) *Secular Education and the Logic of Religion*. London, Faber & Faber.

Stonier, J. (1997) A chorus of voices. In T. Andree, C. Bakker and P. Schreiner (eds), *Crossing Boundaries: Contributions to Interreligious and Intercultural Education*. Munster: Comenius Institut, pp. 169–74.

UK Government (1988) *Education Reform Act*. London: Her Majesty's Stationery Office.

UK Government (1993) *Education Act*. London: Her Majesty's Stationery Office.

Warwickshire (1996) *Warwickshire Agreed Syllabus for Religious Education*. Warwick: Warwickshire County Council.

Watson, G. (1990) *The Report of the Ministerial Inquiry on Religious Education in Ontario Public Elementary Schools*. Toronto: Government of Ontario.

Weisse, W. (ed.) (1996) *Interreligious and Intercultural Education: Methodologies, Conceptions and Pilot Projects in South Africa, Namibia, Great Britain, the Netherlands and Germany*. Munster: Comenius Institut.

Weisse, W. (1997) Dialogical religious education. In Trees Andree, C. Bakker and P. Schreiner (eds), *Crossing Boundaries: Contributions to Interreligious and Intercultural Education*, Munster: Comenius Institut, 33–44.

Westhill College (1989) *Attainment in RE*. Birmingham: Westhill College.

Westhill College (1991) *Assessing, Recording and Reporting RE*. Birmingham: Westhill College.

Wilkins, R. (1991) How can an evangelical Christian teach multi-faith RE? *Resource* 13 (3), 1–3.

Wintersgill, B. (1995) The case of the missing models: exploding the myths. *Resource* 18 (1), 6–11.

Wright, A. (1996) Language and experience in the hermeneutics of religious understanding. *British Journal of Religious Education* 18 (3), 166–80.

10 Religious Education: Cinderella Does Go to the Ball

DEREK BASTIDE

The history of religious education in recent decades has been one of a remarkable adaptation to changing attitudes and circumstances and, although it is operating against a background of diminishing formal religious practice, it seems to be emerging at the end of the process in a stronger position than it was in at the beginning. This chapter will focus upon developments since the 1944 Education Act which established RE firmly on the school curriculum, pick out the landmarks on the way to the new RE settlement in the 1988 Education Reform Act and then on to developments which have followed it. The two underlying questions are: What should RE be aiming to do? and What should the content be?

Prior to the Foster Education Act of 1870 most schools were maintained by voluntary organisations, mainly religious, the two principal ones being the National Society (Church of England) and the British and Foreign Society (Non-Conformist). It was natural, therefore, that religious teaching and observance should have a significant place in these schools. When the 1870 Act embodied a vision of universal elementary education, it was agreed that local School Boards should be set up to establish schools in areas where one did not already exist. This policy of filling the gaps meant that publicly funded Board Schools were set up alongside voluntary schools and so, incidentally, the dual system was established which still exists today. In early considerations as to nature of the curriculum to be offered in these new Board Schools, an inevitable question referred to religion: should religion appear in the curriculum and, if so, what form should it take? The latter question was resolved by the Cowper–Temple clause, which laid down that religious teaching in the new schools should not be given 'by means of any catechism or formulary which is distinctive of any particular religious denomination'. This usually meant that RE was developed as Bible teaching, the Bible being one of the few things which all the Christian churches had in common; and thus began the tradition that the syllabus for RE was the Bible – a situation which was to remain for almost a century.

Religious education in the 1944 Education Act

The next major landmark in the story of RE was the 1944 Education Act. In this Act RE was made a required part of the school curriculum; in fact it was the only subject in that position. The Act had four main requirements with reference to RE (or RI (religious instruction) as it was called in the Act):

1 that religious instruction should be given in every county school;
2 that each day should begin with an act of worship;
3 that there should be a right of withdrawal on the grounds of conscience from both RI and worship by both teachers and parents (on behalf of their children);
4 that each local education authority should formulate its agreed syllabus for use in its area (or alternatively adopt as its own the agreed syllabus of another authority).

Although it is not stated explicitly, it was assumed universally that religious instruction meant Christian instruction. This can be seen clearly from the record of Parliamentary debates in *Hansard* and also from the way in which the Act was implemented. It is also clear that what the Act had in mind was *teaching Christianity* and not *teaching about Christianity.* This is strongly implied by the introduction of the conscience clause – teaching *about* Christianity should hardly offend the conscience – and also by the act of worship.

In addition to this, the more detailed arrangements for drawing up an agreed syllabus are a further indication of the overwhelmingly Christian nature of the enterprise. The syllabus had to be agreed by those who were felt to have a special interest in the teaching of RE, namely elected councillors (representing the local education authority and the electorate at large), the Church of England (as the established church), other denominations and teachers themselves (normally through their unions or professional associations). These four groups together formed what was called a Standing Conference whose responsibility it was to see to the creation of a syllabus on which they all agreed. It was very clear that the other denominations referred to are other *Christian* denominations such as Methodists, Baptists, Quakers and so on. It might be possible for a humanist or a member of another religious faith to be a member of a Standing Conference but this would be in a private capacity as a councillor or as a teacher representative.

The overwhelmingly Christian nature of the enterprise is reinforced by the agreed syllabuses which emerged in the 1940s from the many standing conferences. The following two extracts on the aims of RE from two syllabuses of this vintage illustrate this very well:

> Finally it is well to remember that the ultimate aim in religious education is not to get over to the child a body of facts – or 'inert ideas' to use Professor Whitehead's phrase – but to inculcate and foster a comprehensible Way of Life. This Way of Life is summed up in the words of Our Lord: 'Thou shalt love the Lord thy God with all thy heart, and with all thy soul, and with all thy mind . . . and thy neighbour as thyself.' (LCC, 1947)

> The aim of the Syllabus is to secure that children attending the schools of the County . . . may gain knowledge of the common Christian faith held by their fathers for nearly two thousand years; may seek for themselves in Christianity the beliefs and principles which give true purpose to life; and may find inspiration, power and courage to work for their own welfare, for that of their fellow creatures, and for the growth of God's kingdom. (Surrey County Council, 1947)

It is clear from these two syllabus aims that religious education was seen, to use a technical expression, in *confessional* terms. In other words, the assumption upon which RE was taught was the truth of Christianity, both as an interpretation of the nature of existence and as a set of principles and values which could or should be the basis of individual lives. It is probably true to say that this reflected the views of the large majority of the population at that time. However, there were groups such as the British Humanist Association and the National Secular Society which were outside this consensus and they naturally adopted a hostile stance to such an approach to the teaching of religion in county schools. For them a right to withdraw from RE and the act of worship was a necessary legal mechanism to protect the integrity of both non-believing teachers and parents. Ideally, though, they wanted what they saw as religious 'indoctrination' removed from the county school.

It is clear from this that there was a general consensus during this period that RE should be confessional in aim and this is reflected in the wide range of agreed syllabuses which appeared at this time, of which the two quoted above are examples. The main concern, therefore, which confronted standing conferences, given the generally agreed framework of aims and purposes, was what *content* should they agree. Here a survey of a number of agreed syllabuses of the period shows again that the chosen subject was the Bible, which became a textbook for RE. Along with the Bible went a consideration of key Christian festivals, but the recommended work there was largely the biblical stories which formed the origin of the festival.

To take the London Syllabus of Religious Education (LCC, 1947) as an example: for infants (from 5 to 7+ years) the content lays down that pupils should learn about the festivals of Christmas, Epiphany, Easter, Ascension, Whitsun and Harvest and then encounter other Bible stories under the following themes: the childhood of Jesus; the work and teaching of Jesus; Old Testament stories heard by Jesus; kind deeds of Jesus; some stories told by Jesus; and people who helped Jesus.

For juniors (from 7+ to 11+ years), three sections were laid down: (a) the Bible; (b) the Christian life; (c) Christian worship. In this all the content was drawn directly from the Bible with the exception of a section entitled 'Heroes of Christianity' which listed significant saints and martyrs, missionaries and social reformers who drew their inspiration from Christianity.

At secondary level (from 11+ to 18), pupils returned again to the Bible and looked at similar issues but at a deeper level. The structure consisted of three sections: the Old Testament: the New Testament; and Christian thought and history. It is interesting to note that other world faiths are mentioned in the third section under the sub-heading of 'Religions contemporary with Christianity'. Here there are notes on Judaism, mystery religions, gnosticism, Hinduism, Buddhism, Islam, Confucianism, Taoism and Shintoism, but there is a tendency to represent them negatively through critical Christian eyes.

This syllabus is a fair example of the agreed syllabuses which were being produced across the country at this time and represented the sort of religious teaching which most pupils received in school. In broad terms it was generally acceptable because it represented the general view of most people of the period. The general approach can be characterised as a form of *Christian nurture* in that children were being inducted into a culture of Christian thought, language and literature. However, in the late 1950s and the 1960s changes began to take place in the religious composition of the country and, in addition to this, research into children's understanding of religious concepts and ideas began to have a profound effect upon both the aims and the content of RE which led to a transformation of the agreed syllabuses which had emerged at this period. Before that happened, though, there was a 'final' attempt to resurrect the Christian nurture approach in a guise that was less Bible centred and more attuned to the needs and interests of children and young people.

The contribution of Goldman and the neo-confessionalists

In the late 1950s concern was growing among many concerned with RE in schools about what might be seen as the failure of RE. In the fifteen years of religious teaching after the passing of the Butler Act in 1944, there seemed to be evidence of widespread ignorance of religion. One significant survey in 1961, undertaken by the University of Sheffield Institute of Education, presented the results of investigations by a group of teachers into the levels of attainment of 14- and 15-year-old pupils. This survey showed that after ten years of schooling following agreed syllabuses which were

largely Bible centred there was widespread ignorance of matters religious. The report showed, for example, that the ability of pupils to put into chronological order key events in the history of Israel was poor and that many pupils had no notion of what a prophet was and only a quarter could name even one. Although these may not be regarded by all as the best markers of a religious knowledge, this ignorance was seen as significant because it was clear evidence that the material taught was not being absorbed by the pupils and so was not sticking. Further to this, the report noted:

> One significant result of the survey was to supply evidence that for many children there was little correlation between the factual knowledge gained through education and a faith by which to live.   (University of Sheffield, 1961)

It was this concern about the lack of success of RE in fostering either an information approach or a faith-nurturing approach to RE which led a number of liberal Christian educators to pioneer a new approach, an approach which has often been described as 'neo-confessional'. This approach was still at root faith-nurturing but rather than being Bible-centred it took as its starting point the experience of the pupil. One of the best known of this group was Harold Loukes whose *Teenage Religion* (1961) was a formidable force in the development of discussion methods in school which attempted both to lead pupils from where they actually were in their thinking and also to show how Christianity had a relevance to the daily acts and issues of life.

While Loukes was of considerable importance in the development of the teaching of RE in secondary schools in this period, the figure of Ronald Goldman was beginning to build his influence on RE across all phases of education but perhaps mostly in the primary school. Goldman, who was a psychologist by training, shared this concern about the apparent failure of RE, or perhaps more precisely, of Christian nurture in schools. Again a neo-confessional – 'we teach Christianity because it is true' – Goldman was concerned about such research findings as the Sheffield report and became deeply interested in the way that children are able to develop religious *concepts*. Out of his research, Goldman produced the highly authoritative *Religious Thinking from Childhood to Adolescence*, (1964) and from this, in the following year, he produced *Readiness for Religion* (1965) which examined the implications of his work for teachers and for schools. It is important to note that Goldman's research was concerned with the understanding of concepts – not, for example, with religious feelings.

While it is not necessary to go into detail about Goldman's work here, it is important to note a few key points. Goldman's research and particularly his interviewing of children convinced him that much of RE in his day was unsuited to the conceptual development of the children it was seeking to nurture. His findings led him to posit a Piagetian model of conceptual development in which children passed through stages. He found that many of the stories from the Bible presented to children were complex and that children were often confused by them. In his interviewing, Goldman focused upon three Bible stories: Moses and the burning bush; the crossing of the Red Sea; and the temptations of Jesus in the wilderness. His detailed questioning of children aged from 5 to 15 revealed a large number of misunderstandings and muddles, many of which might make charming reading but they did have serious implications for the development of the children's religious understanding. While others argued that children inevitably resolve their muddles as their understanding develops, Goldman retorted that immature understanding of religious concepts could lead to negative attitudes to religion. When this happened, and Goldman found it all too commonly, the child dismissed religion altogether, and so immature ideas and understanding were never challenged and therefore continued into adulthood.

Goldman characterised his first main stage, which equated roughly with key stage 1 (that is, up to the mental age of 7), as *pre-operational*: in which the child's thinking is limited by egocentricity and monofocalism. He saw this as a *pre-religious stage* in which the child is largely incapable of understanding religious concepts. He called his second main stage *concrete operational* (roughly, mental age 7–12/13 years) which he characterised as *sub-religious*: in which the child is capable of grasping religious ideas but understanding is limited by a difficulty in grasping *abstract* concepts. After this stage, pupils finally pass into the *abstract operational* stage: in which these earlier limitations of understanding largely cease to operate. There has been much discussion of Goldman's research methods and conclusions over the years and he has both supporters and detractors. Our concern in this

chapter is not the extent to which Goldman was right but the influence he had upon the development of RE.

From his work, Goldman drew the considerable conclusion that the Bible was not a children's book and that it was therefore unsuited to be the centre of an RE syllabus. He did not say that all of the Bible was unsuitable for children but that a teacher needed to select biblical material carefully – and there was a lot to choose from. Like Loukes, Goldman advocated working from children's first-hand experience and developed what he called Life Themes which started from the child's experience and sought to develop and explore this in depth. Examples of Life Themes were homes, families, friends, hands, journeys and many, many more. There was a theology behind these themes and this drew on the work of a number of theologians notably Paul Tillich whose writings were very popular at the time. In addition to Life Themes, Goldman also advocated Bible themes such as sheep and shepherds, bread and light, in which children explored biblical imagery which was now largely outside their immediate experience. The London Agreed Syllabus *Learning for Life* (ILEA, 1968) is a good exponent of this approach.

Goldman, although now largely unknown to the younger generation of RE teachers, had two considerable effects upon the development of RE. First, he made teachers and planners aware that RE was no different from mathematics and all the other subjects which make up the curriculum: that children's understanding of religious concepts does develop and it is most important that the child's level of understanding is a foremost priority in decisions about the content of RE. As Goldman often remarked: no one would dream of reading a *Times* leader to 5-year-olds but often in RE a biblical account of similarly difficulty would be read to the children without even a thought. After Goldman it would be difficult to imagine this occurring. Perhaps his most enduring contribution is therefore the way he introduced a more professional and educational approach to the planning and teaching of RE based upon an understanding of the way in which children learn.

Second, and this is a more negative legacy, it could be argued that he had a large responsibility for the disappearance of RE in many primary schools, certainly among the younger children. Many teachers, already aware of the difficulties of teaching RE, simply lost their nerve. This seems to have come about partly because, although Goldman himself was very careful to correct the impression in his writings, the message spread among teachers that the Bible was not a suitable book for the primary school and therefore was best avoided in case children became confused. Unfortunately, the rationale behind Life Themes, intended by Goldman to form the new approach to RE, was quite subtle and it eluded many teachers who were unfamiliar with the work of Tillich. Proponents of Life Themes often talked about the RE being implicit, but this often confused non-specialist teachers even more. So RE, certainly among young children in the primary school, foundered and Life Themes were reduced to such topics as 'People who help us' and even to the care of pets. Of course, these two should not be seen as unimportant but few would agree that this is really the stuff of RE.

Changes in British society and their implications for RE

During the 1950s and 1960s other changes were taking place which were to have considerable implications for the development of RE. The principal change was caused by the arrival in Britain of passport holders from the West Indies and from the Indian sub-continent. While very many of the Afro-Caribbean immigrants were of Christian background, the large majority of those from the Indian sub-continent were practising members of other religions, notably Hinduism, Islam and Sikhism. These groups, for a variety of social and economic reasons, tended to settle in specific areas of the country, and as family and community life was established in Britain, mandirs, mosques and gurdwaras appeared and schools received pupils who were believing and practising members of religions other than Christianity. This could not help but have an impact upon the teaching of RE, especially in those schools and indeed in those areas where other religions were represented in the classroom, and inevitably it challenged the traditional confessional (and indeed neo-confessional) approach to RE with its nurturing overtones. Allied with this was a loosening of the attachment to Christianity. The 1960s, in particular, saw a steep drop in Christian practice especially in terms of church attendance.

These two developments taken together raised strong questions about the sort of aims which were appropriate to teaching RE in a multifaith situation. Inevitably the questions were asked more insistently in schools and localities which were multicultural and multifaith than they were in rural fastnesses, but it soon became clear that these questions were being both raised and addressed at a national level. Two instances of this are the Durham Report (Commission on Religious Education, 1970) and the Schools Council (1971) Working Paper 36, *Religious Education in the Secondary School*.

The Durham Report

The Durham Report, the name given to the Church of England Commission on Religious Education in Schools (1970) chaired by the Bishop of Durham, although set up by a religious body was in no doubt that Christian nurture in any form was no longer appropriate for the county school and it drew a clear distinction between the aims in religious teaching of the church or mosque on the one hand and of the county school on the other. It argued that RE should be much more concerned with skills and understanding:

> The aim of religious education should be to explore the place and significance of religion in human life and so to make a distinctive contribution to each pupil's search for a faith by which to live . . . The teacher is thus seeking rather to initiate his [*sic*] pupils into knowledge which he encourages them to explore and appreciate, than into a system which he requires them to accept. To press for acceptance of a particular faith or belief system is the duty and the privilege of the churches and other similar religious bodies. It is certainly not the task of the teacher in the county school. If a teacher is to press for any conversion, it is conversion from a shallow and unreflective attitude to life. If he is to press for commitment, it is commitment to the religious quest, to that search for meaning, purpose and value which is open to all men.

Working Paper 36

The Durham Report had a considerable impact on thinking about the nature and purpose of RE, not least because it was produced by a major religious body. It was followed in the succeeding year by the Schools Council Working Paper 36, *Religious Education in the Secondary School* (a working paper intended to raise questions for discussion and not a report), which was to prove seminal in the development of RE. The Schools Council Project on Religious Education in the Secondary School based at the University of Lancaster produced the working paper. The director of the project was Ninian Smart, Professor of Religious Studies at the University of Lancaster, and the Deputy Director, Donald Horder. The working paper was highly significant for three main reasons:

1   it proposed aims which were more appropriate to the changing composition and climate of society;
2   it proposed a definite focus upon the teaching of a range of religions;
3   it introduced the work of Ninian Smart to a wider range of people.

Ninian Smart had developed a radically new approach to the study of religion in the university, very different from the traditional approach of theology, and it was his ideas which began to provide the theoretical undergirding of the recommended approach to RE.

The working paper took the view that the 'confessional' approach to the teaching of RE, though entirely proper in a faith community, was inappropriate in schools which served a multifaith society. What it took to be appropriate for the county school was that children should have an opportunity to study religion in an open way so that they could gain some appreciation of what it meant to people to belong to a religion and to be introduced to those existential questions of meaning and purpose which religions deal with and most people ask of themselves at some point in their lives. A central maxim of Smart's approach is that religious education must transcend the informative. Pupils should be helped to see religions from the inside so that they can begin to appreciate attitudes and feelings of those within: to stand in other people's shoes.

If it is to be effective with lively minded pupils, RE must also be *open* and recognise that there are differences of belief and approach. What is expected of teachers is that they should be able and willing to portray fairly and without bias any viewpoint, which might arise in their teaching. In this way an agnostic teacher should be able to present a religious faith with sympathy and understanding and also a religiously committed teacher should be able to present a philosophy such as Humanism or Marx-

ism in a way which would seem fair to its subscribers.

This *open* approach automatically assumed that RE in schools must deal with a range of religions. This was entirely appropriate for a multifaith society but the working party also raised questions about what was meant by a religion. Traditionally (and this can be seen in the historical approach to RE), religion tends to be seen principally as a system of beliefs out of which arises a code of conduct. The working paper argued that this is a totally inadequate view; there is far more to a living religion than that:

> For example, when studying a given religion, one might distinguish first the 'observable' aspects – ritual, custom, buildings, books, etc. One might then study the teaching of the religion, the ideas and beliefs which underlie the observable aspects. After this one could go on to discover what these external phenomena mean to the people involved in and committed to the religion – the 'experiential' or existential aspect. In fact, without this data, a true understanding and appreciation of the religion will not be possible.   (Schools Council, 1971, p. 47)

This new understanding of religion (for many RE purposes at least) as a living activity is further supported by Smart's (1968) analysis of religion as a six-dimensional activity (in 1989 this was extended to a seven-dimensional activity, though this makes little difference to our understanding here). Smart identified the doctrinal, the mythological (that is, story), the ethical, the ritual, the experiential and the social dimensions. These dimensions, which, of course, are all interrelated, attempt to describe how wide an activity any religion is and they have subsequently formed a very solid foundation for the development of RE in both primary and secondary schools and as such have been of immense influence across the country.

Not only did the working paper encourage teachers and others to see religion in a wider sense, it also tried to extend the notion of what might constitute a faith and would therefore be appropriate for inclusion in an RE agreed syllabus. For example, Humanism is a movement, which in no way draws upon the supernatural and as such would not normally be classified as a religion. However, it does respond, as religions do, to the fundamental questions of existence and its response to them has many of the qualities of a faith. From this faith flows also a morality. Movements such as Humanism –

and also Marxism – have often subsequently been described as 'non-religious stances for living' and have found their way into some agreed syllabuses.

The legacy of Working Paper 36

The working paper contributed considerably to the direction in which RE developed in the country, and its emphases upon personal search, upon a study of religions as living activities based on Smart's six dimensions, upon an open treatment and upon a desire to help pupils to achieve a level of understanding and empathy by seeing a religious faith through the eyes of a follower have all become accepted aspects of most, if not all, agreed syllabuses. It is probably fair to say that little of what appeared in the working paper was original. Its real contribution to the future direction of RE was in bringing together much thought and practice into one publication; above all, from this publication it was able to provide a coherent framework for RE.

The working paper's influence was mainly felt among those involved as RE specialists whether in teacher education, in the LEA advisory service or in secondary schools. Here it seemed to give RE, grown tired in many schools, a new spurt of life. Gradually too it began to influence standing conferences as they came to revise agreed syllabuses. One especially notable one, the Hampshire Agreed Syllabus for RE, was adopted by a number of other LEAs.

Its stance was not without detractors. Not all agreed that it was the business of RE to move from a confessionalist position. Others were suspicious of the move to cover a range of religions. This was especially true of the primary school where many felt that to study a range of religions would be highly confusing for children. Perhaps more seriously, the new thinking was slowest to make its impact on the majority of primary schools. Here there seemed to be a number of problems: first, the message had percolated (erroneously) to many teachers that Goldman had said that RE was not really a suitable subject for younger children; second, most teachers felt insufficiently informed to teach religions other than Christianity: third, children had enough difficulty understanding Christianity without introducing other religions as well; fourth, many teachers, who could see that with some personal research they would be able to gain the necessary knowledge to teach about a number of religions felt inadequate to deal with the focus upon the pupil's personal search.

Whatever the difficulties some people felt with the content of the working paper, there can be no doubt that it was seminal in the development of the new approach to RE. After it had been absorbed into educational thinking, it was widely accepted that the aims of RE were concerned both with helping pupils to develop a knowledge and understanding of a range of religious traditions and also with assisting them to develop a personal response to the fundamental questions which religions address and in so doing begin to work out their own personal framework of meaning. After the working paper it was widely accepted that any new or recently agreed syllabus must be multifaith in content and that all positions taught must be treated openly and fairly. Religions were seen less as static systems concerned with doctrines and morality and more as living and changing activities marked as much by what people do and feel as by what they believe. Attitudes to encourage in pupils are understanding, tolerance and empathy. Over the succeeding years this spread across the 'professionals' in the field of RE and became the new orthodoxy. There were, of course, hiccups: there was, for example, a furore in 1975 when the Birmingham Agreed Syllabus and Handbook advocated that all pupils in the secondary schools should undertake a minor study of two 'non-religious stances for living', namely Humanism and Marxism. Despite this, the movement along the lines of the working paper continued.

The Education Reform Act, 1988

By almost any standard the Education Reform Act (ERA) marked a change of direction in the English educational system. Many of the changes are not relevant for our purposes here but it is important to note the introduction of a National Curriculum. For the first time Parliament laid down what ought to be taught in schools rather than leaving that to the discretion of individual schools, and in many cases to individual teachers. Terms such as 'a child's entitlement' and 'delivering the curriculum' came into use. This change in school culture had quite a striking effect upon RE as schools no longer felt able to leave out areas of the curriculum in which they felt less competent; the net result was that much more RE began to be taught. Inspections of schools no doubt assisted in this.

Parliamentary debates prior to the passing of the Act threw up some very interesting discussion about the nature and content of RE – and this merits a chapter in its own right. A group of peers in the House of Lords, led by Baroness Cox, argued strongly for a much more strenuously Christian approach to both the aims and content of RE. This naturally caused concern among the leaders of other faiths in the country, and the Bishop of London, then the chairman of the General Synod Board of Education, and his officers negotiated a settlement which was acceptable to most parties.

The Education Reform Act introduces the notion of a *basic* curriculum which is the entitlement of all pupils and to be provided in all schools. This shall be a 'balanced and broadly based curriculum which promotes the spiritual, moral, cultural, mental and physical development of pupils at the school and of society' (ERA, 1988, s. 1:2). This basic curriculum consists of RE and the ten foundation subjects which form the National Curriculum. Of these foundation subjects, three (English, mathematics and science) are further described as core subjects. RE differs from the other subjects of the basic curriculum in that it does not have nationally laid down attainment targets, programmes of study and assessment arrangements. RE still remains under local control in that each LEA retains responsibility for creating or adopting an agreed syllabus as its own.

However, the Act is very clear about the way in which RE should be taught and how it should develop and in a broader way enshrines in law the developments which have been traced in this chapter.

First of all, the Act substitutes the term religious education for the religious instruction of the 1944 Act, acknowledging the changing and broadening role of RE in the school curriculum and in the personal development of pupils. The major change, however, is that, for the first time, a general account of the content of RE was written into an Education Act: it requires that all new agreed syllabuses must

> reflect the fact that the religious traditions in Great Britain are in the main Christian whilst taking account of the teaching and practices of the other principal religions represented in Great Britain.

This is very interesting for a number of reasons. First, an acceptable agreed syllabus must contain teaching about a number of religious traditions. Second, the reference to the religious traditions (in the plural) being in the main Christian places Christianity as one of (albeit the major one) a number of religious traditions and accepts the religious pluralism of the country. Third, the geographical requirement that the other principal religious traditions are those which are represented in Great Britain implies both that religions not significant in Great Britain should not appear in syllabuses and that every LEA standing conference must plan a syllabus which reflects a national picture rather than a local one. An education authority which has little in the way of other religions present must still provide a syllabus which reflects the religious situation in the country as a whole. This is, of course, a limitation on the local control of the agreed syllabus.

This recognition of the religious pluralism of the country is further reinforced by a clarification in the membership of the standing conference and the Standing Advisory Council for Religious Education (SACRE). SACREs are bodies established in each LEA; they were permitted under the 1944 legislation but were made mandatory in 1988. Their function is to oversee and monitor the provision of RE and collective worship in their own local authority. Under the old rules they were made up of the four groups mentioned earlier; these groups continued but with a useful clarification. The 'other religious denominations' group was previously seen as composed of Christian denominations other than the Church of England; under the new legislation any ambiguities are removed and now members of other religious traditions can belong to a SACRE on equal terms with those of Christian denominations if, in the opinion of the LEA, they 'appropriately reflect the principal religious traditions of the area' (ERA, 1998, s. 11:4(a)). Since the 1988 Act a further requirement has been laid upon LEAs to ensure that membership of this group on SACRE reflects the numbers of the different groups living in the authority.

Religious education since the 1988 Education Reform Act: stick and carrot

Although the Education Reform Act in this way made a very clear statement about the nature and content of RE in county schools and that no one could any more question the movement away from confessionalism and the need to treat a number of religious traditions, it still left a number of questions unanswered, notably the identification of the principal religion traditions of Great Britain and any consideration of how teaching time should be allocated between them. These two issues have not proved to be the problem they were initially seen to be. Buddhism, Christianity, Hinduism, Islam, Judaism, Sikhism soon became with very little controversy secure components of any syllabus. The teaching time distribution has still to be resolved but has been formally left to local decision.

Since the 1988 RE settlement, things have continued to move apace and there has developed an interesting struggle between central and local control. At a national level the National Curriculum Council (NCC) was set up to oversee and to direct the development of the National Curriculum. Although RE was not strictly a National Curriculum subject, a professional officer for RE was appointed after a period and this was continued in the School Curriculum and Assessment Authority (SCAA) which succeeded it. Both NCC and SCAA have in turn been powerful influences in the development of RE.

Although the Education Reform Act opted to leave RE under local control, probably partly because it seemed a less controversial solution, central government has been loath to leave developments completely in local hands. It approached this partly by a process of monitoring and partly through the dissemination of ideas and proposals. One instance of the monitoring process was the approval of agreed syllabuses. The approval of agreed syllabuses, which had generally been taken to be routine, was now taken very seriously and in 1993 a number of LEAs were informed that their new agreed syllabuses did not meet the necessary conditions. This was largely on the grounds that the proposed content to be taught was not sufficiently clear or detailed; but it did make the point very clearly to LEAs that their developments were being watched and, of course, it provided very powerful guidance for those embarking upon a revision of their agreed syllabus. This was further followed up by a requirement that each LEA must review its agreed syllabus every five years.

If this monitoring was the stick, the production of high-quality guidance was the carrot. In this respect this chapter will note two developments. First, there was the question of guidance as to what should be taught. Although it was now widely accepted that RE must deal with a number of religious traditions there were still questions asked about the detailed content of the teaching. In par-ticular there was a concern among many that, say, non-Muslims were selecting what should be taught about Islam. Would Christians be happy for Muslims to select what should be taught about Christianity? Guidance was needed here. Second, there was the question of broad guidance to standing conferences to avoid some of the difficulties identified by the monitoring.

These two issues were addressed through a request from the Minister of State in 1993 to produce model syllabuses for religious education and that members of faith communities and teachers be involved in this work. It was made very clear that the model syllabuses were not statutory documents, and that they were intended for use by standing conferences and not for use as schemes of work for schools. What was most interesting about this development was that the faith communities were all invited to establish groups which would make recommendations about a desirable content for their own faith for the four key stages. This extremely valuable material was then used to develop two model syllabuses, both of which had variations in focus. These appeared in 1994 and their value was widely appreciated (see SCAA, 1994).

Although the model syllabuses have no legal status, they are beginning to prove highly influential. Certainly the two attainment targets identified in the syllabuses – Learning about Religion and Learning from Religion – have passed into RE language and are a very helpful way of balancing the twin focuses of Working Paper 36: understanding religion and the notion of personal search. The introduction to the model syllabuses contains very clear statements of aims, purposes, skills, attitudes and progression, and the syllabuses themselves contain the content as provided by the faith communities. Although, as has been said, the model syllabuses have no legal standing at all, their influence is beginning to spread. It is clear that in teacher education courses, for example, they are being used to fill the gap created by the lack of a National Curriculum document.

This brings the journey right up to date. It will be interesting to see how extensive this influence is as many LEAs begin to review their agreed syllabuses in the next year or two

Conclusion

The old story of Cinderella tells of a very deserving

young girl who slips down into a life of neglect and low self-esteem. From this she is lifted up through a beautiful new gown and coach provided by her fairy godmother and is allowed to go to the ball. There she finds to her amazement and pleasure that she is more widely admired than she had imagined. In some respects the story of RE has similarities. During the post-war years, RE slipped down in significance in the curriculum. It was often neglected and teachers responsible for it frequently had low expectations of support in terms both of finance and classroom time. The government, through the Education Reform Act, played the part of the fairy godmother and gave it the opportunity to put on a beautiful gown (in the form of its multifaith approach, in this case already in the wardrobe) and to go to the ball. There the RE world found that it was more highly regarded than it had ever suspected. It is to be hoped that there will be no disastrous midnight chimes! Given the pressures on the core subjects of the National Curriculum it is highly unlikely that the glass slipper will fit and RE marry the handsome prince. But whether English, mathematics or science eventually becomes the princess, RE should be a confident and attractive bridesmaid at the wedding.

References

Bastide, D. (1992) *Good Practice in Primary RE*. London: Falmer Press.

Choice and Diversity: A New Framework for Schools (Cm 2021) (1992) London: Her Majesty's Stationery Office.

Church of England Commission on Religious Education in Schools (1970) *The Fourth R: The Report of the Commission of Religious Education in Schools* (The Durham Report). London: National Society/SPCK.

City of Birmingham (1975) *Agreed Syllabus of Religious Instruction*. Birmingham: Birmingham City Council.

City of Birmingham (1975) *Living Together: A Teachers' Handbook of Suggestions for Religious Education*. Birmingham: Birmingham City Council.

Goldman, R.J. (1964) *Religious Thinking from Childhood to Adolescence*. London: Routledge & Kegan Paul.

Goldman, R.J. (1965) *Readiness for Religion*. London: Routledge & Kegan Paul.

Inner London Education Authority (ILEA) (1968) *Agreed Syllabus: Learning for Life*. London: ILEA.

London County Council (LCC) (1947) *The London Syllabus of Religious Education*. London: LCC.

Loukes, H. (1961) *Teenage Religion*. London: SCM Press.

School Curriculum and Assessment Authority (SCAA) (1994) *Model Syllabuses for Religious Education*. London: SCAA.

Schools Council (1971) *Religious Education in the Secondary School*, Working Paper 36. London: Evans/Methuen.

Smart, N. (1968) *Secular Education and the Nature of Religion*. London: Faber & Faber.

Surrey County Council (1947) *Syllabus of Religious Education*. Esher: Surrey County Council.

University of Sheffield Institute of Education (1961) *Religious Education in Secondary Schools*. London: Nelson.

11 Values, Virtues, Voluntaryism: the Contribution of Anglican Church Schools to Education in a Multicultural Society

MARIAN CARTER

National debate

National debate was stimulated in January 1996 following a conference convened by the School Curriculum and Assessment Authority (SCAA) entitled 'Education for adult life: the spiritual and moral development of young people'. The necessity for such a focus arose from a series of consultations on the revised National Curriculum, the Model Syllabuses for Religious Education and Sir Ron Dearing's review of qualifications for 16–19-year-olds which together revealed 'concern about a lack of focus on pupils' spiritual and moral development and its consequences'. A series of reports had been published (DfE, 1994; NCC, 1993; OFSTED, 1993, 1994) to which SCAA's response was to signal its intention to take a fresh look at section 1 of the Education Reform Act 1988. This states that the purpose of education is to promote the 'spiritual, moral, cultural, mental and physical development of pupils at the school and of society' and to prepare pupils for the 'opportunities, responsibilities and experiences of adult life'.

The January conference set up a national forum for 'Values in education and the community' consisting of ten representative groups,[1] on the premise that 'schools alone cannot be held responsible for the spiritual and moral development of young people, although they should, and do, play an important role'. The Forum was asked to make recommendations to SCAA on: (a) ways in which schools might be supported in fulfilling their role to contribute generally to pupils' spiritual and moral development; and (b) whether there is any common agreement on the values, attitudes and behaviour which schools are promoting on society's behalf, and whether these values, attitudes and behaviours are promoted elsewhere in society.

The groups, one of which this author was a member (the Initial Teacher Training section), met at regular intervals over the period of a year. An interim SCAA discussion paper (no. 6) was published on 6 July 1996 and engendered considerable press publicity, as did the speech by Dr George Carey, the Archbishop of Canterbury, on morality to the House of Lords on 5 July 1996. The ensuing Lords debate ended with Dr Carey concluding 'You cannot take moral behaviour for granted. It needs to be redefined, re-examined, and nurtured again and again. It is my hope that we will find ways of strengthening the moral fibre of the nation in the days ahead.[2] The final summary of recommendations of the Forum was equally controversial, particularly in relation to the family and the significance of marriage. It contained an analysis of shared values noting them to be in four main areas:

1 values related to self;
2 values related to relationships;
3 values related to society;
4 values relating to the environment.

The moral values which occurred most commonly were: compassion, equality, freedom, justice, respect, responsibility, truth and fairness. The values include a mixture of attitudes and the need for knowledge to inform moral judgements. The former may require little educational policy change: the latter suggests a new look at the National Curriculum since at present the weight of teaching about moral values is assumed by PSHE (personal, social, health education), RE and collective worship[3] while the recommendations of the report presume a teaching of moral values across the entire curriculum. Why are moral values headline news? Answers appear to lie in a perceived lack of societal values.

An influential sector of the Lords' debate recognised the contemporary context in which moral values are exercised as representing an 'assault on traditional values'.[4] The general perception, expressed through, for example, the setting up of the SCAA forum is that currently there is a lack of any common, overarching system of values. Assuming this to be true, and the work(s) of MacIntyre, especially, demonstrates that it is probably the case, it is necessary to examine the possible reasons. First, there is a loss of authority. Traditionally Christian belief has been a major source informing moral values. In Britain the established church has been challenged by internal division, controversy over homosexuality, and financial and sexual scandals, thus diminishing its credibility as an authority and standard-bearer of truth and values. Second, there is a loss of influence. Institutions have failed to reach ordinary people. There is a lack of trust in institutions and an ensuing individualism: the Archbishop expressed it as 'people now see what is good and right as a matter of private taste and individual opinion only'. Societal values have given way to a 'moral and cultural relativism' of the supermarket, 'take it or leave it', 'pick-and-mix' variety. For MacIntyre (see, for example, 1981, 1988, 1990), this leads to emotivism, the moral theory in which the self-interested preferences of the autonomous individual reign supreme. For example, the institution of the family is perceived to be under threat and frequently children are receiving mixed and even contradictory messages from school, home and the media, of the 'you must make up your own mind' variety. Third, there is a loss of certainty. Post-modernism, varied as it is, has made us aware that values, choices and cultural priorities are contextual and ephemeral, influenced by social factors such as economics, class, race, historical and community memories in addition to factors of our own subjectivity formed by heredity and environment. Post-modern claims of context dependence have challenged the universalist claims of religion to truth and the good (see, for example, Bauman, 1993). Fourth there is a loss of social responsibility. Society's emphasis on individualism and competitiveness has encouraged a materialism which has diminished a sense of society and responsibility for one another (see Jordan, 1989). Education has experienced the entrepreneurial spirit of the market-place ethic, with calls for schools to 'opt out', 'go it alone' seek grant maintained status, and the competitive emphasis on so called 'league tables'. The emphasis on basic skills appears politically driven by the ethic of greater productivity and economic recovery rather than a desire for the realisation of the child's full potential. Fifth, there is a loss of religious belief. Instead, there is a wide range of beliefs and values in society for which the terms pluralism and secularisation are commonly used.[5] These characteristics are examples of a societal ethos which is the context of the morality debate in education.

Education through the school system is a major influence on the moral development of children, alongside the family, the media, the peer group and society. The task of the school is essentially the transmission of accumulated wisdom and knowledge to the next generation, although 'education' is, of course, a much contested concept (see, for example, Gutek, 1988). Education is embedded in the life of society, it reflects the society of which it is a part and also plays a part in shaping that society through teaching the next generation. Sometimes education is prophetic (it can be subversive!), challenging the mores of society. Currently, increasing levels of power are given to governing boards. The membership of boards reflects the pluralism of society. It is not therefore surprising that education is influenced by society's uncertainty over moral values.

For a decade in the 1960s and 1970s, educationalists worked with the concept of value-free, neutral education. Rationality became a key word: children must be taught 'the facts' and allowed to decide for themselves. Behaviour must be based on reason. 'Indoctrination' was a word bandied about, particularly in the area of the teaching of religious education where it was thought beliefs were being taught as facts. The strands of the argument for neutrality were many, and will not be developed here (for a fairly comprehensive analysis, see Kleinig, 1982). Suffice it to say that it became increasingly obvious that daily choices were being made in the classroom, for example, that there was not time to learn x but y must be given priority. The choice of which concept/skill to impart presupposes an implicit understanding of what is morally of worth. More recently local management of schools (LMS) has involved budgeting decisions, all of which involve choices dependent on relative values. No education is value free. Decisions on budgets, staffing, curriculum presentation, teaching methods, documentation (prospectus, mission statements and intentions), pastoral care and discipline procedures all reflect what is considered to be of worth in the particular community making the decisions. Every school is therefore involved in the process of value transmission by its documents, how it carries out its function, what it says and what it does.

The debate has raised several questions about what is meant by moral values, moral development, the relationship of moral values, education and cultural pluralism. Are there common values held by society? How are these values decided and recognised? Does pluralism in morality matter? What might it mean? How are values transmitted? It is to these questions we now turn.

Moral values and the Anglican church school

The Latin word *mores* means 'custom', 'manners', a way of life which is characteristic of a society: it is the Latin translation of the Greek term *ethos/ ethikos*, meaning both 'custom' and 'character'. Moral development is about a growing awareness of and a positive response to the demands of living as an individual with others in community.[6] It 'is concerned with fundamental judgements and precepts about how we should behave and act and the reason for such behaviour. It includes questions of intuition, motive and attitude' (OFSTED, 1994, p. 10). Values do not emerge in a vacuum, they are societal. A child learns right and wrong from a moral framework in the home. This may not be the same value system as the school but it is the 'inheritance' of the child and forms a base line for growth. The child enters school to find an expected form of behaviour, rules derived from the value system of the school. This chapter is looking at a particular sector of the maintained system: that of the church school, and the Anglican school in particular. Why?

Historically the Anglican church as the established church in England and Wales has had a significant involvement in education both through its own schools and through a commitment to education. The SCAA debate failed to acknowledge this history of education through the church, an education founded on moral values. For centuries the church was the only provider of education in many areas of England and Wales (see, for example, Silver, 1983). Schools were attached to cathedrals, monasteries and hospitals, though chiefly for the sons of the wealthy and those who could afford to pay. Historians indicate the seeds of change leading to a rudimentary education for all in the eighteenth century. Such events as the Methodist revival with its appeal to the working classes, the American War of Independence and the French Revolution were warnings to Britain of the power of the working masses and engendered a desire to prevent revolution. One hope was in the education of the masses: the extension of the franchise in the Reform Acts of 1832 and 1867 further challenged the need for an educated electorate. The church[7] was a pioneer in initiating education for the lower classes; for example, in 1698 the Society for the Propagation of the Gospel encouraged the establishment of charity schools with a curriculum based on the catechism and the '3 Rs';[8] Robert Raikes in 1780 established Sunday Schools which became so popular that they were extended to other days of the week. The National Society was founded in 1811 to promote 'the education of the poor in the principles of the established church' though the Royal Commission of 1818 made it clear that 'the church catechism is only taught and attendance at the established place of worship only required of those whose parents belong to the established church'. From the beginning education involved values, since Christian beliefs are expressed in a way of life, a moral system. This ethos was explicit in the Trust Deeds, the foundation documents of all church schools.

The church built schools, particularly for the working class, at a period when the state did not think it necessary to make public provision. The motivation for establishing the first church schools was largely philanthropic and altruistic: 'parish schools for the children of the poor'. In Victorian England Christianity was assumed: and of the Anglican tradition. An East End of London church school illustrates the point. It was formed by a Victorian evangelical tradition in 1870 'to educate the children of seamen who had settled in the neighbourhood'; 'to feed, clothe and educate the poor of the parish'. Its mission was to serve the community: it was not intended to be a confessional school. The log books of the school indicate that from the beginning, though a Christian foundation based on a particular set of values, pupils of other faiths were present and welcome. Today, of the 245 pupils, 200 are Muslims from a dozen or so ethnic groups. Other trust deeds had a different focus requiring the daily reciting of the Apostles' Creed. Such deeds were explicit in providing 'a Christian education' and in teaching the doctrines of the established church for the children of Christian parents and for non-Christians prepared to accept this condition.

The present dual system whereby church and state provide education side by side – voluntary schools and county schools – and the fact that Religious Education and collective worship,[9] unlike in the United States, are part of the curriculum for every child, is a consequence of the past history of the country. It is a direct result of the church's initiative in education and the church's continuing resourcing of education;[10] the desire of parents for church schools; and an ongoing relationship between established church and education. In a church school the ideal is a school where in the daily life the Christian faith[11] and belief are lived out in a moral code.

Voluntary schools today

Today there are 22,598 maintained schools in England providing education for 6,985,753 pupils. One-third are voluntary[12] schools, largely from religious foundations: 4864 schools are Church of England (184 Church in Wales) providing for 12 per cent of the children of school age in the maintained sector, representing a quarter of the nation's primary schools and educating one-sixth of the nation's children (Church of England Schools and Colleges Handbook 1993–4). There are 40,000+ teachers and 70,000 governors working in these schools, supported by Diocesan Boards of Education through their directors and teams. The Anglican church has traditionally been involved predominantly in primary education, particularly in rural areas where schools are small. At the secondary level the Church of England's contribution has never been large. In 1992 there were 225 schools, which include middle schools, 72 deemed to be primary, 69 deemed to be secondary, giving 142 purely secondary, of which 48 were controlled and 94 aided.

The Roman Catholic Church has schools in the primary and secondary sector in more balanced numbers. There are 1856 Roman Catholic aided primary schools catering for 434,104 pupils and 2,258 aided secondary schools catering for 746,220 pupils (*Catholic Schools Statistics*, January 1995). There are 31 Methodist primary schools, some joint Anglican/Methodist schools and 17 Jewish aided primary schools. The Muslim community has a small number of private schools and is seeking government permission to enter the special arrangements for voluntary schools. When the schools in the voluntary sector are added together they provide places for 32 per cent of the maintained sector.

Values derive from shared societal beliefs. Haldane (1993, p. 191) reminds us that 'we are not of our own creation and cannot bring knowledge and value into being *ex nihilo*.' He points out that values change but we must work with existing material: 'If we are to question the direction of inquiry, or the values to which we find ourselves committed, we must recognize their pre-existence and understand their character.' British society is broadly Christian, not church-going, but our institutions and values are only intelligible by reference to the influence of Christianity. For many citizens the Christian heritage is muddled and implicit (shaped by other beliefs such as astrology)[13] rather than explicit. This folk religion is evidenced in the attendance at midnight Christmas communion and requests for baptism.[14] For many Christianity exists as a folk religion which is present and can be built upon.[15] Without an accepted moral code of shared values, society ceases to have moral authority and the culture disintegrates. What are the values explicit in Christianity and therefore deemed to undergird the church school?

At the centre is the command of Jesus: 'You must love the Lord your God with all your heart, with all your soul, with all your mind and with all your strength. You must love your neighbour as yourself' (Mark 12: 29–30; Matthew 22: 39; Luke 10: 27). Christianity uses scripture, tradition, reason and experience. It is a search for truth discovered in the truth which is God. It believes that each person is valued as of dignity and worth, created in the image of God. Each lives in integrity and is a moral agent with responsibility/accountability for the neighbour, whoever that is. Each respects the dignity and worth of the other since neighbour love is communal. Each recognises his or her human inability to live up to the ideal of love even in the face of the suffering of others. Each holds the vision of life as it could be, believing that transformation is possible. Each person is responsible for the whole of creation, resulting in the care of the environment and the willingness to work for sustainable and just life styles, in the recognition that we live in a symbiotic relationship with nature and are not the centre of the universe. Each lives with a reverence and respect for limits. This is the Christian tradition and heritage.[16] Jesus did not prescribe values but gave a set of principles for living which need to be worked out in experience. The rise of religious fundamentalism may be fuelled by the prevalent consumerist culture of individualism but this is in distinction to a Christianity which has frequently presented itself as a counter-culture challenging individualism and materialism. If it is Christian values that have informed our culture, how are they transmitted? Have the values changed from the inception of church schools to the present?

The church's self-critical analysis of the role of the church school

There has been considerable self-critical analysis of the role of the Anglican church school in a society which has dramatically changed religiously since many of the schools were founded in the last century. For example in the 1970s the Durham Report (Church of England, 1970) provided a useful focus to the debate by recognising a two-fold role for church schools: 'It was general, to serve the nation through its children, and domestic, to equip the children of the church to take their place in the Christian community.' The Report recognised the two roles of service to the community and nurture – that is, that of encouraging children from Christian homes – as historically indistinguishable, since state and church were coextensive. It recommended that the church should 'see its continued involvement in the dual system principally as a way of expressing its concern for the general education of all children and young people rather than as a means for giving denominational instruction.' The issue of the role of a church school has been raised strongly in areas where the church school was the only school, especially in rural areas. It was raised, second, by the pluralism of faith or lack of faith of staff and pupils; and third, by the arrival in the late 1960s of families from former British colonies, some of whom belonged to non-Christian faiths. Some members of non-Christian faith communities opted to send their children to church schools believing that in a church school there was a recognition of the divine/transcendent lived out in an ethical framework which would pervade all that was said and done. This was in contrast to what was perceived as a rationalist, secular ethos in county

maintained schools. Immigrants from the Indian sub-continent and Amin's Uganda who were Muslim had a high regard for education but of a particular kind: 'For Muslims, education without an awareness of God is meaningless, and not education at all but indoctrination into a particular world-view' (Mabud, 1992, p. 90). The purpose of education for Islam is 'the total balanced growth of a man's personality, in order to make man a true servant of God, and lead him in the path that would enable him to become, or draw near to the stage of, khalifatullah, viceregent of God on earth' (Ashraf, 1991, p. 42). Every single action of a human being must be a meaningful worship of God in one way or another. Islam parallels Christianity in the belief in a Creator God whose followers are called to reflect God's nature of peace and justice in their lives; thus education and values coexist in Islam as in the church school.

The debate about the role of the church school within educational provision was highlighted further in two reports in the mid-1980s produced by the NUT (1984) and the government funded Swann Report (DES, 1985). Each report was concerned with combating racism, promoting multicultural understanding and providing equality of educational opportunity. They argued that church schools were socially divisive and demanded special funding, encouraged religious intolerance and were educationally suspect, giving time to RE and collective worship to the detriment of other parts of the curriculum and using methods more closely resembling indoctrination than education. Subsequently the latter objections were also addressed to non-denominational schools in their provision of RE and worship. The implication was that the dual system should be abandoned and possibly the religious agreement of the 1944 Butler Act.

Some Muslim communities in Bradford and Brent sought permission from education authorities to establish state-aided Muslim schools parallel to church schools. The NUT report argued for the integration of Muslim children within the state sector to encourage cultural pluralism and the teaching of RE in an objective way, giving equal weight to each religious faith, allowing the children to make the choice of which faith, if any, they pursued. The Swann Report also wrestled with the type of RE. It advocated a phenomenological approach to religion 'to understand the nature of religious belief, the religious dimension of human experience and the plurality of the faiths in modern Britain'.

'We believe that religious education can play a central role in preparing all pupils for life in today's multi-racial Britain, and can also lead them to a greater understanding of the diversity of the global community' (ibid., p. 518). The report advocated a neutrality of teaching method while recognising the important role of RE in a multicultural education. The comparative religion offered by both reports was inconsistent, trivialising genuine religious difference while failing to recognise that respect for the faith of another does not mean necessarily sharing that faith. Both reports seem to have failed to recognise that cultural diversity emerges from a faith commitment. Differences in food, dress, festivals are not simply additions, social dimensions of a phenomenon called religion, but emerge from deeply held ethical and religious beliefs. An example is of a church school featured in *The Times Educational Supplement* (9 October 1987): of 160 children only 38 speak English as a first language, there are no fewer than 24 mother tongues. The head teacher stated: 'food is more of a worry than religion . . . the ethos of Christianity pervades the school, but its dogma is notably absent.' While this happy relationship of coexistence is not always the case, it nevertheless witnesses to the sharp issues of multiculturalism in a church school.

The church has wrestled with issues of its relationship with non-Christian faiths; in particular the special place that it gives to Jesus, which has been used as claiming religious superiority. A church school faces these issues as it serves a racially diverse local community. It is able to provide a unified and coherent set of values based upon Christian belief. Can it also be true to its Trust Deed and to an open mission of service to the community?

> Central to Christian moral teaching, as summarised by Jesus, is the love of God and the love of one's neighbour as oneself. The second commandment derives from the first and is subordinate to it. These commandments at once expressed so simply and yet so demandingly, lie at the heart of the Christian Gospel and provide Church schools with a foundation for their provision for the spiritual and moral development of pupils.   (Bath and Wells Diocesan Board of Education, 1994, pt 5)

The Judaic–Christian faith has a tradition stretching back to its beginnings which encourages and commands love of the stranger: this can be, and has been, interpreted as the person of a different faith. There is commonality of belief in a creator God from whom each person is uniquely created and respected and treats his or her neighbour in word and action as s/he has been loved. Often the motivation for behaving morally is linked directly to the voluntary exercise of religious beliefs. A framework is then provided in which attitudes of personal and social responsibility can be developed. There are differences in belief between faiths and this must not be minimised, but there is also a commonality of searching for truth and a basing of this quest on the transcendent. Robert Runcie, the former Archbishop of Canterbury, recognised this when, speaking on interfaith matters, he said:

> We must move on from dialogue to partnership. We can work together on the basis not of common belief but of common values. None of this is easy because the debate about values often runs through the middle of religious communities rather than between them. Yet there is sometimes a sharp contrast between the values of an unreflective secular world and reflective religious traditions with a transcendent dimension.   (Runcie, 1990)

Within the area of multicultural education the importance of religion has been recognised. Christianity itself is a world faith, expressed through a diversity of cultures ranging from the Black Pentecostals of the Caribbean, through the Indian Christian ashrams to the British liturgists. The population of the British Isles in 1991 was 51.8 million in the white ethnic grouping, 500,000 black Caribbeans, 212,000 black Africans, and 78,000 black 'others'; 840,000 Indians, 477,000 Pakistanis, 163,000 Bangladeshi, 157,000 Chinese and 198,000 Asians (see Bruce, 1995, p. 80). Many Afro-Caribbean people are Christian, most Pakistani and Bangladeshis are Muslims – between 900,000 and 1.3 million. Britain is a multicultural society though the statistics indicate that 95 per cent of the population are white and have been influenced by a Christian culture, although they themselves are not necessarily Christian, and other faith groups are represented in small numbers. I am not thereby suggesting that the latter are insignificant. Each person is of worth and of respect, simply indicating the ambiguity of the word 'pluralism'. It is also significant that modern communications place us in a 'global village' where we are very aware of the influence of, for example, Islamic states and the Middle East crisis, and the ethnic and religious strife in Bosnia. The presence of British Jews and second and third generation immigrants who are members of Islam, Hinduism and Sikhism, coupled with awareness of the influence of faith in daily life and commerce on the world scene, witnesses to the necessity to study and explore these cultures and faiths to understand our world. The church school is a place where through the concept of 'love of neighbour', education affirms and rejoices in difference.

School values

The values in a church school are informed by the Christian faith. A distinction between a county school and a church school is that the latter is from its beginning, whether built in the last century or more recently, the result of a conscious and deliberate act of a group of committed Christian people. It has been noted that, from the first church schools, motivations varied yet the commonality was a desire to continue the nurture in Christian faith either because it is within the home culture or a faith stance which parents have chosen deliberately by seeking a church school for their child. This foundation philosophy of the church school is expressed in the trust deed.

The government now requires every school to produce a prospectus which begins with a mission statement on the ethos and shared values promoted by the school. This statement is the bedrock from which school policy on admissions, curriculum and discipline derives:

> The set of shared values which a school promotes through the curriculum, through expectations governing the behaviour of pupils and staff and through day to day contact between them will make an important contribution to pupils' spiritual, moral and cultural development and should be at the heart of every school's educational and pastoral policy and practice.   (DfE, 1994)

For the church school it is the trust deed which informs the mission statement and this is rooted in a Christian commitment. The Trust Deeds dating from the mid-1850s may seem anachronistic at the end of the twentieth century, yet they have the power of legal documents. The interpretation of the deeds is central. Many governing bodies adhere to the spirit rather than the letter and follow the recommendations of the Durham Report in offering a service to the local community of whatever faith or of none.

A church school is created by the trust deed which declares the distinctive education that it is called to deliver. It needs the conscious deliberation of the staff working together with parent representatives and the governing board of the school to decide the nature of the distinctiveness which is expressed in the ethos/values of the school. Subsequently the need is to discover how to make the values evident in the daily life of the school. The National Society, which is the Anglican Synod's representatives to advise Church of England schools, stress that 'Ethos cannot be left to chance; it must be thought about and patterns of action tried and assessed' (National Society, 1984). The ethos has to be regularly reappropriated and discussed by the staff and governors so that it is held in common. New members of staff are aware of this when they apply for a post in a church school. The ethos and values of a church school are often expressed in symbols reminding the school community of the mission of service to the neighbourhood: these may be through a displayed cross; a school Eucharist; a leavers' service; and working with the local church which is a lived faith community.

The values of a school are worked out in the documents guiding its life. These are not fixed but are open to respond to changing needs. Documents guiding admissions policy are of particular importance and have given rise to criticisms of exclusivism and racism (noted in the Swann and NUT reports mentioned). Some deeds stipulate clearly a credal statement, and the requirement for children to be church-going (the nurture role); others are more open, with the mission of service. In a voluntary controlled school the policy is laid down by the LEA, after consultation with the governing body. In a voluntary aided school the admissions policy is considered and decided, by the governors, 'for the benefit of the school and taking into account the numbers of the pupils in each class'. Schools draw up a list of criteria which are very significant, particularly if the school is one in which a place is desired by parents because of its good reputation, is central to an urban community, or is the only school in a village. In these situations it is important that the governors are sensitive to the needs and values of the local community. Governors through the admissions policy must tread a fine line so that the church responds to the feelings of the local community without compromising its own tradition in the Trust Deed: with sensitivity and care in most cases this is possible. I have recently been involved in a new suburban housing estate where a new VA school had been planned. Parents moving on to the estate were very aware of the necessity for a school and glad that it was to be built, but had not been alerted to the fact that it was to be a church school. As the board went up and building commenced there was much anguish and indeed anger on the estate, since the local Anglican church was known to have a strict policy on baptisms and marriage and to be in an evangelical tradition. 'It will be just for them, the church people' was one of the comments. Fortunately, the incumbent heard of the disquiet and was bold enough to persuade the governors that the admissions policy should have as its first priority that children should live on the estate. A balance was achieved between the good will of the local community, the Trust Deed of the school, and mission seen as a service to the community through providing a Christian environment informed by Christian values as the cultural heritage of Britain.

Values in the mission statement are evident in the daily life of the school. They are manifest in attitudes which give worth to individuals, attitudes of respect for others, ranging from the statemented child to the head teacher and the cleaning staff, and how people speak to each other. Values are evident in the use of power in the school when it is constructive, not abused nor hierarchical. Values are reflected in how deficiencies and handicap are handled, how credit is given to talent and success without further belittling those who have failed, and how the offender is treated. Values are reflected in positive attitudes and respect for property: for example, by displaying children's work, by care of the fabric of the building, by the sharing of finite resources. Values are witnessed in respect for non-human life: the pets in the classroom, creatures in the school pond. Children learn to respect as they themselves are respected and through watching the respect and courtesy shown by adults to one another within the school. Values are caught and taught. The way that values are lived and fostered by the religion of the head teacher, staff and governing body will penetrate the life of the school.

A school needs to have a firm framework evidenced, for example, in rules that are discussed with the children, that are minimal but that are held by all for the good of all. Attitudes can be discussed and a base of moral knowledge begun in the primary school. Morality needs to be discussed with the children so that gradually they recognise and accept the need for rules and want to keep them. The discipline policy of the school will reflect the values of the school, it

> should always be designed to provide a basis of self discipline. If it becomes too dependent on the staff enforcing the acceptable standards, then it does not carry the seeds of further growth to maturity. It only has within it the seeds of increased dependency. This implies that there must always be trust. It is only by being trusted that we learn to be trusted. Within a school where every human being is accorded that respect shown to unique human beings loved by God, this should come naturally, and where there are failures, as there will be, these can be dealt with, not as disasters, but as experience from which learning can grow. (Lankshear, 1992b, p. 64)

In a church school discipline may be characterised and informed by Christian understanding and acceptance of the person who has done wrong: condemning the sin, not the sinner, dealing with the consequences, showing that forgiveness is available, and showing that reconciliation is possible.

Values across the curriculum

The mission statement in a church school encourages values not only in RE and collective worship but is underlying and explicit across all the subjects of the curriculum. Values will underline the subject and form part of the reflection in the teaching. In language teaching attitudes will be reflected in communication which is caring, positive and affirms the individual: the beauty of good language within poetry and symbol, story and myth. Content will be informed by the choice of literature that gives exposure to the rich resources of stories that excite and depict virtues and that build character, such as the use of biographies of those who have struggled to overcome handicap and disadvantage. Maths need not be simply instrumental but may be about discovering the awe and wonder which underlie order and pattern, discovering beauty in mathematical formulae and recognising the insights given to maths through the Muslim culture of Arab and Indian scholars.

Often in the past science has been taught as being in opposition to religion, the former considered as deriving from objective facts, the latter from faith and speculation (see, for example, Brooke, 1991). Gradually schools have come to realise that scientists have been saying science can never be objective; it works by using models and probability. Observation is theory-laden, since as observers of biological or physical phenomena we bring with us our own assumptions. Values underlie the teaching of the subject dependent on intuition and inspiration. The development of judgement is required in assessing evidence. Science can be taught which challenges dualism, and sees the interrelatedness of the natural world, valuing the physical world, care of animals, respect for non-human life, for example, by observing creatures in their natural habitat and context if possible rather than in the classroom. Science can engender feelings of awe and wonder in the face of rich diversity and interdependence of the natural world, the mystery of life.

Sex education has been controversial sometimes, since it appears to have been taught with the emphasis on physical processes only, leaving no room for personal, moral and emotional development. In a church school it is expected that this area of the curriculum will be treated with seriousness, reflecting concepts such as the recognition of ourselves as created, sexual beings. Pupils are encouraged to marvel at difference, delight in complementarity and understand how sexuality may be expressed in life-giving ways, in giving and receiving. Pupils will learn the relation of the physical, spiritual, emotional and moral; that all good gifts are capable of misuse; the consequences of misuse; and the Christian belief that there is an opportunity to make amends and to start again. These are some of the ways in which the values of a church school will underpin the curriculum.

Conclusion

The church school is called to reflect Jesus's great commandment: to love God and love neighbour as self. This belief and the values that derive from it will be reflected in the mission statement of the school, 'a Church school will include within its framework for action a theological understanding which cannot be present in quite the same explicit way in a school which does not have a Christian Foundation' (Lankshear, 1992a). The mission statement is interpreted in the school policy documentation and manifest in the relationships between people, young and old alike, who are involved in the life of the school. Attempting to work out the mission and documents of the school in the light of the gospel is

not easy; time commitment and energy is necessary. It may not mean that the school is very different from the county school but it will emerge from and be true to the challenge of Christian faith.

The National Society was the founding group for the establishment of church schools in the nineteenth century. It continues to support church schools through its regular termly newsletter and regular publication of booklets which raise awareness of contemporary issues. Recently published are documents on culture in the curriculum. Nationally the Diocesan Directors of Education meet to share the responsibility of church schools, while locally the Diocesan Director works with the diocese in resourcing church schools, through in-service training, advice and funding.

The church school can offer a model of values in education:

> we have to demonstrate the effectiveness of living within the context of a shared set of values and a shared practice of moral discernment and decision . . . [this is] no easy matter and never one free from disagreement and, at times, personal pain. But we can confidently say that the Christian community has been dealing systematically in such matters for centuries and, properly understood, has much to offer from its experience and teaching. (Catholic Education Service, 1996, p. 19)

Notes

1 The forum included representatives from the teaching profession, school governors, parents, teacher trainers, academics, the legal profession, principal religions, youth workers, employers and the media.

2 *The Times*, 6 July 1966, p. 9. This kind of critique and analysis has been undertaken especially in moral philosophy by writers such as MacIntyre (1981) and Murdoch (1985).

3 The final report of the forum has not been published (May 1997) although two consultations were held to develop materials for schools based on the statement of values: 15 April 1997 at Brasenose College and 22 April at Newcombe House, home of the SCAA.

4 *The Times*, 6 July 1966, p. 9.

5 A working definition of pluralism is the presence of different ethnic and faith identities and a growing number of alternatives to Christian belief among the nominal Christian population, yet frequently derived from Christian roots; secularisation refers to the decline in institutional adherence and specifically Christian commitment.

6 It is, of course, about much more than this, as the

range of competing, and often conflicting, moral theories clearly demonstrates. See, for example, Singer (1993).

7 Although I am emphasising the Anglican involvement in education, other Christian traditions were involved. The British and Foreign Schools Society had emerged in 1798, established by a Quaker, Joseph Lancaster, consisting primarily of non-conformists and liberal Anglicans. It aimed to 'promote the education of the labouring and manufacturing classes of society of every religion'. The repeal of the Test and Corporation Acts in 1828 removed discrimination against non-conformists; and the Catholic Emancipation Act in 1829 thus made possible Christian pluralism in education. In 1843 the Methodists and 1847 the Catholics established Boards of Education.

8 W. M. Jacob in Wood (1994). In almost all cases of the establishment of a school the motive would seem to be religious. But this was not a clerical movement. The Norfolk town of Diss in 1715 is quoted as proclaiming: 'Whereas Prophaneness and Debauchery are greatly increased owing to a gross ignorance of Religion especially among the lower sort and nothing is more likely to promote the practice of Christianity and Virtue than an early and pious Education.'

9 The entitlement of every child is the product of a series of Acts of Parliament, beginning with the 1870 Education Act, ss 25–30 of the Butler 1944 Education Act and the Education Reform Act of 1988 and 1993. These two subjects are chosen because Department for Education and Employment and School Curriculum and Assessment Authority reports have acknowledged the key role in moral education played by religious education/collective worship, while recognising that spiritual and moral development must inform the whole curriculum.

10 For example, budget cuts in some local authorities have resulted in cutting the post of adviser in religious education. When this happens the LA may, and rightly does, look to the local Anglican Diocesan Director of Education for support for the subject within in-service training.

11 Examples of Christian beliefs and values are found in numerous National Society Reports and diocesan literature, for example, 'A Church school is well placed to provide a unified and coherent set of values based upon the Christian faith' (*Handbook for the Inspection of Schools*, Diocese of Bath and Wells, Part 5, p. 4); 'Relationship between the school and members of the wider community are founded on the teaching of the gospels' Lankshear, D. W., Looking for Quality in the Church School, N.S., 1992.

12 Voluntary aided and voluntary controlled.

13 David Young, Bishop of Ripon, in submission to SCAA.

14 Grace Davie (1994, p. 199) argues that for the great majority there is both 'a lack of attachment to religious organizations' and an openness 'to the widely diverse

forms of the sacred which appear within contemporary society'.

15 Parents give as the reason for retaining RE/collective worship in school that 'it teaches the ten commandments', that is, it is seen to be connected in some way with a moral standard.

16 Christians have constantly fallen short and recognise their own oppression of others by, for example, unjust colonial structures.

References

Ashraf, S.A. (1991) Islamic studies in British schools. *Muslim Educational Quarterly* 3 (3): 41–6.

Bath and Wells Diocesan Board of Education (1994) *Handbook of Inspection of Church of England Schools*. Wells, Som.: Diocesan Office.

Bauman, Z. *Postmodern Ethics*. Oxford: Basil Blackwell.

Brooke, J. (1991) *Science and Religion: Some Historical Perspectives*. Cambridge: Cambridge University Press.

Bruce, S. (1995) *Religion in Modern Britain*. London: Oxford University Press.

Catholic Education Service (annual) *Catholic Schools Statistics*. London: Catholic Education Service.

Catholic Education Service (1996) *Spiritual and Moral Development across the Curriculum: A Discussion Paper for the Professional Development of Teachers in Secondary Schools*. London: Catholic Education Service.

Church of England Commission on Religious Education in Schools (1970) *The Fourth R: The Report of the Commission ...* (The Durham Report). London: National Society/SPCK.

Church of England Schools and Colleges Handbook, 1993–4. Redhill, Surrey: School Government Publishing.

Davie, G. (1994) *Religion in Britain since 1945: Believing without Belonging*. Oxford: Basil Blackwell.

Department for Education (DfE) (1994) *Religious Education and Collective Worship*, Circular 1/94. London: DfE.

Department of Education and Science (DES) (1985) *Education for All* (The Swann Report: final report of the Committee of Inquiry into the Education of Children from Ethnic Minority Groups), Cmnd 9543. London: Her Majesty's Stationery Office.

Francis, L.J. and Lankshear, D.W. (1993) *Christian Perspective on Church Schools*. Leominster, Herefs: Fowler Wright.

Francis, L.J. and Thatcher A. (1993) *A Christian Perspective for Education*. Leominster, Herefs: Fowler Wright.

Gutek, G. (1988) *Philosophical and Ideological Perspectives on Education*. New York: Allyn and Bacon.

Haldane, J. (1993) Religious education in a pluralist society: a philosophical examination. In L.J. Francis and A. Thatcher (eds), *Christian Perspectives for Education*. Leominster, Herefs: Fowler Wright.

Jordan, B. (1989) *The Common Good*. Oxford: Basil Blackwell.

Kleinig, J. (1982) *Philosophical Issues in Education*. London: Croom Helm.

Lankshear, D.W. (1992a) *Looking for Quality in the Church School*. London: National Society.

Lankshear, D.W. (1992b) *A Shared Vision*. London: National Society.

Mabud, Shaikh Abdul (1992) A Muslim response to the Education Reform Act 1988. *British Journal of Religious Education* 14: 88–98.

MacIntyre, A. (1981) *After Virtue: A Study in Moral Theory*. London: Duckworth.

MacIntyre, A. (1988) *Whose Justice? Which Rationality?* London: Duckworth.

MacIntyre, A. (1990) *Three Rival Versions of Moral Enquiry*. London; Duckworth.

Murdoch, I. (1985) *The Sovereignty of Good*. London: Ark.

National Curriculum Council (NCC) (1993) *Spiritual and Moral Development: A Discussion Paper*. London: NCC; reprinted as SCAA, 1995.

National Society (1984) *A Future in Partnership*. London: National Society.

National Union of Teachers (NUT) (1984) *Religious Education in a Multi-faith Society*. London: NUT.

Office for Standards in Education (OFSTED) (1993) *Framework for the Inspection of Schools*. London: OFSTED.

Office for Standards in Education (OFSTED) (1994) *Spiritual, Moral, Social and Cultural Development*. London: OFSTED.

Runcie, Robert (1990) 'Christianity and the world religions' (the Younghusband Lecture), unpublished.

School Curriculum and Assessment Authority (SCAA) (1995) *Spiritual and Moral Development*. London: SCAA; reprint of NCC, 1993.

Silver, H. (1983) *Education and History*. London: Methuen.

Singer, P. (ed.) (1993) *A Companion to Ethics*. Oxford: Basil Blackwell.

Wood, D. (ed.) (1994) *The Church and Childhood* papers read at the 1993–4 meetings of the Ecclesiastical History Society. Oxford: Basil Blackwell.

12 Values Education in Bahá'í Schools

JENNIFER CHAPA AND RHETT DIESSNER

The state of human society today can be characterised as one of rapid and accelerating change in all its aspects: social, political, economic, cultural, and moral (Commission on Global Governance, 1995). Chaos and confusion plague humanity; civil wars and unrest, increased incidents of domestic and international terrorism, growing materialism, acts of moral depravity, and economic hardship are seen world-wide. People everywhere have become disenchanted by ineffective, traditional systems of government and social organisation, while new solutions are yet to be discovered. The social needs of a world that has shrunk to a village, owing to the incredible advance of science and technology during the past century and a half, require us to forge new relationships and organizational structures and to develop a conscious understanding of the transformation which society is undergoing (United Nations Research Institute for Social Development, 1995; Commission on Global Governance, 1995). Confronted by such a distressing situation, more and more people are searching for ways to resolve it. Signs of hope and a vision of a 'new world order' are becoming increasingly evident as world leaders gather more often to deal with global issues and as the grassroots arise together to address local problems (Mathews, 1997); the need to cooperate is apparent (Havel, 1995).

One sign of humanity's desire to overcome the current state of affairs is a world-wide trend towards emphasising values or moral education in schools in order to prepare children to assume their future societal roles (Etzioni, 1993; Sandel, 1996). Bahá'ís are among those who recognise that an academic education devoid of an explicit values education, sensitive to a multicultural world, will not create the kind of citizen who contributes to the progress of human civilization (Bahá'í International Community, 1995). In fact, Bahá'ís believe that the foundation of a proper education is the acquisition and implementation of sound values and virtues.

The Bahá'í view of education is based on the teachings of Bahá'u'lláh, prophet-founder of the Bahá'í Faith, and of 'Abdu'l-Bahá, Bahá'u'lláh's son and chosen interpreter of his teachings. Bahá'u'lláh (1976, p. 213) advised his followers to 'Be anxiously concerned with the needs of the age ye live in, and center your deliberations on its exigencies and requirements'. Hence, the aim of Bahá'í education is the process of learning how to apply Bahá'u'lláh's spiritual and moral teachings to the problems of the world in order to effect a positive transformation in the individual and collective lives of humanity.

Bahá'u'lláh (in Shoghi Effendi, 1991, p. 186) taught that religion is 'the greatest of all means for the establishment of order in the world and for the peaceful contentment of all that dwell therein'. The purpose of religion in this world is to 'effect a transformation in the whole character of mankind, a transformation that shall manifest itself, both outwardly and inwardly, that shall affect both its inner life and external conditions' (Bahá'u'lláh, 1950, p. 240). Examining the history of humankind, we find that religion has been the impetus for the rise of many great civilisations. Consider the transformation in the Arab people which resulted from their acceptance of the teachings of Muhammad. Warring tribes were united under one faith and developed the most advanced civilisation at the time.

Notwithstanding, the perversion of religion, the abuse of religious authority and religious fanaticism are responsible for many of the problems of the world today. Faced with the current state of religion, people have turned elsewhere for solutions to society's ills: 'they have turned either to the hedonistic pursuit of material satisfactions or to the following of man-made ideologies designed to rescue society from the evident evils under which it groans' (Universal House of Justice, 1985, p. 6). How many of these ideologies have resolved or mitigated the vast problems facing our world today? By ignoring spirituality and pursuing contentment through material means, disillusionment has only increased.

According to Bahá'u'lláh, human beings have a dual nature – spiritual and material. As the creation of God, humans are essentially spiritual beings. Their purpose in the material world is to draw ever closer to God through the acquisition of spiritual qualities and virtues which, when applied through service to others, contribute to the progress of society. By neglecting the development of spiritual capacities and needs, and focusing solely on achieving material pleasure, humans become worse than animals. The animal lives according to its instincts; it does not have the capacity to be consciously aware of and understand its environment and the consequences of its actions. Humans, however, do have this capacity; when they do not use it and allow their base desires and passions to rule their behaviour, they remain more savage than the animal. 'Abdu'l-Bahá (1990, p. 4) wrote:

> how wretched and contemptible, if he [man] shuts his eyes to the welfare of society and wastes his precious life in pursuing his own selfish interests and personal advantages . . . this is man's uttermost wretchedness: that he should live inert, apathetic, dull, involved only with his own base appetites. When he is thus, he has his being in the deepest ignorance and savagery, sinking lower than the brute beasts.

On the other hand, human beings educated in spiritual and moral virtues who use their knowledge in service to others and society are indeed noble. From a Bahá'í perspective, the purpose of education is to cultivate children's spiritual capacities so that they will contribute nobly to the betterment of the world. Bahá'u'lláh (1976, p. 260) wrote: 'Regard man as a mine rich in gems of inestimable value. Education can, alone, cause it to reveal its treasures, and enable mankind to benefit therefrom.' Because education is so important for the progress of civilisation, Bahá'u'lláh made it obligatory. The education of all, whether male or female, is absolutely necessary if humankind hopes to des-

troy the 'foundations of war and contention' and establish peace in the world ('Abdu'l-Bahá, in Research Department of the Universal House of Justice, 1976, no. 82).

Bahá'í education begins in the home. Although fathers play an important role in raising children, the mother, as the primary caretaker of a newly born infant, is the first educator of the child and is responsible for the child's initial development:

> For children, at the beginning of life, are fresh and tender as a young twig, and can be trained in any fashion you desire. If you rear the child to be straight, he [sic] will grow straight, in perfect symmetry. It is clear that . . . it is she [the mother] who establisheth the character and conduct of the child. ('Abdu'l-Bahá, in Research Department of the Universal House of Justice, 1976, no. 96)

When a child is old enough, he or she begins school. The aim of a school should be to cultivate not only a child's intellect, but to help it develop good character and behaviour. The child's education should be 'of three kinds: material, human, and spiritual'. The first refers to 'the progress and development of the body', its nutritional and other needs. The second concerns the various aspects of human endeavour and civilisation such as 'government, administration, charitable works, trades, arts and handicrafts, sciences, great inventions and discoveries, and elaborate institutions, which are the activities essential to man as distinguished from the animal'. The third involves the cultivation of spiritual qualities, virtues and attitudes which form the basis of human social relations ('Abdu'l-Bahá, 1981). Bahá'í-inspired schools strive to educate children in all three areas.

Common principles and features of Bahá'í-inspired schools

Bahá'í-inspired schools aim to translate the Bahá'í teachings into practice. There is no universal 'model' of Bahá'í education; rather, Bahá'í-inspired schools may be seen as laboratories for learning how to apply Bahá'í principles to the conditions of the populations which they serve to educate. Although Bahá'í-inspired schools are found on every continent and serve many types of people from many different backgrounds, they are based on the same principles and share common features and aims. The latest available statistics note that, on a world-wide basis, there are 178 academic and 488 tutorial Bahá'í-inspired schools (Bahá'í World Centre, 1996, p. 319).

Moral and spiritual education

Moral training is the most essential feature of a Bahá'í school. 'Abdu'l-Bahá (in Research Department of the Universal House of Justice, 1976, no. 74) explained that 'the basic, the foundation-principle of a school is first and foremost moral training, character building, and the rectification of conduct.' In fact:

> Training in morals and good conduct is far more important than book learning. A child that is cleanly, agreeable, of good character, well-behaved – even though he [*sic*] be ignorant – is preferable to a child that is rude, unwashed, ill-natured, and yet becoming deeply versed in all the sciences and arts. The reason for this is that the child who conducts himself well, even though he be ignorant, is of benefit to others, while an ill-natured, ill-behaved child is corrupted and harmful to others, even though he be learned. If, however, the child be trained to be both learned and good, the result is light upon light. ('Abdu'l-Bahá, 1978, pp. 135–6)

Some of the qualities emphasized in Bahá'í schools are truthfulness, trustworthiness, integrity, humility, love and kindness, courtesy, cleanliness, determination, excellence, obedience, patience and tolerance. 'Abdu'l-Bahá counselled:

> The more cleanly the pupils are, the better; they should be immaculate . . . The children must be carefully trained to be most courteous and well-behaved. They must be constantly encouraged and made eager to gain all the summits of human accomplishment, so that from their earliest years they will be taught to have high aims, to conduct themselves well, to be chaste, pure, and undefiled, and will learn to be of powerful resolve and firm of purpose in all things. ('Abdu'l-Bahá, 1978, p. 135)

> First and most important is training in behaviour and good character; the rectification of qualities; arousing the desire to become accomplished and acquire perfections, and to cleave unto the religion of God and stand firm in His Laws, to accord total obedience to every just government, to show forth loyalty and trustworthiness to the ruler of the time, to be well wishers of mankind, to be kind to all. (In Research Department of the Universal House of Justice, 1976, no. 80)

Through the loving encouragement and nurturing of the school teacher, a child acquires the desire to strive for excellence in all realms of learning – whether spiritual or academic. 'Abdu'l-Bahá (in Research Department of the Universal House of Justice, 1976, no. 62) advised:

> Strive thou with heart and soul; see to it that the children are raised up to embody the highest perfections of humankind, to such a degree that every one of them will be trained in the use of the mind, in acquiring knowledge, in humility and lowliness, in dignity, in ardour and love.

Every human being is endowed with the capacity to manifest spiritual qualities and moral virtues. Education is the process that draws out these potentialities. Sometimes,

> certain qualities and natures innate in some men [*sic*] and apparently blameworthy are not so in reality. For example, from the beginning of his life you can see in a nursing child the signs of greed, of anger and of temper . . . greed, which is to ask for something more, is a praiseworthy quality provided that it is used suitably. So if a man is greedy to acquire science and knowledge, or to become compassionate, generous and just, it is most praiseworthy. If he exercises his anger and wrath against the bloodthirsty tyrants who are like ferocious beasts, it is very praiseworthy. But if he does not use these qualities in a right way, they are blameworthy. ('Abdu'l-Bahá, 1981, p. 215)

Thus, how one utilises the qualities one possesses is of key importance. 'Abdu'l-Bahá (1990, p. 59) explains that one of the characteristics of the spiritually learned is the ability to oppose one's passions:

> This is the very foundation of every laudable human quality. How often has it happened that an individual who was graced with every attribute of humanity and wore the jewel of true understanding, nevertheless followed after his passions until his excellent qualities passed beyond moderation and he was forced into excess.

Children must learn how to use their spiritual qualities to overcome their physical desires. They do not have an innate ability to do this; they must be educated. 'Abdu'l-Bahá (ibid., pp. 97–8) explains further:

> There are some who imagine that an innate sense of

human dignity will prevent man from committing evil actions and ensure his spiritual and material perfection. That is, an individual who is characterized with natural intelligence, high resolve, and a driving zeal, will, without any consideration for the severe punishments consequent on evil acts, or for the great rewards of righteousness, instinctively refrain from inflicting harm on his fellow men and will hunger and thirst to do good . . . We also observe in infants the signs of aggression and lawlessness, and that if a child is deprived of a teacher's instructions his undesirable qualities increase from one moment to the next. It is therefore clear that the emergence of this natural sense of human dignity and honour is the result of education.

Children must develop good character through discipline and order. They must be trained systematically – rewarded and punished as necessary. Bahá'u'lláh (1988b, p. 27) wrote: 'That which traineth the world is Justice, for it is upheld by two pillars, reward and punishment. These two pillars are the sources of life to the world.' The teacher must be very careful to properly encourage and counsel children in a loving and caring manner so that they will become obedient. At times, however, children may need to be carefully punished, though never through verbal or physical abuse.

To summarise: the most important aspect of Bahá'í education is acquisition of moral and spiritual qualities. All children possess the potential to develop these virtues, but a loving education is necessary to actualise them. If a child manifests spiritual and moral attributes through good conduct and a praiseworthy character, that child will benefit others. Children learn good behaviour in an orderly and disciplined environment and through constant encouragement from their teachers.

Religious education

As mentioned previously, religion has been the primary cause of the rise of civilisations throughout history. 'Abdu'l-Bahá (1990, p. 94) writes: 'the religions of God are the true source of the spiritual and material perfections of man, and the fountainhead for all mankind of enlightenment and beneficial knowledge'. Moreover:

> Universal benefits derive from the grace of the Divine religions, for they lead their true followers to sincerity of intent, to high purpose, to purity and spotless honor, to surpassing kindness and compassion, to the keeping of their covenants when they

have covenanted, to concern for the rights of others, to liberality, to justice in every aspect of life, to humanity and philanthropy, to valor and to unflagging efforts in the service of mankind. It is religion, to sum up, which produces all human virtues, and it is these virtues which are the bright candles of civilization.   (Ibid., p. 98)

Bahá'ís believe that God has sent a progressive series of Divine Educators or Prophets throughout the ages to guide humankind. The religions founded by these Prophets, such as Judaism, Christianity, Zoroastrianism, Islam, Buddhism, Hinduism, and Bahá'í, came from the same God. In light of this belief, Bahá'ís are encouraged to educate their children not only in the teachings, principles and history of the Bahá'í Faith but of past religions as well. From their earliest days, children should be exposed to the Word of God and learn religious concepts, for:

> God sent His Prophets into the world to teach and enlighten man, to explain to him the mystery of the Power of the Holy Spirit, to enable him to reflect the light, and so in his turn, to be the source of guidance to others. The Heavenly Books, the Bible, the Qur'an, and the other Holy Writings have been given by God as guides to the paths of Divine virtue, love, justice and peace. ('Abdu'l-Bahá, 1995, p. 57)

For Bahá'ís, religious training is an aspect of moral and spiritual education. Bahá'u'lláh (1988b, p. 68) taught:

> Schools must first train the children in the principles of religion, so that the Promise and the Threat recorded in the Books of God, may prevent them from the things forbidden and adorn them with the mantle of the commandments; but this in such a measure that it may not injure the children by resulting in ignorant fanaticism and bigotry.

Children who gain insight into religious teachings and establish a relationship with God are more likely to be able to develop their spiritual natures and oppose their material inclinations. Thus, the regular recital of prayers and readings from Sacred Scriptures are an essential feature of Bahá'í-inspired schools.

Acquisition of knowledge and skills

'Following religious training, and the binding of the child's heart to the love of God, proceed with his education in the other branches of knowledge', advised 'Abdu'l-Bahá (in Research Department of the Universal House of Justice, 1976, no. 70). As ignorance is the primary cause of the problems of the world, education in the various fields of knowledge is of crucial importance:

> The primary, the most urgent requirement is the promotion of education. It is inconceivable that any nation should achieve prosperity and success unless this paramount, this fundamental concern is carried forward. The principal reason for the decline and fall of peoples is ignorance. Today the mass of the people are uninformed even as to ordinary affairs, how much less do they grasp the core of the important problems and complex needs of the time.   ('Abdu'l-Bahá, 1990, p. 109)

When the peoples of a nation are educated, the nation progresses. 'Observe carefully how education and the arts of civilization bring honor, prosperity, independence and freedom to a government and its people' (ibid., p. 111). Hence, taught Bahá'u'lláh (1988a, pp. 26–7), education should be compulsory:

> Knowledge is as wings to man's life, and a ladder for his ascent. Its acquisition is incumbent upon everyone . . . knowledge is a veritable treasure for man, and a source of glory, of bounty, of joy, of exaltation, of cheer and gladness unto him. Happy the man that cleaveth unto it, and woe betide the heedless.

As the 'purpose of learning should be the promotion of the welfare of the people', all people must be educated in the 'branches of knowledge as are of benefit' to humankind (Bahá'u'lláh, in Research Department of the Universal House of Justice, 1976, nos 26, 17). Therefore, in school, children must learn to read and to write. They must study foreign languages so that they can communicate with people of other countries. They must be educated in music and other arts and study the sciences. They must be trained in crafts and other practical skills (Bahá'u'lláh and 'Abdu'l-Bahá, in Research Department of the Universal House of Justice, 1976). Consequently, they must pursue a profession in order to earn their livelihood as adults. Bahá'u'lláh (1988b, p. 35) taught that 'man standeth in need of wealth, and such wealth as he acquireth through crafts or professions is commendable and praiseworthy'. He wrote that the 'best of men are they that earn a livelihood by their calling and spend upon themselves and upon their kindred for the love of God' while the 'basest of men are they that yield no fruit on earth' (Bahá'u'lláh, 1975, nos 82, 81). Hence, children must discover their calling through their school experience so that they may be able to acquire the material means to support themselves and their families and to contribute to the well-being of the community. The teacher's role, then, is to help the child to be trained in a 'field for which he hath an inclination, a desire and a talent' ('Abdu'l-Bahá, in Research Department of the Universal House of Justice, 1976, no. 79).

As knowledge is such a powerful tool, it must be exercised wisely and moderately. The spiritual and moral virtues one develops assist one to use knowledge for good and useful purposes. 'Knowledge is praiseworthy when it is coupled with ethical conduct and a virtuous character; otherwise it is a deadly poison, a frightful danger', writes 'Abdu'l-Bahá (in Research Department of the Universal House of Justice, 1976, no. 74). We need only to look at the lessons of history to realise the truth of this statement. 'Abdu'l-Bahá (ibid., no. 79) explains further:

> If . . . an individual hath spiritual characteristics, and virtues that shine out, and his purpose in life be spiritual and his inclinations be directed toward God, and he also study other branches of knowledge – then we have light upon light: his outer being luminous, his private character radiant, his heart sound, his thought elevated, his understanding swift, his rank noble.

Thus, the aim of Bahá'í-inspired schools is to integrate spiritual and moral concepts into every aspect of the academic curriculum, and to create an environment conducive to the practice of spiritual, moral and religious values as well as the achievement of excellence in intellectual pursuits.

Oneness of humanity

According to the Bahá'í teachings, all human relationships must be based on the principle of the oneness of humanity if peace and unity are to be established in the world. Human society is seen as one organic whole made up of individual yet interconnected parts. Like a human body, society 'functions through the unified, specialized functions of all its constituent parts. Every human being is a part of this organic entity, and his health or illness, his exaltation or debasement, his joy or sorrow, ultimately affects the whole organism' (Danesh, 1986, p. 32).

Science has proved that the human race is one species, although physical characteristics may differ. Bahá'ís believe that God created all humans 'from the same dust' so that 'no one should exalt himself over the other' (Bahá'u'lláh, 1975, no. 68). A sense of superiority by one people prevents others from prospering. Although the heart is one of the most important organs of the human body, it cannot function properly if the other organs of the body are not healthy. All the parts must work in unison for the maintenance and health of the entire body.

Bahá'u'lláh (1976, pp. 94–5) taught that rather than exalt oneself over others, one should 'hold fast unto whatsoever will promote the interests, and exalt the station, of all nations and just governments', and in personal relationships, 'consort with all men . . . in a spirit of friendliness and fellowship' (ibid., p. 289).

Unity in diversity

The principle of the oneness of humanity as a foundation for world unity does not preclude an appreciation of diversity. Although all humans are created essentially the same, as spiritual and material beings they do differ in physical appearance and cultural experience. Bahá'u'lláh likened the diversity of the human race to a flower garden:

> He has declared that difference of race and color is like the variegated beauty of flowers in a garden. If you enter a garden, you will see yellow, white, blue, red flowers in profusion and beauty – each radiant within itself and although different from the others, lending its own charm to them . . . If all the flowers in a garden were of the same color, the effect would be monotonous and wearying to the eye. ('Abdu'l-Bahá, 1982, pp. 68–9)

Therefore, the differences which exist between human beings should not be the cause of disunity and contention, rather they should be celebrated as contributions to the beauty of the whole of humanity: 'The diversity in the human family should be the cause of love and harmony, as it is in music where many different notes blend together in the making of a perfect chord' ('Abdu'l-Bahá, 1995, p. 45).

Peace and world citizenship

'Religious, racial, political, economic and patriotic prejudices destroy the edifice of humanity. As long as these prejudices prevail, the world of humanity will not have rest' ('Abdu'l-Bahá, 1978, p. 299). These prejudices and the resulting divisions between races and cultures are manmade and not based on religious truth nor on sound scientific knowledge ('Abdu'l-Bahá, 1995). Bahá'u'lláh

> has said, and has guarded His statement by rational proofs from the Holy Books, that the world of humanity is one race, the surface of the earth one place of residence and that these imaginary racial barriers and political boundaries are without right or foundation. ('Abdu'l-Bahá, 1982, p. 232)

Humanity is crying out for peace, which, as Bahá'ís believe, is an inevitable stage in the evolution of human civilisation (Universal House of Justice, 1985). Gone are the days when one nation could live in isolation. The world is manifestly interdependent and a world civilisation is beginning. Recognition of the interdependence of peoples and nations, founded on the principle of the oneness of humanity, requires one to view the world as a single entity. Bahá'u'lláh (1976, p. 250) wrote, 'The earth is but one country, and mankind its citizens.' The children of such an interconnected, global society must be trained as citizens of the world. Each must feel a 'profound sense of responsibility for the fate of the planet and for the well-being of the entire human family' (Bahá'í International Community, 1993, p. 1). Although this requires that one's primary loyalty be towards the whole of humanity and not solely to one's own people or nation, it 'does not, however, imply abandonment of legitimate loyalties, the suppression of cultural diversity, the abolition of national autonomy, nor the imposition of uniformity' (ibid., p. 2).

Service

One of the most crucial requirements of world citizenship is the development of a sense of service towards others and towards the common good. 'Abdu'l-Bahá (1990, p. 103) asks:

> . . . is there any deed in the world that would be nobler than service to the common good? Is there any greater blessing conceivable for a man, than that he should become the cause of the education,

the development, the prosperity and honor of his fellow-creatures?

He furthermore counselled:

> Be ye loving fathers to the orphan, and a refuge to the helpless, and a treasury for the poor, and a cure for the ailing. Be ye the helpers of every victim of oppression, the patrons of the disadvantaged. Think ye at all times of rendering some service to every member of the human race. ('Abdu'l-Bahá, 1978, p. 3)

Bahá'ís believe human beings were created to serve. Bahá'u'lláh (1988b, p. 138) wrote that 'man's merit lieth in service and virtue and not in the pageantry of wealth and riches'. Serving others not only brings happiness to those who receive, but those who give as well. 'Happy the soul that shall forget his own good, and . . . vie with his fellows in service to the good of all' ('Abdu'l-Bahá, 1990, p. 116); and, 'Blessed and happy is he that ariseth to promote the best interests of the peoples and kindreds of the earth' (Bahá'u'lláh, 1976, p. 250).

Consultation

One of the most important skills for cooperative decision-making is the ability to consult in a group. Bahá'u'lláh (1988b, p. 168) advised: 'Take ye counsel together in all matters, inasmuch as consultation is the lamp of guidance which leadeth the way, and is the bestower of understanding.' Through discussion and sharing of ideas and opinions, participants strive for consensus in decision-making. Because of the diversity of views of a number of individuals, the solutions resulting from consultation are sure to be more creative than those devised by one person alone.

Consultation is based on several key principles. First, information on the problem or topic to be discussed should be gathered from many diverse sources. Second, in order to gain the most from the opinions of the participants, each must strive to be as open and honest as possible while remaining courteous and avoiding statements that might be viewed as prejudicial. Third, once an idea has been shared it becomes the property of the entire group, thereby requiring individuals to avoid defending their ideas. Finally, the group must try to reach unanimity of thought and action, although a majority vote decision is acceptable if consensus is not reached (National Spiritual Assembly of the Bahá'ís of the United States, 1994).

Bahá'u'lláh (in Research Department of the Universal House of Justice, 1980, no. 2) explained that 'no welfare and no well-being can be attained except through consultation', because it 'bestows greater awareness and transmutes conjecture into certitude' (no. 3).

Some examples of Bahá'í-inspired schools

Schools founded on Bahá'í principles may be officially sponsored by Bahá'í administrative institutions or may be private ventures owned and run by Bahá'í-inspired agencies or individual Bahá'ís. There are Bahá'í-inspired schools and educational projects in many countries and in every continental area. Some of the schools are fairly traditional in their organisation, while others provide alternative educational opportunities for disadvantaged populations. The schools and programmes highlighted below represent a diversity of approaches to the implementation of Bahá'í teachings and principles.

School of the Nations, Macau

Founded in 1988, the School of the Nations is a private, non-profit international school licensed by the Government of Macau. It offers from pre-school through to secondary education to nearly 500 students. Although most of the students are from Macau, Hong Kong and China, the students and teachers together represent more than 30 cultures and five continents. Classes are taught in English to allow students greater access to information, and in Mandarin to prepare them for Macau's return to China in 1999. In the secondary school, students prepare for the International General Certificate of Secondary Education (IGCSE).

One of the key features of the school is its moral education programme which aims to develop students' moral capabilities. The term capability refers to 'a developed capacity to carry out actions purposefully in a well-defined field of endeavor' (Nogouchi *et al.*, 1992, p. 14). A moral capability is concerned with the field of morality and, therefore, 'results from the interaction of certain related qualities, skills, attitudes and knowledge that enable a person to make moral choices' (ibid., p. 14) which affect his or her personal life as well as social relations. The kindergarten and secondary school programmes are the most developed.

At the kindergarten level, the building blocks of moral capabilities – spiritual qualities, skills and abilities, attitudes and knowledge – are integrated into all subjects across the curriculum. For example, in science, students learn the concept of the oneness of humanity through studying the family as a system. Once the children understand the nature of the family and how its members cooperate, the concept is expanded by looking at how families within a community are related and interact, and so forth. In maths, the concept of the oneness of humanity is conveyed through lessons on the mathematical concept of a set. The children look at larger and larger sets of children – in their class, in the country and then in the world. Separate moral education classes, in which children learn about virtues such as courtesy, sharing, service, love, cooperation and generosity through prayers, stories, games, role plays and other activities, are also given.

The secondary school moral education programme emphasises five specific capabilities: to create a healthy family; to empower others, to bring joy to others; to preserve the environment and use its resources soundly; and to consult effectively. Each week students spend two hours either serving various organisations and projects or in class consulting about and evaluating their experiences. Students keep journals about their activities.

In the first year of the programme (Form 1), students learn about the education of children and practise their knowledge by assisting in the school's kindergarten or by tutoring primary school students. Once confidence in their ability to serve is gained, the students begin to work with agencies outside of the school. In the second year, students learn about environmental conservation, manage the school's recycling programme and educate other students, teachers and parents about the need to recycle. They also work with the Park Service to clean designated public areas. In the third year, students learn to document the history of Macau, particularly its social service organisations, in order to produce materials, such as videos, for the education of the public. During the fourth year, students work with the elderly in nursing homes under the direction of social workers. In the fifth year, the students choose the type of social service organisation that they would like to serve.

The moral education programme not only helps the students to develop a sense of service to others and the community but also to learn about themselves and realise their responsibility to contribute to the betterment of society. The school also takes care to educate parents about the programme and to enlist their support. It has been so successful that the social service agencies have come to depend on the volunteer assistance of the school's students.

System for Tutorial Learning, Colombia

The System for Tutorial Learning (SAT) is a secondary-level rural education programme developed by the Foundation for the Application and Teaching of the Sciences (FUNDAEC), a non-profit development agency based in Cali. In the early 1970s the founders of FUNDAEC, most of whom were Bahá'ís, became aware of the lack of opportunities for secondary education in the Cauca region, due to a paralysis of poverty and urban migration. Realising that traditional schooling methods would not solve the region's problems, they began to develop the SAT programme according to the need and realities of rural life, with an emphasis on the sciences.

Today the SAT curriculum is recognised by the government and is offered to 15,000 students in thirteen of Colombia's 30 departments. It is also being used in an increasing number of Latin American countries. Although FUNDAEC trains tutors and administers the programme, tutors may start classes in any community through seeking the sponsorship of the municipal government, a non-governmental organisation or a religious group. Tutors form small groups of students who study together for 15–20 hours per week. The tutor guides the students through a series of workbooks. By participatory learning methods, students acquire the practical skills needed for rural life and gain a deeper understanding of their connection to and responsibility towards the environment.

The curriculum is not divided into subject areas, but rather integrates them to be more meaningful to the students. For example, in the series of workbooks called 'Descriptions', students learn words and concepts that help them describe the world around them. When learning about systems and processes, the students look at the example of the human body, thereby learning anatomy and physiology. Moral and spiritual concepts and principles gleaned from the Bahá'í teachings are incorporated into the curriculum. Service to the community and virtues such as honesty, trustworthiness and love are emphasised.

Maxwell International Bahá'í School, Canada

The Maxwell International Bahá'í School, established in 1988 at Shawnigan Lake, British Columbia, is a residential secondary school beginning with grade seven. It is officially sponsored by the National Spiritual Assembly of the Bahá'ís of Canada. It offers a standard academic curriculum approved by the provincial government which is integrated with Bahá'í moral and spiritual concepts and principles. In addition, the school provides visual and performing arts and physical education programmes. Approximately 240 students from more than twelve countries attend the school.

The Maxwell School is concerned with the spiritual, intellectual, social and physical development of its students. Its goal is to prepare its students as world citizens and, therefore, the entire school environment as well as the curriculum revolve around this aim. Students are encouraged to study a diversity of subjects and to learn about the contributions the world's peoples, cultures and religions have made toward human civilisation. Courses in history, geography and other social sciences examine the connections between peoples and their cultures and investigate the needs of human society in the present age. The mathematics programme, which includes computer programming, teaches students how to measure relationships, processes and changes in nature and society and in one's own life. The science programme assists students to understand their relationship and responsibility towards nature and the establishment of sustainable environments. The health and physical education programme helps students to care for and develop the strength of their bodies, and offers a variety of sports and other recreational activities. To learn to communicate more effectively, students study English and French, paying particular attention to effective speaking and listening as well as writing. Study of music and art allows students to express themselves artistically, while study of the world's religions leads to greater understanding of the spiritual and moral foundations of social life. A service programme offers students the opportunity to put their knowledge into practice through serving their fellow students and the community at large.

Bahá'í Vocational Institute for Rural Women, India

Established in 1983, the Bahá'í Vocational Institute for Rural Women works towards the improvement of the social and economic condition of twenty tribal communities in seven districts surrounding the city of Indore. The people living in this region are among the most marginalised in Indian society and few opportunities for education exist there. In 1981, the census showed that only 7 per cent of the rural population was literate and only 3 per cent of the rural women.

The Institute has established courses and other programmes which focus on changing traditional attitudes and practices based on the prejudices of caste, tribe, religion and gender that have prevented men and women from working together for community improvement. Every year the Institute trains 50 to 60 women as community workers during a three-month residential programme. The majority of these women are between the ages of 15 and 20 and are illiterate. The three-month course emphasises literacy and numeracy in Hindi, health and nutrition education, spiritual education based on the Bahá'í teachings and focusing on the principle of the oneness of humanity, and the development of skills such as sewing, embroidery, growing vegetables, and cycling. The programme involves participatory learning activities and consultation to help women gain self-confidence. When graduates of the programme return to their villages, they are capable of starting small income-generation or community-improvement projects, teaching children's or literacy classes, and educating others in health matters. The Institute also trains annually, during a one-month course, ten area coordinators who visit the community workers to help them utilise their newly acquired skills, establish and encourage local women's committees to organise activities for education and income-generation, identify and recruit students for future courses, and collect data for evaluation. By June 1996, the Institute had trained more than 700 women.

In 1992, the Institute was recognized with the Global 500 Roll of Honor award by the United Nations Environment Program for its role in the complete eradication of Guinea worm from the region as a result of education.

School of the Nations, Brazil

Founded in 1980 by a group of Bahá'í educators, the School of the Nations is a private bilingual, international primary school offering education from kindergarten through to the eighth grade. The curriculum is taught in both Portuguese and English and meets all government standards. Approximately 230 students representing more than 25 countries attend the school. Located in the capital city, Brasilia, the school attracts children of many foreign diplomats interested in the school's emphasis on world citizenship.

Through exposure to many cultures and religions, students learn to respect diversity but also to see the connections between the world's peoples. In grades 5–8, students go through a comparative religion programme looking at the historical context of the Bible in the first year, followed by study of the New Testament, Islam and the Bahá'í Faith in each of the remaining years.

The School of the Nations also offers a strong science programme focusing on the environment. In 1993, the School of the Nations collaborated with the Office of the Environment of the National Spiritual Assembly of the Bahá'ís of Brazil and UNICEF in developing an environmental education programme for primary school children. The School's students in grades 2–6 wrote four skits about the elements of earth, fire, water and air which they performed as part of the overall programme for thousands of children. The school is also in the process of developing a science and ethics curriculum for grades 1–4 based on Bahá'í teachings.

Bahá'í pre-schools and teacher training programme, Swaziland

In 1986, a national pre-school curriculum plan based on the experiences of several Bahá'í pre-schools in Swaziland was approved by the Ministry of Education in order to establish standards for a growing number of pre-schools run by various organisations throughout the country. The curriculum incorporates moral and spiritual education in basic virtues such as love, respect for parents and teachers, unity, courtesy and service, as well as other activities, to prepare children for primary school. To ensure that teachers for the Bahá'í schools are adequately trained, a teacher-training programme was developed which is also offered to students selected by the Ministry of Education.

Implications of Bahá'í education in the context of a culturally diverse world

As noted above under the heading 'Common principles and features of Bahá'í-inspired schools', Bahá'í educational curricula not only explicitly emphasise tolerance of diversity, but go beyond that to advocate 'unity in diversity'. No Bahá'í-inspired school is without instruction in:

1   respect for cultures other than one's own;
2   recognising the divine foundation of the major world religions, thus decreasing religious prejudice;
3   recognising the essential oneness of humanity, thus decreasing ethnic and racial prejudice; and
4   emphasising world citizenship and not nationalism, yet respecting a sane patriotism to one's native country.

Besides 'direct instruction' in these values, Bahá'í education seeks to practise these beliefs. Bahá'í-inspired schools welcome and invite members of all races, religions and nations to attend them, while continuing to respect the individual student's, and the student's family's, belief system. As shown in the examples of Bahá'í-inspired schools above, students in these schools participate in '*service practica*' in which they provide some form of social service to the community surrounding them. They perform this service without regard to the religious, racial or class background of those they serve.

Although Bahá'í-inspired schools tend to be non-government affiliated, they generally meet government standards for education and often assist the secular government in its goals to educate the people of that country. Bahá'ís believe in, and explicitly teach, loyalty to the secular government of the lands in which they reside, therefore governments tend to encourage Bahá'í-inspired educational innovations (see, in particular, the example in Colombia, above). Additionally, individual Bahá'ís and Bahá'í institutions encourage and support government schools' efforts to increase the focus upon and quality of the moral education in government-run schools. Bahá'ís, though exceedingly cautious not to be involved in partisan politics of any kind, encourage their school boards, and governmental schooling agencies, to place prominently in their curricula: education for world citizenship; understanding of the teachings of the various world religions; oneness of the races; equality of the sexes; respect for nature and the environment; and the learning of skills that will allow students to become productive members of a world society.

In summary

In this chapter we aimed to introduce the reader to a Bahá'í view of the purpose of education, along with a review of common principles and features of Bahá'í-inspired schools. The Bahá'í perspective emphasises that values education (especially in the context of moral and spiritual values) is of greater importance than intellectual education, and high-quality schools must give careful attention to both. Various goals of a Bahá'í curriculum, related to a values education that is multiculturally sensitive, were then examined. Those goals are:

- teaching content knowledge of the various world religions;
- studying and experiencing the oneness of humanity;
- appreciating unity in diversity;
- striving for peace and world citizenship;
- developing a life of service to humanity; and
- gaining the skills to conduct consultative dialogue.

To illustrate the educational process of attaining those goals, descriptions of particular exemplar Bahá'í inspired schools were sketched. It was emphasised that students of all cultural and religious backgrounds are welcome in Bahá'í schools, and that these school's *service practica* are aimed at serving others of a variety of ethnicities and religious beliefs.

References

'Abdu'1-Bahá (1978) *Selections from the Writings of 'Abdu'l-Bahá*. Haifa: Bahá'í World Centre.

'Abdu'l-Bahá (1981) *Some Answered Questions*. Wilmette, IL: Bahá'í Publishing Trust.

'Abdu'l-Bahá (1982) *Promulgation of Universal Peace: Talks Delivered by 'Abdu'l-Bahá During His Visit to the United States and Canada*. Wilmette, IL: Bahá'í Publishing Trust.

'Abdu'l-Bahá (1990) *The Secret of Divine Civilization*. Wilmette, IL: Bahá'í Publishing Trust.

'Abdu'l-Bahá (1995) *Paris Talks: Addresses Given by 'Abdu'l-Bahá in 1911*. London: Bahá'í Publishing Trust.

Bahá'í International Community (1993) *World Citizenship: A Global Ethic for Sustainable Development*. New York: Bahá'í International Community.

Bahá'í International Community (1995) *The Prosperity of Humankind*, a statement released by the Office of Public Information on the occasion of the World Summit for Social Development, Copenhagen. Haifa: Bahá'í World Centre.

Bahá'í World Centre (1996) *The Bahá'í World 1994–95: An International Record*. Haifa: World Centre Publications.

Bahá'u'lláh (1950) *The Kitáb-i-Íqán: The Book of Certitude*. Wilmette, IL: Bahá'í Publishing Trust.

Bahá'u'lláh (1975) *The Hidden Words of Bahá'u'lláh*. Wilmette, IL: Bahá'í Publishing Trust.

Bahá'u'lláh (1976) *Gleanings from the Writings of Bahá'u'lláh*. Wilmette, IL: Bahá'í Publishing Trust.

Bahá'u'lláh (1988a) *Epistle to the Son of the Wolf*. Wilmette, IL: Bahá'í Publishing Trust.

Bahá'u'lláh (1988b) *Tablets of Bahá'u'lláh Revealed After the Kitáb-i-Aqdas*. Wilmette, IL: Bahá'í Publishing Trust.

Commission on Global Governance (1995) *Our Global Neighborhood: The Report of the Commission on Global Governance*. Oxford: Oxford University Press.

Danesh, H. B. (1986) *Unity: The Creative Foundation of Peace*. Ottawa: Bahá'í Studies Publications.

Etzioni, A. (1993) *The Spirit of Community: Rights, Responsibilities, and the Communitarian Agenda*. New York: Crown Publishers.

Havel, V. (1995) The need for transcendence in the postmodern world. *Futurist* **29**, 46–9.

Mathews, J. (1997) The age of nonstate actors. *Foreign Affairs* **76**, 50–66.

National Spiritual Assembly of the Bahá'ís of the United States. (1994) *Unity and Consultation: Foundations of Sustainable Development*. Wilmette, IL: National Spiritual Assembly of the Bahá'ís of the United States.

Nogouchi, L.M., Hanson, H. and Lample, P. (1992) *Exploring a Framework for Moral Education*. Riviera Beach, FL: Palabra Publications.

Research Department of the Universal House of Justice (comp.) (1976, rev. 1987) *Bahá'í Education: A Compilation of Extracts from the Bahá'í Writings*. London: Bahá'í Publishing Trust.

Research Department of the Universal House of Justice (comp.) (1980) *Consultation: A Compilation*. Wilmette, IL: Bahá'í Publishing Trust.

Sandel, M.J. (1996) *Democracy's Discontent: America in Search of a Public Philosophy*. Cambridge, MA: Belknap Press.

Shoghi Effendi (1991) *The World Order of Bahá'u'lláh*. Wilmette, IL: Bahá'í Publishing Trust.

United Nations Research Institute for Social Development

(1995) *States of Disarray: The Social Effects of Globalization. A United Nations Research Institute for Social Development Report for the World Summit for Social Development.* London: KPC Group.

Universal House of Justice (1985) *The Promise of World Peace: To the Peoples of the World.* Wilmette, IL: Bahá'í Publishing Trust.

Further reading

Ayman, Iraj (ed.) (1993) *A New Framework for Moral Education.* Germany: Asr-i-Jadid Publisher.

Bahá'í International Community, Office of Public Information (1995) *The Prosperity of Humankind.* New York: Bahá'í International Community.

Johnson, Barbara (1991) Multicultural education and the oneness of humanity. *World Order* **23**, 29–38

National Bahá'í Education Task Force (1995) *Foundations for a Spiritual Education: Research of the Bahá'í Writings.* Wilmette, IL: Bahá'í Publishing Trust.

Nikjoo, H. (ed.) (1990) *Trends in Bahá'í Education: Proceedings of the 2nd Symposium on Bahá'í Education 1989.* London: Bahá'í Publishing Trust.

Rost, H.T.D. (1979) *The Brilliant Stars.* Oxford: George Ronald.

Tailor, B. (comp.) (1986) *The Power of Unity: Beyond Prejudice and Racism.* Wilmette, IL: Bahá'í Publishing Trust.

13 Denominational Schools in the Netherlands

DORET DE RUYTER AND SIEBREN MIEDEMA

Introduction

This chapter is devoted to the Dutch school system. We shall present and discuss this system quite extensively and from different perspectives. The Dutch school system is unique in the world, but uniqueness naturally does not imply worth and value, nor a system which is unquestionable or unproblematic. We think we can elucidate some general questions about separate schools by focusing on our system and its history.

We shall start with a historical survey of the origin of the Dutch educational system within the context of our former strongly segregated society. This society was called a 'pillarised' society, a metaphor for a society divided into four highly segregated groups, namely Roman Catholics, Protestants, Socialists and Liberals. In the third section, we shall describe three characteristics of the Dutch educational system, namely its constitutional basis, the complete subsidy by the state and the restricted role of the state. In the fourth section we go deeper into the difference between state schools and denominational schools regarding their stance towards world views and religions. The major difference between the two kinds of schools is not that religion is absent in state schools compared to denominational schools, but that denominational schools are faith-orientated while state schools are not. We also show that state schools can handle religious matters in different ways.

In the final two sections we shall evaluate the Dutch system. In the fifth section we describe two possible justifications of denominational schools. These justifications are related to rights of parents and children. In the last section we describe two restrictions to denominational schools that should

be taken into account by these schools in order to make the given justification plausible.

The history of the Dutch educational system

The more or less denominational segregation or pillarisation of public life was characteristic of Dutch society from the French Revolution up till the 1960. This pillarisation was the result of a struggle for emancipation by Roman Catholics and Protestants that started around 1830 and became manifest in the second part of the nineteenth century. This emancipation movement initially focused on the school. Both groups wanted to have their own religion-based curriculum. They had serious doubts whether the pluralistic public schools could be adequate vehicles for the transmission of their specific religious cultures. They strongly argued against any form of pluralistic public schooling (the form originally intended in the state-Protestant tradition) in which all religious denominations had their place.

Although from 1857 it was legally possible for parents to start denominational schools and give their children the education they wanted, it was not until 1917 that the controversy about school funding was settled by the Pacification Act. It resulted in an equal financial treatment of state schools and private (denominational) schools. Very important to this settlement was the role played by the new political movement of Socialism. The Socialists did not want to lose or alienate the Christian labourers from the socialist movements. In the words of one of the socialist leaders, Troelstra: 'In order to save the class struggle, we leave the religious struggle untouched' (De Jong Ozn, 1992, p.28). The

Protestant and Catholic schools received freedom of direction and freedom of organisation and were to be governed by a school board or a school corporation. The state only laid down general quality criteria for all schools, private as well as state (see also the third section).

The process of giving form and content to the permitted educational autonomy went hand in hand with a general economic and political emancipation, resulting in a total pillarisation of public and political life in Dutch society. From 1920 onwards this process of pillarization resulted in a fragmentation of almost all societal institutions and groups along denominational lines. So pillarization was not restricted to education, but the entire public and political life of society became organized along segregational lines: universities, political parties, trade unions, welfare work, hospitals and so on (cf. Lijphart, 1975). This, which can be characterised as vertical pillarisation, resulted in a specific plurality of our society. The effect of this *politics of pillarisation* was a strong separation between the various denominational groups, each locked up in their own organisations and institutions. This blocked the way for value exchange and for the sharing and mutual construction of values.

Due to the influences of secularisation and individualisation, during the 1960s and 1970s the de-pillarisation of Dutch society began. The overall impact of the church diminished in public and political life, and many organisations merged across denominational lines.

Just when the rigid system of the politics of pillarisation was past its zenith and *intracultural plurality* was unlocked, Dutch society was confronted much more than before with *intercultural plurality.* In the 1960s people from Morocco, Spain, Portugal, Turkey and Yugoslavia came to the Netherlands in an attempt to improve their situation. They were welcomed as, literally translated, 'guest labourers'. This name stood for the idea that the men would come to the Netherlands to work for several years, leaving their families in their countries of origin. But the reality was different. After several years their families came to the Netherlands as well. After these immigrant workers, people from our former colonies came to the Netherlands in larger groups. In particular, just before the declaration of independence of Surinam, people moved from Surinam to the Netherlands as they expected to have a better future there.

Thus, nowadays Dutch society is multicultural and multireligious in two senses. Not only has the number of cultures and religions increased, but so have the ways in which religion is practised become individualised and enormously varied. One would think that this would be reflected in the educational system, but interestingly, until now the denominational borders between the schools still exist. Today the division between state schools and Christian schools is still evident, and it is exactly the same 1:3 ratio as it was in the days when Dutch societal pillarisation was at its height. So about 75 per cent of the schools are denominational, and this in spite of the enormous secularisation that has taken place during the last decades.

Constitutional right to denominational schools

Since 1917 and the already mentioned Pacification Act, parents have had a constitutional right to send their children to the school of their choice. This includes a constitutional right to send their children to religious schools. Being a constitutional right expresses the great importance given to that right. For, in our political system, the constitution cannot be changed easily. A change needs two successive governments carrying the proposed change. Although parents have this right, it is restricted in one way: denominational schools, contrary to state schools, are allowed to refuse admittance to children. If for example, the principal of such a school has serious doubts about the way in which parents deal with religious matters that are important to the school, the principal has a right to advise them to try to find another school for their child.

Section 2 of Article 23 of our constitution states that teaching is free, except for inspection by the government of the capability and moral behaviour of the teachers. Though this section does not say anything about parental freedom of choice, it has acquired this interpretation during this century. Parents not only have the right to send their children to religious schools, they also have the right to found a school based on their religion or world view, if this is distinctive enough from schools in the nearby area and if the group of children that will attend the school is large enough. The issue is sometimes under discussion in the Netherlands. For instance, a few years ago a group of liberal Hindu parents wanted to found their own school in The Hague. This was not allowed by the government, because it was argued that there was already a Hindu school in the city. Though this was a school with a more traditional stance towards religion the government did not think it different enough *qua* direction to grant the liberal Hindu parents a separate school. Only after a hunger strike by the parents did the government decide to subsidise a liberal Hindu school. But, though 'direction'[1] sometimes poses problems, we have an enormous number of state-subsidised religious or ideologically bound schools. To mention just a few, we have Roman Catholic, Protestant, Dutch Reformed, Baptist, Jewish, Hindu, Islamic, and Waldorf primary and secondary schools. Recently, a Transcendental Meditation primary school opened its doors.

We learned that in the United Kingdom direction and size of group are also requirements parents must meet in order to found a school; but there is another demand, which is absent in the Netherlands. In the United Kingdom it must be shown that a new school is required in an area: that there are too many pupils for the existing schools. If this had been the same in our country, we would never have had the existing pluriformity of schools.

Against the constitutional right of parents, it is interesting to notice that children are not given a right to a certain kind of education. Legally they have no rights to education at all, but a duty: children have a duty to attend school from the age of four until they are sixteen. This compulsory education has been present in the Netherlands since 1901 and has extended in length during this century. Since children are obliged to go to school and receive education, it is apparent they also have the right to do so. The content of the education they have a right to receive is not explicitly formulated in our law. However, in the Netherlands several international conventions in which statements are made on the content of education have been ratified. Among these are the International Covenant on Economic, Social and Cultural Rights (IVESCR) and the Convention on the Rights of the Child. Article 29 in the latter Convention describes the aims of education. It says:

1. State Parties agree that the education of the child shall be directed to:
   (a) the development of the child's personality, talents and mental and physical abilities to their fullest potential;
   (b) the development of respect for human rights and fundamental freedoms, and for

the principles enshrined in the Charter of the United Nations;
   (c) the development of respect for the child's parents, his or her own cultural identity, language and values, for the national values of the country in which the child is living, the country from which he or she may originate, and for civilisations different from his or her own;
   (d) the preparation of the child for responsible life in a free society, in the spirit of understanding, peace, tolerance, equality of sexes, and friendship among all peoples, ethnic, national and religious groups and persons of indigenous origin;
   (e) the development of respect for the natural environment.[2]

The child's right to the particular kind of education defined in sub-sections (a), (b), (e) and especially (d) can be different from or even in opposition to the right of the parents to a specific kind of education. For it is not in every school that the educational aims mentioned under (a), (b) and (d) are striven after. We shall see in the examples given in the rest of this chapter that in the Netherlands the right of the parents tends to prevail over the right of the child to the mentioned aims of education (see also Van der Ploeg, 1994).

The constitutional right of parents has led to two other characteristics of our system, namely complete governmental subsidy and a restriction of the influence of the government in denominational schools. The practice of complete state subsidy is based on the principle of justice. The argument is that if the right to found denominational schools and maintain them is considered so important that it is a constitutional right, everybody must, within the restrictions given by the constitution, have the opportunity to enjoy this right. Thus, it should not be dependent on the financial situation of the group whether they can have their own specific school. This is different from other countries. Though other countries have different kinds of schools as well, they are in many countries more or less paid for by the parents themselves.

The other characteristic mentioned is that the government has a limited influence in the curriculum and practice of denominational schools. We shall give two examples of the boundaries of that influence. The first example is a project launched in 1992 by the democratic-socialist Dutch Minister of Education and Sciences, Jo Ritzen. This project was named 'The pedagogical task of the school: an invitation to joint action' (Ritzen, 1992). Ritzen believed that the school should take its responsibility in filling the vacuum of norms and values in Dutch society, which results in over-individualised and criminal behaviour. A revitalisation of the pedagogical task of the school was needed, a striving for a new equilibrium between individuality and communality, between individual freedom and responsibility for others. As he knew he was treading on delicate ground, he stated that his project was not intended to be a policy statement, but should be interpreted as a position at the outset of a dialogue, hopefully leading to collective action (ibid., p. 2). One year later in an article published in a national Dutch newspaper, the Minister elaborated on his view of the pedagogical task of the school. In order to defend his interference with the denominational schools as well as to explain why he had stayed on his side of the line, he made a distinction between three aspects of the pedagogical task of schools and related these to different kinds of (shared) responsibility of state and schools. The first aspect is civic education: mindful of its interests, the Minister is of the opinion that the state should be involved. The second aspect concerns the relationship between school education and the world view: here the Minister thinks it necessary for the state to be very reserved. But although this particular relationship is the responsibility of those in charge of the schools, the Minister stresses their responsibility to explicate the world view identity of the schools, and is pleading for processes of exchange of ideas and dialogue between the participants in the schools in which norms and values show up. The third aspect deals with the pedagogical relations and processes in the school which he takes to be the complete responsibility of those involved (cf. Ritzen, 1993).

The second example of the restrictions of state involvement in denominational schools concerns a more recent discussion in our country. Though the state was said to have no influence on the content of the curriculum, it has influence in a quite distinctive way in secondary schools. The final examinations are coordinated centrally, so that every student has the same chance of passing. But this implies that the subjects of the examinations are also decided upon centrally. In the case of the biology examination this has become an issue. The problem, that even made it to parliament, is whether in the central examination questions about Darwin's evolutionary theory

can be included. Several denominational schools opposed this, claiming that they should not be forced to teach about Darwin's theory as a possibly true theory of evolution because this is in conflict with their faith in creationism. Being a subject of examination would imply this obligation, for schools must give their students a fair chance in the exams. It was finally decided that this was such a problematic subject related to matters of faith, in which the government could not have a say, that it would not be part of the examinations. Thus, the schools are free to decide whether they will teach about evolutionary theory or not. This example shows the way in which the tension noticed regarding the article in the Convention of the Rights of the Child is resolved in favour of the religious communities.

Denominational schools and state schools on conceptions of the good

As our system is segregated along denominational lines, we shall elucidate the distinction in the way in which denominational schools and state schools deal with conceptions of the good. 'Conception of the good' is described by Rawls (1987, p. 16) as 'a determinate scheme of final ends and aims, and of desires that certain persons and associations as objects of attachments and loyalties should flourish. Also included in such a conception is a view of our relation to the world – religious, philosophical or moral – by reference to which these ends and attachments are understood.' We prefer to use the term conception of the good instead of religion, because it has a broader content than religion and because it is not necessarily religious.

Characteristic for state schools is that their education must be conscious of the multiformity of the conceptions of good in society. Because no child can be refused admittance to the state school, these schools need to be aware of the diverse world views represented by the children attending the school. This multiformity must, by law, be reflected in the curriculum. Not one conception of the good or one world view is to be directive for the process of introduction into cultural, moral and religious meanings. The state schools are required to take a non-preferential stance against the diversity of world views; this does not imply that these schools are neutral or that the teaching in these schools is neutral, but state schools should not favour a particular world view.

A non-preferential stance against world views can be interpreted in two radically different ways, both of which can be found in Dutch public schools. The first interpretation can be described as 'passive non-preferentiality'. In this conceptualisation teachers must refrain from influencing pupils in any possible way regarding conceptions of the good. The conception of every pupil in the school is to be fully respected, and in accordance with this, the teacher is not allowed to influence the pupils towards any conception of the good which might be different from the pupils' conceptions. Thus, conceptions of the good that are specific in character are only put forward in the school as a subject of knowledge, as part of the subject-matter of the curriculum. The second conception of non-preferentiality can be described as 'active non-preferentiality'. In this conception the teachers must give attention to all the conceptions of the good that are prevalent within the school. By refraining from influencing the pupils with her or his own conception and by giving attention to the different conceptions of the pupils, respect is actively shown. However, both interpretations of non-preferentiality have the common factor of not being faith-orientated. Precisely at this point the approach of world view, of conceptions of the good in state schools differs greatly from those practised in denominational schools.

In denominational schools children are raised within one specific conception of the good, that is, one specific world view. It is a characteristic of these schools that one specific conception of the good is dominant and that teachers aim for the embracing of this conception by the children.

The difference can also be explained by means of the concepts 'teaching about' and 'teaching into'. Characteristic of teaching about is that a religion is offered as a scholarly topic without any evangelical intentions on the part of the teacher. The teacher can deal with the topic as neutrally as possible and teach the pupils about the religious tradition, its holy books, its rituals and its morality. In this interpretation teaching religion can be compared to teaching languages: teaching English or German is not teaching pupils to become an Englishman or a German, but is about acquiring knowledge of the country and its history and skills to speak the language (see Holley, 1994; Sealy, 1994). When religious education is thought of as teaching about several religions, it is of course possible to implement this subject in the curriculum of all schools, similarly to history and geography. In fact, since 1985, every elementary school in the Netherlands is obliged to teach its pupils about the major religions or world views.

Characteristic of teaching into religion is that the teacher or parent intends that the child should become a committed religious adult. This is explicitly not non-preferential. On the contrary, the educators think that the religion they are teaching the child into is the best and most worthwhile, and they hope the child will share this opinion.[3]

Though religion has been the basis of justification of our system, it is under pressure nowadays. Due to secularisation not only are many children who attend denominational schools not raised by their parents in that specific conception of good, but also many teachers at denominational schools no longer hold that specific conception. This poses problems for denominational schools, especially with respect to justifying their existence. For why should a Christian school, for instance, remain a Christian school when there is hardly anything Christian left? This situation is, however, not unexceptional in the Netherlands. This tendency has been called 'changing colour': schools that were denominational change into schools with a different direction or into a school without a clear and distinct kind of direction.

Defence of denominational schools

In this section we shall describe two justifications of denominational schools based on parental and children's rights.

The extension argument

Parents have the legitimate right to send their children to specific denominational or world view based schools. We may wonder, however, whether parents should have this right. The answer to this question depends on the way in which the education which takes place in the school is related to the upbringing in the family. In the Netherlands there is a broad consensus about the normative status of denominational schools. These schools are not value-free in respect to world view. Norms and values related to teaching and learning play a role, and the impact and content of the underlying world view or embraced world views should be articulated. School practices are not restricted solely to teaching knowledge and skills, but are embedded in and related to normative and/or world view frameworks. We can say that in the Netherlands denominational schools are looked upon as communities in which children are not only taught subjects, and not only learn, but also live together on the basis of shared or at least respected world views. This view on denominational schools can also be seen in the remarks of authors that religion should not be restricted to moments of religious education, but should permeate throughout the entire school. This is called the broad identity of schools (Miedema, 1994).

Denominational schools are thus regarded as an extension of parental education, not because they teach knowledge and skills which the parents themselves have not mastered, but precisely because they teach within a specific conception of the good, which gives parents the right to have a say about the kind of conception they want their children to be raised in. This right is not unrestrained. Parents cannot claim their parental right to raise their children according to their world view if the conception of the good they want their children to be educated in is in flagrant opposition to the laws of our society.

The coherence argument

Do children have a particular right to denominational education as well? To this, two related answers can be given. Our first answer focuses on the importance for children's development to be raised within a specific conception of good. Our second answer concentrates on the desirability for coherence between the primary culture in the family and at school.

Schools have an important role in the identity development of children.[4] Schools are communities in which the child participates for at least twelve years and for about seven hours a day. Within schools, fellow pupils and the formation of peer groups contribute to a child's identity. Teachers, however, will have as much influence, not only by direct education, but also by the way in which they behave in social situations, the way in which they support the child if he or she is outcast or the way in which they correct a child's behaviour in relation to other children.

Various philosophers (of education) claim that a stable primary culture or framework in which children can develop their identity is necessary (see, for example, Taylor, 1989, 1992). Children need values and ideals with which they can identify or which they can reject in the formation of their identities. So, children have to be raised within a situation in which parents and teachers hold a conception of the good, live according to it, and share that conception with the children. Teachers and the school community can and will influence children's formation of their conception of good, that is the values and ideals they comprise within their identities. This claim is valid not only for denominational schools, but for all schools that educate within a specific conception of the good. Within our multicultural, depillarised society it is all the more important that children should be provided with frameworks within which they can form their identities. Without it, choice options would be so overwhelming that children would become too paralysed almost to begin to make choices.

The argument that all schools should transmit a specific conception of the good is not a sufficient justification for the existence of denominational schools or for the right of children to denominational education: state schools also educate children within a conception of the good. So, for the interest of a child to denominational education, we need an additional argument. This is the coherence argument.

In our opinion, children of primary school age have a need for coherence between the primary culture they are raised in at home and the primary culture of the school. A stable primary culture of beliefs, practices and values is significant for a child's development (see McLaughlin, 1994). In a religious family, the religious beliefs and practices (rituals) are part of the primary culture as well. Children join their parents in religious practices and parents transmit their religious values to their children. Since we in the Netherlands have schools with a religious primary culture, broadening the primary culture to a stable primary culture at school as well is in the young child's interest. As we have said, in such a school the specific religion (or conception of the good) is not presented as a knowledge subject to be studied within religious education, but is prevalent in all aspects of the school, for instance in the pedagogical stance of the teachers, and the sphere of the school. This kind of school, in which the conception of the good is highly prevalent and which is coherent with the conception within which the child is raised in the family, is beneficial to children.

This argument is valid only if the pupils in a school have generally the same specific conception of the good; thus Christian schools are attended by Christian children only, and Islamic, Hindu and Jewish schools are attended only by children with that specific conception of the good. This, however, is no longer the case in the Netherlands. If we take the child's interest in a coherent primary culture seriously, we either have to guarantee a specific denominational school for all children, or we have to change our specific denominational schools into multidenominational schools, of which there are already a few examples in The Hague, Rotterdam and Amsterdam. The intended approach is sometimes characterised by these Christian schools as precisely the distinguishing feature of the identity of such a Christian primary school. In practice this implies that attention is given to the core religious and cultural narratives from the different traditions present in the school. An indication of such an approach might be that the school explicitly tries to hire teachers from the different traditions represented in the school. But this implies that we cannot speak of a Christian school any more. Such a school should be called multireligious or interreligious.[5]

Limits of the Dutch school system

We have described several arguments in defence of denominational schools. Now, we shall focus on the limits of our school system. As we have hinted at some points in the chapter, our system has its weak sides as well. Arguments against the system of segregated schools are quite strong (see, for example, Snik and de Jong, 1995). One of these is that educating a child within a specific religion is incompatible with the aim of autonomy. It restricts the choice of the child by suppressing the influence of other religions present in society. If in a pluralistic society it is in a child's interest to become autonomous, then religious schools are detrimental to the child's interest. This argument can, however, be denounced in part. It can be argued that initiation into a tradition is a necessary step for critical thinking: one has to have some content about which one can be critical; being critical about nothing is impossible. Initiation is also argued to be necessary from a psychological point of view: children are not able to reflect critically about subjects until a later age. Finally, one could claim that it is pedagogically

necessary: children need a stable primary culture, firm ground while they are young. Only when children are older is it responsible to encourage children to be critical about things they take for certain. However, these arguments presuppose that children are not initiated in such a way that critical thinking is made impossible. They exclude indoctrinary practices. Thus, the argument given by the opposition must be taken seriously. Another disadvantage mentioned is that separate schools can lead to fragmented, segregated society of fairly closed groups, which diminishes the integration of groups into an open democratic society.

We believe the system is defensible, but there are constraints. We shall describe the two most important ones in the remainder of this chapter, namely the complete development of the child and civic education.

The first restraint can be derived from the right of the child to education which aims for the development of the child to its fullest potential. This means that schools are not allowed to transmit a conception of the good that conflicts with this aim. For instance, some highly traditional denominational schools teach girls that they have to fulfil a specific role. They have to learn the capacities of being a housewife and mother and most certainly not those of striving in a career or of a political citizen. This is an indefensible limitation of the development of children. In our opinion, these schools should be made to change their educational policy.

Civic education is necessary for a flourishing pluralistic society (see Tamir, 1995; Walzer, 1995). The interaction between different groups with specific ways of life and values and norms is not self-apparent. A peaceful and respectful coexistence is only possible if citizens keep the necessary rules. These rules are learned within civic education. The Netherlands, as almost all western countries, is a liberal democratic society. Thus, civic education should comprise knowledge about and the capacities to live in such a society. From the start it must be clear that although civic education is education for citizenship in a democratic liberal society, it is not to be confused with a comprehensive liberal education. Civic education focuses on the lives of persons as citizens, not on their lives as a whole.

What are the aims of civic education? We cannot deal with this topic extensively, so we shall focus on several central aims. First, children must acquire knowledge about the way in which a democratic society functions and about the laws that underlie it (see Walzer, 1995). Children must know their rights and duties as citizens of a democratic society. In addition, children should also learn to reflect on laws, practices and attitudes, for a democratic society can only function properly if its citizens play a constructive and critical role.

Second, in learning the laws that underlie a liberal democracy children learn the principles and rules of public morality. Of course, they not only have to know the rules, they must also have the disposition to keep those rules. Especially important is that children learn to tolerate and respect other people who have different values and traditions (see Tamir, 1995). Children have to learn to respect others as equals in their membership of the political system. This means that children must learn that in the eye of the state all citizens are equal and that they, as citizens, should also take that stance. They must be exposed to the religious diversity of their society for the sake of learning to respect as fellow citizens those who differ from them in matters of religion (Macedo, 1995). In the debate on evolutionary theory, this would imply that this subject must be taught but that children should not be forced to question their own beliefs. However, pupils must know that other people may hold different ideas about the creation. This brings us to the third aim.

This aim is that children must be taught that critical thinking and public argument are the appropriate means of political justification (Macedo, 1995). We agree with Macedo that educators must realise (and teach the children) that, though critical thinking is necessary for political reasonableness and good citizenship, questions of religious truth should be left aside. Religious differences must be respected (ibid., p. 226). Based on Rawls's description of one of two moral powers of citizens in a liberal democracy, Spiecker and Steutel (1995) argue that critical thinking must be stimulated in every school by the government if the government takes the powers seriously. This moral power is the capacity for a conception of good, being 'the capacity to form, to revise, and rationally to pursue a conception of one's rational advantage or good' (Rawls, 1993, p. 19). This, according to Spiecker and Steutel, implies the capacity to submit such conceptions to critical thought. And this takes them one step further than Macedo. They argue that in liberal civic education the child 'also has to acquire the equipment to engage in critical examination of

conceptions of the good that are permitted by this framework, including the ideal of the good life into which she or he was initiated' (Spiecker and Steutel, 1995, p. 392).

As was shown in the debate on evolutionary theory, critical thinking poses a major problem for schools in the Netherlands that are of a 'closed' kind. In these schools thinking critically about or having doubts about religious principles, values and norms is blasphemous and thus could not be part of education at all. These schools put pressure on the justifiability of the Dutch educational system. We do think that a segregated school system is defensible within a liberal society, except when the denominational schools take full account of their complete pedagogical task: that is not only to transfer a specific conception of the good to the children, but also to do their duty to educate children to become full persons and citizens of a liberal democracy.

Notes

1 By the end of 1996 the government had decided to change the strictness of the term direction. Based on the advice of the Dutch Education Council, private schools are no longer obliged to demonstrate that they have a recognised world view. As a result of this change, the government is released from the task of passing judgement on whether the school has a specific direction. This policy makes it easier for schools to change the specific colour of the direction of their school. For instance, Christian schools can easily change into Islamic schools or into interreligious schools.

2 In the second section it is stated that individuals and bodies have the liberty to establish and direct educational institutions, but that these are subject to the mentioned principles as well as the minimum standard as may be laid down by the state.

3 The most obvious objection to teaching a certain faith is that it is indoctrinary. For reasons of space, we can only mention this problem here. Indoctrination can be said to have four characteristics, namely (a) the educator has to have the aim or intention to indoctrinate; (b) the educator uses specific methods, such as suppressing critical thinking and instilling fear; (c) the content of indoctrination is (religious) doctrines; (d) the consequence is that the indoctrinated has irrational emotions, and is unable to think critically about the doctrines he believes in (see Spiecker and Straughan, 1991). Teaching into a specific faith can be indoctrinary if this education can be shown to have the given characteristics. In discussion about this subject on Christian education, authors have claimed that critical thinking and open mindedness are characteristic of

Christian education. Thus, in this interpretation, Christian education is by definition not indoctrinary. (See, for a discussion on Christian education and indoctrination, Thiessen, 1993, and reactions on Thiessen by Spiecker 1996, and Miedema 1996).

4 We adopt Flanagan's (1991) description of identity as an integrated, dynamic system of a person's description of his or her identifications, desires, commitments, aspirations, beliefs, dispositions, temperament, roles, acts, and action patterns as well as his or her evaluations of these. A person's identity consists of the characteristics of the person (his or her body and temperament), the characteristics, values and ideals derived from the different communities he or she is part of, and of the characteristics, values and ideals of the society he or she is part of (see De Ruyter and Miedema, 1996).

5 Interreligious schools must comprise at least two religions. In the Netherlands there is one officially acknowledged interreligious school in which the Islamic and Christian faiths are prominent. The extent of the religions is dependent on the population of the school and the compatibility of the religions. We could think of a Hindu, Islamic and Christian interreligious school.

References

De Jong Ozn, K. (1992) Het ontstaan van de onderwijspacificatie van 1917 [The start of school pacification in 1917]. In R.J. Rijnbende (ed.), *Een onderwijsbestel met toekomst*. Amersfoort: Unie voor Christelijk Onderwijs.

De Ruyter, D.J. and Miedema, S. (1996) Schools, identity and the conception of the good: the denominational tradition as an example. *Studies in Philosophy and Education* 15, 27–33.

Flanagan, O. (1991) *Varieties of Moral Personality: Ethics and Psychological Realism.* Cambridge, MA: Harvard University Press.

Holley, R. (1994) Learning religion. In J. Astley and L.J. Francis (eds), *Critical Perspectives on Christian Education*. Leominster, Herefs.: Gracewing.

Lijphart, A. (1975) *The Politics of Accommodation: Pluralism and Democracy in the Netherlands.* Berkeley, CA: Berkeley University Press.

McLaughlin, T.H. (1994) The scope of parents' educational rights. In M. Halstead (ed.), *Parental Choice in Education*. London: Kogan Page.

Macedo, S. (1995) Multiculturalism for the religious right? Defending liberal civic education. *Journal of Philosophy of Education* 29, 223–38.

Miedema, S. (1994) *Identiteit tussen inspiratie en engagement* [Identity between inspiration and engagement]. Amsterdam: VU Uitgeverij.

Miedema, S. (1996) Teaching from commitment: a developmental perspective. In A. Neiman (ed.), *Philosophy of Education 1995*. Urbana IL: University of Illinois Press.

Miedema, S., Biesta, G. J. J. and Van der Kuur, R. (1995) De pedagogisering van het onderwijs als nationale zorg [The pedagogisation of education as a national concern]. In C. Dietvorst and J.P. Verhaeghe (eds), *De pedagogiek terug naar school.* [Pedagogy back to school]. Assen: Van Gorcum/Dekker en van de Vegt.

Miedema, S. and De Ruyter, D.J. (1995) On determining the limits of denominational school communities. *Panorama: International Journal of Comparative Religious Education and Values* 7(2), 75–82.

Rawls, J. (1987) *Liberty, Equality, and Law: Selected Tanner Lectures on Moral Philosophy.* Salt Lake City, Utah: University of Utah Press.

Ritzen, J.M.M. (1992) *De pedagogische opdracht van het onderwijs. Een uitnodiging tot gezamenlijke actie* [The pedagogical task of the school. An invitation to joint action]. Zoetermeer: Ministry of Education.

Ritzen, J.M.M. (1993) School moet uitleggen wat democratie inhoudt [The school needs to explain what democracy means]. In L. Dasberg, *Meelopers en dwarsliggers.* Amsterdam: Trouw.

Sealey, J. (1994) Education as a second-order form of experience and its relation to religion. In J. Astley and L.J. Francis (eds), *Critical Perspectives on Christian Education*. Leominster, Herefs.: Gracewing.

Snik, G.L.M. and De Jong, J. (1995) Liberalism and denominational schools. *The Journal of Moral Education* 24, 395–408.

Spiecker, B. (1996) Review article: Commitment to liberal education. *Studies in Philosophy and Education* 15, 281–91.

Spiecker, B. and Steutel, J.W. (1995) Political liberalism, civic education and the Dutch government. *Journal of Moral Education* 24, 383–94.

Spiecker, B. and Straughan, R. (eds) (1991) *Freedom and Indoctrination in Education.* London: Cassell.

Tamir, Y. (1995) Two concepts of multiculturalism. *Journal of Philosophy of Education* 29, 161–72.

Taylor, C. (1989) *Sources of the Self.* Cambridge, MA: Harvard University Press.

Taylor, C. (1992) *The Ethics of Authenticity.* Cambridge, MA: Harvard University Press.

Thiessen, E.J. (1993) *Teaching for commitment: Liberal Education, Indoctrination and Christian Nurture.* Leominster, Herefs.: Gracewing.

Thiessen, E.J. (1996) Liberal education, public schools and the embarrassment of teaching for commitment. In A. Neiman (ed.), *Philosophy of Education 1995*. Urbana, IL: University of Illinois Press.

Van der Ploeg, P. (1994) Recht op onderwijs versus vrijheid van onderwijs [The right to education versus the freedom to educate]. *Nederlands Tijdschrift voor Opvoeding, Vorming en Onderwijs,* 10(6), 360–9.

Walzer, M. (1995) Education, democratic citizenship and multiculturalism. *Journal of Philosophy of Education* 29, 181–90.

14 The Values of Grant-maintained Status: the Case of Catholic Schools

ANDREW HANNAN

Introduction

Values in education are manifested in different ways. They may be explicitly taught as part of some deliberate programme or stated in the goals set out in a school mission statement. They may be transmitted as an aspect of a school's 'ethos' or hidden curriculum or, more implicitly still, institutionalised in the very fabric of the education system. In the case of grant-maintained (GM) status the values have been those championed by what was a reforming Conservative government, suspicious of local education authorities (LEAs), admiring of the mechanisms of the market place and apparently anxious to give more power to parents whilst expanding central controls over the curriculum and tightening up compliance to its agenda through inspection and the publication of tables measuring school performance against its own criteria. The debate about 'opting out', the term used to describe the process by which schools left their LEAs to take on GM status, and about fee-paying independent schools 'opting in' to take state funding through becoming GM, however, was particularly beset by questions of the morality involved, especially in the case of schools with a religious affiliation. This chapter makes use of a variety of sources, including a survey of all the Catholic GM schools in England, an interview with a bishop at the centre of such a debate in his own diocese, and a number of documents, to analyse the issues and to derive insights about the processes involved. These matters, it is argued, have a more general relevance in understanding the relationship between church and state and have implications for those of other faiths who may be implicated in similar controversies.

GM status and voluntary-aided schools

The 1988 Education Reform Act simultaneously concentrated power at the centre by establishing a National Curriculum and a national system of assessment whilst devolving it to governing bodies (through financial delegation) and to parents (through enhanced entitlement to choice of schools and access to information about the performance of their children and of schools generally). The power thus redistributed was taken from LEAs and teachers themselves, both categories being identified as the source of problems such as political indoctrination and falling standards. On the one hand, teachers, pupils and parents were judged incapable of choosing what should be taught and, on the other, schools were being invited to compete with one another in terms of their performance on league tables of exam and test results in order to offer themselves up for parental choice. Schools which succeeded in these terms were to be rewarded with higher pupil intakes, more funding and so on, and those doing less well were to suffer declining rolls and eventual demise unless they could learn to compete in the new market place.

However, given the existence of a centrally determined curriculum, there seemed to be little choice to be exercised in terms of the nature of the goods or services provided. The Education Act of 1993, based on a White Paper entitled *Choice and Diversity* (DfE, 1992a), was designed to put this right. The idea here was to encourage schools to develop different characteristics in terms of style and emphasis (with selection on the basis of 'ability' a possibility which was given explicit support by the Conservative government more recently). The principal method of achieving this diversity was the encouragement of more schools to attain the goal of GM status, which had originally been provided for in the 1988 Act. These would then receive their finance from the central government via the Funding Agency for Schools (a centrally appointed quango) rather than from their LEAs (which were at least theoretically accountable to their local constituencies). In GM schools the governing body (including five elected parent governors in secondary schools and three to five in primary) were the employers of the staff, not the LEA. The pamphlet issued by the Department for Education to explain the proposals made it clear that: 'The government hopes that all schools will eventually become grant-maintained' (DfE, 1992b: 2).

The 1992 White Paper and the various pronouncements of the then Secretary of State, John Patten, also built on elements of the 1988 Act in stressing the importance of the 'spiritual, moral and cultural development' functions of schooling. Religious education was seen as making an important contribution here, with voluntary-aided schools given particular encouragement. In the UK such schools do not require parents to pay fees; they are funded through a combination of church and state, with the former providing 15 per cent of capital and external repair costs and the latter paying all the rest, including teachers' salaries. Voluntary-aided schools have been established for Anglicans, Catholics and Jews (although some pupils not from these faith communities also attend such schools and other pupils who are members attend non-denominational schools) but not for Muslims. Such schools were portrayed in *Choice and Diversity* as bastions of virtue, transmitting values which were essential for the regeneration of our modern society:

> The government continues to attach great importance to the dual system of County and voluntary schools which stems from the Education Act 1944 and the religious settlement which underpins it. The contribution of voluntary schools provided by the churches and others cannot be overestimated. They are popular with parents, and enhance choice. They provide powerful reinforcement of the spiritual and moral dimension of education which is of great importance to children. The government wishes to see the role of the churches and other voluntary bodies in education preserved and enhanced. (DfE, 1992a, p. 32)

Here the spiritual and moral 'dimension' (with an assumption that each element was merely a side of the same coin) was combined with choice and diversity to produce a vision of mutually reinforcing harmony to the benefit of all.

The position of the Catholic Church

John Patten (himself a Catholic) when Secretary of State told schools that they had a responsibility for teaching children the difference between right and wrong (Patten, 1994). Schools are often told by politicians that they are to blame for the breakdown in moral values as exhibited by events such as urban riots or young people engaging in violence. It is difficult to deny that schools are involved in moral education, indeed sociologists have made great play of the fact that the 'hidden curriculum' often looms larger than the formal curriculum in the processes of schooling. Patten seemed, however, to have seen a particular role for religious education and the awareness of the spiritual, even the prospect of eternal hell fire for wrongdoers. Perhaps this was why he was so keen on church schools.

However, the admiration seemed far from mutual, even though the various rearguard actions fought by the bishops and their allies in the House of Lords were hugely successful in obtaining concessions about the place of religion, and particularly teaching about Christianity and Christian acts of worship, in the education reforms which took place under the Conservative governments from 1979 onwards. One of the bones of contention was opting out. Thus, the Catholic Education Service's response to *Choice and Diversity* argued that the GM option:

> intensifies financial and curricular inequalities between schools and creates new inequalities. It also supposes that schools derive their strength from their own autonomy without any sense of having a wider responsibility (the common good). Moreover there is no reason to believe that the growth of the GM sector will do other than undermine the financial ability and reputation of those schools which remain outside the GM sector. It is difficult to see how a tiered system can be avoided. (Catholic Education Service, 1992, p. 4)

All this despite the best efforts of the government to offer reassurance about the maintenance of church control and a significant financial inducement.

GM status builds upon the existing freedoms available to voluntary-aided schools. In particular, the governors of ex-voluntary aided GM schools are not liable for a 15 per cent contribution to capital and external repair costs. The position of the foundation is guaranteed by the foundation governors' having a majority on the governing body. The established character and ethos of the school is thus protected. Voluntary schools, therefore, have a lot to gain by becoming grant-maintained. (DfE, 1992a, p. 32)

The gift-horse, however, has not been readily accepted, and relatively few Catholic schools have opted for GM status (by August 1996 there were 144 Catholic GM schools out of a possible total of 2502). This advice from one Catholic bishop to parents of children at Catholic schools stated some of the reasons for reluctance:

> Present government policy seeks to give you more influence in schools. In order to exercise our influence responsibly we need to assess its effect on other people's lives. Perhaps the best use of our influence in schools is in collaboration with others – other parents, teachers and those in Church and State whose task is to provide education not just for you and your children, but for those who live alongside or who come after us.
>
> As government often reminds us, especially when advocating grant-maintained status for schools, educational choices include the type of school, its size and the range of abilities for which it caters. In a Catholic perspective, I would wish to add that preferences in education will also involve a school's relationship with other schools. We have to show our concern for our own children, but we must not forget the children of other schools or the children of future generations or children who are in any way disadvantaged.
>
> Whilst considering our influence in education, perhaps a word of caution is appropriate. Those who seek to increase your influence could also be seeking to achieve their own ends. A good test of proposed educational changes is what happens to the most disadvantaged. We should never allow our influence to be used to the detriment of our more vulnerable brothers and sisters.
>
> If defending true human values and our Catholic faith obliges us to adopt a position where we are financially disadvantaged perhaps we have to endure that and do our best to provide what we can from our own limited resources. It would be a sad day if those who come after us say that we gained every possible financial advantage and every degree of excellence in secular terms to the detriment of gospel values. (Extracts from letter to parents, October 1992)

Such concerns were later echoed in the words of Bishop David Konstant of Leeds, who acts as national spokesperson on Catholic education matters:

> one policy clearly underlying current government thinking is that market forces are intended to regulate the pattern of educational provision. The Bishops' Conference has consistently warned against such an emphasis because it considers regulation by market forces to be quite wrong for a service like education and incompatible with the Church's obligation to provide equal opportunities for all its members. I continue to have certain reservations about GM schools, arising from inequalities of resourcing, from the emergence of a two tier system of schools and from the loss of democratically elected local regulatory and planning bodies.
>
> . . .
>
> I would urge all governors of our diocesan schools to ensure they and their parent bodies are fully informed about all the issues which relate to GM status and to take great care not to precipitate action in order to obtain short term gains or ones that are at the expense of any other school, whether Catholic or County. (From letter to 'all those concerned with the Catholic schools of the diocese', February 1994)

An alternative view of the motives involved is given by Arthur (1994), who presents an account of events as a rearguard action which has been fought by the Catholic bishops to resist the growth of parental power. That effort is portrayed as a defence of the power of the church, of the clerical hierarchy against the laity, of the cosy relationship between the LEA and the diocese against the uncertainties of the market place and the power of parents (many of whom may well not be Catholics even though their children go to such schools). Kenneth Baker, Secretary of State when the Education Reform Act was passed, gives a colourful account in his memoirs (Baker, 1993, pp. 217–18) of negotiations with the Catholic church which strongly supports the view that the overriding concern was about loss of control. The Conservative government did its best to assuage these fears in the terms described earlier. However, such worries continued to plague those involved, as evidenced by the fact that Bishop Konstant quoted the following extract from a booklet produced by Local Schools Information in a letter to his diocese of February 1994:

> Parents are being asked to make a very important choice ... If they choose to opt out, it is an irrevocable choice, for opting out is a one-way door. A change of government, however, is likely to lead to an end to GM status. Both Labour and Liberal-Democrat parties have clear policies to restore GM schools to the democratic account-ability of elected local authorities. This could be a particular issue for voluntary-aided schools, as it is difficult to see how schools which choose to give up voluntary-aided status in return for 100 per cent State funding can expect to have it restored to them in the event of such a change. Also, as the financial contribution of the churches diminishes, the basis of their current authority over Church schools is simultaneously eroded. (LSI, 1994, p. 8)

When the government tried to entice more voluntary-aided schools to opt for GM status by offering them a 'fast track' (suggesting such meas-ures as by-passing the normal requirement for a bal-lot of parents providing the governing body were in agreement; making all voluntary-aided schools GM from a certain date unless the governing bodies were in opposition; and removing LEA appointees to voluntary-aided governing bodies) this was firmly rejected by the Catholic Bishops' Conference. The government was severely lambasted and the proposals judged 'discriminatory and divisive':

> Schools are under severe financial pressure because of cuts in education funding, both centrally and locally. This is the context in which these proposals are being put forward. The cost of establishing new self-governing schools, if taken from the main edu-cation budget, would mean less funding for other maintained schools and would exacerbate the pres-ent under resourcing of education. (Bishops' Conference Statement on the Government's Pro-posals on Self-Government for Voluntary-Aided Schools, November 1995)

It is apparent, though, that the Catholic church's resistance to GM status has not held firm over time, nor is it uniform across the country. Thus, when a Catholic secondary school (run by a religious order) opted for GM status in March 1993 it did so against the advice of the local Catholic bishop (quoted above and interviewed as part of the research reported here). However, since late 1995 an independent Catholic school in that diocese has

been strongly supported by the same bishop in its efforts to 'opt in' as a GM school. More broadly, a survey in November 1992 carried out by *The Times Educational Supplement* (Maxwell, 1992) found that 18 (62 per cent) of the 29 Catholic and Angli-can bishops or diocesan education officers who replied believed that opting out was either divisive, against the interests of all pupils or undermined the position of their schools. However, in August 1994 another survey by the same journal (Dean, 1994) reported that a quarter of Catholic bishops in Eng-land and Wales had been privately promoting GM status for more than a year.

The survey

How have Catholic GM schools themselves experi-enced these conflicting pressures? To find out, a postal questionnaire survey was conducted of every Catholic GM school in England in September 1996, a total of 144 schools; 80 replies were received, giving a response rate of 55.55 per cent, a high level of return for a data collection exercise of this kind. The characteristics of the respondent population were as follows:

- 37 (46.3 per cent) were primary schools (two of these were for the junior age range), 40 (50 per cent) were secondary schools (seven of which were for 11–16-year-olds, 33 of which have sixth forms) with three respondents not provid-ing this information;
- the three smallest schools had between 100 and 199 pupils, the eighteen largest between 1700 and 1799, with 55.2 per cent having fewer than 700;
- nine schools (11.3 per cent) were single-sex boys, six (7.5 per cent) single-sex girls;
- 38 schools (47.5 per cent) had less than 10 per cent non-Catholic pupils, 19 (23.8 per cent) had between 10 per cent and 19 per cent, nine (11.3 per cent) had between 20 per cent and 29 per cent, another nine had between 30 per cent and 39 per cent, four (5 per cent) had between 40 per cent and 49 per cent, and just one had between 70 per cent and 79 per cent;
- two of the schools were previously independent, that is, fee-paying and outside the state system, all the others had been voluntary-aided (except one which had a 'special arrangement' status largely similar).

In almost all cases the respondent was the headteacher although some schools were represented by the responses given by a deputy head. The questions asked were designed to reveal their perception of the issues raised in the light of their own experiences.

Reasons for going GM

In response to the open-ended question (which allowed for a number of reasons to be given by any one respondent), 'Why did your school apply for GM status?' 39 respondents (48.75 per cent) identified reasons of a financial nature, concerning the budgetary advantages with particular reference to capital spending and building improvement, as typified by the following responses:

Headteacher 01: Inability to meet 15 per cent commitment to capital works – cumulative effect of this on basic infrastructure.
Headteacher 03: To better use the 12 per cent of our budget being retained by our LEA.
Headteacher 04: Financial reasons – underfunding by LEA in comparison to LEA schools.
Headteacher 06: To obtain funding for capital works as the diocese/LEA were not able to help.
Headteacher 12: (a) To gain more funding for capital building; (b) to improve the physical environment of the school.
Headteacher 70: (a) For a level playing field with county schools, whose funding has always been 100 per cent as opposed to the 85 per cent rate for new build and external repairs, maintenance attracted by/incurred by the voluntary-aided sector; (b) to escape the cumbersome bureaucracy which accompanied the grant system administered partially via county; (c) to know where we stood financially in a clearer more immediate way than before; (d) to allow us to plan ahead more effectively; (e) to relieve the diocese of incurring further debt because of our legitimate needs.

It is noticeable that for many of these headteachers, the advent of GM, rather than being a morally dubious means of acquiring financial advantage at the expense of others, gave them the chance to put things right, that is, to make up for the underfunding they felt they had suffered in the past. To a large extent, the LEA was blamed for this. The need for greater autonomy and the attractions of relative independence was referred to in their response by

25 headteachers (31.25 per cent), as exemplified in the following examples of reasons given for seeking GM status:

Headteacher 02: To have the facility to make our own decisions. We believe we know what our children need.
Headteacher 23: Greater freedom. We were sick of the 'politically correct' manoeuvres of the LEA. Set our own priorities and spending patterns, and not have county hall spending money on our behalf. A chance of a building programme following 13 years of refusal.
Headteacher 32: (a) For the greater management flexibility to provide a quality education and environment for our pupils; (b) we were convinced we could provide a better education than our partnership with the LEA.
Headteacher 35: A desire for greater control at a school based level on spending and in decision making by both staff and governors. A strong feeling that better value for money could be achieved and that resulting benefits would improve educational provision for our pupils.

Six of these and a further 20 others blamed their LEA for deliberate underfunding, prejudice, intransigence or negligence, giving a total of 45 (56.25 per cent) who were keen to 'opt out' to escape their LEA, in terms such as the following:

Headteacher 28: Dissatisfaction with the services offered by the LEA and their response to the school's needs.
Headteacher 31: (a) Lack of confidence in an LEA which had over the previous 26 years displayed an arrogance and contempt for the mission of a Catholic school; (b) to control our own affairs and to give to our community many powers previously held by the LEA; (c) to restore the financial cuts imposed in the previous two years of £100,000.
Headteacher 52: Because a newly formed LEA gave scant regard to the Catholic school and was underfunding church schools in comparison to county schools.
Headteacher 57: . . . Because it was the worst funded school bar one in the borough (proportionate to numbers) . . . Because we wanted our Catholic children to be put on an equal footing as non-Catholic neighbours – staffing, curriculum, buildings and site development.

Other reasons given by more than one of the Catholic GM schools were: the need for greater efficiency (seven); because managing a Catholic school was almost like being a GM school in any case (five); better educational provision for pupils (four); to secure the future (three); to establish or save a sixth form (three); to escape an LEA which favoured selective schools (two); inability of the diocese to provide for growing needs (two); and to avoid staff redundancies (two). So although many of the headteachers considered underfunding and lack of support under the voluntary-aided system a distinct problem, only three explicitly referred to the need to opt out to avoid closure.

Moral issues

When asked 'What moral issues were involved in taking the decision to apply for GM status?', the possibility of disadvantaging other schools was by far the most frequently cited, with 36 headteachers (45 per cent) doing so, in terms such as the following:

Headteacher 34: Only one – the question of whether GM status for some schools meant reduced funding for other schools.
Headteacher 38: Equal opportunities – considered to have been discriminated against in past, but concerned about taking too much in future.
Headteacher 41: The need to continue providing Catholic secondary education at a high level overrode any other moral considerations but concern was expressed about how the share out of money would affect non-GM schools.

Nine headteachers (11.25 per cent) cited 'justice' or 'equality' when identifying the moral issues involved, for example:

Headteacher 10: Primarily our concern to make provision for our Catholic children which will be at least on a par with that provided with the LEA. Basically a question of justice.
Headteacher 33: The Catholic students were entitled to the same benefits as those in state education.
Headteacher 45: Governors felt the school had been unfairly treated for years!
Headteacher 48: The basic moral issue was to achieve 100 per cent funding for the pupils at the school who were being denied it by a dictatorial and high-handed LEA.
Headteacher 61: Equality.
Headteacher 65: The school was underfunded by

county relative to county schools. We wished to rectify that immoral position.

Other reasons cited by more than one were: the dangers of exclusivity and elitism (seven); the danger of undermining the LEA (five); to provide what is best for their pupils (five); and the need to continue to provide Catholic education (three). However, 21 headteachers (26.25 per cent) answered 'none'.

Advice from the local diocese

When asked 'What advice did you receive from your local diocese?', 24 headteachers (30 per cent) answered 'none' or 'very little'; fifteen said that they were advised against applying for GM status; ten that they were advised in favour; seven that they were advised that it was 'up to you'; five that they should keep to Catholic principles; nine that the advice was neutral or balanced; and nine that it was confused or contradictory. The following responses represent the range:

Headteacher 09: Diocese not in favour but willing to respect the views of all associated with the school. Very much a 'local' decision.
Headteacher 13: That GM status would be good for us and would benefit the children.
Headteacher 16: Answer the moral questions. Act in good faith. Accept community decision.
Headteacher 22: Little or none. They simply wanted to be reassured that we would remain a Catholic school in touch with the diocese.
Headteacher 38: The diocese suggested the change.
Headteacher 39: They felt it was the right decision for us and backed us in it.
Headteacher 41: Conflicting. Luke-warm opposition from archbishop's house. Strong opposition from local dioceses.
Headteacher 52: If the school gave an undertaking to operate as a Catholic school within the framework of diocesan policy the diocese would not oppose an application for GM status.
Headteacher 75: The diocese wanted to close the school and were thus opposed to GM status. Advice was not sought.
Headteacher 79: Diocese advised that community links were essential and we should not see this as a means of becoming selective in any way.

On being a GM Catholic school

When asked 'Has being a GM school made it harder or easier to be a Catholic school?', and given the scale 'harder – easier – no difference', only one headteacher indicated 'harder'. An explanation was given for this response in the following terms:

Headteacher 52: Pressure to act unilaterally like other GM schools with no regard for the Catholic 'community of schools'.

However, this was very much the exception: 36 (45 per cent) of the headteachers thought being GM made being a Catholic school 'easier' and 40 (50 per cent) that it made 'no difference', while three did not reply to this question. The most common points referred to by those who indicated 'easier' were to do with aspects of 'transmission' (passing on the faith, improving support for instruction in Catholicism); 'social purpose' (providing for those with special needs, better provision for each pupil); 'strengthening the community of the school' (giving all a common purpose, taking responsibility for own future as a Catholic school); and 'autonomy' (escaping from the perceived bias of the LEA against voluntary-aided schools, being able to prioritise on the basis of being a Catholic school). Examples of each follow:

'Transmission'
Headteacher 21: More money given to religious education (RE). Appointment of a chaplain. More RE teachers. 10 per cent RE curriculum time.
Headteacher 62: Now heavily oversubscribed with first-class Catholic applicants. More financial freedom has allowed us to spend more on RE and the development of our Catholic ethos, for example, the appointment of a lay chaplain.

'Social purpose'
Headteacher 04: (a) We have increased funding to devote to the integrated resources in the school catering for physically handicapped children; (b) we can support a range of activities, including residential study visits, for children from socially deprived/impoverished backgrounds who previously missed out on such experiences.
Headteacher 39: We have the freedom to use our money as we choose in certain areas, for example, supporting children with special educational needs (SEN) by the provision of extra SEN classroom

assistants. This comes out of a budget we are able to use more creatively for the good of the children.
Headteacher 68: Because we do not have to be part of the LEA's selection process, we can celebrate the achievement of all our children, regardless of ability and without any of them having been rated as success or failure at age 11. We recognise the wealth of talents and gifts in all our children, and staff, as unique individuals.

'Strengthening the community of the school'
Headteacher 31: 1 Apart from the obvious implications of increased funding no material changes can be discerned. 2 Advantages: (a) the Diocesan Trustees through interview appointed the majority of the Foundation Governors. The Governing Body is now fully committed to govern the school for the benefit of our Catholic community both local and diocesan; (b) the 'network' is stronger than before as other schools and parishes expressed support for this school during the 'campaign'; (c) our relationship with the LEA is the best we have had in 28 years. They provide the services which we think are valuable and the client/provider situation is one which is to be singularly recommended; (d) becoming GM has dramatically increased the already close relationship the school had with parents. Additional parents on the governors provides a wider 'window' for parents to be involved. Far more parents now offer their services as classroom helpers and there has been a marked increase in the number of parents involved in the weekly school meetings, class meetings, etc. This has come about because the parents became involved in the school before and during the changeover to GM. What happened then gave them a unique insight into the values which the school represents and many responded accordingly; (e) a similar increase in cohesion and common belief has also been evident in teaching and non-teaching staff. We are now a much stronger Catholic school and community than we were as a beleaguered maintained institution.

'Autonomy'
Headteacher 35: We are able to exercise a greater Catholic independence as we are no longer driven by LEA initiatives that were not always favourable to voluntary-aided schools.
Headteacher 50: Easier, because of our autonomy.
Headteacher 58: We control our own destiny!!

The moral dilemmas: the bishop's view

On 16 September 1996, I conducted an interview with the Catholic bishop referred to earlier and quoted above, who had been much involved in the debate about GM status, having in 1992 and 1994 made statements which reflected the caution voiced by the Bishops' Conference, having publicly opposed the 'opting out' of a voluntary-aided school in his diocese in 1993 and having strongly supported the 'opting in' of a Catholic independent school since the end of 1995. The following extracts from the transcript identify some of the key points:

AH: What do you consider to be the most important issues raised for the Church by the possibility of schools opting for GM status?

Bishop: I think for me the issue is not funding and grant maintained status, for me it is the risk of slight distancing of the school from its roots in the Catholic community. I suppose that's apropos the Catholic schools but I see it also in terms of county schools distancing themselves somewhat from the communities which have set them up and have set them going, to which they have related. That's for me one of the important things. . . . The other issue is that of partnership which we have been heavily involved in as a Catholic community. . . . We feel that we have a partnership which we've worked long and hard to achieve and somehow GM status is pushing that on one side and saying that doesn't matter, that it's the school which is valid in its own right and, OK, we have some sort of relationship, but we're the centre stage. There's that sort of issue around, I think. Yes, and I suppose there's atomisation that goes on with the schools standing on their own two feet totally, competing with each other and of course this is reinforced by league tables, all the paraphernalia of competition being brought to bear on something which is really much more fundamentally important than competition. It's about boys and girls being educated.

I went on to ask about the issues of funding and control:

AH: Is that one of the concerns about going GM, 100 per cent state funding?

Bishop: It is. I suppose there's a fear in the background, if you go for fears, that the one who pays the piper calls the tune. In the end, and given other governments coming in as they do every five years, they may say we're paying all the money therefore we'll call the tunes. In that sense the religious dimension of the education which we particularly want to relate to and have a very heavy stake in could well be eroded and pushed to one side.

AH: One of the things for me that came through strongly in the statement from the Bishops' Conference and in the paper from Bishop Konstant was the feeling that it was wrong to set up a two-tier system where some schools which had GM status had certain privileges, funding privileges.

Bishop: That's right. I think that was around when we were talking about this. I suppose there was a certain amount of ambivalence in our discussions because we realised that it would be very nice to get this burden off our shoulders in terms of the 15 per cent finance we had to provide, to unload it. But we were also thinking that if another 15 per cent was to come out of the coffers of the education budget someone else was going to be lacking, it might well be a number of county schools and we should have their benefit to mind as well as our own. So we were caught between that and 'let's go and get the best deal for ourselves' sort of thinking. But then, of course, that got mixed up with a concern that if we didn't have a stake expressed financially in one of our schools, what leverage did we have? What control did we have, not heavy-handed control, but what sort of guarantee did we have of the Catholicity of that particular school?

When I put to him the contrast between his opposition to voluntary-aided schools 'opting out' and his support of an independent school 'opting in' he replied in the following terms:

AH: What about the governors of Catholic voluntary-aided schools, is this a green light for the GM option now?

Bishop: I wouldn't see it like that although you know I can understand the interpretation you've outlined. I think it's very different psychologically, that the dynamics of the thing are very different when you get a school which has been very solidly part of the voluntary-aided system suddenly saying we want to become an independent unit totally, really that's what they're saying, and opt out of the local community, local authority. They'll say 'well, we're not opting out of the diocese, were still Catholic', but you know that's a matter of discussion. I think they're opting into the competitive. All the things we don't like about GM, the things I've tried to say and David Konstant tried to say about GM, I think they're very clearly opting for. What we're doing in the case of the independent school 'opting in' is finding a way of actually providing a school from the beginning for our secondary pupils, building on the original foundation of an independent school. I think to that extent this is opting into the public sector and therefore the school is going to start relating to at least some public bodies in a way it didn't need to before. One of those public bodies being the diocese, of course. The regret I've got is that they won't be relating to the local authority ... But I think the two, the dynamics of the two are different; the position we are at with the school opting in compared to that when a school is actually a part of the system, part of the partnership, part of a family and says no, we're going 'independent'.

When asked about the future for Catholic education he replied as follows:

Bishop: I don't know. One question is, how long can we afford to keep our Catholic schools in the present voluntary-aided system because it's getting more and more expensive? The number of Catholics is diminishing, let's be honest. Therefore we've got a smaller income coming in, so we've got a financial question there.... I think the key question is, are we going to be able to afford to continue paying for our Catholic schools? The GM option, if it remains in its present form, is one way we could go to try and unload some of the financial responsibility, but there's a price for that. As I said at the beginning, if we cease to be a financial stakeholder, to use the contemporary jargon, we're running the risk of whoever is paying all the money saying 'I'm going to call more of the tune'. There's the potential government could do that in time. The GM thing I think is very dangerous. The way that power is being put into central government hands, I think, I find dangerous, not just politically now but in the light of the principles of subsidiarity and solidarity. A strong central government could be bad news. We only need a government to get in which wants to secularise everything in sight and we're in trouble. We lose then.

Discussion

There is obviously a wide range of moral issues

identified here, the most prominent of which seem to be the following:

- competition versus cooperation;
- autonomy versus control;
- justice versus privilege.

However, as is often the case, none of these can be understood as simple oppositions since the definition of terms is not shared and the perspectives of those involved differ significantly. For the headteachers of many of the Catholic schools which attained GM status, 'cooperation' was not a term which aptly described their relationship with their LEA and 'competition' was in any case part of the new reality for all schools which therefore needed to ensure they, and their pupils, were not disadvantaged. For many of them 'autonomy' was a highly desirable means of escape from what was seen as the unequal treatment they had received from the LEA, or the restrictions imposed by having to rely on 15 per cent funding from the diocese for new building and external maintenance. They saw GM status as giving the opportunity to be closer to their local Catholic community and to better serve its children. For these headteachers the idea that they were receiving more than their fair share of education funding was a misunderstanding of the way GM schools are financed (although the House of Commons Public Accounts Committee did not agree with them: see Dean, 1995, and Bevins, 1995) and in any case might be said to be no more than a correction of the previous position where they felt they suffered what amounted to discrimination. For a minority GM status was practically unavoidable, given the predominance of such schools in their area or through their desire to avoid becoming selective when this was the policy of the LEA.

For the Catholic church, the dilemmas have been very difficult to manage. On the one hand, GM status destroyed the old pact reached between church and state and the partnerships established with LEAs. The bishops were affronted by the new language of competition and the market place, much preferring notions of 'the common good' (Catholic Bishops' Conference, 1996). They feared the centralising tendencies of a Conservative government, which were seen as reducing the powers of the diocese as well as of the LEA. On the other hand, they were being presented with the opportunity to guarantee the full funding of Catholic schools without having to find ways of providing the 15 per cent of capital and external repair finance which was necessary to provide for the growing needs of voluntary-aided schools at a time of falling church income. The 'opting in' facility made the temptation too great to resist when it meant providing a Catholic school for a community where no such provision had previously existed (except for those who could afford it through the payment of fees). The moral imperative of 'catechesis' is clearly greater than any considerations about 'subsidiary' or 'solidarity' when such an opportunity presents itself.

Conclusion

The GM experiment has provided a means by which schools with a religious foundation, including Jewish, Seventh-Day Adventist, Muslim and Catholic independent schools, have been given the opportunity to 'opt in' to full state funding. For Muslim schools in particular this has provided a means of overcoming the barriers represented by the path to voluntary-aided status, obstacles which they have not been able to overcome despite repeated efforts. For at least one Muslim and one Seventh-Day Adventist school, it looks as if GM status will be obtained. However, by August 1996 the only independent schools which were operating as such were both Catholic. At that date there were four Jewish, 140 Church of England and, as noted above, 144 Catholic GM schools out of a total of 1117 GM schools then in operation.

The relationship between church and state is highly problematic and the situation has been further complicated by the GM option. The moral dilemmas confronting churches, schools and parents have been prominent also in the lives of politicians making decisions for their own children as well as in the sphere of public policy. The Conservative government seemed to want to promote church schools via the GM device as transmitters of moral order. The public have often favoured such schools for perceived advantages in terms of both discipline and academic success. The creation of a GM sector has served to highlight the inequalities of provision which are a feature of the diversity which is part of the education system in England.

Clearly, when education reforms are subject to scrutiny in terms of the morality involved, opinions can differ quite markedly. The overriding pressure from religious groups for state support for educational institutions which will transmit their faith is difficult to resist if the government concerned is insistent on the importance of religion in reproducing social order through such mechanisms as the collective act of worship in schools. The investment of public funds via the GM device in church schooling represents a remarkable sponsorship of religious values, with the state taking up costs previously incurred by the religious groups concerned (the 15 per cent of new building and maintenance costs for formerly voluntary-aided schools and the full 100 per cent for formerly independent schools after their establishment with GM status) whilst giving the 'foundations' continued control of the schools' governing bodies. It remains to be seen, however, if this 'pact with the devil' is a success in the long term, with a significant number of church schools now so dependent on funding from the central state. As the case of Catholic schools illustrates, the GM experiment has added to the diversity and exacerbated the contradictions whilst failing to resolve the fundamental issues of the relationship between church and state in matters of education.

References

Arthur, J. (1994) Parental involvement in Catholic schools: a case of increasing conflict. *British Journal of Educational Studies* **42**(2), 174–90.

Baker, K. (1993) *The Turbulent Years: My Life in Politics.* London: Faber & Faber.

Bevins, A. (1995) Bonanza for opt-out schools. *Observer*, 7 May, 8.

Catholic Bishops' Conference (1996) *The Common Good and the Catholic Church's Social Teaching.* London: Catholic Bishops' Conference of England and Wales.

Catholic Education Service (1992) Education: a response to the White Paper. *Briefing* **22**(2) 22 October, 2–5.

Dean, C. (1994) Churches fear loss of power. *The Times Educational Supplement*, 12 August, no. 4076, 1.

Dean, C. (1995) MPs defied over £40m bonus for GM schools. *The Times Educational Supplement*, 9 June, no. 4119, 1.

Department for Education (DfE) (1992a) *Choice and Diversity: A New Framework for Schools.* London: Her Majesty's Stationery Office.

Department for Education (DfE) (1992b) *Education into the Next Century: The Government's Proposals for Education Explained.* London: Her Majesty's Stationery Office.

Local Schools Information (LSI) (1994) *Opting For What? A Choice for Parents*, 4th edn. London: LSI.

Maxwell, E. (1992) 'Divisive' opting-out worries bishops. *The Times Educational Supplement*, 13 November, no. 3985, 1.

Patten, J. (1994) Invaluable values: address to the Oxford Conference on Education (an 'In brief' report). *The Times Educational Supplement*, 7 January, no. 4045, 2.

15 How Local should a Local Agreed Syllabus for RE be?

VIVIENNE BAUMFIELD

Religious education (RE) appears destined to occupy an anomalous position within the English education system. In 1944 it was the only nationally prescribed subject in the curriculum when the Education Act stated that all registered pupils were to receive RE. The fact that no thoughts of including religions other than Christianity crossed the minds of the legislators of the Act at that time should not detract from our appreciation of the effort necessary to achieve cooperation between different groups within Christianity. The price of securing agreement was that decisions as to what should be taught were to be made locally by an Agreed Syllabus Conference consisting of representatives from the Christian denominations, the local education authority and teachers. Provision for RE in the locality could be monitored by a Standing Advisory Council for RE (SACRE), if one was constituted. Also, parents who could not agree to the principle of locally agreed RE had the right to withdraw their children from RE lessons. Teachers were also given the right to withdraw from teaching RE.

The solutions in 1944 to the problems raised when RE was included in the state's provision for education were to devolve decisions about content to a local forum, in which the views of the different groups within the Christian community were represented, and the provision of a conscience clause for dissenters. In 1988 the Education Reform Act established the National Curriculum, which prescribed programmes of study for pupils across five key stages from ages 5 to 18. The first drafts of the Act did not include RE and a vigorous campaign was launched to retain the subject as part of the maintained school curriculum. The campaign was successful in retaining RE as a subject to be studied by all registered pupils but it was not included in the National Curriculum. RE was to continue to be agreed locally using the mechanisms established in 1944, although faiths other than Christianity represented in the locality were now to be included in the Agreed Syllabus Conference and the setting up of a SACRE was mandatory. The conscience clause was retained.

The decision not to include RE in the National Curriculum and the retention of its distinctive local character have been presented as both positive and negative moves by the Department for Education (DfE). Supporters of the local agreed syllabus for RE present their arguments as a defence of a principle. According to this view, RE is placed outside of nationally agreed assessment arrangements in order to ensure that syllabuses reflect local circumstances and to enable the different interest groups, predominantly faith communities, to participate fully in decision making. Bolton (1997) claims the local agreed syllabus as a powerful manifestation of the non-conformist conscience and vital to democracy. The local control of RE should be cherished by teachers faced with the moves towards ideological control through a centrally determined National Curriculum:

> it permits us to feel supported by a consensus of local councillors, faith communities and educationalists and ask critical questions of the promotion of national consciousness in education. (Bolton, 1997, p. 137)

Whilst the defence of local determination in the face of the campaign during the debate on the National Curriculum to secure RE as the basis of a defence of the hegemony of Christianity in British society[1] may be understandable, the issues it raises must be considered if we are to be fully appraised of the possible long-term costs. The issues can be grouped under two broad headings: the question of local as opposed to national agreement on the syllabus for RE in a multicultural society, and the role of faith group representatives in determining what should be taught.

The principle of advocating local agreement on the syllabus for RE renders the subject vulnerable to further localisation or devolution down to an individual school level. Neo-liberal comments on state education take the position that modern society is too heterogeneous for supposedly 'common' schooling to be other than a matter of uneasy and unstable compromises. If, as current research suggests, effective schools are characterised by a clear sense of purpose and direction there is a strong case for uncommon schools which embody the distinctive religious and educational philosophies of their parents. The concept of 'schools of choice' is thereby extended beyond curriculum diversity to specialisation by ethos and values. The consequent cultural segregation of intakes is approved of, or at least accepted (Edwards, 1996). Rather than removing RE from ideological control, advocates of local determination risk supporting an ideology which undermines the contribution RE makes to multi-cultural education and threatens the viability of the subject in the mainstream curriculum.

The mosaic of learning

David Hargreaves (1994, p. 56) describes modern society as a 'mosaic of institutions and life patterns in which boundaries weaken, edges blur, colours blend, lines curve, shapes fragment; and patterns, though undoubtedly present, are less easily discerned'. He argues that schools in the next century must respond to diversity by providing greater parental choice in terms of curriculum specialisation and along philosophical, ideological or religious lines. Parents should be able to choose a school which promotes a distinct and particular ethos. At the same time, all schools should teach civic education as the source of a common core of values that is shared across the communities which make up our pluralistic society; these common values will form the cement which will bind together the individual pieces of the mosaic. He finds support for this view in Chief Rabbi Jonathan Sacks's notion of bilingualism whereby we all learn the language of citizenship as our first language whilst retaining as our second language our own local, family, tradition 'language'

(Sacks, 1991). Religion is a second language and whilst religious schools should be provided for those who want them, it has no place in the common school. For Hargreaves, religious education in schools has failed on three counts: parental demand for RE is really a cry for moral education and is unlikely to be satisfied by the current non-denominational, multifaith provision; the 'pick'n mix tour of religions' of the contemporary agreed syllabus trivialises each faith's claim to truth; and finally, pupils lack the intellectual maturity to engage in the study of religion as an academic discipline. Government should acknowledge that attempts to bolster and rationalise RE since 1988 have failed and replace RE in schools with the teaching of citizenship.

It is hard to see why civic education should succeed where RE has been deemed to fail. Concepts of justice or citizenship require as much intellectual maturity as anything one might encounter in the study of religion and the problem of conflicting truth claims is common to both areas of study. Only when the values of a Western model of liberal democracy are taken to be self-evident can there be no worries about indoctrination when teaching civic education as opposed to RE. No evidence is offered to support the claim that parents will be more satisfied with civic education than they are with RE. Hargreaves's argument exemplifies how reliance on addressing diversity through local determination could result in a syllabus for RE reflecting an individual school ethos. The need for agreement to be reached between heterogeneous groups would be replaced by a tacit consensus within the homogeneous school population resulting from the admissions policy. In practice the mosaic fixes limits and boundaries as each local group defines itself and only adds to the larger society by providing one distinct part of a larger picture. This image raises two immediate questions: who enjoys the vantage point from which the 'picture' composed by the individual tiles in the mosaic can be seen; and what provision can there be for accommodating change?[2] Perhaps the notion of a mosaic is, after all, not a happy one, and comparison with a kaleidoscope would be more apposite at least in regard to encompassing a dynamic of change. The role of RE in promoting dialogue between viewpoints arising from different perspectives, religious and non-religious, is significant in its absence from neo-liberal accounts which prefer to see belief as a private affair.

'We are not complete unless we are with others'

Dr John Habgood, the former Archbishop of York, advocates an approach he calls critical solidarity as a means of meeting the charges against the value of RE in maintained schools. The willingness to question provides the critical edge to the study of religion and the understanding that the inquiry also requires an openness to dialogue is the source of solidarity as we identify with each other's common concerns. Habgood is aware that conversation with others will also require the exploration of differences but the discussion will be conducted in the spirit of a mutual search for truth. Genuine dialogue involves a commitment to the possibility of change. However, change need not be equated with conversion as it can also mean a growth in understanding of existing beliefs in the light of new ideas. Critical solidarity provides a tough-minded approach to RE which Habgood believes will secure it a proper academic status. The fostering of a positive attitude to pluralism which is inherent in the idea of dialogue also means it has something important to offer the curriculum as a whole:

> We are not complete unless we are with others. The more we can broaden our understanding and our sympathies the more fulfilled we should be as communities and individuals. (Habgood, 1995, p. 14)

The sentiments expressed in Habgood's critical solidarity have been expressed by other writers: the dialogical approach to teaching RE promotes a sense of identity achieved by including other points of view because it is through encountering others that we discover truth (Hull, 1991). Jackson (1999) develops this point when he warns of the dangers inherent in RE of 'locking members of different religious groups, especially their young people, into stereotypical religious and cultural identities'. Religions should be presented as changing and evolving; as negotiated and sometimes contested 'processes'. The interpretative approach to RE developed by the Warwick RE Project offers an alternative methodology derived from ethnography, in which the relationships between individuals and groups are examined against the background of the wider tradition. Learners are encouraged to move back and forth from one perspective to another in such a way that a 'hermeneutic circle' is instituted and their understanding is increased as the challenge of interpreting another world view transforms the learner.[3]

Critical solidarity and other dialogical approaches to RE focus on a process of understanding rather than the acquisition of a body of knowledge about a faith tradition. The methodology is applicable in any context and, because identifying specific content is less important, does not require local interpretation through an agreed syllabus. Habgood is not convinced of the benefits deriving from the local agreed syllabus and has petitioned for a National Curriculum for RE as the only guarantee of the proper status and resourcing of the subject. Hull has also voiced concerns about the detrimental effect of a policy of devolving responsibility for determining the syllabus for RE to a local committee which receives no delegated funding, results in a variety of syllabuses across the country and makes training and resourcing difficult. If the syllabus for RE is based on educational criteria reflecting the capabilities of the child in each key stage, as is the case elsewhere in the curriculum, then estimations of the appropriate knowledge, skills, attitudes and understanding need not vary greatly, wherever the child might be attending school. The sound educational tenet of using the child's own experience to promote learning need not be confused with a need to provide a locally agreed distinctive syllabus for RE.

The integrity of a faith tradition

The constitution of Agreed Syllabus Conferences can encourage a view of RE in which children learn about those traditions most heavily represented in their locality. The faith representatives, as the 'owners' of a tradition, may then determine what is taught in schools. On first impression this appears to be a plausible approach to the problem of what to teach in schools; if there is only a limited amount of time available, there must be criteria for selection, and who better to determine the specific content than the experts in those traditions selected? Closer examination renders the situation more problematic as issues of principle emerge.

Any criteria for selection based on the extent to which a particular faith is represented locally must be clear as to what 'representation' might mean. For example, how large must a faith community be before it can be invited to participate in the Agreed Syllabus Conference or compete successfully for time allocation within the syllabus? If it is a question of counting heads, then what does it mean to be a member of a faith community? We would arrive at very different estimations of which faiths were actually represented in a locality if we were to take active participation rather than nominal ascription of membership as one of the criteria. Decisions based on representation, however the accounting is managed, risk promoting separation of one group from another and the exclusion of faith groups not present in sufficient numbers to warrant attention. In 1944 the representation of the different Christian denominations on the Agreed Syllabus Conference was intended to promote ecumenicity. The extension of the franchise to include faiths other than Christianity in 1988 was long overdue but the absence of any serious consideration of how this might affect the nature of representation has led to a potentially divisive situation. In fact most agreed syllabuses do strive to give acknowledgement to a spread of religious traditions in their programmes of study as is recommended in the 1988 Education Reform Act (ERA). However, decisions about what should be required, as opposed to recommended, and time allocations still tend to be susceptible to justifications based on local representation. The extent to which any consideration is given to RE as an academic subject requiring the study of forms and varieties of religious traditions, or non-religious philosophies, which may or may not be represented locally is dependent on the quality of support available from (unpaid) consultants rather than on the formal constitution of the Agreed Syllabus Conference. Also, despite the protests of bodies such as the Humanist Association, there is no place within the current arrangements for non-religious viewpoints to be represented; a situation which tends to confirm the impression that RE is only the concern of the 'religious'.

The status of faith representatives as experts is also in need of careful consideration. It is evident that as believers and practitioners they have an insight and understanding of their faith tradition denied to anyone else and so their contribution to RE is unique. However, when the issue of who is best equipped to decide what should be taught in RE is raised the question is not so easily resolved. In the first place, to decide in favour of the faith representative would be to weigh the balance too much in favour of religion as understood by a practitioner rather than RE conducted by a professionally qualified teacher. It may also encourage a view of RE

which prizes authentic transmission of a tradition above the mediation of what, if anything, a particular tradition might mean when encountered by 'outsiders' who may belong to another religious tradition or none.[4] Promoting transmission above interpretation can be a way of avoiding difficult questions of meaning and relevance but, I would argue, ultimately reduces the educational validity of RE. The kind of RE advocated by Habgood and Hull assumes a mediated process of understanding where particular viewpoints and traditions meet in the public domain and enter into dialogue. Teachers, rather than faith representatives, have an important role to play in introducing children to the language of the dialogue and equipping them to participate. If the role of the teacher is viewed in this light, any inadequacy of detailed knowledge of a particular tradition can be balanced by their expertise in children's learning and understanding.[5]

The importance of preserving the integrity of faith traditions was a dominant theme in the debates surrounding the introduction of the 1988 ERA. Multifaith RE, the common practice in most schools since the early 1970s, was challenged on the grounds that it was detrimental to the integrity of individual traditions. The term 'mishmash' was used to denigrate current practice and the study of religious traditions as separate systems advocated. As Hull demonstrates in his study of this phenomenon, the food metaphors which characterise multifaith RE as a mishmash are intended to ridicule the dialogue of faiths and powerful food aversions are evoked in order to arouse emotions in favour of confining religions to separate compartments (Hull, 1991). Those who have a fear of mishmash are deeply respectful of the faith of others but see each religion as a kind of separate classification. For a faith tradition to preserve its integrity, it must maintain a separation and avoid the risk of comparison inherent in a multifaith approach. According to this view, to enter into dialogue is to risk contamination of one tradition by another, respected but separate, tradition to the detriment of both parties: truth lies within a tradition and is not sought in any public understanding or shared meaning. Antipathy to any approach which seeks to look across traditions and promote dialogue, given the constraints of the curriculum time available for RE, leads to a competitive situation in which each tradition vies for adequate coverage of specific content.

How local *can* a local agreed syllabus for RE be?

Two sources of non-statutory guidance, Circular 1/94 from the DfE (1994) and the model syllabuses for RE developed by the Schools Curriculum and Assessment Authority (SCAA, 1994), provide support for an approach to RE which gives precedence to the separatist interpretation of the principle of the integrity of a faith tradition. The Circular reflects three basic principles: integrity of religion whereby religions are taught one by one in separate compartments; Christianity is conceived of as national tradition, as heritage; Christianity is predominant. Faiths other than Christianity are marginalised as a distinction is made between the religion which is the heritage of this country and those which are merely represented here. The SCAA model syllabuses were the response to the cry for a National Curriculum for RE and function as models for Local Agreed Syllabus Conferences to emulate. The syllabuses present RE as the systematic study of a series of religions and provide minimal scope for dialogue between traditions or perspectives from outside any religion. Faith group representatives from six major world religions contributed to the model syllabuses through Faith Group Working Parties. Their involvement has been seen as one of SCAA's major achievements and no one would dispute the extension of a privilege previously confined to the main Christian denominations. However, by arranging for the groups to meet separately and discuss what children should learn about their faith an opportunity to develop interfaith dialogue on the provision for RE in schools was missed.[6] Subsequently, when attempts were made to incorporate the lists of content offered by each group into a realistic time frame, some groups felt aggrieved that expectations raised by the form of the consultation could not be met. Attempts to develop alternative models were discouraged and did not receive support from SCAA.[7]

Circular 1/94 and the model syllabuses set parameters which exert a powerful influence on local agreed syllabuses. By offering guidance which is not statutory, national prescription is effected without apparently challenging the local determination of RE. Not everyone is of the opinion that the level of prescription is such that a truly local interpretation is impossible:

The model syllabuses are helpful – not the answer to ultimate questions – but useful as a basis to teach RE. Leaving aside political elbowing, there is little in them to offend for they do lay out very clearly *what* should be taught and *when* and even if one disagrees with their content there is sufficient flexibility for most Syllabus Conferences to manage comfortably. (Brown, 1995, p. 40)

However, if, as I have argued, the assumptions implicit in the structure of the Local Agreed Syllabus Conference replicate a tendency to preserve the integrity of faith traditions through separation and achieve consensus through devolution to self-selected like-minded groupings (whether they are faith group representatives or 'schools of choice') then there is little room for manoeuvre. It may be that fudging the issues or 'managing comfortably' by retreating from national debate to local interpretations will not result in a syllabus for RE that adequately addresses the issue of diversity in a multifaith society.

Conclusion

Attempts to promote debate on contentious issues should be careful not to present polarised views which obscure the 'broken middle', the area of confusion and difficulty which lies between antithetical states and is the source of a grounded critique (Rose, 1992). Writers such as Bolton (1997) subscribe to a dialogical approach to RE whilst also supporting the Local Agreed Syllabus Conference, and Habgood (1995), who first called for a National Curriculum for RE, advocates 'sensitive adaptation to local circumstances'. Hargreaves (1994) offers the 'Mosaic of Learning' as a means of avoiding the imposition of one set of beliefs in a multifaith society. I have tried to demonstrate that the solution found in 1944 to the issues arising from the decision to include RE as a compulsory subject within a state education system has had a very different effect 50 years on. The structures which promoted dialogue and a shared vision of the form and purpose of RE are no longer capable of performing that function. Studying different faiths is not the same as studying the common ground shared by the different Christian denominations. The contribution of faith representatives to the education of children cannot be the same in our contemporary multicultural, and largely secular, society as it was in the Britain of the 1940s. We have not given sufficient attention to examining the assumptions underlying the structure of the local agreed syllabus; our failure to do so has jeopardised the contribution of RE to the development of a shared understanding within a culturally diverse society. Whether the syllabus for RE is local or national, it should, above all, be agreed.

Notes

1 See Hull (1991).

2 Hargreaves's reference to civic education as the 'concrete' which will bind society together would seem to confirm a rather rigid view of the management of plurality by fixing groups into a frame rather than promoting a process of encounter and change.

3 The hermeneutic circle is derived from the work of Rorty and involves a search for what he has called the 'strands in a possible conversation' which lead to 'edification'.

4 The Warwick Project values the perspective of members of faith communities and has criticised the tendency to generalise from an apparently objective standpoint which was characteristic of scholars of religion who manufactured descriptions of entities such as Hinduism which did not actually reflect the beliefs of the members of the tradition. However, they do reserve the right to mediate the contributions they elicit in their ethnographic studies of faith communities:

> In arriving at our interpretations we needed to be aware that some 'insiders' with interests in portraying the tradition in a particular way might wish to influence us (e.g. in representing only 'orthodox' examples). A pragmatic solution was usually achieved through consultation and negotiation. (Jackson, 1999, pp. 204–5)

5 Wright (1997) provides a critique of the current tendency to polarise debate around specific 'theologies' of RE which have been variously described as generic versus nominalist or thematic versus systematic. He offers a modified version of Cooling's (1994) hermeneutical model as a means of moving the debate on so that common ground can be established and the entitlement of the child is acknowledged. The argument is too complex to be adequately addressed here but it does highlight the extent to which RE seeks to develop theological literacy (Wright's term) within a tradition, across traditions and, I would add, perhaps even beyond traditions if humanism, agnosticism or atheism are accepted as legitimate outcomes of a successful religious education.

6 Interestingly, the process used by the Values Forum to draw up a set of common values for schools was very similar. The groups constituting the Forum met separately and at no stage in the process was provision made for discussion between groups or of the whole Forum. Consequently, a set of values emerged in a compartmentalised form reflecting the absence of any debate as to what should happen when one set of values comes into conflict with another. The Forum also proscribed any discussion of the source of authority for the values or how they should be applied because the assumption was made that there could not be agreement on these matters.

7 For example the Third Perspective was produced independently of SCAA with support from the Conference of University Lecturers in RE (CULRE). See Baumfield *et al.* (1994a, 1994b and 1995).

References

Baumfield, V., Bowness, C., Cush, D. and Miller, J. (1994a) Model syllabus consultation period: a contribution. *Journal of Beliefs and Values* **15**(1).

Baumfield, V., Bowness, C., Cush, D. and Miller, J. (1994b) *A 3rd Perspective: RE in the Basic Curriculum.* Exeter: 3rd Perspective Group, Exeter University.

Baumfield, V., Bowness, C., Cush, D. and Miller, J. (1995) Model syllabuses: the debate continues. *Resource* **18**, 1.

Bolton, A. (1997) Should religious education foster national consciousness? *British Journal of Religious Education* **19**(3), 134–42.

Brown, A. (1995) Discernment: the last word. In *World Religions in Education 1995/96.* London: Shap Working Party on World Religions in Education.

Cooling, T. (1994) *Concept Cracking: Exploring Christian Beliefs in School.* Stapleford, Essex: Association of Christian Teachers.

Department for Education (DfE) (1994) *Religious Education and Collective Worship*, Circular 1/94. London: DfE.

Edwards, A.D. (1996) Changing relationships of producers to consumers in public education. Unpublished paper.

Habgood, J. (1995) Keynote Address at the St Gabriel's Conference on RE, *National Collaboration in RE: Conference Proceedings.* Abingdon: Culham College Institute.

Hargreaves, D. (1994) *The Mosaic of Learning: Schools and Teachers for the Next Century.* London: Demos.

Hull, J. (1991) *Mishmash: Religious Education in Multicultural Britain*, Birmingham Papers in RE, no. 3. Derby: Christian Education Movement.

Hull, J. (1993) *The Place of Christianity in the Curriculum: The Theology of the Department for Education.* London: Hockerill Educational Foundation.

Hull, J. (1995) Religion as a series of religions: a comment on the SCAA Model Syllabuses. In *World Religions in Education 1995/96.* London: Shap Working Party on World Religions in Education.

Jackson, R. (1999) The Warwick RE project: an interpretive approach to religious education. *Religious Education* **94**(2), 201–16.

Rose, G. (1992) *The Broken Middle*. Oxford: Basil Blackwell.

Sacks, J. (1991) *The Persistence of Faith: Religion Morality and Society in a Secular Age*. London: Weidenfeld & Nicolson.

Wright, A. (1997) Mishmash, religionism and theological literacy: an appreciation and critique of Trevor Cooling's hermeneutical programme. *British Journal of Religious Education* **19**(3), 143–56.

16 The Rationale of the Charis Project

JOHN SHORTT

Introduction

The promotion of the spiritual and moral development of pupils was regarded, until fairly recently, as the more or less exclusive preserve of religious education and of personal, social and moral education lessons in the school timetable. It is now increasingly being recognised that all subjects of the curriculum can play a part in this central aspect of education. It is also recognised that many subjects probably still fail to do so. The Office for Standards in Education discussion paper (OFSTED, 1994) stated: 'To move towards a position where subjects see themselves in this way might seem to require a sea-change in attitudes and approaches, but certainly the potential is there.'

It was to help to bring about this sea-change in attitudes and approaches that the Charis Project was set up. The project commenced in autumn 1994 and, in its first three-year phase, teacher resource books were produced for mathematics, English, science, French and German. The materials were written by teams consisting mainly of practising teachers and were designed for use with 14- to 16-year-old pupils.

The project was modelled to some extent on the already established SATIS (Science and Technology in Society) Project. Both projects were sponsored by charitable trusts set up by members of the Sainsbury family. Both were developed by teacher associations – the SATIS Project by the Association of Science Education (ASE) and the Charis Project by the Association of Christian Teachers (ACT). Both projects produced resource books of photocopiable material written by teams of teachers. Both were concerned to bring issues of personal and social morality into the teaching of curriculum subjects.

The Charis Project added to the SATIS Project's concern with moral and social aspects an emphasis on the spiritual dimension of education. It goes further still in setting out to produce resource materials that are, in some significant sense of the word, *Christian* and, at the same time, acceptable to teachers and pupils of a wide range of faith backgrounds and of none.

This chapter is concerned with the rationale for producing Christian resources for the promotion of spiritual and moral development across the curriculum. What does it mean to describe such resources as Christian? What has Christianity got to contribute to the teaching of mathematics or other subjects?

In attempting to answer these and other questions, the chapter seeks to throw some light on the relationship between the beliefs central to world views – whether Christian or any other – and the teaching of the different 'secular' subjects of the school curriculum. In these days when curriculum content and educational processes are seen to be 'value-laden' or, at least, not value-neutral, and when values are seen, in their turn, to be related to basic beliefs and outlooks, this curriculum project provides a good case-study for the exploration of these important questions.

The kinds of issues involved

A curriculum innovation such as the Charis Project brings together Christianity, spiritual and moral development and the 'secular' subjects of the school curriculum. It raises issues of many kinds.

First, there are issues to do with the nature of, and relations among, the different areas or forms of human knowledge. Some may argue that Christian beliefs are religious in nature and can therefore have nothing to do with the content of subjects like mathematics or science. Each area or form is concerned with distinct and different types of explanation. Each has its own key ideas and ways of proceeding. That which is true or false in one area does not affect the truth or falsity of statements in another area. In other words, the different subject areas have a logical autonomy which places a question-mark against talk of providing Christian resources for spiritual and moral development through modern foreign languages, mathematics or other 'secular' subjects. The issues here are *epistemological*: they have to do with matters of the logic of the structure of knowledge and whether it makes sense to talk in such terms across the boundaries between the subject areas.

A second set of issues are *ethical* in nature. They have to do with whether or not it is morally acceptable to produce Christian curriculum resources for the common schools of a plural democracy. These issues are not related to the structure of knowledge but rather to the nature of our society, the different sets of basic beliefs and values which are held among its citizens, and the rightness or wrongness of producing curriculum resources which are somehow based in or proceeding from a particular set of beliefs and values held within a particular community or tradition of thought.

Ethical issues are distinct from those which I shall term *prudential*. These have to do with whether or not, given a set of aims, it is wise to proceed in a certain way. There may be no moral objection to a course of action but it may still not be the most advisable. Issues here include, for example, practical ones to do with marketing of curriculum resources like these. Questions to be answered are of a 'how best to proceed' kind, but as these are less likely to be of interest to the general reader I will leave them to one side.

Both epistemological and ethical issues will be explored in relation to different aspects of the curriculum project. We shall look in turn at aims, content and method. The *aims* of the project will be looked at to see in what sense they may be said to be Christian and to explore the epistemological and ethical issues raised as a result. The *content* of the resource materials for the different subject areas can be classified under several headings. Christian beliefs and values are involved in several different ways. Again both epistemological and ethical issues arise. The third aspect of the project is that of the

teaching *methods* it makes use of in the way the material is presented and the kinds of tasks that are set and the methods it recommends that teachers use in the classroom. Methodology immediately raises ethical issues of the possibility of indoctrination and the like but it also raises issues to do with the nature of knowledge. What has Christianity to contribute to an understanding of teaching methods?

There is still another issue raised by this project. It has to do with what might be understood by the word 'Christian' and it is the subject of the next section.

Uniquely Christian or shared with others? And does it matter?

Although Christians differ among themselves on many issues (as indeed do those of other world views) and some of these disagreements can seem quite fundamental at times, I am assuming that there are basic beliefs and values which can be generally characterised as Christian and that these form a more or less coherent set. They have what Wittgensteinian philosophers term 'family resemblances' which are generally sufficient to enable us to distinguish between beliefs and values which are Christian and those which are not.

What is of importance for this chapter is not differences among Christians but the extent to which these identifiably Christian beliefs, values, attitudes and practices overlap also with those of other world views. In other words, there is an important distinction between, on the one hand, a belief, a value, a teaching method, the content of a curriculum resource or an educational aim which is *uniquely* held or advocated by Christians and, on the other hand, those which are *also* held or advocated by those of another tradition or other traditions.

This 'common ground' of 'shared beliefs and values' can occur both with basic beliefs and values and also with those which depend on them. Christians generally hold as a basic belief that God is personal but this is not a uniquely Christian belief. They also hold that God is three persons and one being and, in this respect, their belief would seem to be unique. The situation can be depicted as shown in Figure 16.1. If this line of argument is along the right lines, curriculum resources may be Christian either because they are uniquely based on Christian beliefs and values or, alternatively,

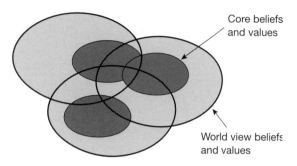

Core beliefs
and values

World view beliefs
and values

Figure 16.1   A common ground of shared beliefs and values

because they comport well, although not uniquely, with basic Christian beliefs and values and also with the basic beliefs and values of other world views

If then it is the case that there are many beliefs, values, attitudes and practices which are common to Christians and to those of other faiths and, indeed, to those who would disavow any religious commitment at all, why not focus on what is common? Why should anybody be concerned to produce curriculum resources which are, in some significant sense, Christian? After all, one of the things that seems important with the move to recognising a need to promote spiritual and moral development across the curriculum is that teachers and pupils realise that values come into everything. Why go beyond that and bring different religious outlooks and other world views into the picture?

It seems to me that the objection expressed in such questions fails to take sufficient account of the importance of such matters as the wholeness, coherence and adequacy of foundation of a person's set of beliefs and values. The School Curriculum and Assessment Authority's National Forum for Values in Education and the Community produced a list of shared values and principles for action.[1] These were categorised in relation to society, (human) relationships, the self and the environment. However, the fact that such values and principles are shared or common is not sufficient to establish their moral or spiritual authority over the individual. Pupils may still respond, 'It may well be the case that most adults in our society hold these values but why should *I* hold them?' An adequate values education making use of such a statement of shared values will need to show also the importance of having reasons or grounds for holding them and to recognise that these reasons or grounds are not the same for everybody.

Common or shared values are neither free-standing nor worldview-neutral. Common ground is not neutral ground. If we remove from the figure the different sets of core beliefs and values, we effectively remove everything. Shared beliefs and values are only so because they are *shared* among those of *different* basic outlooks. They gain their authority not from the fact that they are shared but from the different basic sources from which people of different world views derive them. It is important that we have shared beliefs and values so that we can understand, communicate with and cooperate with one another. It is also important that we recognise that they have different bases – not least when we come to work through our disagreements.

An adequate values education will also need to show how the whole domain appears very differently to people of different world views (and it can do so without necessarily conceding anything to the unsophisticated relativism which the Forum's deliberations were meant to falsify). Christians, for example, who add values in relation to God to those listed in relation to society, (human) relationships, the self and the environment, are not adding just *another* category to the list: it is the kind of addition that can transform the whole perspective and provide both justification and motivation for adopting the values in question. To them it can make a great difference that God is seen as three persons-in-relation because this sets human relationships in an altogether different light. That God is seen to be love and that such love is believed to have taken Jesus Christ to death on a cross can make an ethic of enlightened self-interest seem seriously deficient. That Jesus Christ is regarded as having risen from the dead can bring a sense of meaningfulness to mortal life that might not otherwise be there.

The Charis Project materials do not go into detail on these central Christian beliefs because, as I shall attempt to show later, this would not be appropriate to lessons in subjects like mathematics. On the other hand, they do not exclude all mention of such beliefs in an exclusive focus on shared moral and spiritual values because this would be to suggest that such values do not need a basis in a particular view of reality. Pupils may be helped to develop their own integrated view of life and reality through coming to see that basic beliefs undergird the values that pervade the whole of the school curriculum and the whole of life. Christian beliefs and values can provide a helpful example of how this happens.

Bracketing 'Christian' with 'spiritual and moral'

There is another objection to the idea of Christian resources for the promotion of spiritual and moral development. This is that moving from talk of spiritual or moral to *Christian* spiritual or *Christian* moral is illegitimate. Ethics is an autonomous domain. Morality does not require religious underpinning, it is said, and anyway non-religious people are often very moral and sometimes more so than some religious people. A similar claim may be made for spirituality: people can discuss spiritual issues and be spiritual without being religious. Religious beliefs and values, it may be argued, are of a different kind from moral and spiritual beliefs and values.

This objection brings the relation between the different forms of human knowledge and understanding into sharper focus. I shall therefore take the relation between religion and ethics as a case-study of how it may be possible to integrate Christian beliefs with beliefs in other 'non-religious' areas of understanding.

It is undoubtedly the case that non-religious people are often very moral and sometimes seem rather more so than some religious people. However, it does not follow from this that it is not possible to base morality on religious beliefs and, in particular, on those of the Christian religion. The absence of agreement on the foundations of ethics, after centuries of debate, would seem to make it at least a bit premature to rule out the possibility of a Christian foundation.

However, there is an argument which, if successful, would rule out talk of a Christian basis for ethics. It is the 'open-question argument'. According to this argument, 'good' cannot be defined in terms of what God is or wills or commands because it is open to question whether what God is or wills or commands is really good. The purported definitions can, it is claimed, be denied without self-contradiction. But I am not sure that it is so clear that it 'makes sense' to ask whether what God is or wills or commands is really good. For some, it seems that it does but for others it doesn't. From within a Christian perspective on reality, it may not make sense to ask at all whether God is good. Granted the question may be grammatically meaningful so that it does make a kind of *sense*, but the Christian may not see any *point* in asking it. It is not really meaningful to ask it. Or perhaps, bearing in mind those times of anguished doubt and questioning that most Christian believers will admit to if they are honest, it does not *generally* make sense to ask it.

If this is a reasonable counter to the open-question argument, it would indicate that some approaches to morality are rooted in world views which recommend definitions of ethical terms while others are rooted in those which reject all such definitions and insist on the autonomy of ethics. If so, the open-question argument itself may express nothing more than a recommendation from within a particular kind of world view.

What this suggests to me is that at the core or basis of our world views, there are beliefs *and values* Some, if not all, of our basic beliefs are themselves value-laden. It is not a case of moving from a 'factual' domain of religious beliefs or of those of other world views to a separate domain of moral (or spiritual?) values. Right down there at base (or right in there at the core), our key beliefs have facts and values all bound up together within them. If so, it would seem acceptable for Christians to bracket 'Christian' with 'moral' and, in like manner, with 'spiritual'.

On the bracketing of religious and spiritual, it can at least be argued against the strict autonomy of a spiritual domain that not just any spirituality, or any spiritual experience, will do. In an article in the *Guardian*, Albert Radcliffe (1995) wrote:

> The most spiritual man of the 20th century was also the most evil, that is the most destructive of humanity. . . . To be spiritual is not necessarily to be on the side of the good angels, let alone your neighbour. Tomorrow is the 50th anniversary of the suicide of Adolf Hitler; a man so gifted in manipulation and whose mind was so in tune with the dark fears and anxieties of his time that he was able to seduce and draw into his baleful fantasies millions of baptised Christians.

It could be argued that this is an unusual usage of 'spiritual' but the reason why it is unusual is surely because we tend to link together the spiritual and the good in a way that is similar to that in which, I have suggested, Christians tend to link ideas of God and goodness. Bracketing 'Christian' with 'spiritual' or 'moral' in this way is not obviously as unacceptable as it is sometimes claimed to be.

I turn now to look in turn at the aspects of aims, content and method and in doing so I shall take examples from the Charis resources to illustrate how Christianity, spirituality and morality may possibly be integrated with the different subject-areas of the curriculum.

Aims of the curriculum resources

The aims of the Charis Project as stated in the Introduction to the resource books (ACT, 1996a, 1996b, 1996c) are as follows:

- to enable teachers to respond to the challenge of educating the whole person;
- to help teachers to focus on the spiritual and moral dimensions inherent in their subject area;
- to encourage pupils towards a clearer understanding of Christian perspectives on the fundamental questions that arise in all areas of knowledge; and
- to contribute to the breadth, balance and harmony of pupils' knowledge and understanding.

These aims have an emphasis upon wholeness – both the wholeness of personal development and the wholeness of knowledge and understanding. At a conference at Westhill College in January 1993, the then Chief Inspector for Schools, Professor Stewart Sutherland, suggested in the context of remarks about spiritual development that schools should have among their aims 'the integration in the pupil's personality of some overall view of knowledge and of the world' (Sutherland, 1995). It is this concern that the listed aims (particularly the fourth of them) seek to state.

At the same time, there is a concern with the integrity of the subject areas as they are at present constituted. The concern is not to add on artificially from without that which does not arise from within the mathematical, scientific or other topic. Spiritual and moral dimensions, it is stated, are present *within* the subjects and fundamental questions arise *in* all areas of knowledge. In an unpublished paper, a member of one of the project's writing teams has this to say on this subject:

> There is a thin line between, on the one hand, materials for *teaching mathematics* which aim to expose the spiritual dimension of such study, and materials which *teach theology* using mathematics merely as illustrative material, somewhat in the manner of a sermon illustration. This has sometimes been referred to as the issue of integration versus pseudo-integration – exploring the very real faith dimensions of all human activity versus downgrading other areas of study to handy raw material to be used in support of another, more narrowly religious agenda. This does not mean that religious belief should be absent from other curriculum areas, but rather that it can arise for consideration in ways which are integral to each area – where, for instance, it has shaped a certain work of literature, mathematical development, or historical event.

How Christian are the aims listed above? Three of the four make no explicit reference to Christianity and would seem acceptable regardless of faith commitment. The only reference to 'Christian' is in the third aim where it is seen as important that pupils develop a clearer understanding of Christian perspectives on fundamental questions. Even this is an aim that might be shared by those of other world views since, across the curriculum as in RE, it could well be maintained that the influence of Christianity on the history and culture of the western world justifies giving particular attention to Christian ways of responding to deep questions.

It seems therefore that the expressed aims, as they stand, are not *uniquely* Christian. They comport well with basic Christian beliefs and values but, at the same time, they may also be held by people with other perspectives on life and reality. This is also true of the specific aims stated for the different subject areas. For example, the introductions to *Charis Français* and *Charis Deutsch* (ACT, 1996b, 1996c) list the following aims:

- to promote a sense of the meaning and the wholeness of life;
- to challenge materialism and self-interest as a basis for life;
- to explore moral aspects of relationships, including truthfulness and the role of language;
- to encourage students to look positively and critically at other cultures and to question narrow stereotypes;
- to help students to identify with the experiences and perspectives of people in other countries and communities;
- to encourage an understanding of diversity of values, beliefs and customs; and
- to generate appreciation of the foreign culture, by exploring aspects such as spirituality, faith, self-sacrifice, wonder, worship, freedom and responsibility, suffering, forgiveness, hope, love, compassion and received truth.

In this list there is no explicit reference to Christianity and only brief references to faith and worship.

The aims could again be shared by people of a wide range of faith commitments and of none.

So it would seem that the aims of the project are Christian, but not uniquely so. Others may share them and hold them just as dearly. But, as I have suggested earlier, different basic beliefs can put shared aims in an altogether different light. They may be viewed differently by people of different basic outlooks. References in these listed aims to wholeness, spiritual, moral, fundamental questions, meaning, faith, self-sacrifice, suffering, forgiveness, hope and love will, I suggest, be seen differently depending on a person's world view. A Christian outlook with a particular regard for the love of Christ who suffered death on a cross will fill a concept like forgiveness with distinctive meaning. We may agree on the need of whole person development but what kind of person do we mean, characterised by what virtues? Christians generally hold that wholeness has ultimately to do with personal relationship with God.

To find what may be written into these statements of aims, we need to look at how they are worked out in practice in the content and methods of the resource materials.

Content of the curriculum resources

The topics in the various resource books produced by the Charis Project are dealt with in several different ways. Some of these are unique to particular subjects while others are found in several of the resource books. They illustrate a range of ways whereby spiritual and moral dimensions to the teaching of the subjects can be made more explicit.

Mathematics

The introduction to *Charis Mathematics* identifies three approaches to be found among the units making up the book. The first recognises that mathematics has been developed and applied in a wide range of human situations. This approach uses contexts which allow pupils to develop and use their mathematics while, at the same time, reflecting upon and discussing spiritual and moral dimensions of human issues which arise in those contexts. A unit using the 1991 Census as a context provides work on number and data-handling while, at the same time, encouraging pupils to consider the value of the individual 'lost' when population numbers

are rounded or when people are missing from a census return. A unit on mortality statistics encourages reflection on attitudes to life and death. Another unit on statistics of literacy in different parts of the world seeks to remind pupils of the value of being able to read and write. Another unit in the mathematics resources counters the me-first view of life by focusing on giving to charity and making use of calculations of the extra amount received by the charity when gifts are covenanted. Traditional exercises in mathematics textbooks have tended to take for granted a different approach to life as, for example, when they ask for calculations of the amount of interest gained from a method of saving. The surprise of realising this for the first time shows how easy it is to proceed on the basis of a particular evaluative stance without ever questioning it.

A second approach identified in the mathematics materials makes use of the way in which people have explored mathematical ideas in order to gain understanding of related ideas in other areas of knowledge. One unit explores the truth and falsity, proofs and refutations of a series of statements about prime numbers and goes on to raise wider issues about belief, truth and proof of statements of kinds other than those of mathematics. In this case, a concept which occurs in several disciplines is investigated by initially looking at it in a mathematical context. Another unit takes the concept of infinity, looks at the mathematical idea of infinity and its paradoxes and then moves out to other contexts. The teacher's notes to the unit point out that the massive contributions of Georg Cantor to our understanding of mathematical infinity were motivated by his Christian concern to understand the infinity of God. The pupils are encouraged to reflect on the bigness of the numbers of stars in the sky or grains of sand on the seashore (and here there is reference to the Genesis account of God talking in these terms to Abraham). Yet another unit studies the normal probability distribution and leads into a consideration of what we mean by being 'normal' and how we can be pressured into conformity with the expectations of the majority. It encourages consideration of the attitudes we take to minorities.

Here (and elsewhere) in the mathematics units, biographical information on famous mathematicians is introduced in order to show the human face of mathematics. This includes information on their religious beliefs and, as in the case of Cantor, the religious motivations of their mathematical work.

A third approach adopted in the mathematics materials makes use of the ways in which mathematics can model the physical universe and seeks to lead pupils to develop a sense of wonder at the reality around them. One unit provides an introduction to fractals and leads into consideration of the images of startling beauty and complexity through which it is now possible to model such natural features as the shapes of coastlines, trees, fern leaves and clouds. The teacher's notes make reference to the description of Mandelbrot's fractal as 'the thumb print of God'. Additional sources recommended to teachers include a book with the title *Does God Play Dice?*. Another unit studies the mathematics of networks and leads into consideration of the Anthropic Principle (on how perfectly suited the universe is for intelligent life to exist) and the impossibility of intelligent life in two dimensions.

The three approaches identified could be summarised as:

1 using mathematics in contexts where human issues are considered;
2 exploring key ideas that occur in mathematics and in other disciplines; and
3 exploring mathematical models of phenomena in the physical world.

To these could be added a fourth which is found across several units using these three approaches:

4 studying mathematicians as 'whole people' with moral and spiritual concerns.

Science

The units in *Charis Science* are likewise concerned to present scientists as whole people. One unit sets out potted biographies of four important scientists and goes on to show how their discoveries can be used for both good and harmful ends. Brief biographical information also appears in some other units.

Environmental and human issue concerns are, not surprisingly, present in several units which deal with applications of science. There is a unit on fuel consumption which seeks to encourage stewardship of natural resources. Another unit looks at waste products and seeks to promote reflection on inter-

dependence and on personal mortality. There is a reference here to 'a Jewish teacher' who said that all must return to dust. Yet another unit considers healthy and unhealthy lifestyles and encourages consideration of how we treat our bodies. In this unit there is a brief section which outlines the different attitudes to the human body taken by Hedonists, Stoics and Christians.

Another concern in some of the units is to show some of the limitations of science and the fallibility of scientists. Linked with this is an expressed concern to oppose scientific reductionism. These concerns are particularly evident in two of the units which respectively present the stories of the development of continental drift theory and of atomic theory. At this point, the materials differ in an important respect from what might find a place in a course on science and religion as, say, part of RE or sixth form general studies. They work from *within* science rather than from outside it and are designed for use by science teachers rather than teachers of RE or general studies.

Several units set out to promote wonder at the immensity, beauty, order and mystery of the universe. One of these focuses on origins and looks particularly at the Big Bang theory. The Anthropic Principle occurs in another science unit – and also, as I have mentioned above, in one of the mathematics units. Another science unit focuses on the wonder and the value of human life and suggests that some medical judgements can devalue life. It contains in a 'pause for thought' section a quotation from Psalm 139 on the development of the human embryo.

Again, as in mathematics, it seems that there are four general kinds of approach to be found in the science units. Briefly put, they are as follows:

1 applications of science leading into consideration of human issues;
2 consideration of the nature and limitations of scientific explanation (and pointing to other kinds of explanation);
3 reflection on life and the universe as understood scientifically leading to encouragement to wonder at its beauty and mystery; and
4 studying scientists as 'whole people' with moral and spiritual concerns.

These four approaches are quite similar to those identified in the mathematics material.

English

The first book published by the project for English teachers is a set of units which could be integrated into work on Shakespeare's *Macbeth*.

Several of the units of material explore themes in the play which lead directly into consideration of moral and spiritual issues. There are units on: relationships in *Macbeth*; good and evil in *Macbeth*; questions of responsibility, order and disorder; supernatural influences; and Macbeth's moral decline. There is an expressed concern to 'allow students to pursue their own responses as the text speaks for itself' which is based on the belief that 'teaching that has integrity will focus *on the text*, not on an accepted reading of it'. In these units there are some references to Christian belief and some quotations from the Bible but these are mainly in the teacher's notes rather than in the student material. For example, Macbeth's search for a 'balm for his guilt-ridden conscience' is contrasted with King David's finding of forgiveness for heinous sins recorded in Psalm 51. The 'bleak fatalism' of Macbeth's despairing soliloquy should be countered, we are told, by literary examples of optimism and hope, and suggestions here include John Bunyan's *Pilgrim's Progress*. In a section with the title 'Fighting against evil' (this time in the pupil material), quotations from the play are juxtaposed with a couple of biblical quotations which contain some of the same ideas of supernatural power and grace. Again, in an exercise of building up a log of Macbeth's moral decline, pupils are referred to C.S. Lewis's *Screwtape Letters* as a source of ideas for this.

A second approach to spiritual and moral development in the English materials brings out the importance of world views in writing and interpreting literature. A unit on the historical and religious background to *Macbeth* outlines the Elizabethan world view. A unit entitled 'On stage and screen' looks at ways of staging and filming the play. This contrasts Shakespeare's ending of the play with the defeat of evil with the way in which Polanski leaves the struggle between good and evil continuing without a necessary prospect of an end. It is suggested that Shakespeare's view corresponds more with orthodox Christianity than Polanski's 'dualistic world-view'. In this unit, one of the exercises for the pupils invites them to write a critical comparison of the portrayals of the witches in two or three different productions of the play.

The unit on the historical and religious background to the play also incorporates a third approach when it explores the nature of literature and the nature of history and asks: 'Is there a moral dimension to Shakespeare's distortion of history?'. Here, as in the mathematics and science units, there is a concern with the nature of truth in different subject areas and with different kinds of explanation.

A fourth approach used in *Charis English* is found in two units which focus particularly on aspects of language and deal, respectively, with the imagery used in the play and with the different kinds of prose and verse in the play. The unit on imagery makes the point that many of the image patterns echo those used in Christian liturgy and the Bible (light and darkness, washing and water, blood, and clothing). In this respect, this unit also brings out the importance of world views to literary studies. It goes on to consider the effectiveness of Shakespeare's imagery. The unit on the different kinds of prose and verse in the play encourages pupils to consider the moral and spiritual implications of the power of words. That our use of language itself is not value-neutral is no longer as radical a suggestion as it was before it was realised how sexist and racist assumptions could be so easily built into it.

To sum up, four approaches used in the *Charis English* materials are as follows:

1 exploring moral and spiritual issues that arise directly from the text of a piece of literature;
2 exploring the influence of world views on writing and interpreting literature;
3 considering the nature of literature and history and of different kinds of truth; and
4 exploring the moral and spiritual dimensions of the ways in which we use language.

Modern foreign languages

The units in *Charis Français* and *Charis Deutsch* illustrate several approaches to the integration of moral and spiritual issues with teaching modern foreign languages.

Some units make use of biography to explore the role of faith in people's lives, their goals and sacrifices and the way they respond to experiences of suffering. The materials deal with the White Rose (a student resistance group in Hitler's Germany); the experiences of a lady who was born into a German-speaking community in the Ukraine and who with members of her family fled before the Red Army to Germany; and the life and work of St Martin of Tours. The role of faith in people's lives is also explored in a German unit on faith which seeks to show that German speakers hold the same diversity of beliefs as the pupils would find in their own school. The material in this unit makes use of surveys of young people's religious beliefs and there is a section which outlines similarities and differences between Jewish, Christian and Islamic beliefs.

Another unit looks at the work of *L'Arche* communities among the mentally handicapped in France and around the world. The focus here is on people with particular need and the expressed concern is to encourage pupils to become more aware of the feelings and situations of others. The unit includes a brief exercise on the story of Noah's Ark.

A unit which appears in both the German and French books takes the beauty of the natural world as its theme. It makes use of black and white photographs and of translations of Psalms 8 and 23. The teacher's notes suggest that a group of pupils might present an assembly based on one of these psalms.

Another approach deals fairly directly with moral and spiritual issues. One of the French units, for example deals with issues of lying and truth-telling. Traditional proverbs and interviews with French teenagers are made use of in this unit. Another French unit considers the symbolism of bread in life and in Christian thinking and goes on to consider priorities in life. A German unit on kissing uses the different significances of a kiss to explore the moral aspects of relationships. The different kinds of kiss include the Judas kiss, referring to the kiss of betrayal by Judas Iscariot of Jesus.

To summarise, the approaches in these units are of the following kinds:

1 exploring the role of faith in people's lives, mainly through biographies;
2 looking at the different kinds of situations in which people live and particular needs that some people have;
3 looking at the natural world, leading into reflection on its beauty; and
4 exploring moral and spiritual issues more directly.

Summary

Bringing together the results of this brief survey of the contents of the books produced by the Charis Project, the approaches used are of a number of kinds. Some are subject-specific while others occur (with variations) in more than one subject. It therefore does not make sense to attempt to bring the different sets of approaches together into a single list. However, there are a number of general observations to be made.

Several subject books make use of an approach which explores the influence of world views and the role of the moral and spiritual in people's lives and work. Extensive use is made of biography: of great mathematicians and scientists, of saints of old and of twentieth century figures (not all well known). Closely related to this approach is the emphasis on world view in the work of playwrights and that of their interpreters in film and on stage or, as mentioned earlier in connection with one of the science units, in the outline of Hedonist, Stoic and Christian views of the human body.

Human issues which involve moral and spiritual questions are explored either (a) directly or (b) by looking at the different kinds of situations in which people live and particular needs that some people have or (c) as they arise in a work of literature or the contexts in which the technical knowledge of a subject area like mathematics or science is applied.

Key philosophical ideas, such as truth, proof, infinity, time, are explored, beginning from their use within a particular subject area and moving out to other subject areas as well. Closely related to this approach is a concern to explore the nature, powers and limitations of the subject areas of human knowledge.

The beauty, order and mystery of the universe, the natural world and human life is reflected upon from within a range of subject areas with a concern to promote a sense of awe and wonder.

As regards the influence of Christian beliefs and values in the selection of content, *shared* beliefs and values predominate throughout. Relationships, truth-telling, concern for the needy, human dignity, the beauty of the natural world, stewardship of natural resources, healthy life-styles, courage in the face of suffering and the like are all valued by people of many different world views. At the same time, there is a concern to show that different basic perspectives underlie these values and make a difference to how we view and apply them. It is evident too that Christian beliefs have a role in the selection of themes and examples. The symbols of bread, the ark, blood and so on are particularly (albeit not exclusively) important to Christians. References to Mandelbrot's fractal as 'the thumb print of God' or to Bunyan's *Pilgrim's Progress* or Lewis's *Screwtape Letters* show Christian preferences. Quotations from the Bible or from well-known Christians appear fairly regularly where they relate to the content but often as 'pauses for thought' without elaboration or set tasks.

One reviewer said of *Charis Mathematics*: 'Suffused with a Christian flavour, there is nevertheless much of value here for even the most devout atheist.'[2] If this is true of all the materials from the Charis Project, it would seem to indicate that the Christian content has been integrated in an acceptable way. Whether or not it really has done so is not only a matter of content but also of method. It is to this latter aspect that we now come.

Methodology of the curriculum resources

Here I shall make some general remarks about the Charis books rather than look at each in turn.

Remarks from two of the writing team members in unpublished papers prepared for recent conferences point to the importance of methodological considerations. One (Marfleet, 1997) writes:

> The thinking behind the Charis Project . . . is based on the belief that it is credible to bring a discussion of values into the whole curriculum. Some would say that it brings risk of one point of view dominating the teaching; we would argue the reverse, that it will lead to greater breadth and balance in the pupils' knowledge and understanding.

The other (Smith, 1996) has this to say:

> If writers of Christian educational materials give careful attention to content, making it interesting, accessible and integrally Christian, without giving at least as much thought to questions of methodology, the results can be an approach which delivers Christian content by methods which both undermine the content and sit uncomfortably with a Christian view of the learner.

The units of Charis material are designed to be used in situations where there is provision for both open-ended discussion and quiet personal reflection. It is recognised in the introductions and sets of teacher's notes that this is something with which teachers of English will generally be more at ease than teachers of science and, particularly, of math-

ematics. The underlying conviction is that teachers of all subjects are inevitably engaged in value-laden activities and the danger of the apparently neutral approach is that it communicates a set of values which are taken for granted and made neither explicit nor open to question. The provision for reflection on these issues and discussion of them is therefore seen as de-indoctrinatory.

It is also recognised that it is very difficult to promote any in-depth discussion of moral and spiritual issues using the medium of a language in which the pupils may be very far from fluent. Both French and German books contain several worksheets labelled, respectively, '*a considérer*' and '*zum nachdenken*' and the teacher's notes suggest that the pupils be allowed time to reflect on what they have learned, to note their thoughts in either the foreign language or English, so that they interact with a text and respond at a personal level without being required to share their responses with others. In similar manner, the other Charis books include a number of 'pause for thought' items in their units.

Even though there is, as we have seen, a 'Christian flavour' to the content, the concern is that the materials should stimulate thought and elicit genuine personal responses rather than that the pupils should complete activities and tasks in a mechanical and unreflective way with minimal personal involvement. This is not incompatible with activities which are concerned to help pupils to learn the subject matter. An interesting example of this is an activity in the French unit which explores the symbolism of bread. Pupils are asked to work in pairs to work out a shared hierarchy of values that they place on bread, money, water, family, friendship, faith, education, television, love. These words (in French) are cut out and the pupils are required to place them on a grid. One of them places a word on the grid and says (again in French) something along the lines of 'I think the most important thing is bread'. The other takes another word and places it on the grid, perhaps moving the first word from its place, with a statement like 'No, I think water is more important than bread'. This activity provides for what one of the writing team terms a 'multi-layered response' (Smith, 1996) in that the students may be considering their priorities in life at the same time as they practice over and over again comparative and superlative phrases, using model phrases provided.

Such methods are, of course, not uniquely Christian. Indeed, they are probably methods which any good teacher would be happy to endorse. But, as Paul Ernest (1991; see also Ernest, 1989) has pointed out in relation to mathematics education, teaching method is affected by underlying ideology even in such an apparently uncontroversial subject as mathematics. It is therefore significant that shared methodology be founded in basic beliefs about reality, knowledge and human nature. The methods advocated in the Charis Project materials comport well with a Christian view of human nature with an emphasis on the importance of free and informed choice. They would not comport well with, for example, a behaviourist view of the person.

Conclusion

Of course, in all this there has to be a recognition that much depends on the active involvement of the teacher. The Charis Project resources consist of photocopiable pupil worksheets with notes for teachers. They are not textbooks or a complete curriculum for values education in any of the subject areas. They are produced merely as aids in a process where values are, most importantly, incarnated in the teacher's person, attitudes and activity. It would be easy to claim too much for the resource materials. At the same time, they are intended to point the way to how a mix of the ingredients of shared beliefs and values along with foundational beliefs and values distinctive of particular world views can contribute to the spiritual and moral development of young people in our contemporary plural society.

Notes

1 Published in QCA (1997).
2 John Bibby in 1996 catalogue of resources for teachers of mathematics published by QED of York.

References

Association of Christian Teachers (ACT) (1996a) *Charis English*. St Albans, Herts.: ACT.

Association of Christian Teachers (ACT) (1996b) *Charis Français*. St Albans, Herts.: ACT.

Association of Christian Teachers (ACT) (1996c) *Charis Deutsch*. St Albans, Herts.: ACT.

Ernest, P. (1989) The impact of beliefs on the teaching of mathematics. In P. Ernest (ed.), *Mathematics Teaching*. London: Falmer Press.

Ernest, P. (1991) *The Philosophy of Mathematics Education*. London: Falmer Press.

Marfleet, A. (1997) The Charis Project. Paper presented to Conference on Values in the Curriculum at the University of London Institute of Education, April 1997.

Office for Standards in Education (OFSTED) (1994) *Spiritual, Moral, Social and Cultural Development*. London: Her Majesty's Stationery Office.

Qualifications and Curriculum Authority (QCA) (1997) *The Promotion of Pupils' Spiritual, Moral, Social and Cultural Development*, November 1997, London: QCA.

Radcliffe, A. (1995) Faith on the dark side of spirituality. *Guardian* 29 April.

Smith, D. (1996) A Christian approach to cross-curricular moral and spiritual development: personal reflections on the Charis Project. Paper presented to *Reclaiming the Future*, International Conference on Christian Education, Sydney, July.

Sutherland, S. (1995) Speech to a Consultation at Westhill College, Birmingham, on 'Inspecting Pupil's Moral and Spiritual Development', unpublished.

17 The End of Religion in the UK and Beyond

BRIAN E. GATES

Humanity is waving farewell to religion

There is a dominant myth that religion is in decline in the UK and that, in so far as it thrives elsewhere in the world, this is a sign of social backwardness. For instance, Richard Dawkins (1997, pp. 64–9), the public advocate for better understanding of science, wastes few opportunities to belittle religion as inheritor of pre-scientific beliefs which will not bear sustained rational scrutiny. Or again, commentators on world development attribute to Hinduism a major responsibility for slow economic growth in India, and dismiss it accordingly (see Siegel, 1986, ch. 8). Such judgements are commonplace in the western world view which inducts us into Marxist and Freudian ways of thinking. Religion belongs in our childhood, both as individuals and, more collectively, as the human race. Whether in the form of some all powerful, parent-like, protective power or a back-to-the-womb mysticism it is there as consolation in the face of misfortune and as promise of alternative compensation in some future world beyond the present. Accordingly, how can it be other than patently false? It has no more credibility than the self-projected belief in Father Christmas, or the fleeting internal glow induced by one or other of the socially accepted drugs, contemporary opiates of the people.

The evidence of decay

The numerical decline of organised religion

The evidence on which the myth is based is of two kinds. First, there are the annual inventories of church-going, conducted by the churches themselves, such as the Church of England's returns on Easter communicants, or the Marc Europe/Christian Research surveys of all the Christian churches (see *Church of England Yearbook*, 1997; Brierley, 1997). They reveal that only 10–12 per cent of the population are in active membership, as measured by regular and frequent church-going, of whom the majority are under 15 years of age or over 50.

By all accounts, the other established religions show similar seepage. In the case of the Jewish community, the statistics are scarcely more encouraging and a special initiative entitled Jewish Continuity has been launched to attempt to reverse the trend.[1] For a variety of reasons, comparable figures for the other faith communities are difficult to obtain. Complications include debate over who should 'count' as a Hindu, Muslim or Sikh. Ethnicity may be a guide, but only partially so. The reintroduction of a question about religious identity in the next census might therefore in this regard be very revealing.[2] In the meantime, however, there is extensive concern expressed from within these communities regarding the perceived trends towards 'fall-out'.[3] Similarly, Buddhist societies and meditation centres are popular, but the scale of active membership remains quite modest.[4]

In hard-edged institutional terms, traditional religious belonging no longer has the strength it once had. Even the pattern of preferred arrangements for marriage and the ceremonies associated with it confirm that this is so.[5]

The dubious worth of religion

This impression of religion as a minority activity is further reinforced by the impression advertised in the media that religion fuels extreme fanaticism and conflict, on the one hand, and quaint superstition, if not endemic corruption, on the other. Thus, a Rabin or a Gandhi is killed by a fellow Jew or Hindu. There are riots between Hindus and Muslims in India over the site of the Ayodhya mosque, or between Buddhists and Hindus in Sri Lanka, between Shi'ite Muslims in Iran and Shi'ite Muslims in Iraq, and remnants of mistrust between Protestants and Roman Catholics in Ireland. In Japan the determination of the Aum cult to engage in large-scale extermination of the general public is as grim as that of the Hayley Bop enthusiasts to take their own lives and so hasten transition to another planet. And still the millennium is yet to arrive. Religion on this evidence is a destructive force and we are to be thankful that the majority are not touched by it.

At the same time, there are reports of church statues which weep tears of blood, or of stone figures which drink milk in Hindu temples. The faith which is shown may be touching, but in the eyes of an independent observer it is gullible and naive. The fantastic history of relics in medieval Christendom or of self-serving gurus in India today expose very clearly how vulnerable individuals can be abused and exploited in the name of religion (see Duffy, 1992, chs 5 and 8; Mehta, 1980). With such track records as these, the sooner religion is dispensed with the better. It is perhaps no great surprise that Dawkins compares it to a genetic disease which warrants urgent eradication.[6]

Counter-evidence

Such data of religious decline give only a partial picture. There is a wider context and there are other perspectives.

Any established institution is vulnerable to the effects of rapid change

The context is one of extraordinary social and technical change, along with the unsettling of familiar social forms; all this impacts on religion. Worldwide urbanisation, air travel, electronic media, artificial birth control, longer life expectancy, transplant surgery and all such new phenomena together entail that human life today is a different experience from when we were born. Moreover, because the process is continuous, this is true whatever our age. Alcopops, Aids, attention deficit syndrome and computer-animated pets will give way to, or be joined by, other striking developments within the year.

In the midst of such dramatic change, it is no surprise that all established institutions, social and economic, religious and political, are experiencing some turbulence and disaffection. The family is a typical example. In the UK, the rate of family breakdown has never been higher. This is evident in the figures for divorce, the incidence of pregnancies outside of marriage and of child abuse.[7] In each case there are qualifications to be made. For instance, in spite of the high divorce rate, remarriage is very popular. Unmarried mothers may be more numerous, but a higher proportion (80 per cent) of them have their babies also registered with their father's name, suggesting a continuing relationship. And the known extent of child abuse may be more a reflection of our greater sensitivity to its likelihood than of any sudden growth. The overall effects, however, are unsettling and there is crisis talk about the family's future (see Berger and Berger, 1983; Davies, 1993).

Similarly, there is talk of alienation from the political process, exemplified by the numbers, including young people, who do not vote in elections. Accordingly, political parties and trade unions are restructuring their operations; but so too are banks, hospitals, law courts and schools. Change is evident on every institutional front. In some respects this is indicative of decay, but just as frequently it is a sign of rethinking and new growth. Arguably, therefore, it would be surprising if the same mixture of elements were not also at work in the sphere of institutional religious life.

The persistence of religion in personal experience

Many other perspectives on religion are less jaundiced. The sociologist of religion, like the opinion pollster, may well point out that religion is more organically present in the interstices of family life and personal conviction than church attendance figures by themselves would suggest (see Davie, 1994; cf. Greeley, 1992). They may go on to draw attention to the reported incidence of individual religious experience as far more widespread, even in modern western societies, than might ever easily have been guessed. This indeed has been remarked by a range of investigators, with and without any 'religious axe' to grind. In this vein Alister Hardy (1980), Edward Robinson (1977) and David Hay (1982), successively directors of the Religious Experience Research Unit, remarked on the widespread incidence of the wider population's readiness to acknowledge such experiences as their own. Marghanita Laski (1980) independently came to the same conclusion, as did Andrew Greeley (1974) in North America. Yet others, associated with the Implicit Religion Network coordinated by Edward Bailey, have drawn attention to the vitality of religion, living as it were unassumingly in the plain clothes of everyday life. Thus, they point to functional alternatives to traditional religion, not only in the labelled form of cults, but also in the less obvious ways in which a particular company, leisure enthusiasm, or even television can take over the role of providence and direction in life.[8] To the list might well be added the incidence of religious motifs in fantasy forms of Hollywood sci fi and horror movies, or of computer adventure games.

Religion as a continuing feature of national and international constitutional debate

It is significant too to observe the persistence of the religious ingredients in fundamental debates about national and international constitutions. Whenever the identity and future of a nation is 'up for review', it seems that religious considerations are commonly called into play. This has been evident in the UK throughout its history with respect to the monarchy, or, more particularly but perhaps less noticed, in England and Wales whenever, since 1870, there has been debate about a national curriculum. In Parliament, the shape of provision for education has invariably been associated with lengthy and acrimonious debate in which religion has loomed much larger than might have been anticipated by the politicians of the day. This happened in the 1987–8 debates about the Education Reform Bill, and it will happen again. Further afield, religion has featured directly in the constitutional reviews that have been taking place over the last decade in Eastern Europe, for instance in Bulgaria, Hungary, Poland or Russia.[9] Similarly, it has warranted deliberate attention in the peace talks in Bosnia and the Middle East, as well as in the Punjab and Tibet. Indeed, at least one observer

speaks dramatically of religious nationalism as a challenge world-wide to western secular assumptions (Jürgensmeyer, 1993).

At one level this might be interpreted as a lingering hangover of the unfortunate influence of institutional religion amongst people who have yet to come to terms fully with the sober realities of living in a free society. At another, it would be recognised as sensing that in any discussion of human boundaries, far-reaching questions will arise which have to do with the bases for believing and valuing within which that humanity is rooted (see Bowker, 1997, xvi–xxiv).

Cosmic wonderings

Another area of evidence which provokes scepticism regarding the myth of religion on its last legs comes from reaction to scientific and technological achievements. One effect of these is that awareness of mortality and of the cosmic dimensions of life has been magnified. In a curious way, the very technology, which in other ways is associated more with mechanical control and technical mastery, serves to highlight precariousness and contingency in our existence. Accordingly, consciousness that we are mortal or that the universe is of mind-boggling proportions still arouses in human beings sensations and wonderings that put more immediate and functional preoccupations in the broader setting of concern over what we are to make of living in the first place. After all, we might never have been, either as the individuals we are or in more collective and organic connectedness.

Dependence is not a state of being which autonomy usually celebrates, but in so far as we might ever be moved to acknowledge the giftedness of life, we may find ourselves individually admitting there is that which is beyond us, on which we do depend. This might be a parent, the sunshine, or perhaps even the internet. Whichever it may be, these in turn may point beyond themselves. And therein lies the stuff of religion (cf. 'theistic evidences' in Richmond, 1970).

Alternative sources of salvation

In one sense it is too easy to invoke religion. Whenever that is done, proper scrutiny is called for lest indeed it serves to confine and constrain the human spirit. One example of over-easy religious embrace may be seen in a general reaction to the experience of change and uncertainty or of contingency as just described. Unnerved by one or more of these experiences, there is a rush to find immediate certainty. This simple and appropriate observation is all too quickly turned into dismissive explanation, heard alike from secularist social commentators and from defenders of established religions against more authoritarian versions of their faith or to counter the rise of the cults (see Evans, 1973, Introduction; Marty and Scott Appleby, 1991–5, passim.).

The distinction needs to be made between shrewd comment and reductive explaining away. Another example of how the one can elide into the other is apparent in the magnetic attraction which the national lottery so evidently has for a substantial majority of the British population. It is certainly true that human beings enjoy gratification. It is also true that the mood of the moment is to prefer this gratification to be granted in the present rather than delayed. What is more contentious is whether, when presented with the opportunity to engage more subtly with questions of longer-term meaning in their own lives, people will be driven by whatever instant scratch card solutions they can find in charisms, cults or casinos. 'Playing the final meaning game' may be an aspect of what is involved in both institutional religious behaviour and seeking salvation by lottery, but it begs the question to explain away either as only to do with materialistic intent or alternatively with yearning for spiritual release.

Arguably, it is in the interests of any society in its provisions for public education to want to challenge unthinking credulity as demeaning the human propensity for freedom and truth. By a similar line of argument, religious traditions of any standing in the world arena will be no less enthusiastic in encouraging their inheritors to use their hearts and minds fully in making the faith their own. There is a coincidence of potential opposites here: if closed-mindedness is the enemy of participational democracy, then it is no less the enemy of truth in religion.

The public credibility of religions

The established religions owe it to the world, to their present followers and to patrons from of old,

to represent themselves in ways that compel good sense. This is true of every faith. It is the reverse of any flight from reason, as represented by some cults and closed-minded forms of fundamentalism, but it is more easily pointed out than acted on. In each religious tradition there are those who are more preoccupied with maintaining the purity of the inheritance than with translating it into contemporary expression. This is their prerogative, as it often was for the followers of what we now remark as the dead religions which litter the past of human civilisation (see Bowker, 1978, ch. 1). It might be argued that the future of contemporary living religions may actually be better preserved by the path of separate conservation than by that of engagement. However, if that were the typical response then their opportunity to enrich present and future generations would be considerably reduced and the dominant myth, with which we began, might after all come more closely to match reality.

It is perfectly possible to present each of the traditions, identified since 1988 as the principal religions of England and Wales,[10] in ways that demonstrate their internal coherence and consistency. In terms of their own theological (or Buddhalogical) circle, they have their own credentials which deserve to be understood. What is trickier, yet no less crucial, is the degree of mutual questioning which is seen as a proper part of the process. In so far as each tradition makes claims to truth that go beyond the confines of its immediate followers, that is of double interest. First, the followers themselves will wish to demonstrate that their claim will stand close scrutiny; and, second, those outside the faith might, for their own sake, reasonably wish to check that this is so (see Christian, 1987).

The common human discourse for such exchanges is reason. Again, some parts of some traditions will find it more or less acceptable to trade in these terms. Depending on how Revelation or Illumination is understood and appropriated within the tradition, open, rational enquiry may be welcomed or avoided. For instance, if Biblical or Qur'ánic Revelation were perceived as only to be heard and never argued with for fear of offending God, that would reduce the degree of engagement with either or both religious traditions which could be effected within the sphere of publicly funded education. In fact, this is not the only view which is found in either community (see Barr, 1993; Hourani, 1985).

In highlighting the importance of reason, there is always the risk of becoming so rationalistic as to ignore the depth of human logic that is conveyed in forms other than verbal formulae. Fortunately, those studying religion from the outside are increasingly as sensitive to this point as those practising the religion from within. In good faith, and in the interests of mutual understanding, religions need to demonstrate a readiness to be subject to exploration and experiment that test the claims to truth which they advance. From their own heartlands they may then find they stand on common ground in asserting the wider, even universal, import of humanity (Green, 1988).

Partnership in groundwork on beliefs and values

Religious education, as developed within the public educational provision of England and Wales introduced in 1870, can itself help with this process. Its potential to do so is there, in principle, throughout the tradition of agreed syllabuses, and also in the dual system. The syllabuses are envisaged as controlling the content of RE teaching in such a way as to avoid religious strife and to be acceptable within a legal framework which expressly rules out denominationally specific teaching.[11] The dual system was a constitutional commitment to a national educational system provided by a partnership of church and state[12]. Both of these aspects of the provision are in process of being extended, but they are faced with two foes.

Agreeing the syllabus

LEA agreed syllabuses emerged in the 1920s and 1930s as a means of managing the religious diversity which was already apparent. They applied in both county maintained schools and those church schools which were designated 'controlled' rather than 'voluntary aided'. They avoided denominationally specific catechisms and formularies, as legally proscribed, for divergent priorities and emphases were evident between the different Christian denominations as well as with the still largely self-contained Jewish community and with the growing secularist movement. Instead, the biblical common denominator found in all these syllabuses until the late 1960s was set out as common ground

and may have contributed to a prevailing sense of national cohesion and identity.[13]

Since 1975 the extension on the syllabus front has gone beyond agreement primarily between the different Christian churches with a sideways look to the Jewish community. It has extended to other religious communities that are part of modern Britain, and this inclusiveness was reinforced by the wording of the 1988 Education Reform Act which makes it illegal for any syllabus not to give due regard to any of the principal religious traditions which now form part of the national community (see Hull, 1989; Marratt, 1989). In place of the biblical core that was normative for the older agreed syllabuses, there are new agreed cores for each of Buddhism, Christianity, Hinduism, Islam, Judaism and Sikhism. These are intended as norms for each of the traditions, which local syllabus conferences can work to (SCAA, 1994).

Considering the decades and even centuries that can pass before agreement may be reached in efforts to define the beliefs and values of a particular religious tradition, it is remarkable that these cores, and the national model RE syllabuses based on them, were produced within a two-year period. They are the fruit of collaboration between representatives of the different faith communities and professional educators, who met sectionally, according to faith, as well as all together. It is not clear that the cores have yet been fully scrutinised by authoritative councils in the respective faith communities or indeed by the specialist academic networks (Everington, 1996). There are issues of 'ownership' in which the self-definition of any one faith community may be challenged by an independent scholarship which might find more fluidity in the tradition and individual sense of religious identity than 'official' versions would immediately acknowledge (see Jackson, 1997). Nevertheless, until there is further revision, the realm of public education is promoting the understanding of individual religions as determined at least in part from within the self-definition of each of them.

Extending the partnership of churches and state

Enlargement of the dual system of partnership between the churches and the state, in together providing for the nation's educational needs has moved more slowly. In part, that may reflect some confusion within the thinking of the two churches (Anglican and Roman Catholic) most involved in partnership provision with the state. Are the church schools for the whole community or for boys and girls from the one denominational background? In general, the Roman Catholic emphasis has been more on education for families from that denominational background, whereas the Churches of England and Wales have usually served the wider neighbourhood (Church of England Commission, 1970, ch. 7). Admissions policies vary, however, from school to school, with some Catholic ones having more open access and some Anglican ones, most especially secondary, becoming more selective (O'Keeffe, 1986, chs 2 and 3; Catholic Commission, 1984; Chadwick, 1994, ch. 2). That said, both churches accept that their receipt of public funding depends upon their willingness to deliver the agreed National Curriculum in all the other subjects, even if they choose to do their RE differently.[14]

The number of other Christian denominational schools is small,[15] as is that of any other religious community. Amongst those schools which are Jewish, there are the same variations in admissions policies, but at least they do exist.[16] By contrast, the development of state-funded Buddhist, Hindu, Muslim and Sikh voluntary aided schools has been scandalously slow.[17]

The implication must be that schools with non-Christian religious affiliation are perceived as politically suspect and likely to encourage divisiveness. This is all too reminiscent of the religious intolerance of 1902, when people campaigned against 'Rome on the rates'. The lack of financial support from the public purse to help the different faith communities to develop at least a few schools of their own is in sharp contrast to what happened in the early decades of public education. Then, large numbers of church schools were judged to be making only poor-quality provision, which could only be improved by the injection of public funds; accordingly, these were provided (Evans, 1985, pp. 69, 76, 94). In the interests of community relations and good education, it remains a disappointment to many that the historical generosity of this dual partnership has yet to be extended to a more plural one, encompassing other faith communities. Their members pay the same taxes as Christians or any other citizens of the UK.

Further opposition to open collaboration

The foes of such extension continue to mount a rearguard action. On the one hand, latter-day Christian imperialism still seeks to reassert a more exclusively closed establishment position. This has been evident in the wholesale resistance to public endowment of any Muslim schools, but also in the triumph of the lobby which engineered the notorious Circular 1/94 (DfE, 1994, for fuller discussion, see Gates, 1995; Robson, 1997). At a stroke this Circular interpreted the law as requiring schools, as never before, to conduct confessional Christian worship. Such interpretations which had already appeared in the draft version of the Circular had been expressly castigated by representatives of the churches, other faith communities and educationists, but their advice was overruled.

Narrowness such as this serves only to reinforce the impression that religion is self-seeking and out to achieve its own sectional superiority. Where it appears in the name of Christianity, it displays a curious lack of theological imagination in respect of the biblical God of creation, who is more comprehensive in cover and care than any localised boundary, whether national, racial or indeed religious.

On the other hand, persistent secularism also acts in opposition to any collaboration involving religion. Thus, there is a tendency within the educational system wilfully to play down the religious ingredients in school assembly, as also in moral, personal and social education.[18] To some extent this is made into a more justifiable position as a consequence of the infelicitously presumptuous wording of Circular 1/94. That apart, there are creative opportunities waiting to be opened up that would find focus in school 'collective worship'.

Of course, if such school assemblies have the connotation of corporate worship in church, mosque or other faith community, then it is the more intelligible that they should succumb not only to secularist critique, but also to an educational one. By contrast the tradition maintained in primary school assemblies, as also in a minority of secondary schools, is one that explores and affirms practical expressions of basic beliefs and values. With appropriate investment of resources and professional energies there is scope for these integral gatherings to be redeveloped. They would serve very well as centre points for highlighting the moral, social, spiritual and cultural dimensions of the school curriculum and community. And, without presumptions as to any particular religious belief on the part of those present, they would include overt reference to the resources of religions.[19]

Threats to confidence in the future

Whether such optimism is realistic, however, is another matter. Looking to the future, outside of school it is difficult to avoid a sense of foreboding. Television and related revolutions in electronic communications magnify the extent of social and moral disorder. It is abundantly visible on every front: in family violence and breakdown; disparities of poverty and wealth that appear obscene; impending environmental disasters; and persistent prejudice and strife that defies reconciliation. Teachers and children bring these concerns with them into school every day, from the wider society if not also from their own homes. Within school itself there may be struggles arising of a different kind, for example, from new curricular expectations, record-keeping arrangements, and inspection preparations. Putting all this together the prospect is daunting.

In response, the actual need for resilience in personal and professional terms is great. The sources for that resilience lie largely within the individuals concerned. Their inner springs have to do with senses of purpose and meaning, sensitivity to human delight and sorrow, and visions of what might be, combined with a determination to bring it to fruition. In principle, every one of these aspects can be fed creatively from the combined institutional strengths of religion and education. In practice, either or both of these can also be drudging and draining. Accordingly, if either is intellectually enfeebled or they fail to collaborate effectively, the worst foreboding will materialise.

Shared values and a global ethic

To anyone who is at all sensitive to the ambiguities of religion in human experience, the suggestion that religion might actually have some direct relevance to addressing the position we find ourselves in might seem almost risible. How and why should we look with any positive expectation to resources associated with religion, when it is religion itself which is claimed often to be at the root of the problems themselves?

The answer to this challenge lies in the nature of humanity. Intrinsic to being human is a preoccupation with meaning. It has arisen continually from a universal experience of life bounded by death. It has worked itself out from earliest times in the fabrication of cave paintings, carved figurines and stone circles, or in the more developed cultural forms, both religious and scientific, in subsequent civilisations. These forms have served to bond and unite, but also to estrange and divide.

Men and women have created and articulated a communal sense of order, as in the varnas and the doing of dharmic duty, the sangha and eightfold path, the priesthood of all believers and the pilgrim's way, or the lifelong haj. At the same time, they have sometimes experienced that very order finding them, as it were, 'from beyond' themselves. They have talked of the voice of the ancestors, the word of the Lord, or light from another dimension. Best estimates suggest that such language characterises the experience of over 80 per cent of the present population of the world.[20] Even if it were strange to any particular educationist or politician, it would be an act of extraordinary arrogance to dismiss it all as worthless.

Yet it does remain true that the different beliefs and values, enshrined in separate religious traditions, can trip each other up. Closer scrutiny reveals that this may more often be true when the religious reference becomes identified with spatial, ethnic or other localised boundaries. In any case, they can only effectively be challenged, accepted or transformed if they are first understood. And that is why what schools do with religious education is so important globally.

Over the years there have been initiatives that seek to identify values that are shared across religions and cultures, and with which education itself can resonate. Some naivety may be involved in these pursuits, for the historical and anthropological evidence of cultural diversity is hard to deny. For instance, how shall we reconcile animal, let alone human, sacrifice with the Jain ahimsa which hesitates even to quench a living flame? Is the prevalence of patriarchy entirely a coincidence in Semitic religious traditions? What possible compatibility might there be between an All Powerful Cosmic Force and a crucified Palestinian? Beliefs as well as values are all too relative.

However, religious and cultural relativism is not the whole story. There is a philosophical tradition of very long standing that is not confined to

Graeco-Roman roots, but which finds echoes in ancient China, India and Israel.[21] It is known as natural law, and its contemporary exposition by social scientists looks for transcultural continuities and a common rationality. One of its examples of pan-human valuing is the taboo against incest; those instances involving the acceptance of incest do indeed appear to be quite exceptional. Another is the acknowledgement of truth-telling as a precondition of life in community (Bok, 1978): without trust, people perish. Yet another might be sympathy for suffering as a taboo against torture (see Little, 1993).

It was the claim that there is a universal pattern of individual moral development, to be observed throughout the world in any and every culture, which gave Kohlberg his pre-eminent significance over twenty years. Empirical evidence does not entirely bear this out, at least not in Kohlberg's fully elaborated stage sequences; nevertheless, his concern to identify a universality of moral sense is one that continues to exercise all those who speak of moral education.[22]

A different initiative seeking similar effect was promulgated by the Centenary Parliament of the World's Religions in Chicago in 1993 in the form of a 'Declaration Toward a Global Ethic'. This is designed expressly to address what is diagnosed as a fundamental crisis of economics, politics and ecology, and, for its further development, acceptance and application, Hans Küng and others continue to work. They bring together the perspectives of religious diversity in a common focus on the global challenges to human survival (Küng and Kuschel, 1993; cf. Küng, 1991, and Braybrooke, 1992).[23]

The educational relevance of such initiatives warrants more direct attention from public educational agencies than they have so far been given. In the UK they deserve to be added to the formulations which have come from the Schools Curriculum Assessment Authority's Forum on Moral Values;[24] indeed, they were more than hinted at in the Inter Faith Network for the UK's Consultation on Shared Values (see Pearce, 1997). What is critical in all the discussion is that the reference to religious sources and resources is freely admitted.

The Commonwealth of human diversity

In British constitutional terms this process could be given a significant boost by celebrating the multi-

faith character of the Commonwealth. It is from our historical past in empire that the present ethnic and religious diversity of Britain largely derives.[25] Instead of playing down that diversity, near and far, its affirmation by politicians and church leaders, as also by representatives from other faiths, could be very positive and powerful.

The point is still valid even if links with the European Community and with the United States are coming to be of greater significance. For in the USA the constitutionally induced reluctance faced by religions over their admittance to the realm of public schooling has concealed much of the now extensive religious diversity of the nation from everyday understanding on the part of the population at large (Carter, 1993). More immediately from within Europe there is much learning yet to be pursued about religious diversity, such as in France and Germany with Algerian and Turkish Muslims respectively, or in Russia and other former Soviet territories where for instance Buddhism, Islam and Shamanism have a powerful presence. Europe, America and indeed the wider world may have insights to gain from a common wealth tradition.

In the UK, as mooted by Prince Charles, the role of the monarch as the Defender of Faiths, and not only of Christianity, need not be the 'oddball' idea it is sometimes presented as being (see Dimbleby, 1994, pp. 528–34). It could be a highly creative symbol for a confederated framework guaranteeing the integrity of each religion and recognising the import of faith, whether natural or supernatural, in the personal identity of individual human beings. Thus, it would indicate that the diverse faith communities now thriving in this country are actually valued in their own right as part of the national establishment. It would also demonstrate a deliberate valuing of the importance in the lives of individual citizens of their personal beliefs.

The inclusivity of the notion of 'faith' and of 'personal belief' is a critical aspect of this principle.[26] It would be as simplistic in the name of science to urge that all elements of faith should be expunged from the daily lived experience of individuals throughout the world as it is in the name of religion to proclaim that rational exploration and experiment bespeak an inferior logic. Quite deliberately, secular humanism has contributed to the Chicago statement on global ethics, also to the British consultations about shared values. In its own terms it sees itself as a living faith. It looks for an education for all which includes critical appreciation of secular perspectives, as well as enrichment by reference to the more explicitly religious faith of others.[27]

Wider recognition of this common grounding of humanity in faiths which are diverse and open to mutual scrutiny might actually make a direct contribution to health and peace. Accordingly, it is highly appropriate for the slogan 'Defender of Faith(s)' to be attached to a nation's chief constitutional office, whether royal or republican. It brings together the commitment to individual freedom and to companionability.

The articulation of such Commonwealth reference points could bring to negotiations on the future of the European Community a charity and vision that might enable Europe, both eastern and western, to come to terms with the anti-Semitism that has been at its heart and which is still latent, and at the same time to become less aggressively suspicious and defensive about Islam (see Runnymede Trust, 1997). Of course, to be true to the founding vision of their faith, Muslims will live in tension with non-Muslims; theologically speaking, Dar al Islam is always at war with Dar al Harb. (summarised in Schacht and Bosworth, 1979, pp. 174–7; cf. Lewis, 1994, pp. 50–3). But, by definition, tension is generated wherever there is difference, and deeply held convictions inevitably call into question those from different starting points. In both political and educational terms, however, the Commonwealth tradition of the UK holds open a moral status for Islam, as for any other faith which accepts humanity as shared and commonly gifted from beyond any one individual or group. It is in the interests of both the European and world-wide communities that tabloid distortions and invective against Islam based on highly particular episodes, should not be permitted to provide the normative framework of perception with which that living tradition is condemned.

Religion and the school's agenda

Any prediction about the imminent ending of religion in the UK and beyond is both naive and pointless, the more so when the present season of the millennium will far more probably generate an excess of its own characteristic genre of religious speculation and reflection. Of far greater significance is the end of religion, in the purposive sense, involving teleological direction. Intrinsic to religious tradition is a directional drive that affects both the individual respondent and the wider community of faith. The drive may be more internally than externally transformative. It may lead to passivity or action, solitariness or sociability. But in this sense, the end of religion is not a tale of termination but of ambition. It strives that life in all its heights and profundity might become more abundantly appreciated by all. This is a far more interesting and challenging goal. To be sure, in its pursuit institutional religions may have some dying to do, but only if this their proper end is achieved.

This end is one to which each boy and girl deserves to be introduced as they are exposed to the fundamental importance of beliefs and values in every school. Only an unthinking scepticism can doubt that questions of overall meaning and purpose for individuals, for local and national community, and for the world at large, deserve to be directly addressed by schools. As an end in itself, critically appreciative attention to religion should be a precondition for any education, religious or secular, which claims public sponsorship in a democratic society.

Notes

1   Thus the Jewish Continuity/Joint Israel Appeal, Chief Executive Jonathan Kastenbuam. Cf. Sacks (1994).

2   Absent since 1851, when fears were expressed that it would not be in the national interest to publish the strength of Christian pluralism alongside the established church.

3   See discussions in religious press.

4   What proportion of the UK Chinese community would describe itself as Buddhist? It is they who might significantly swell the numbers of those meeting regularly in Buddhist centres, viharas and monasteries. Cf. Weller (1997).

5   Not only has the number of weddings decreased by two-fifths in the last 25 years, but of those only 49 per cent are held in church (Church, 1996, ch. 2, tables 14–16).

6   'In the history of the spread of faith you will find little else but epidemiology, and causal epidemiology at that . . . Happily, viruses don't win every time. Many children emerge unscathed from the worst that nuns and mullahs can throw at them.' (Dawkins, 1993).

7   Cf. Church (1996, table 2.11) on divorce, which has doubled since 1971; table 2.1 on births outside marriage, now four times as many as in 1971 and accounting for a third of all live births. Reliable data on child abuse are more difficult to come by. There were 90,000

emergency calls to Childline in 1995–6, which is four times as many as in 1986–7.

8 Cf. Centre for the Study of Implicit Religion and Contemporary Society, recently established at Middlesex University, see Bailey, (1986 and 1997).

9 Cf. *Religion State and Society*, quarterly journal of Keston Institute, 4 Park Town, Oxford.

10 Although not named in the text of the 1988 Education Reform Act, Buddhism, Hinduism, Islam, Judaism and Sikhism were identified as the principal religions of Great Britain, alongside Christianity. This was so in publications from the National Curriculum Council and including new agreed syllabuses from local education authorities.

11 Hence the famous Cowper–Temple amendment in the 1870 Forster Education Act which specified that in schools 'hereafter established by means of local rates, no catechism or religious formulary which is distinctive to any particular denomination shall be taught'.

12 For historical background, see Cruickshank (1963) and a more recent treatment: Waddington (1984).

13 On the evolution of syllabuses, see Hull (1975). The claim of contribution to ecumenical cohesion was made more than 30 years ago by the then Bishop of London (1966, pp. 11–29).

14 Hence the arrangements for public inspection. Whereas the school as a whole, and the curriculum delivered within it, is scrutinised by OFSTED on the same basis as in any other, special arrangments are made for the inspection of religious education. The legislation specifying this is contained in section 13 of the 1992 Education Act. Cf. Keiner (1996).

15 There are 96 primary schools (24 voluntary aided, the rest controlled), and four secondary (only one of which is voluntary aided) related to the Free Churches, as compared with nearly 6500 CE and RC primaries and 600+ secondaries.

16 There are seventeen primary and five secondary Jewish voluntary aided schools.

17 The racial dimension of the slowness of this change was apparent in the recommendation against 'separate schools' in the Swann Report (Church of England Commission, 1970) and is discussed again in Comper (1994, ch. 12).

18 The evidence from OFSTED reports on school inspections is highly revealing in these respects; cf. National Association of Head Teachers, (1994). For a more general review of the debates surrounding collective worship, see Religious Education Council of England and Wales (1996).

19 On the joint initiative of the Inter Faith Network UK, the National Association of SACREs, and the RE Council of England and Wales a year-long consultation is taking place with a view to establishing what consensus there might be that would achieve such changes as would effect greater sensitivity to educational priorities and the range of religious and secular sensibilities.

See *Collective Worship Reviewed*, Culham College Institute, 1998.

20 See *Worldwide Adherents of All Religions by Six Continental Areas Mid-1995* available on: http://www.zpub.com/un/pope/relig.html. This information is developed from a combination of recent UN population figures, the data in the 1982 *World Christian Encyclopedia*, edited by David Barrett, and other sources.

21 Not in any fixed and static sense, but dynamic and evolutionary, rooted in a purposive sense of humanity seeking fulfilment.

22 A recurrent theme within the *Journal of Moral Education*'s Moral for the Millennium conference held in Lancaster in July 1996 and of the pages of that journal.

23 As an indication of the proponents' interest in engaging a consensus of world with the specific text of the Global Ethic, specially created web pages invite browsers to indicate their preferences for alternative wordings on the more contentious statements in the original; see http://www.silcom.com/~origin/poll.html.

24 Cf. SCAA's Revised Consultation Document arising from the National Forum for Values in Education and the Community, January 1997.

25 Principally from India, Pakistan and Bangladesh (in part, via the Commonwealth East Africa of Kenya and Uganda), from the Caribbean and Cyprus. This is not to imply, however, that the Jewish, Chinese and Vietnamese communities are accordingly of any less importance. The Commonwealth connection for the Jewish community dates back to 1656 when, in the days of the Protectorate, they were readmitted to the UK.

26 This point is systematically expounded in the work of James Fowler, amongst others. Faith is understood generically as a human universal, including but not limited to or identified with religion (Fowler, 1981); cf. Smith (1979).

27 From within the British Humanist Association, this is the position which has been consistently maintained by its representatives on the Religious Education Council of England and Wales since its foundation in 1973, and also on such local SACREs as have chosen to include Humanists as members. Its advocates from the BHA Education Committee include David Bothwell, Harry Stopes-Roe, and John White.

References

Bailey, E. (1986) *A Workbook of Popular Religion*. Dorchester, Dorset: Partners Publications.

Bailey, E. (1997) *Implicit Religion in Contemporary Society*. Kampen, Netherlands:

Barr, J. (1993) *Biblical Faith and Natural Theology: Gifford Lectures for 1991*. Oxford: Clarendon Press.

Berger, B. and Berger, P. (1983) *The War over the Family*. London: Hutchinson.

Bok, S. (1978) *Lying: Moral Choice in Public and Private Life*. Hassocks, Sussex: Harvester Press.

Bowker, J. (1978) *The Religious Imagination*. London: Oxford University Press.

Bowker, J. (1997) *Oxford Dictionary of World Religions*. London: Oxford University Press.

Braybrooke, M. (ed.) (1992) *Stepping Stones to a Global Ethic*. London: SCM Press.

Brierley, P. (1997) *UK Christian Handbook, 1998–9*, vol. 2: *Religious Trends*. London: Christian Research.

Carter, S.L. (1993) *The Culture of Disbelief: How American Law and Politics Trivialise Religious Devotion*. New York: HarperCollins.

Catholic Commission for Racial Justice (1984) *Learning from Diversity*. London: Catholic Media Office.

Chadwick, P. (1994) *Schools of Reconciliation: Issues in Joint Roman Catholic–Anglican Education*. London: Cassell.

Christian, W.A. (1987) *Doctrines of Religious Communities: A Philosophical Guide*. New Haven, CN: Yale University Press.

Church, J. (ed.) (1996) *Social Trends 27*. London: Her Majesty's Stationery Office.

Church of England Commission on Religious Education in Schools (1970) *The Fourth R: The Report of the Commission . . .* (The Durham Report). London: National Society/SPCK.

Church of England Yearbook 1997 (1997) London: Church House Publishing.

Comper, P. (1994) Racism, parental choice and the law. In J.M. Halstead (ed.), *Parental Choice and Education Principles*. London: Kogan Page, ch. 12.

Cruickshank, M. (1963) *Church and State in English Education*. London: Macmillan.

Davie, G. (1994) *Religion in Britain since 1945: Believing without Belonging*. Oxford: Basil Blackwell.

Davies, J. (ed.) (1993) *The Family: Is It Just Another Lifestyle Choice?* London: Institute of Economic Affairs Health and Welfare Unit.

Dawkins, R. (1993) Viruses of the mind. In Bo Dahlbom (ed.), *Dennett and his Critics: Demystifying Mind*. Oxford: Basil Blackwell. Available http://www.physics.wisc.edu/~shalizi/Dawkins/virusesofthemind.html.

Dawkins, R. (1997) *Climbing Mount Improbable*. Harmondsworth, Middx: Penguin.

Department for Education (DfE) (1994) *Religious Education and Collective Worship*, Circular 1/94. London: DfE.

Dimbleby, J. (1994) *The Prince of Wales: A Biography*. London: Little Brown.

Duffy, E. (1992) *The Stripping of the Altars: Traditional Religion in England, 1400–1580*. New Haven, CN: Yale University Press.

Evans, C. (1973) *Cults of Unreason*. London: Harrap.

Evans, K. (1985) *The Development and Structure of the English Education System*. London: Hodder & Stoughton.

Everington, J. (1996) A question of authenticity: the relationship between educators and practitioners in the representation of religious traditions. *British Journal of Religious Education* 18 (2), 69–77.

Fowler, J. (1981) *Stages of Faith: The Psychology of Human Development and the Quest for Meaning*. San Francisco: Harper & Row.

Gates, B.E. (1995) Secular education and the logic of religion: shall we re-invent the wheel? In P. Masefield (ed.), *Aspects of Religion: Essays in Honour of Ninian Smart*, Toronto Studies in Religion, vol. 18. New York: Peter Lang.

Greeley, A. (1974) *Ecstasy: A Way of Knowing*. Englewood Cliffs, NJ: Prentice-Hall.

Greeley, A. (1992) Religion in Britain, Ireland and the USA. In R. Jowell *et al.* (eds), *British Social Attitudes: Social Attitudes, 11*. Aldershot, Hants: Dartmouth, pp. 51–70.

Green, R.M. (1988) *Religion and Moral Reason: A New Method for Comparative Study*. Oxford: Oxford University Press.

Hardy, A. (1980) *The Spiritual Nature of Man: A Study of Contemporary Religious Experience*. Oxford: Clarendon Press.

Hay, D. (1982) *Exploring Inner Space*. Harmondsworth, Middx: Penguin.

Hourani, G.F. (1985) *Reason in Islam Ethics*. Cambridge: Cambridge University Press.

Hull, J.M. (1975) Agreed syllabuses, past, present and future. In N. Smart and D. Horder, *New Movements in Religious Education*. London: Temple-Smith.

Hull, J.M. (1989) *The Act Unpacked*. London: Christian Education Movement.

Jackson, R. (1997) *Religious Education: An Interpretative Approach*. London: Hodder & Stoughton.

Jürgensmeyer, M. (1993) *The New Cold War? Religious Nationalism Confronts the Secular State*. Berkeley, CA: University of California Press.

Keiner, J. (1996) Opening up Jewish education to inspection: the impact of the OFSTED inspection system in England. *Education Policy Analysis Archives* 4 (5).

Küng, H. (1991) *Global Responsibility: In Search of a New World Ethic*. London: SCM Press.

Küng, H. and Kuschel, K.-J. (eds) *A Global Ethic: The Declaration of the Parliament of the World's Religions*. London: SCM Press.

Laski, M. (1980) *Everyday Ecstasy*. London: Thames & Hudson.

Lewis, P. (1994) *Islamic Britain: Religion, Politics and Identity among British Muslims*. London: I.B. Tauris.

Little, D. (1993) The nature and basis of human rights. In G. Outka and J.P. Reeder Jr (eds), *Prospects for a Common Morality*. Princeton, NJ: Princeton University Press.

Marratt, H. (ed.) (1989) *Handbook for Agreed Syllabus Conferences, SACREs and Schools*. Lancaster: Religious Education Council of England and Wales.

Marty, M.E. and Scott Appleby, R. (eds) (1991–5) *Fundamentalism Project*, vols 1–5. Chicago: Chicago University Press.

Mehta, G. (1980) *Karma Cola: Marketing the Mystic East.* London: Jonathan Cape.

National Association of Head Teachers (1994) *Survey on RE and Collective Worship: A Policy Statement.* London: NAHT.

O'Keeffe, B. (1986) *Faith and Culture and the Dual System: A Comparative Study of Church and County Schools.* Brighton: Falmer Press.

Pearce, B. (ed.) (1997) *The Quest for Common Values: Report of a Seminar.* London: Inter Faith Network UK.

Religious Education Council of England and Wales (1996) *Collective Worship in Schools.* Abingdon, Oxon: Culham College Institute.

Richmond, J. (1970) *Theology and Metaphysics.* London: SCM Press.

Robinson, E. (1977) *The Original Vision.* Oxford: Religious Experience Research Unit.

Robson, G. (1997) Religious education, government policy and professional practice, 1988–95. *British Journal of Religious Education* **19** (1) 13–23.

Runnymede Trust (1997) *Islamophobia.* London: Runnymede Trust.

Sacks, J. (1994) *Will We Have Jewish Grandchildren? Jewish Continuity and How to Achieve It.* London: Valentine Mitchell.

Schacht, J. and Bosworth, C.E. (1979) *The Legacy of Islam*, 2nd edn. London: Oxford University Press.

School Curriculum and Assessment Authority (SCAA) (1994) *Model Syllabuses for Religious Education*, 2 vols: *Model 1: Living Faiths Today*; *Model 2: Questions and Teaching.* London: SCAA.

Siegel, P.N. (1986) *The Meek and the Militant: Religion and Power Across the World.* London: Zed Books.

Smith, W.C. (1979) *Faith and Belief.* Princeton, NJ: Princeton University Press.

Waddington, R. (1984) *Future in Partnership.* London: National Society.

Weller, P. (ed.) (1997) *Religions in the UK: A Multifaith Directory*, 2nd edn. Derby: University of Derby and Inter Faith Network.

18 Mission Impossible? Religious Education in the 1990s

JUDITH EVERINGTON

Religious education (RE) is in need of a new direction and a new identity. This is a view expressed in different quarters of the profession and in an increasing number of its publications. Why this need has arisen and the direction in which the subject might develop are matters considered in this chapter. For some, the new direction should be towards a greater emphasis upon the moral and spiritual development of pupils (see, for example, Robson, 1996). For others, the future of the subject lies in the development of its academic 'respectablity' (for example, Wintersgill, 1995) or in its role in promoting intercultural harmony (for example, Bigger, 1995). These different views indicate that at the heart of the debate about identity and direction lies the question: What is of greatest value to teachers and students of religious education?

Although this chapter examines a situation which is peculiar to religious education, there is a sense in which the dilemmas it describes are shared by all those who are concerned with the education of children in a culturally plural society. For there is a tension

> between the recognition that individual children are both valuable and to be valued, whose spiritual and moral development are to be promoted by the school and a 'nationalised curriculum' where market forces and school league tables are seen to prevail. There is a tension also between the call for greater emphasis on spiritual and moral development and the call for more didactic styles of teaching and a content-led curriculum. (Miller, 1996, p. 4).

The problem

'We stand at a cross-roads, uncertain as to which path to go down' (Wright, 1993, p. 2). 'There is a need for much debate to find a new consensus for the future shape of religious education' (Miller, 1996, p. 6). 'Between now and the year 2000 there will be substantial changes . . . in the RE field. . . . [there is a need to] establish a long term development plan' (Rudge, 1996, p. 8).

What lies behind these calls for greater clarity or for redefinition? Two recent developments have stimulated and lent urgency to the debate. In the late 1990s an unprecedented amount of attention has been paid, by educators and politicians, to the spiritual, moral, social and cultural development of pupils (Blaylock, 1996). The recent formation of SCAA's National Forum for Values in Education and the Community is indicative of the growing concern. If, as seems likely, this body is soon to recommend that schools give more emphasis to moral and spiritual development, and if every area of the curriculum is to be called upon to account for its contribution, then religious educators are understandably concerned to clarify their own, distinctive role. In recent years too, the profession has been called upon to give serious consideration to the idea that RE might relinquish its independent status and enter the National Curriculum (Hull, 1996; Habgood, 1995). The proposed revision of the curriculum in 2001 would provide an opportunity for religious education to be incorporated, but this would require the disempowerment of local Standing Advisory Councils for Religious Education (SACREs) – which at present produce the agreed syllabus for religious education to be followed in the local education authority (LEA) – and the establishment of a national body. This body would need to arrive at a consensus about the purpose, identity and direction of the subject.

While these developments have added a sense of

urgency to the debate surrounding the nature and purpose of RE, it will be argued that there are more fundamental reasons for religious educators' concern about the identity and direction of the subject. Since the 1960s, religious education has been in a state of 'transformation'. There has been a series of 'new directions', 'new movements' and 'new perspectives' and, as each new development has been superseded by another, so religious education has gained another 'aim'. The result has been an accumulation of aims each representing a different view of the nature and purpose of the subject. Although it is common to view these various aims as complementary, each makes its own demands in terms of curriculum structure, content and teaching strategies. For teachers attempting to give equal time and attention to each aim there is not only confusion about the direction of the subject, but also a sense of despair at the enormity of the task:

> Teachers and other educators have the unenviable task of tying together these many, sometimes opposing strands and weaving them into a pattern which is acceptable to the children, the school, the community and to society as a whole. The philosophical complexities and practical difficulties of this undertaking are vast and this is depressing. (Miller, 1996, p. 6)

The first government-sponsored and controlled attempt to produce 'model' syllabuses for religious education and the debate that these have stimulated will serve to illustrate the nature of the problem. Section 8(3) of the Education Reform Act 1988 requires all agreed syllabuses for religious education to 'reflect the fact that religious traditions in Great Britain are in the main Christian whilst taking account of the other principal religions represented in Great Britain'. In its letter of 18 March 1991 to Chief Education Officers, the Department of Education and Science (DES) advised that an agreed syllabus should be sufficiently detailed to give clear guidance to teachers as to what is to be taught about Christianity and the other principal religions. In order to assist Agreed Syllabus Conferences in the task of producing syllabuses which conform to these requirements, the Schools Curriculum and Assessment Authority (SCAA) undertook to develop a 'model syllabus' and in 1994 the Authority published two syllabuses. Two claims were made for these: first, that they reflect 'a broad consensus about the subject's educational rationale and purpose' (SCAA, 1994, p. 4); second, that agreement

had been reached upon the content to be taught at key stages 1–4 (3). The 'broad consensus' about the subject's purpose, expressed as a series of aims, had been arrived at by analysing the aims and attainment targets of existing agreed syllabuses. The content of the syllabuses had been agreed by representatives of the six 'principal religions' represented in Britain. At an elaborate and highly publicised launch in 1994, the syllabuses were hailed as a 'major achievement' (Dearing), 'a moment of history' to be grasped (Patten), 'a major positive step forward' (Khan-Cheema) and 'a milestone in Religious Education', (Maddox).

Since 1994, many Agreed Syllabus conferences have made use of the Model Syllabuses in revising or replacing their own documents. However, in the years since their publication the syllabuses have been subjected to a barrage of criticisms (Baumfield *et al.*, 1995; Brown, 1995; Everington, 1996; Edwards and Newell, 1994; Hull, 1995; Wright, 1997) and, more significantly, they have been ignored in discussions about the future direction of the subject. Thus, at an 'RE Futures' seminar on RE and values, where there were calls for a new consensus on the future shape of RE and for a reassessment of its role and identity, no mention was made of the Model Syllabuses (Miller, 1996). In the same year, John Hull suggested that SCAA should be asked to set up another working party to draw up a national curriculum for RE and Linda Rudge called upon the profession to develop a development plan which would take into account the views of many different bodies, but not those of SCAA. So why have the SCAA syllabuses, which, it is claimed, reflect a broad consensus about the purpose of RE, failed to provide an acceptable direction, role or identity for the subject? One answer to this question is offered below

The list of aims featured in the introduction to each of the SCAA syllabuses includes:

- acquiring and developing knowledge and understanding of Christianity and the other principal religions represented in Great Britain;
- developing the ability to make reasoned and informed judgements about religious and moral issues;
- enhancing pupils' spiritual, moral, cultural and social development by: developing awareness of the fundamental questions of life raised by human experiences; responding to such questions with reference to the teachings and

practices of religions and to their own understanding and experience; reflecting on their own beliefs, values and experiences in the light of their study;

- developing a positive attitude towards other people, respecting their right to hold different beliefs from their own and towards living in a society of diverse religions (abridged from SCAA, 1994, p. 3).

To assist planning and assessment, the aims are translated into two attainment targets which are to be given equal weight. These are: Learning about Religions (acquiring, developing and deepening of knowledge and understanding of), and Learning from Religions (enhancing their own spiritual and moral development by) (ibid., p. 6).

It would appear that these are all aims that religious educators would view as appropriate and worthy and that SCAA has provided a balanced educational rationale which should provide a clear direction and role for the subject. But this has not been the case and there are two, related, reasons for this. First, in their attempt to reflect a 'broad consensus' about the purpose of RE, by restating what have come to be seen as the aims of the subject, the syllabus constructors have not provided a clear answer to the question: What is the purpose of religious education? Rather, their apparently complementary aims represent several different answers to the question, each reflecting a different strand of thinking in RE and each making different demands on syllabus constructors and, ultimately, on teachers. As such they are no help to those who are seeking clarification about the role and direction of the subject.

Second, because the aims are not different aspects of a single purpose but reflect different views of what this purpose should be, the syllabus constructors were required to decide which aim to prioritise. So, in spite of a commitment to achieving a balance between aims, when aims are related to content in order to produce key stage plans, it is clear that priority has been given to the acquisition of knowledge and understanding. It is this aim which steers the construction of the syllabuses so that content is put in place first and in such a way that the 'integrity' of each religious tradition is respected. After this has been achieved, guidance is given (by means of various headings and suggestions for questions and activities) on how learning about religions can be used to achieve other aims. It

is this prioritisation of the acquisition of knowledge and understanding of religions that has led to the strongest criticism of the Model Syllabuses and to the publication of an alternative, independently produced syllabus (Baumfield *et al.*, 1994). For critics, the Model Syllabuses do not represent a new or agreed direction but a return to the 'transmissionist' model of the 1940s and 1950s RE (Baumfield *et al.*, 1995) or to 'the academic study of contemporary religions' (Bigger, 1995). Thus the syllabuses are viewed as failing to take account of the needs, questions and interests of young people and therefore as failing to make adequate provision for their spiritual and moral development.

No attempt will be made to adjudicate between the critics and supporters of the Model Syllabuses. The debate surrounding them has been introduced in order to suggest that the current concern about RE's lack of direction stems from the fact that religious educators are required to pursue aims which pull them in different directions; that it is not possible to construct syllabuses which give equal weight to all of these aims and that there are very real disagreements over priorities. In order to support these propositions, I intend to examine the different strands of thinking reflected in the SCAA aims and in the aims of agreed syllabuses and to demonstrate how each represents a particular understanding of what religious education is 'for' and of the contribution that it may make to pupils' development. Each different understanding of the purpose of RE requires teachers to select particular content, to organise this in particular ways and to employ particular teaching strategies. Ultimately, it also requires them to place greater value on some things than on others. This being the case, it will be argued that there is a very real need for the profession to examine its aims and their implications, to decide what is of greatest value to teachers and students of religious education and to agree upon priorities.

The aims of religious education

It will be suggested below that the aims included in the SCAA Model Syllabuses and in agreed syllabuses reflect three different views of the purpose of religious education:

1 The purpose of religious education is to enable

pupils to gain knowledge and understanding of religion(s).

2   The purpose of religious education is to promote understanding of and respect for people whose cultures and beliefs are different from one's own and to promote a positive attitude towards living in a plural society.

3   The purpose of religious education is to promote the personal, moral and spiritual development of pupils.

The purpose of religious education is to enable pupils to gain knowledge and understanding of religion(s)

> The great purposes of Religious Education . . . are to learn and to understand others; to learn about and understand ourselves; to ponder the great questions about life and the universe; to develop understanding . . . between people of different faiths and cultures and, *above all*, to know and understand the core elements of the Christian and other main faiths of this country. (Dearing, 1994; italics added)

> What RE offers uniquely is a study of religion. (Wintersgill, 1995)

In every strand of thinking about the purpose of religious education and at every stage in its development, it has been recognised that pupils must acquire knowledge and understanding of religion or religions. However, for several decades there has been disagreement about the extent to which RE should be concerned with knowledge and understanding and this reflects disagreement about the purpose of acquiring knowledge and understanding. For some, knowledge and understanding are to be acquired as a means to an end; for others, their acquisition is an end in itself.

In the 1960s and early 1970s, those who wished to see a clear separation between religious education and Christian education were forced to grapple with the question: If RE is not to be concerned with nurturing children in the Christian faith, what justification is there for including it in the school curriculum? One answer to this question was to be found in the work of the philosopher Paul Hirst: 'Hirst . . . understands education as the initiation of pupils into . . . forms of knowledge which he sees as necessary and worthwhile in themselves. Thus we have the grounds upon which some . . . have argued for the inclusion of the study of religion in

the school curriculum' (Grimmitt, 1987, pp. 21–2). It was this understanding of the purpose of religious education that underpinned the work of Ninian Smart (Jackson, 1978, p. 5), widely regarded as the father of multifaith religious education.

From the 1970s to the present day, the work of Smart and of the curriculum development project that he directed has been hugely influential. For Smart, the aim of religious education was to create 'certain capacities to understand and think about religion'. These included the capacity to understand religious phenomena, to discuss sensitively religious claims and to see the interrelations between religion and society. These capacities were to be developed in a number of ways. Amongst the strategies that Smart proposed, the most influential has been the phenomenological method, which requires pupils and teachers to 'bracket-out' their presuppositions and experiences in order to enter, empathetically, into the thoughts and feelings of others. This enables religious phenomena to be understood in the believer's own terms. Smart also envisaged that religious education would induct pupils into the various disciplines of religious studies including the history, sociology and philosophy of religion and that pupils would study the 'ideologies' of Humanism and Marxism alongside the world religions. In this way, pupils would acquire the necessary insights and skills to undertake a 'rational' evaluation of religious phenomena (Smart, 1968). The Schools Council Project on Religious Education, which Smart directed, promoted the phenomenological or 'undogmatic' approach to religious education and through its working paper and curriculum materials influenced the teaching of the subject at school level. Although the project team 'incline(d) to the view that religious education must include both the personal search for meaning and the objective study of the phenomena of religion', it is clear from their 'consensus as to the aims of religious education' and their objectives that it is the 'objective study' which is to receive most attention (Schools Council, 1971, pp. 44–5).

In the 1990s, Smart's understanding of religious education can be seen most clearly in GCSE Religious Studies courses which have been characterised as: starting with religions; emphasising learning about religion; having a curricular agenda set by religions; avoiding the personal; challenging students to academic excellence; and succeeding when knowledge and understanding of religions are developed (CEM, 1995, p. 8). This view is also reflected in the SCAA Model Syllabuses, in the decision to promote knowledge and understanding as an aim in itself; in the elevation of this aim to one of two attainment targets and in the adoption of this particular attainment target as the planning principle for the syllabuses. While the Model Syllabuses are offered as one way of structuring a syllabus for religious education, it is clear from the statements of Ron Dearing and Barbara Wintersgill, quoted above, that SCAA is seeking to persuade the profession that this is the direction in which the subject should develop.

What, then, are the values underlying this view of the purpose of religious education and what are the implications for the shape and direction of the subject, of giving priority to this view? There is a long tradition in religious education of associating the acquisition of knowledge and understanding 'for its own sake' with academic rigour and 'standards'. The current concern with the subject's academic respectability dates back to the pioneering work of Smart who sought to lift religious education above the level of the Sunday School class by introducing a study of religions which would parallel that undertaken in university departments. In Smart's view there should be no difference in the essential aims and character of religious education in schools and religious studies in universities (Smart, 1968). In more recent times, the association of learning about and understanding religions with academic standards has been reflected in the fact that pupils wishing to be certificated have been obliged to undertake a course which is primarily concerned with the acquisition of knowledge and understanding and which is entitled 'religious studies', rather than religious education. This association is also reflected in the justification given for the emphasis upon knowledge and understanding in the SCAA Model Syllabuses. In the words of Barbara Wintersgill (1995, p. 10), professional officer for RE at SCAA:

> This approach provides rigour, clear learning expectations and standards . . . The subject must be presented for what it is; a demanding, challenging, thought provoking discipline with a clearly defined content base . . . RE needs to lose its (sometimes deserved) reputation for long winded sentimentality and adopt the rigorous language of the National Curriculum.

In this view of religious education, high value is placed upon the body of knowledge to be acquired and upon the internal logic of that body of knowledge. For both Hirst (1970) and Smart (1968), the curriculum should be constructed according to this logic and this is the principle followed in the SCAA syllabuses as the following statement from Model 2 suggests:

> In each section, knowledge and understanding have been presented in a way that preserves the integrity of the religions and ensures that pupils will develop a coherent understanding of each religion. (DfE, 1994, p. 8).

In practical terms, a religious education which is concerned primarily with the acquisition of knowledge and understanding is one in which other aims must be given less attention. Acquiring knowledge is time-consuming for pupils and when time is spent on this activity it cannot be spent on others, such as the exploration of pupils' own experiences, feelings and beliefs. This common-sense observation is reflected in a report on the views of secondary school teachers who 'felt that the overloaded consent of GCSE Religious Studies is problematic and leaves little time for pupils to engage in a personal search for meaning' (CEM, 1995, p. 6).

A religious education which places a high value on the acquisition of knowledge and on academic standards is one in which other aims and concerns will not only receive less attention but may also be devalued. This is suggested in the statements and tone employed by Wintersgill when defending the SCAA syllabuses against their critics. Thus, RE needs to lose its deserved reputation for long-winded sentimentality and adopt the rigorous language of the National Curriculum; religious educators are derided for preferring the word 'explore' to 'investigate' and the word 'experience' to attainment targets and we are informed that, without rigour, RE is in danger of 'leading children down the path of the Midsummer fairy' (Wintersgill, 1995, pp. 10–11). In this defence of the SCAA syllabuses, it is possible to discern a conflict between two competing ideologies of education, characterised by Clive Lawton (1973, p. 24) as the 'classical' – which values standards, structure and rationality – and the 'romantic' – which values expression, style and experience.

A view of religious education which puts a high value on the acquisition of knowledge and understanding is one in which the internal logic of the body of knowledge dictates the structure of the curriculum. Wintersgill illustrates this point when she explains that, during the development of the Model Syllabuses, an attempt was made to create a syllabus which took as its starting point the spiritual and moral development of pupils. However, this approach was found to 'distort' the material relating to religious traditions and on these grounds, the personal development of pupils was rejected as an organising principle for a syllabus (Wintersgill, 1995, p. 8).

The purpose of religious education is to promote understanding of and respect for people whose cultures and beliefs are different from one's own and to promote a positive attitude towards living in a plural society

> We believe that religious education can play a central role in preparing all pupils for life in today's multi-racial Britain and can lead them to a greater understanding of the diversity of the global community. We feel that religious education . . . can contribute towards challenging and countering the influence of racism in our society.   (DES, 1985, p. 496)

The view that religious education should make a major contribution to promoting intercultural harmony has a long history. In the 1960s, Harold Loukes (1965, p. 161) was recommending that RE should include an examination of 'group relations and the hostilities that spring from class, national and racial differences'; the West Riding Agreed Syllabus included a unit of work on 'The Colour Problem' (1966, p. 82) and Colin Alves was urging religious educators to recognise the seriousness of their responsibility to 'curb' racial conflict (1964, p. 39). As these examples suggest, at this stage in the evolution of the subject, the focus of concern was racism and its place in the RE curriculum was alongside other 'moral issues' such as premarital sex and drug abuse. This kind of study has remained a feature of secondary school RE syllabuses to the present day, but with the appearance of the 'world religions approach' in the 1970s, a different view of the profession's responsibilities emerged. This emphasised the role of religious education in promoting an understanding of different cultures and peoples through the study of world religions. In this view, the acquisition of knowledge and understanding serves to dispel the ignorance and suspicion which give rise to prejudice and to engender an attitude of mutual respect between people of different backgrounds. This was the view accepted and promoted by the Swann report (DES, 1985).

Although the report recognised that racism and injustice were examined within the 'moral dimension' of the subject (ibid., p. 470) it laid greatest emphasis upon RE's role in enhancing pupils' 'understanding of a variety of religious beliefs and practices thus offering them an insight into the values and concerns of different communities' (p. 466) and 'encouraging an atmosphere of mutual respect and understanding between all groups in today's multi-racial society and the wider world' (p. 469).

The Swann report provided welcome support for religious education; at the same time it established, in the minds of many within and outside the profession, the view that a major, if not *the* major, purpose of RE was to promote intercultural harmony through the acquisition of knowledge about and understanding of religious traditions. Throughout the 1980s and 1990s agreed syllabuses and teachers' handbooks have continued to promote this view (Everington, 1993; AREIAC/NASACRE, 1996).

In recent years, serious doubts about both the validity (Troyna, 1987; Troyna and Hatcher, 1992) and the pedagogical implications of this claim have led some religious educators to treat it with caution. Nevertheless, speeches made at the launch of the SCAA Model Syllabuses in 1994 demonstrate that the role of religious education in promoting intercultural harmony is strongly suppported by representatives of the faith communities (Carey, 1994; Khan-Cheema, 1994; Maddox, 1994; Newton, 1994; Singh, 1994). A continuing commitment to this view of RE is also evident in the views of practitioners. As Joyce Miller (1996, p. 5) suggests, despite growing interest in the promotion of spiritual and moral values, 'Many RE professionals would be very wary of moving too far from an explicit, phenomenological approach for that is where RE's current identity and status predominantly lie. It is perceived to be of fundamental importance in promoting a harmonious, multiracial society.'

What, then, are the values underlying this view of the purpose of religious education and what are the implications for the shape and direction of the subject, of giving priority to this view? Of greatest value, in this view of RE, is the multicultural, multifaith society and the 'harmony' of this society. High value is also placed upon religion: 'A common assumption . . . is that religion, in whatever form, has a positive function at both individual and collective levels . . . [it] enhances the positive growth and development of individuals and society' (Wright, 1993, p. 58).

Also valued are the different cultures and religions which constitute the plural society. These are viewed as equally valid and important and as serving equally to 'enrich' society. At the level of the individual, value is placed upon attitudes of respect, tolerance and openness and upon skills such as to empathise and to set aside one's own beliefs and values in order to gain a deeper insight into those of others.

In Britain, a religious education which enables pupils to understand and respect fellow citizens of differing cultural and religious backgrounds must provide a curriculum which covers at least six religious traditions, the so-called 'principal religions'. As the Education Reform Act 1988 requires schools to take into account the backgrounds of their pupils, in some areas other traditions will need to be included. Such a curriculum will be heavy in content. As we have already suggested, a curriculum which is content-heavy is one which requires teachers to devote a large proportion of the limited time available to the acquisition of knowledge and understanding and, in real terms, this must be at the expense of other concerns and aims, including those which have to do with the spiritual and moral development of pupils. This being the case, it is little wonder that teachers feel torn between their responsibility to the 'social good' and their responsibility to the personal development of individual pupils. However, it might appear that a view of religious education which places a high value on intercultural harmony has much in common with a view which places a high value on the academic study of religions. Both give priority to the acquisition of knowledge and understanding and both therefore require a content-heavy curriculum. Also, the phenomenological method which is central to Smart's academic study of religions is a very useful tool for the teacher who wishes to promote a respectful attitude to the religions of Britain. However, there is a difference between the use of the phenomenological method in Smart's approach and its use in much multifaith teaching and this reflects a fundamental difference between the 'academic study' and the 'social harmony' views of religious education.

In Smart's own understanding of religious education, the 'bracketing out' of presuppositions and the empathetic understanding of religious phenomena are stages in the process of learning. Both Smart and the Schools Council project referred to earlier envisaged pupils proceeding from knowledge and understanding to a 'rational' evaluation of the truth or value of religious claims. However, there has been a tendency, in much multifaith teaching, to restrict learning to an understanding of religious phenomena in the believers' own terms. This has led critics to 'blame' the phenomenological method for denying pupils the opportunity to develop the skills of critical evaluation, but it can be argued that it is not the method itself which turns religious education into little more than a descriptive exercise, but those who have adopted the method as a means of promoting intercultural harmony.

In the 'academic view' of religious education, the study of religions is to be objective and impartial. The tools of scholarship are to be used rigorously to understand and then to undertake an informed and rational evaluation of religious phenomena. For Smart, this 'open approach' would require pupils to study 'anti-religious' ideologies as well as religious traditions. In the 'social harmony' view, the aim is not just to enable pupils to acquire knowledge and understanding, it is also and more crucially to enable them to develop a positive attitude towards and a respect for the people, beliefs, values and practices that are studied. In curriculum and pedagogical terms this is a fundamental difference. In crude terms, if the principal aim is to promote respect there will be a tendency, first, to select material which provides a positive and 'respectable' view of the tradition and of believers, and second, to present religious traditions in such a way that they will seem, to pupils, to be worthy of respect. In the view of critics, this pressure to 'process' religious phenomena into a form that will be acceptable, even agreeable, to pupils of differing ages, abilities and backgrounds has led to the 'sanitisation' and 'domestication' of the religious traditions. A 'sanitised' view of religions is one in which believers and beliefs are portrayed in ideal terms:

> To offer a picture of believers as those deeply committed to their faith, continuously putting their faith into practice, and united in a 'common denominator' set of universally accepted beliefs is surely to offer an idealistic lie in the face of realistic evidence. (Wright, 1993, p. 58)

A 'domesticated' view of religions is one in which controversial matters, such as the believer's claim to be in possession of the only Truth, are hidden from sight (Grimmitt, 1987, pp. 40–1). A recognition of the demands that this aim makes on the subject and on teachers has led some religious educators to question whether the cost of performing such a role is too high (Watson, 1993; Wright, 1993).

A consequence of selecting and presenting religious material in such a way that it appears 'in its best light' is that pupils receive insufficient information to reach their own conclusions about it. Evaluation is, in effect, excluded from the learning process. But there is another sense in which this approach discourages pupils from forming their own judgements. Where the teacher is required to promote attitudes which (it is believed) will be supportive of a harmonious multicultural society, she or he becomes a vehicle for the transmission of particular values and the pupil becomes the receiver of these values. As we shall see, this understanding of the roles of teacher and pupil and of the relationship between them is in direct conflict with those envisaged in a view of religious education which gives priority to the spiritual and moral development of pupils.

The purpose of religious education is to promote the personal, moral and spiritual development of pupils

> Religious Education is about the pursuit of truth and the acquisition of wisdom; uncertainty and questions, doubts and dialogue are essential elements in such a search and Agreed Syllabuses need to make this absolutely clear in their philosophy and in the organisation of the curriculum. (Baumfield *et al.*, 1995, pp. 5–6)

While the direction and identity of religious education has been redefined many times in the last four decades, the personal, spiritual and moral development of pupils has remained a constant, though not for all a major, concern. In the days of 'confessional' religious instruction, pupils' personal, moral and spiritual development was synonomous with the development of their religious faith and so lay at the very heart of the RE teacher's mission. By the 1960s, attempts were being made to respond to the findings of educational research and to improve the effectiveness of RE by constructing syllabuses based on the capacities, needs and interests of pupils but the fulfilment of these needs was seen to be possible only through an acceptance of the Christian faith. So, while primary school teachers were being encouraged to abandon the presentation of explicitly religious teachings and to adopt a cross-curricular approach in which all work became the exploration of 'life themes', it was expected that they would relate the whole world of experience and discovery to the basic idea that 'this is God's world' (Goldman, 1965). In the secondary schools, however, the work of Harold Loukes began to offer teachers an alternative to an explicitly confessional approach.

Concerned primarily with the needs of non-academic pupils who saw religious education as 'irrelevant', Loukes advocated an approach which viewed RE as a personal quest for meaning in life. Less emphasis was to be placed on communicating information about religion and more on the analysis of experience. In Loukes's view religious education was at root 'a conversation between older and younger on the simple question, "What is life like?"'. The role of the teacher was to set pupils thinking and searching for meaning in an atmosphere of sympathetic dialogue. Though the Christian tradition was seen as providing the framework in which exploration should take place, Christian answers were not to be imposed, the exploration was to be spontaneous, arising from pupil's experience and relating to it (Loukes, 1965).

By the 1970s, a concern to further pupils' personal quest for meaning in life was being linked to the new study of world religions and used as a justification for such a study. In 1978 Robert Jackson (1978, p. 5) summarised this argument:

> World religions should be approached through the exploration of 'ultimate questions' for these ensure the relevance of religious data to the student's life . . . with this approach the relevance of the questions to the pupil's own life provides the motivation for study; the body of knowledge from world religions gives information but primarily stimulates the pupil in his own search for a philosophy or a theology of life.

Throughout the latter years of the 1970s and in the 1980s agreed syllabuses for religious education continued to include moral and spiritual development amongst their aims. However, it was during this period that the phenomenological, approach became influential, and although commentators (Bates, 1996; Robson, 1996) recognise that adoption of the new ideas was slow and patchy at school level, they are agreed that the approach was strongly supported by the professional religious education centres and by other influential agencies. Many school textbooks of the period reflect this support. There is also some research evidence to suggest that by the late 1970s teachers in secondary schools were beginning to show less interest in 'emphasising moral aims' and more interest in the phenomenological approach (Bedwell, 1977). The extent to which pupils' personal search for 'meaning and purpose' had become marginalised during the 1980s is suggested by the emergence of a 'movement' which, in the latter years of the decade, sought to reinstate personal, social, moral and spiritual development as the major concerns of religious education. A key figure in this movement was Michael Grimmitt.

Grimmitt's examination of 'The relationship between studying religions and personal, social and moral development' was published in 1987. In this study, the author drew attention to the superficiality of much teaching and learning in religious education. Multifaith teaching had become multifact teaching and had thus ceased to be relevant to pupils or to make a significant contribution to their education, which Grimmit (1987, p. 198) defines as: 'a process by, in and through which pupils may begin to explore what it is and what it means to be human'. Such an education will provide pupils with the opportunity to become aware of the fundamental questions and dilemmas posed by the human condition; to clarify their own beliefs and responses to such questions and to acquire the knowledge, skills and attitudes necessary to enable them to participate in the processes by which they and their lives are shaped. In order for religious education to make a meaningful contribution to this process, pupils should be encouraged to explore that 'shared human experience' which underlies their own beliefs and values and those of the world religions, and 'traditional belief systems' which represent religious responses to and interpretations of these experiences. In order for the exploration of these two fields to contribute to personal development, careful attention must be paid to the structuring of the curriculum and to the selection of content. The curriculum should be structured in such a way that pupils learn from the interaction between the two areas of study. Interaction takes place when pupils are enabled to use the insights gained in the exploration of shared human experience to understand and evaluate traditional belief systems and to use their knowledge and understanding of traditional belief systems to understand and evaluate shared human experience, including their own. Grimmitt acknowledges that meaningful interaction will not take place simply by placing any piece of religious material next to any example of shared human experience. Material must be carefully selected from both fields, using criteria that will ensure that the content of the curriculum reflects the needs, experiences and questions of the pupils.

While Grimmitt's thesis and 'curriculum illustrations' took account of the spiritual development of pupils, the case for a religious education which gives priority to this aspect of personal development was taken up by other writers and curriculum development teams. In 1992, Nicola Slee noted that during the past decade there had been a renewed concern amongst religious educators for the realms of imagination, spirituality and the arts. She attributed this, in part, to dissatisfaction with the form of religious education proposed by advocates of the phenomenological method, in which questions of personal values, commitments and beliefs are bracketed out. In response to what was perceived to be the impoverishment of religious education, a number of writers had been seeking to develop a more pupil-centred, personalistic approach in which the quest for spirituality is at the centre of religious education rather than at the periphery. For each of these writers:

> religious education is far more to do with method than content, it is essentially process rather than programme. It is a process which is characteristically inquisitive and explorative, rather than instructive and explanatory; experiential and inductive rather than didactic and deductive; . . . personal and relational rather than academic and detached; holistic and integrative rather than abstract and analytical . . . whilst the acquisition of knowledge and the development of understanding are not decried in this process, they are perceived to be secondary to religious education's more fundamental concern with spirituality. (Slee, 1992, p. 42).

In practical terms Slee recognised that it will not be possible to place spiritual development at the heart of religious education without making sacrifices. An emphasis upon spiritual growth requires teachers to choose depth rather than breadth, to select the 'one thing necessary' out of a possible hundred which, within the limited time and space available, will do most to capture the spirit of a tradition, a quest, a life story or an insight. Such an approach also requires the space for free exploration, for reflection and for questioning the boundaries of what is safe, accepted and known. Thus, in order to 'light the flame of learning', stark choices have to be made and priorities formulated and this will involve a recognition that much that is worthy of study will have to be omitted, 'the good must give way to the better' (ibid., pp. 54–5).

While it is difficult to assess the effect that the writers of the 1980s' movement had upon the thinking of their contemporaries, some of the arguments introduced during this period have re-emerged in the 1990s. As we have seen, the publication of the SCAA Model Syllabuses in 1994 gave rise to further debate about the purpose of religious education and to renewed concern about its role in promoting moral and spiritual development. Dissatisfied with the 'unnecessarily narrow' view of religious education promoted by the Model Syllabuses and alarmed at the influence that this might have upon Agreed Syllabus conferences, a group of university-based religious educators determined to design a 'third' syllabus which would provide an alternative and balance to those produced by SCAA. The syllabus was constructed with the explicit intention of making religious education relevant and accessible to all pupils by using their needs, experiences, questions and interests as the starting point for planning. Although the authors accept the importance of providing pupils with knowledge and understanding of religious traditions, these, together with non-religious world views, are seen as contributing to the personal development of pupils. Thus, the first aim of religious education to be defined is 'To assist pupils in their personal search for meaning and purpose in life'. This is to be achieved through the exploration of human experiences which raise fundamental questions about beliefs and values and through knowledge, understanding and evaluation of the world views of the pupils, of the religious traditions and of non-religious ideologies (Baumfield *et al.*, 1994).

Echoing Loukes and Grimmitt, the authors of the syllabus believe that their approach offers a 'religious education for all' which is relevant, stimulating and active and which involves children, rather than adults, in setting the agenda and in asking the questions that really matter to them. Like their pre-

decessors, the authors stress that these aims cannot be achieved within a religion-centred curriculum (Baumfield *et al.*, 1995).

In 1996, the case for a more pupil-centred form of RE was strengthened by the launch of new GCSE Short Courses in Religious Education. The new courses are to be offered alongside the full GCSE in Religious Studies (RS) but have different aims and assessment objectives designed, according to a recent SCAA report, to meet the requirements of agreed syllabuses 'and the interests and questions of 14–18 year olds' (1996a, p. 16). All five examination boards offer a new kind of course in which there is an emphasis upon exploring 'fundamental questions of life raised by religion and human experience'. These 'questions' range from 'What is truth?' and 'The existence of God' to 'Thinking about Morality' and 'Religion and Prejudice'. The launch of the new courses represents more than a new opportunity for pupils. More significantly, it represents a recognition, on the part of SCAA and of the examination boards, that there is a fundamental difference between the academic study of religions, represented by RS courses, and the religious education that teachers have been providing for the majority of pupils. In effect, what have been seen in the past as separate aims have become separate subjects. In the view of one commentator, the courses represent 'A change of direction for RE' and 'an opportunity to offer a clear vision of what RE is trying to achieve' (Wright, 1996). Support for this change of direction is indicated by the results of a survey of teachers' responses to the new courses, which revealed that 76 per cent of those consulted agreed with the proposition that 'Religious studies only indirectly addresses the students' experience. New accreditation should centre on the personal search for meaning that is at the heart of good RE' (CEM, 1995, p. 6).

It is clear, from the account offered above, that throughout the last four decades there has been very considerable support for the view that religious education should be primarily concerned with the personal, moral and spiritual development of pupils. Although the passing of the years has seen different emphases and the development of different methodologies, there has been a common understanding of the values underpinning this form of religious education and general agreement about the implications of providing for it.

In this view of the purpose of religious education, it is the individual child or young person who is valued above all else. More specifically, it is the freedom of children to develop their own beliefs and values and to find their own meaning and purpose in life that is valued. High value is placed upon the imagination and 'vision' of the children and upon those qualities and skills which will enable them to be active in and take responsibility for the development of their own selves and the society in which they live. Also valued is the experience that children bring to the learning situation and the insights that arise from this experience.

Advocates of this view of religious education have stressed that the goal of promoting the personal development of pupils has implications, not just for teaching methods, but also for the structure of the curriculum and for the selection of content. The framework on which content is hung must be constructed from the interests, questions and experiences of pupils. This framework must be flexible, to enable pupils to pursue their own interests and reach their own conclusions in their own time. Content must be selected for its potential to contribute to the personal development of pupils and must be limited, to allow time and opportunity for exploration and reflection and for the development of skills other than those associated with the acquisition of knowledge. At the interpersonal level, a religious education which gives priority to pupils' personal development requires teachers to adopt the role of enabler or facilitator and for pupils to become active participants in the learning process. Together, pupils and teachers will explore values and beliefs in an open-ended search for 'truth' and 'wisdom'.

Conclusion

An attempt has been made to relate what have come to be thought of as 'the aims' of religious education to different strands of thinking about the nature and purpose of the subject. It has been argued that there are three different understandings of what the subject is 'for'; that in each of these, different values are promoted and that each makes its own particular demands in terms of the structure and the content of the curriculum. For several decades teachers have struggled to balance the aims that they have inherited. The historical overview presented above, the arguments of those who have recognised the implications of pursuing particular aims, and recent concerns about the sub-

ject's lack of direction and identity indicate that, in practice, there are very real difficulties in achieving this balance. It has been suggested that these difficulties arise because there is conflict between the demands made by each different aim. Thus, a curriculum which is designed primarily to promote the personal, spiritual and moral development of pupils cannot, at the same time, respect the internal logic of the body of knowledge. A curriculum designed primarily to enable pupils to undertake an 'academic' study of religions or to promote the personal development of pupils cannot, at the same time, ensure that pupils will develop a positive attitude towards the religions under study. A curriculum which is designed to promote the academic skills and achievements of pupils cannot, at the same time, allow pupils the space and freedom to pursue their own interests and reach their own conclusions in their own ways and in their own time.

While religious educators continue to struggle with or to ignore the conflict of interests that exists between the subject's different aims they will continue to feel directionless and, more crucially, they will continue to feel (and be) unable to fulfil all of the expectations that are placed upon them. The time has come for the profession to look seriously at the question of priorities; to decide what is of greatest value to teachers and students of religious education and which of its aims should define and lead the subject in the new millennium.

Reaching such a decision will not be easy. Loyalty to particular theoretical and pedagogical positions and to particular 'client groups' would inevitably lead to some fierce battles within the profession but these could prove to be very creative if undertaken in the right context and in the right spirit. For this reason John Hull's (1966) proposed working party, consisting of educators from primary, secondary and higher education and from the professional associations and the faith communities, would be very necessary. Much of this body's time would be taken up with resolving ideological and philosophical disputes but there would also be a need to consider the practical matter of 'survival'. For many years, religious education has been treated as a 'cinderella subject', it has occupied a marginal position in the curriculum and it has been under-resourced, especially in terms of its specialist teaching force (Gates, 1993). Any attempt to arrive at priorities and to decide upon a new direction must take account of the need to strengthen the position of the subject, but in which direction does strength lie?

It seems that SCAA favour a view of religious education which emphasises the acquisition of knowledge and understanding of religious traditions and in which academic standards are a major concern. Acquiescence to this view may well be a precondition of entering the National Curriculum. The benefits of moving in this direction are clear. The raising of the status of religious education should improve schools' treatment of the subject and pupils' response to it. As a National Curriculum subject RE would be entitled to its fair share of resources and the appointment of greater numbers of specialist teachers would improve the quality of teaching and learning.

The view that RE can play a major role in promoting intercultural respect and harmony may have been called into question in recent years, but it is a view strongly supported by the faith communities and by many within the profession. While such confidence may be unwarranted, the fact remains that this is the only area of the curriculum in which pupils are offered an opportunity to receive an informed, sympathetic and balanced introduction to the differing religions and cultures that constitute our plural society. Moreover, there has been a recognition, amongst those who have been particularly critical of religious and multicultural education, that there is an urgent need to address pupils' misconceptions of religious and cultural practices (Short and Carrington, 1995). We have no reason to believe that this need will disappear in the new millennium.

The personal, moral and spiritual development of pupils is currently receiving a great deal of attention from educators, politicians, religious leaders and employers and there seems to be general agreement that religious education has a major role to play in these areas. Ironically, it is two of SCAA's own publications which provide the strongest evidence for this (1995a, 1996b). If an emphasis upon pupils' personal development is to be a feature of education in the new millennium then religious educators may find themselves viewed as major contributors and as guides in territory that their predecessors have been exploring for several decades.

Clearly, there is strength to be gained in giving priority to and pursuing any of these aims of RE and so the dilemma facing the profession cannot be solved by appeal to the 'survival issue'. There are no easy answers and the decision-making process must be a painful one. However, it has been my intention in this chapter to demonstrate that while the profession continues to ignore or to struggle with the competing demands made by its different aims, there will continue to be confusion and a sense of despair at the complexity and enormity of the task. There is not, nor can there be, any strength in this position, and while religious educators fail to decide upon the direction that the subject should take, there will always be those who are ready to step in and take this decision for them. In the words of Brenda Watson (1992, p. 1): 'Deciding on priorities is an uncomfortable task . . . [but] if we do not choose priorities, they choose us and their effects are inescapable.'

References

Alves, C. (1964) Insights and suggestions. *Learning for Living* **8** (3), 39–42.

Association of RE Inspectors, Advisers and Consultants (AREIAC)/National Association of Standing Advisory Councils for Religious Education (NASACRE) (1996) *Directory of Agreed Syllabuses for Religious Education*. Norwich: University of East Anglia, AREIAC/NASACRE.

Bates, D. (1996) Christianity, culture and other religions, Part 2: F.H. Hilliard, Ninian Smart and the 1988 Education Reform Act. *British Journal of Religious Education* **18** (2), 85–103.

Baumfield, V., Bowness, C., Cush, D. and Miller, J. (1994) *A Third Perspective*. Exeter: School of Education, University of Exeter.

Baumfield, V., Bowness, C., Cush, D. and Miller, J. (1995) Model syllabuses: the debate continues. *Resource* **18** (1), 3–6.

Bedwell, A.E. (1977) Aims of religious education teachers in Hereford and Worcester. *Learning for Living* **17** (2), 66–74.

Bigger, S. (1995) Challenging RE in a multicultural world. *Journal of Beliefs and Values* **16** (2), 11–18.

Blaylock, L. (1996) A blizzard of spiritual and moral development. *Resource* **18** (3), 21.

Brown, A. (1995) Discernment – the last word. *Shap Working Party on World Religions in Education Journal 1995/1996*, 40–2.

Carey, G. (1994) Transcript of a speech given on behalf of the Church of England at the launch of the SCAA Model Syllabuses.

Christian Education Movement (CEM) (1995) *RE at Key Stage 4: A Report on the CEM Teachers' Conference*. London: CEM.

Dearing, R. (1994) Transcript of a speech made at the launch of the SCAA Model Syllabuses.

Department of Education and Science (DES) (1985) *Education for All* (Ethnic Minority Groups) Cmnd 9543. London: Her Majesty's Stationery Office.

Edwards, L. and Newell, M. (1994) RE 1988–1994: a conflict of values? *Journal of Beliefs and Values* **15** (1), 5–10.

Everington, J. (1993) The role of religious education in combating racism and promoting inter-cultural harmony. Unpublished M.Ed. dissertation, University of Birmingham.

Everington, J. (1996) A question of authenticity: the relationship between educators and practitioners in the representation of religious traditions. *British Journal of Religious Education* **18** (2), 69–78.

Gates, B. (1993) *Time for Religious Education and Teachers to Match: a Digest of Under-Provision.* London: Religious Education Council.

Goldman, R.J. (1965) *Readiness for Religion.* London: Routledge.

Grimmitt, M. (1987) *Religious Education and Human Development.* Great Wakering, Essex: McCrimmons.

Habgood, J. (1995) Address to the conference on 'National Collaboration in Religious Education' at the Royal Society of Arts, London, 8 March.

Hirst, P. and Peters, R.S. (1970) *The Logic of Education.* London: Routledge & Kegan Paul.

Hull, J. (1995) Religion as a series of religions: a comment on the SCAA Model Syllabuses. *Shap Working Party on World Religions in Education Journal 1995/1996,* 11–17.

Hull, J. (1996) Editorial: Religious education and the National Curriculum. *British Journal of Religious Education* **18** (3), 130–2.

Jackson, R. (1978) The world religions debate. In R. Jackson (ed.), *Perspectives on World Religions.* London: School of Oriental and African Studies, University of London.

Jackson, R. (1990) Religious studies and developments in religious education in England and Wales. In U. King (ed.), *Turning Points in Religious Studies.* Edinburgh: T. & T. Clark, 102–17.

Khan-Cheema, M.A. (1994) Transcript of a speech given on behalf of the Muslim Education Forum at the launch of the SCAA Model Syllabuses.

Lawton, D. (1973) *Social Change, Education Theory and Curriculum Planning.* London: Open University/ Hodder & Stoughton.

Loukes, H. (1965) *New Ground in Religious Education.* London: SCM Press.

Maddox, R. (1994) Transcript of a speech given on behalf of the Buddhist Society at the launch of the SCAA Model Syllabuses.

Miller, J. (1996) RE and values. *Resource* **19** (1), 4–7.

Newton, J. (1994) Transcript of a speech given on behalf of the Free Church Federal Council at the launch of the SCAA Model Syllabuses.

Patten, J. (1994) Transcript of a speech given at the launch of the SCAA Model Syllabuses.

Robson, G. (1996) Religious education, government policy and professional practice, 1985–1995. *British Journal of Religious Education* **19** (1), 13–23.

Rudge, L. (1996) The future of RE in the school curriculum: trends in England and Wales. *Resource* **18** (3), 4–8.

Schools Curriculum and Assessment Authority (SCAA) (1994) *Model Syllabuses for Religious Education,* 2 vols: *Model 1: Living Faiths Today*; *Model 2: Questions and Teachings.* London: SCAA.

Schools Curriculum and Assessment Authority (SCAA) (1995a) *Spiritual and Moral Development.* London: SCAA.

Schools Curriculum and Assessment Authority (SCAA) (1995b) *GCSE (Short Course) Criteria for Religious Education.* London: SCAA.

Schools Curriculum and Assessment Authority (SCAA) (1996a) *Analysis of SACRE Reports 1996.* London: SCAA.

Schools Curriculum and Assessment Authority (SCAA) (1996b) *Education for Adult Life: The Spiritual and Moral Development of Young People.* London: SCAA.

Short, G. and Carrington, B. (1995) Learning about Judaism: a contribution to the debate on multi-faith religious education. *British Journal of Religious Education* **17** (3), 157–67.

Singh, I. (1994) Transcript of a speech given at the launch of the SCAA Model Syllabuses.

Slee, N. (1992) 'Heaven in ordinarie': the imagination, spirituality and the arts in religious education. In B. Watson (ed.), *Priorities in Religious Education.* London: Falmer Press, 38–57.

Schools Council (1971) *Religious Education in Secondary Schools,* Working Paper 36. London: Evans/Methuen.

Smart, N. (1968) *Secular Education and the Logic of Religion.* London: Faber & Faber.

Troyna, B. (1987) Beyond multi-culturalism: towards the re-enactment of anti-racist education in policy, provision and pedagogy. *Oxford Review of Education* **13** (3), 307–20

Troyna, B. and Hatcher, R. (1992) *Racism in Children's Lives.* London: Routledge.

Watson, B. (ed.) (1992) *Priorities in Religious Education.* London: Falmer Press.

Watson, B. (1993) *The Effective Teaching of Religious Education.* Harlow, Essex: Longman.

West Riding of Yorkshire (1996) *Suggestions for Religious Education.* County Council of the West Riding of Yorkshire Education Department.

Wintersgill, B. (1995) The case of the missing models: exploding the myths. *Resource* **18** (1), 6–11.

Wright, Andrew (1993) *Religious Education in the Secondary School.* London: David Fulton.

Wright, Andrew (1997) Mishmash, religionism and

theological literacy: an appreciation and critique of Trevor Cooling's hermeneutical programme. *British Journal of Religious Education* **19** (3), 143–56.

Wright, Angela (1996) A change of direction for RE: the GCSE (Short Course) RE syllabuses. *Resource* **19** (1), 15–18.

19 Mentoring Religious Education Teaching in Secondary Schools

NICK MEAD

Introduction

The research in this chapter is prompted by three developments: the emerging role of the mentor in school, the expanding recruitment of Religious Education Postgraduate Certificate of Education (RE PGCE) students from diverse backgrounds, and the government's concern with the standards of initial teacher training (ITT). The research identifies the mentoring needs of RE PGCE students in the light of their academic background and personal, religious and philosophical motivations. It then assesses how effectively these needs are met by mentors, and identifies good practice in RE mentoring. Third, the research examines the influence on RE mentoring of the structure and expectations within the training partnership and identifies areas for improvement. The research findings suggest that, given training which links student needs with good practice in mentoring, mentors can turn a diverse intake of students into competent classroom practitioners. However, the research findings also establish that the extent to which RE mentoring needs are met can be influenced by the structure and expectations within the partnership, and recommendations for improvement are made, which should enhance the role of the mentor. The research concludes that the expanding recruitment of RE PGCE students from diverse backgrounds is justified if mentors engage in a training, as opposed to a supervisory role and become equal, proactive partners in the training process. The research was sponsored by the Farmington Institute, Oxford, who are the copyright holders of the data (see Mead, 1996).

The research design

The type of qualitative research used for the project is defined in Maykut and Morehouse (1994, p. 153) as, 'the emergent design case study approach'. Initially, we specified an awareness of RE mentoring needs in the light of the backgrounds and motivations of students. These needs became specific as data were collected and categorised. We then engaged in the process of discovering how well these needs are met by mentors and the emergent design highlighted certain priorities. Significantly, the data generated other factors pertaining to how the training partnership affected the degree to which mentoring needs are met.

This approach was based around contexts in three training partnerships. One was chosen because it is traditional and well established; another is modern and just established; the third offered contexts in which confessionalism was particularly well-handled. The field work lasted seven weeks, covering the PGCE RE course induction period and initial school experiences. Methods of data collection included Graduate Teacher Training Registry (GTTR) document analysis; participant observation in mentor training and student seminars; questionnaires to two student cohorts; and transcriptions of semi-structured interviews with six PGCE course leaders, fourteen mentors and seven observed mentoring sessions.

What are the mentoring needs of RE PGCE students?

Our data identify three broad needs which reflect the diversity of students entering the RE profession. The first is how subject competence is addressed; the second, how varied student motivations are turned into classroom practice; and the third, how subject aims are understood.

Subject knowledge findings suggest that RE PGCE courses run in traditional academic universities, which have theology/RS departments, tend to attract well-qualified theology/RS students. An example is institution E which has 60 per cent of its PGCE intake with theology/RS degrees and 40 per cent with degrees which have an RS component or none at all. More recent courses in more modern institutions which do not necessarily have a theology/RS department tend to recruit a higher proportion of graduates with either combined RS or non-specialist degrees, such as philosophy, social sciences, combined studies. An example is institution D which has 70 per cent of its intake with combined RS or non-specialist degrees. However, both types of institution demonstrate a widening academic base in their intake, following the Gates Report (1993). For example, although traditional Institution B has 58 per cent with Theology/RS degrees, it has 36 per cent with non-specialist degrees which is comparable to the 31 per cent with non-specialist degrees at modern institution F.

The data suggest that there will be gaps in subject knowledge and this has implications for mentoring. It also raises the question about whether a student, with or without a theology/RS background, has the right intellectual orientations for teaching RE. It is possible, for example, that a philosopher may display more appropriate skills than a theologian. There is a wider issue here about the nature of subject competence in RE with which mentors need to engage.

Data from 52 students in two institutions enabled us to identify three key motivations for wanting to teach RE, out of a possible eight: 23 per cent spoke in terms ranging from 'communicating and encouraging ideas in a stimulating environment', of enjoying the challenge of devising programmes to, 'hold their interest and fire their imagination' Although we might call these general teaching motivations, it is possible to discern within them some of the basic intellectual skills required in RE teaching. Of these students, 21 per cent held convictions about the spiritual, moral and cultural value of RE:

> My academic background is in Philosophy but I am keen to teach RE because I am convinced of its importance throughout every pupil's school life. At its best I think RE should provide children with a

context for moral reasoning, a sense of their own identity within the universe and a basis for understanding their own and other cultures, as well as knowledge of particular religions.   (Student F)

This intellectual base is linked by other students to actually wanting to give pupils the means to change and develop and to share in their spiritual development. Students see the outcome of this intellectual enterprise as relating to the dilemma in our society about the relationship between belief, morality and action: there is mention of the influence of personal ideas and values on behaviour, of 'responding to moral dilemmas which dominate our lives', of 'giving pupils convictions and wisdom to change things', and there is a good deal about teaching respect for culture, law and morality.

Of the sample 17 per cent identified skills in RE which they had valued and wished to pass on to pupils. Mention is made of reflective skills: 'the ability to think effectively', 'to think critically' and to use knowledge to understand and accept the 'sheer variety of human nature and its beliefs'.

RE mentors need to understand these motivations which, for many students, are more significant than subject knowledge. They reveal certain intellectual orientations and skills compatible with understanding and evaluating religious ideas. School experience can focus and deepen these or can threaten them. Mentors need to nurture such motivations and shape them into realistic classroom competences.

We went on to find out to what extent these motivations relate to students' understanding of subject aims. Data from questionnaires conducted in week 2 of the course reveals: 19 per cent confused about subject aims; 44 per cent were able to give a basic definition; 12 per cent believed the subject was confused itself; and 25 per cent were able to give a definition pointing to knowledge, understanding and reflection with some understanding of the principle of learning from as well as about religions.

It is evident that, because they have the right intellectual orientations and skills for the subject, students are well ahead on methodology, but this is yet to be matched to a clear understanding of subject aims and progression. Students in the final group are advanced and tutors will be working fast to ensure all gain similarly clear subject aims before they get too far into the first school placement. Mentors will need to be aware of the students' level of understanding of subject aims and progression at the commencement of the course, how tutors address this, and how they will need to develop it in the mentoring process, enabling students to match their imaginative ideas for classroom practice with sound aims and progression.

How do mentors meet the needs of RE PGCE students?

Having identified the mentoring needs, we proceeded to describe the mentoring process in order to measure the degree of good practice in meeting these needs.

The data overwhelmingly point to the mentor–student relationship as the foundation of good mentoring. In RE the relationship provides the context within which motivations are shared:

> It's about building up trust quickly. It does seem to work. I don't know how but perhaps it's because there is no hidden agenda. We're here to help them pass and I am very honest about my own teaching.   (Mentor C)

The honesty mentioned says something about the mentors' need to explain the relationship between their own motivations and what they think they are achieving in the classroom. It is not surprising that effective mentors see their role as more than supervisory and based on mutual respect of motivations. In the process of turning motivations into classroom practice, such mentors are sensitive and supportive, for example in not letting a lack of subject knowledge undermine initial classroom experience. They can also lay the foundations for constructive self-criticism, an essential skill for lone RE teachers, without demoralising the student.

Concerning the mentoring of subject knowledge, mentors seem to be saying two important things: first, there is a certain amount of subject knowledge about six world religions which is needed; second, RE is not the same creature as that which constitutes a so-called specialist qualification:

> Students are often disappointed because it's not the subject they thought it was – often they don't recognize it when they observe because their experience is what they had at university and that is completely different.   (Mentor C)

This suggests that an understanding of subject principles may be more important than the amount of subject knowledge.

Effective subject knowledge mentoring seems to be about providing well-motivated students with strategies and resources for acquiring appropriate subject knowledge. Mentor A talks about 'setting targets in subject knowledge research so that they are aware you have to keep working on it and it is part of good practice'. In order to ensure *appropriate* subject knowledge is selected for the lesson, effective subject knowledge mentoring will be done in the context of planning lesson aims and methodology.

As personal motivations figure largely in RE teaching, mentors are anxious to identify the extremes of indifference and confessionalism:

> I've had one or two students in the past about whom I've had that underlying feeling that they simply wanted to extend their university course.   (Mentor F)

> One student had this view of what he wanted to do and I said this is not on but he felt it was my view against his. He was confessing his own world view and identifying himself with the subject.   (Mentor C)

It seems that both indifference and confessionalism are dealt with effectively by mentors who have worked through, and can account for, the relationship between their own motivations and their classroom practice. This enables the mentor to articulate what the student may be experiencing in the classroom and so facilitate discussion, leading to effective strategies. For example, a female Muslim mentor is very clear in her own mind about avoiding confessionalism, as she explains it to students:

> It is perfectly all right for you to wheel yourself on in the lesson as the personal exhibit, but then wheel yourself out and bring on the teacher. I am a facilitator, a confessional approach wouldn't improve their learning experience. When I offer a Muslim view, it is as acquired knowledge in an educational context.   (Mentor D)

Other mentors talk about the need to encourage students to develop an open, enquiring atmosphere in which spirituality, rather than dogma, is valued.

In order to help students develop clarity in subject aims, mentors need to demonstrate the links between the aims of the agreed syllabus, the school's scheme of work and the RE teacher's lesson plans. Mentors who do this well are usually engaged in reviewing their work; for example, modifying the scheme of work in the light of agreed syllabus revision.

To learn from as well as about religions, through knowledge, understanding and reflection, requires the school scheme of work to employ a variety of teaching styles. The mentor has the task of linking subject aims to teaching styles which is crucial in the mentoring process because it is the means by which the subject comes alive and contributes to the spiritual and moral growth of children. An example follows of Mentor C and Student A building up the links between aims and methodology:

Mentor: What is the aim of this Year 8 lesson?
Student: The aim is to teach the significance of the Seder meal to the Jews.
Mentor: Good. What should the activities try and do?
Student: To get across why the meal is important and goes beyond just eating unleavened bread and bitter herbs, its about evoking sympathy and remembrance
Mentor: That's good, exactly how you approach it – so let's think about activities.
Student: We could ask the pupils how they remember things, for example, toys, photos, then we could go on to Remembrance Day.
Mentor: Good. You are beginning with pupils' experience and then moving from individual memories to collective remembrance.
Student: That's the whole point about Pesach which I want pupils to reflect on, that it's shared thankfulness that you are not in that situation now. The pupils could make up their own symbolic ways of remembering things – or the Exodus and then we could introduce the Seder artefacts which would then mean something, and perhaps act out the meal.

As this mentoring session develops it is clear that the student is being encouraged to link aims and method in a way which will engage pupils in the meaning and value of the RE content for others and for themselves.

Confusion about attainment and progression in RE arises because both theology/RS students and non-specialists have derived their intellectual orientations from university courses which do not relate directly to RE at the different key stages. Mentors need to direct students away from their own experience to the actual *process* whereby pupils grasp an understanding of and are able to reflect on religious concepts. Assessment becomes clearer to students when mentors relate clear subject aims to lesson outcomes.

At the heart of mentoring discipline in RE is the mentor's ability to communicate to both pupils and PGCE students what it is that they are trying to achieve in the lesson. Classroom *ethos* is one of the keys to this:

> Where RE does cause a discipline problem is when the children perceive it as you trying to get them to believe something – the barriers go up. It's not a problem if it's about exploration – everyone has a spiritual element.   (Mentor E)

Holding the line in discussions, a readiness to be genuine and personal and tenacity in the face of what might become personalised anti-RE hostility were other qualities mentors identified as crucial in mentoring discipline.

In the case of both resources and workload, there is a tendency for some mentors to present the worst-case scenario for students in the belief that this will prepare them for anything. There are sufficient data from other mentors to suggest that, given the limitations of the RE situation, it is possible to be creative in the mentoring of these important areas. Some mentors have sessions on creating your own resources and they encourage students to use all the available sources, such as RE centres, the Schools Library Service, the local faith communities and the university. Mentoring workload is not a baptism of fire into an impossible marking load with no time to prepare, let alone reflect. Effective mentors give students strategies for coping but also ensure that there is sufficient time for planning and reflection in a training context.

We would conclude our description of the mentoring process by saying that what we have judged to be good practice are those skills and strategies which seem to be meeting the mentoring needs of the students which we identified earlier in this chapter. Where mentors are not clear about the students' mentoring needs, and where they are not adequately equipped with the necessary mentoring skills, RE mentoring will be less than effective in contributing to the much-needed expansion of the RE teaching force.

On the basis of this assessment, we would argue for an increase in mentor training which might use as an objective starting point the nine recommendations for good practice identified in our research:

1 Establish a training as opposed to a supervisory relationship with students.

2 Encourage students to read up, but mentor subject knowledge in relation to lesson aims and methodology.

3 Discourage indifference and confessionalism as a result of the mentor having worked through the relationship between their own motivations and classroom practice.

4 Demonstrate how the agreed syllabus, the school's scheme of work and lesson plans relate to each other.

5 Enable students to employ different teaching methods to achieve subject aims.

6 Introduce students to differentiation and assessment through *process* and *outcome*.

7 Encourage good discipline through subject ethos.

8 Encourage students to be creative about resourcing.

9 Ensure students have a balanced school experience of RE pressures and time to plan and reflect.

How the training partnership affects RE mentoring

As mentors are partners, it seems inevitable that the structure and the expectations within the training partnership will affect the quality of mentoring, and therefore the extent to which the needs of RE students will be met. Our data suggest that the partnership has a bearing on the quality of RE mentoring in five areas of concern.

The first area is that of responsibility for subject knowledge. PGCE course leaders are committed to recruiting students who have the right motivations, but they are anxious about subject knowledge in the light of the widening intake, and the Circular 4/98 requirement (DfEE, 1998) that PGCE students have 'knowledge, concepts and skills in their specialist subject at a standard equivalent to degree level'. Course leaders do not see themselves as having either the time or the expertise to provide adequate subject knowledge. In their turn mentors are uncertain about who is responsible for subject knowledge. Mentor I demonstrates the sort of confusion to which this uncertainty gives rise:

> I think it is beyond my job to have to teach them the subject matter before they teach the class. I wouldn't want anyone who has done sociology – it's an entirely different appproach.

The perception here is that, if mentors are expected to deal with subject knowledge as well as methodology, they do not wish to be given a non-specialist. However, it seems that the main task for RE mentors is to turn the motivations and intellectual orientations of the likes of sociologists into classroom competences; mentors will not be confident about taking on this task unless subject knowledge responsibility is clarified by the partnership. Clarification will also reassure those mentors who see neither the university nor the school as providing adequate subject knowledge and who realistically judge subject competence according to whether the student has *appropriate* knowledge for the lesson.

We would recommend that, because the right intellectual orientation and enthusiasm figure more largely in student selection than subject knowledge, subject knowledge should be the responsibility of the students if they wish to implement their motivations. Neither the university nor the school are ultimately responsible but both can support the student through lectures, guided reading and distance learning.

Another difficult area is the matching of theory to practice, especially on serial placements. As a result of such a varied intake of students there is pressure to cover a certain amount of theory before students are too far into their first school experience. This puts pressure on mentors in two ways: theory often gets in the way of dealing directly with experiences; and second, mentors may find it difficult to handle the dual role of the trainees as students and professionals, sometimes treating them as less than colleagues and without due attention to their motivations. Course leaders see some of these tensions in school giving rise to an uneven matching of theory and practice for which they feel they need to compensate. For example, in one-person departments there is often neither the time nor the variety of teaching styles to enable a lot of matching of theory and practice. There is also the need to go beyond the often misleading layer of cynicism about RE within the school culture.

The difficulty of trying to integrate theory and practice across uneven school experiences may be overcome if more theory were to arise out of the students' experience in school. To this end students should be trained by the university to approach their mentor in the right way, asking appropriate questions, in order to draw out the mentor's understanding of the relationship between theory and practice. In their turn, mentors should be trained in how to elicit pertinent questions from students about their classroom experience.

The matching of student and mentor seems particularly important in RE because of the variations in students' academic background, personal motivations and faith commitments. Failure to take account of these factors can lead to inconsistent student performance:

> I have been struck by the way different students get on in different schools. Student J was thought to be outstanding by her first mentor, but went on to a school where she found the mentor totally unwilling to help her, and if she hadn't had the first good experience, she would have struggled. (Course Leader E)

What seems to lie behind such inconsistencies is the fact that RE means different things to different people. Teachers tend to create their own RE in a way that does not happen in other subjects. This means that mentors need to be sensitive to individual students' motivations, but it should not mean that student X can only work with mentor Y: there has to be coherence in RE mentoring across schools if students are to develop a professional approach. A similar balance needs to be struck in the placement of students who are committed to a faith and those in danger of confessionalism.

Matching does enhance RE mentoring but it would be less of a problem for course leaders if mentors became increasingly skilful at mentoring students from diverse backgrounds, giving them opportunities to experiment without being afraid that their own good work in RE would be undermined.

A fourth area of concern is the lack of progression in mentoring in RE within the partnership arrangement:

> Some students have a first placement in a school with discrete RE and then move on to one with something much less. It would be nice if they all built up but it doesn't happen like that at all. When you talk to students they usually have a favourite and tend to polarise their experiences. (Course Leader E)

A more coherent, progressive mentoring might be achieved if positive, diagnostic consultation took place between mentors. This would go beyond the limitations of report writing and give the next mentor a real feel for the professional needs of the student, enabling them to address these, albeit in a very different RE context.

The final area of concern is the effect of the partnership on the confidence of RE mentors. The unevenness of RE in existing partnership schools and the isolation of many lone RE heads of department makes for a reluctance to participate if teaching is to be scrutinised by both the university and other schools:

> I feel apprehensive about the role because you wonder if you are going to deliver what the university wants. (New Mentor C)

Our research suggests that there is a correlation between confidence in professional expertise and a desire to take on RE mentoring. Those who are most confident in their mentoring are usually communicating and sharing their understanding of the subject with other professionals. RE would certainly benefit from mentor training becoming part of professional development in school, facilitated by the professional tutor. This would mean that the large number of fairly isolated RE specialists might then be encouraged to become mentors and, through the training, become more confident practitioners, knowing that what they are doing is valued by the school. School-based mentor training would be supported by HE tutors who are not comfortable with the 'big brother' role but would rather disseminate good mentoring practice.

Conclusion

In identifying the mentoring needs of RE PGCE students and then assessing how well these needs are met, we found that where mentors are clear about the mentoring needs and where they are adequately equipped with the necessary mentoring skills, RE mentoring can succeed in turning a diverse intake of students into competent classroom practitioners. However, we also found that the extent to which the RE mentoring needs are met can be influenced by the structure and expectations within the training partnership.

These findings have led us to make the following recommendations:

- Develop mentor training which identifies the mentoring needs of RE students.
- Develop training materials based on observed principles of good practice.
- Establish that the student is ultimately responsible for his/her subject knowledge.

- Tutors and mentors should devise ways to support students in this.
- Students and mentors should be trained to get the best out of each other so that theory and practice are more integrated.
- Matching students with mentors is important but mentors should become skilful in mentoring students from different backgrounds.
- Coherent, progressive mentoring might be achieved within partnerships if positive, diagnostic consultation took place between mentors.
- Mentor training should become part of professional development within schools.
- Higher education institutes should support school-based mentor training by disseminating good practice, for example, through mentor panels.
- A wider forum might be set up which disseminates good practice across partnerships.

There is concern in the RE world that, having finally persuaded the Technical Training Agency (TTA) to recognise RE as a shortage subject, the increased recruitment from such diverse backgrounds will result in RE initial teacher education being found wanting, according to the criteria of Circular 4/98.

It is our conviction that, in this scenario, the relatively recent role of the mentor can come into its own and develop a professional expertise which will ensure the motivations of a diverse intake of students can be turned into excellent classroom competences.

For this to happen, mentors need to be equal, proactive partners in the training process; after all, we have moved on from the old PGCE arrangements in which the university provided the programme of study, and then students came into school to practise what they had learnt.

There is sufficient evidence in our research to suggest that many RE mentors are engaging in a training, as opposed to a supervisory, role. However, much more needs to be done to help mentors identify the training needs of the expanding RE intake and provide them with the skills to address these. Not least in RE is the need to give the large number of isolated specialists the confidence to become mentors, for the mutual benefit of the students and themselves.

We conclude that there are strong grounds for being optimistic about the developing pattern of recruitment and mentoring of RE students, and hope that our recommendations can contribute to further developments which will help justify our optimism.

References

Department for Education and Employment (DfEE) (1998) *Teaching: High Status, High Standards*, Circular 4/98. London: DfEE.

Gates, B. (1993) *Time for Religious Education and Teachers to Match: A Digest of Underprovision*. Report prepared for the Religious Education Council of England and Wales. Lancaster: RE-ME Enquiry Service.

Maykut, P. and Morehouse, R. (1994) *Beginning Qualitative Research: A Philosophical and Practical Guide*. London: Falmer Press.

Mead, N. (1996) Mentoring religious education teaching in secondary schools. Unpublished research paper. Oxford: Farmington Institute.

Collective Worship in a Predominantly Muslim LEA Upper School

R. THOMPSON

It is now accepted that schools are involved in the moral and spiritual development of their pupils, whether they like it or not. Since the Education Reform Act of 1988, the process has become much more explicit . . . more explicit but not more clear. The legislation and its confusion reflect a society undergoing massive changes. At one level there was an attempt to reinforce the dominant white, Anglo-Saxon faith and culture – a push towards 'integration'. Intensive lobbying by those working for a pluralist society had, however, some effect. The result is that, to the chagrin of the traditionalists, there has been some scope for manoeuvre. All-white schools from Truro to Tynemouth have had to bring back assemblies with a 'broadly' Christian ethos. It is however our inner city multiethnic schools which have addressed the real challenge; they have had to fulfil the requirements of the Act in its integrationist aims and yet try to affirm the faith and culture of their own pupils.

Grange Upper School in Bradford has tried to do just this. I, as headteacher, drawing from my personal experience a particular attitude to differences, have used the requirements of collective worship to develop a model which is both 'inclusive' or integrationist and 'exclusive' in so far as it affirms the uniqueness and distinctive strengths of my pupils.

Grange School is a mixed comprehensive upper school of over 1000 students from 13 to 19 years. There is a sixth form of over 250 students who follow a mixture of A level, GNVQ and BTEC courses. The intake of the school is multicultural with 80 per cent of the students from non-white, mainly Asian backgrounds. These are predominantly the children of Muslim Pakistani families, although there is a group of about ten Gujerati Hindu youngsters and a growing number (currently about 50) of Bengali-speaking Bangladeshi

students. Most of our pupils are, therefore, bilingual at least, which the school considers a definite asset. The school has a very positive and practical policy of valuing achievement and stressing the uniqueness of each person, a policy which is integrated into all aspects of the life and work of the school. However, many of our pupils approach education from a position of social and economic disadvantage. The public perception of the school arises from this fact. Grange, as recently as the early 1990s, was perceived as having many pupils with low self- and school-esteem, lack of confidence, low expectations and a tendency to underachieve.

There is now within the school, however, a mood of achievement and improvement. It is as if we have achieved a 'critical mass' of pupils who have internalised the priorities of high achievement, good behaviour and confidence, and these now lift the expectations of everyone else. The major elements of this change of culture have been:

1 our ethos and practice of valuing all our pupils in their faith and culture, underpinned by our motto 'Achieving Together';
2 all staff being involved in the development of language skills as the key to empowerment;
3 the development of targeting in all years, underpinned by the recording of data which demonstrate progress;
4 the establishment of the homework diary and the student planner;
5 our 'Charter for Success' which makes explicit the roles of pupils, teachers and parents.

These initiatives are held together by greater staff consistency and commitment on the fulfilment of development plan priorities.

The school is situated just within the boundary of the 'white highlands' of Bradford but does not attract youngsters from this area. They tend to travel to predominantly white schools. As the proportion of Pakistani pupils from the inner-city wards has increased, progressively we have received smaller white, Hindu and Sikh intakes. The white population has been holding steady for the last few years. Regrettably even some ethnic minority parents and children, particularly those who are upwardly mobile, perceive Grange as 'having too many Asians' and seek white or more mixed schools, however confidently we project a culture of improvement.

Our OFSTED report has acknowledged our efforts. GCSE results represent 'a significant improvement', A levels 'a notable improvement'. Expectations are positive: 'Individual and group targeting works well to persuade pupils to aim high and achieve their best'. Attitudes are positive: 'Pupils generally have a positive attitude, are eager to learn and make progress.' The school works well with parents: 'Care is taken to nurture strong links with the families of pupils and the community served by the school.' The final conclusion of the inspectors was: 'Overall the school makes a positive contribution to the spiritual, moral, social and cultural development of all pupils.'

Our task is clear. It is to empower all our pupils by raising their levels of achievement and self-esteem. We shall thereby demonstrate that young people of minority cultures (including white working class) can maintain their cultural integrity and become full and active members of society. Grange has the potential to be a model for 'Achieving Together', a symbol of the opportunity we have in Bradford of valuing and combining the strengths of different cultures.

An obvious tension

How then did we tackle the requirements of the 1988 Education Reform Act for collective worship and RE? There was an obvious tension. Most of Grange pupils would not pass 'Tebbit's cricket test'. Their identity, their self-concept and source of self-esteem is inextricably bound up with their parents' culture and faith. And yet, they also wish to be fully active citizens of the UK, playing a full part in its educational and economic life.

The Act requires all registered pupils to take part in daily collective worship, the character of which must be, wholly or mainly, broadly Christian. A

school may however seek a 'determination' from the local SACRE (Standing Advisory Conference on Religious Education). Fortunately, we in Bradford have an Interfaith Education Centre which has been able to guide us through the intricacies. I referred to the Interfaith guidelines:

> Schools serving multi-faith areas should be, and should be seen by parents to be, sensitive to the presence of pupils from a variety of cultural and religious backgrounds when they plan the content of collective worship.
>
> The school can apply to the Bradford SACRE for a determination which alters the requirements governing the character of collective worship. The duty to provide daily worship remains. In deciding whether to apply to SACRE the governing body may wish to seek the views of parents. It is for the Headteacher to decide what form worship will take following the granting of a determination by SACRE. Either the acts of daily worship will simply not be required to be broadly Christian in character – and so can reflect the background of pupils better, or the school can provide worship which may be distinctive of a particular faith or religion.   (Interfaith Education Centre, 1996, para. 4)

Exclusive and inclusive

I saw the way forward for Grange as developing two apparently contradictory paths: one 'exclusive', and one 'inclusive'. On one side, I wished to develop the confidence of our youngsters by affirming their faith and cultural identity. On the other, I wanted to use every device possible to move them into mainstream society. The energies of my staff and myself were focused obsessively on our HAPTAM policy (Helping All Pupils To Achieve More), our Quality of Teaching and Learning Priority, our work experience programme, industry links, 'Charter for Success', Parent Volunteers Scheme and our *Parents Curriculum Guide*.

In collective worship, I followed the same dual approach. The exclusive path saw Grange applying for and receiving a determination from Bradford SACRE in 1989. We began separate weekly meetings for Christians, Muslim girls, Muslim boys, Sikhs and Hindus (numbers approximately 25, 150, 150, 2 and 5 respectively). The actual arrangements were an example of trial and error. I presented to staff and governors the basic principles and eight alternative plans.

Principles

1 It is worthwhile trying to develop the spiritual awareness of our pupils.
2 It is important to validate many of our pupils' religious experience. By avoiding the spiritual, we deny it.
3 Assembling pupils of different or no faiths regularly is important for the ethos of the school and for personal development.
4 We must avoid a mechanical, insensitive approach to worship. What we do must be done with integrity, and must be a quality experience.
5 We must find a way which shows we are moving towards implementation of the Act.
6 The key factor is staff participation

The widest possible set of options was canvassed (Appendix A) and one particular set adopted. The staff chose the simplest option of the post-morning registration single-faith meeting once a week (Plan G). The requirements of registration and collective worship are fulfilled. It has become a well-established part of school life. The meetings' leaders are either school staff or staff of the Interfaith Centre. They all meet twice termly across the faiths to share experiences and to make proposals for future improvements. There are occasional cross-references made; for example, Lent and Ramadhan; stories of respect for other faiths. The following is a list of themes covered in the Muslim boys' Meeting. (I now avoid the use of the word 'worship'. A school 'Meeting' is *sui generis* and should not be associated with particular forms of worship).

Topics for Muslim single-faith Meetings

- What is Islam?
- The meaning of the first declaration of faith
- Tawheed – oneness with God
- Risalah – a means of communication from God to man
- Akhirah – life after death
- Isman – its characteristics
- Ihsan – its characteristics
- The jinn
- The Qur'án – its importance
- The revelation of the Qur'án
- Manners and morals
- The significance of prayer
- Prophet Moses (pbuh [peace be upon him]) and his life

- Life of prophet Abraham (pbuh)
- Ramadhan – its benefits
- Ramadhan – its importance
- Importance of last ten days in Ramadhan
- Battle of Badr
- The night of prayer
- Significance of Eid
- Examples from life of Muhammad (pbuh)
- Importance of the Qur'án – its implications in everyday life

Our aims are detailed as follows:

- to be interesting;
- to be informative;
- to involve all pupils;
- we want the students to want to attend the meetings;
- we want to give a positive image to belief in faith;
- we want to give respect and value to all the faiths;
- we want to give equality of esteem to each faith;
- we want to improve the religious knowledge base of the students who attend the meetings;
- we want the students to be active participants in their own spiritual journey.

The faith meetings take place from 8.50 a.m. to 9.03 a.m. and are arranged as follows:

Monday	Years 9 and 11	Muslim girls in the hall
	All years	Hindus in the head's room
Wednesday	Years 9 and 11	Muslim boys in the hall
Thursday	Years 10 and 12/13	Muslim girls in the hall
Friday	Years 10 and 12/13	Muslim boys in the hall
	All years	Christians in the music room

In addition, for Muslims there are additional opportunities: Zohar Namaz (midday prayer) is held during the three staggered lunchtimes; ablution facilities are made available. During Ramadhan, the sports hall is used and up to 200 attend each day, with an equal number of boys and girls in different venues.

A particular problem arises with Juma (Friday) prayers. Devout Muslim boys often request permission to go to the mosque for Juma prayers on Friday during lessons, but I refuse. I maintain that it is my responsibility to ensure 100 per cent attendance to lessons and that Islam must never be seen to be an obstacle to education. A letter is sent to parents; this usually suffices.

The inclusive approach is centred on our daily silence which was established in September 1993.

Every morning at the end of tutor groups/single-faith meetings the whole school observes a silence of two minutes. I introduced the idea to our three separate constituencies of pupils, staff and governors in the spring of 1993. I outlined the three benefits of discipline, inner strength and unity. I had few qualms over the issue of discipline. The Muslim pupils each year in Ramadhan demonstrate ample resources of self-discipline. They rise early, say their prayers, attend to devotional reading, come to school without breakfast then maintain their cheerfulness throughout their fast. Applying the principle of fasting to our daily silence would be merely building on a strength. I presented the silence as access to inner strength, again without difficulty. Our Muslim pupils adhere to their faith – a source of personal strength. Finally, I was able to promote our daily silence as a unifying factor between the world's religions in so far as they all respect the practice of silent prayer. Pupils and governors supported the venture without any hesitation. There were one or two quizzical eyebrows raised by staff when they were reminded that the silence had to be complete. Staff who were not tutors and who were likely to be brewing up an early morning cup of tea had to be in the school corridors being seen to observe the silence like everyone else.

A 'Thought for the Week' was also introduced and posted at the front of the school. Tutors and pupils are encouraged to bring in their own and to share them with the rest of us.

I need not have worried. The Grange silence is now well established. Faith meetings, year assemblies and tutor periods end with us all achieving stillness together.

To what extent do we succeed in, on the one hand, affirming the religious and cultural identity of our pupils and, on the other, preparing them to be fully active members in mainstream society? Conventional wisdom would have us play down the former. One of Her Majesty's Inspectors (HMI) in my early days of headship advised me 'not to pander to the minority communities': schools should offer a standard English product. The customer seems to prefer to follow the dictates of conventional wisdom. There is no lack of upwardly mobile Asian parents seeking admission to schools like the City Technical College (CTC) and Bradford Grammar School, schools which appear to pay little attention to the religious and cultural needs of ethnic minority youngsters.

Conventional wisdom, however, will not help us on the way to a pluralistic society. We are an island race with a recent history of Empire. All differences look very easily like threats. They appear to question our way of doing things. Our immigration policy seems to be based on 'otherness' being a problem, whereas, for instance, in the United States it is a means of attracting special talent. My own personal experience tells me that the differences are in fact enrichments. My approach to differences goes back to the differences in culture between my father, a gruff Yorkshireman, and my wife, who originates from the South of France, and centres on how we touch and even hug each other.

It is perhaps because the matter is so personal that it provides the drive for my work in Bradford. It is, I believe, worth relating briefly. I was brought up to believe that men do not show emotions. On my last evening at home before I left for university and London, my father went off to bed with the advice: 'Take care of thisen, lad.' No contact. No hug. I didn't expect either. Two years later, when my then fiancée introduced me to my future family-in-law, I received the French treatment. I was held and kissed by every member of the family, from grandfather to youngest brother. Now thirty years later, I maintain that the incorporation of this French lesson into my life has enriched and enlarged it.

In conclusion, I maintain that the apparent contradictions of the Grange 'exclusive' and 'inclusive' policies in collective worship will help determine, in a small but significant way, our local and even national approach to being a pluralistic society.

We must overcome our insular and superior tendencies, arising from our geographical position and our history of Empire, which make us perceive differences as threats. Instead, we must accept that there are different ways of living and of worshipping, and that these differences can be strengths. By combining the strengths from our diverse communities, we can build a vibrant, dynamic society.

Appendix

Plan A: the 'added-on' approach

Keep morning tutor groups and assemblies. Friday – revert to tutor groups (6th Form Assembly). Shorten the two afternoon lessons to 60 minutes. Faith groups meet 2.50 p.m.–3.10 p.m.

Head asks SACRE to lift requirements for Muslims, Sikhs and Hindus. Five faith groups using sports hall. Faith groups conclude at 3.10 p.m. Faith adherents return to tutor base for registration. Staff volunteers run faith groups (and outsiders brought in).

Plan B: 'start the day' approach

Faith groups begin at 8.45 a.m., go to tutor groups for 9.00 a.m. registrations. Main tutor period and assemblies 1.00 p.m. to 1.15 p.m. Shorten afternoon lessons to 65 minutes. Latecomers to faith groups go to tutor groups. Tutor informs parents.

Plan C: 'faith groups minus one house' approach

Present system, but faith adherents miss four morning tutor periods. One house assembly takes precedence.

Plan D: 'Multifaith'

House assemblies each day, theme, for example, of 'forgiveness', with readings from major religions. Content issued from central group.

Plan E: theme a week approach

After application to SACRE is accepted, keep present tutorial/form group arrangements. Theme of week has five faith examples. Tutor has reading session in each tutorial for 5 minutes. Principles 4 and 6 out of the window.

Plan F: preregistration approach

Worship groups begin promptly at start of school – 10 minutes and the normal day begins. (Remove 5 minutes from last two lessons.) The day would be as follows:

08.45–08.55 a.m. Faith groups

08.45–09.15 a.m. Tutor groups
08.55–09.15 a.m. Assemblies as now
09.15–10.25 a.m. 1st period
10.25–10.45 a.m. Break
10.45–11.55 a.m. 2nd period
12.55–02.00 p.m. 3rd period
02.05–03.10 p.m. 4th period
03.10–03.15 p.m. Registration

Plan G: post-registration approach

All pupils register in tutor groups at 8.45 a.m. At 8.50 a.m. worshippers go to single-faith groups. Non-worshippers have to opt out. With a meeting hall of 200 and a school population of over 1000, we timetable two year groups at a time of single-sex groups to meet once a week.

Plan H: evolutionary

During summer term, a steering group plans one theme per week and a rota of group leaders. Faith groups meet on Mondays, focus on the weekly theme from their own sources. Coordinator collates all material and issues to year heads, who deliver one multifaith assembly each, treating the theme using the four faith examples. Announcements come at the end. Pupils see what is common in major religions. If there are prayers, they will be prefaced by 'this is a Christian prayer on'. On the remaining three days, tutors take up the theme for part of the tutor period.

A pupil who does not opt out would therefore experience one faith group, three multifaith tutor periods and one multifaith assembly. The school would request the requirements for 'broadly Christian' collective worship to be lifted for all Muslims, Hindus and Sikhs on one day per week.

Reference

Interfaith Education Centre (1996) *Meeting the Spiritual and Moral, Social and Cultural Needs of all Pupils: Parental Rights in Relation to Collective Worship, Religious Education and Related Matters*. Bradford: Yorks.: Interfaith Education Centre.

21 Approaches to Collective Worship in Multifaith Schools

JEANNETTE GILL

The provision of daily acts of collective worship in all maintained schools is probably one of the most controversial elements of the curriculum at the present time. The debate which has surrounded it since the publication of the Education Reform Act of 1988 is not new, however, and during most of the 50 years since collective worship in schools was first made a legal requirement in the Education Act of 1944 there has been a continuing spiral of argument and counterargument. Initially, the debate focused on the validity of compulsory worship in the curriculum of a liberal education and this remains a central issue. However, although this question continues to lie at the heart of the debate, as a consequence of the requirements of the Reform Act it has, during the last decade, been largely submerged in the public realm by arguments of a more practical nature concerned with the type of worship which might be considered appropriate in the schools of a democratic society whose government wishes to maintain its traditional Christian heritage whilst necessarily recognising the pluralist nature of its population. To this circumstance can be added the recent heightening of demands for the provision of stronger moral and values education in schools. These calls have made frequent reference to the potential contribution of collective worship to this dimension of pupil development (Shephard, 1996; Redwood, 1996), and have resulted in renewed demands both for a reinforcement of its provision and for a reduction in its frequency.

To detail here all of the arguments which surround the question of worship in schools and its relationship to values education would be too lengthy. However, they include claims that Britain is a Christian country whose children must be educated in its traditional faith. Closely related to this view is the belief that religion provides an essential moral authority and must therefore be taught to the young. Others argue that the cultural values of Britain are embedded in its historical Christian tradition and it is these which educators have a responsibility to transmit to future generations. At this point, it is possible to identify a divergence of intention behind these positions. For some, the purpose of collective worship is the broad transmission of shared moral and cultural values; for others its function is to inculcate a moral code within a framework of divine authority. A contrasting view, however, perceives its prime focus to be the encouragement of the worship of God:

> A celebration of shared values may be a worthwhile endeavour. But it is a world away from the worship of Almighty God and from sharing the spiritual experience of prayer and praise. That is the heart of the matter. (Cox, in *Hansard*, House of Lords, 1988, vol. 496, col. 1345)

Opponents of collective worship, however, argue that Britain is no longer Christian in its practice but can be described more accurately as secular and pluralist. Morality is not dependent on religion, and worship is a private and personal matter which is the responsibility of the family and faith community. Compulsory worship, therefore, is in clear contradiction to the concepts implicit in the liberal goal of rational autonomy and is contrary to the nature of education itself.

Guidance to schools

At this point it is important to recognise that any attempt to steer a path through the intricacies of the debate which surrounds the provision of worship must take into account the complexity of the human environments in which schools find themselves. The application of the arguments to practice is met by a range of responses from schools which reflect the distinctive nature of each situation. Any attempt, therefore, to impose uniformity of practice without reference to the school context may be self-defeating. However, the guidance provided in Circular 1/94 (DfE, 1994) re-emphasises the government's concern that insufficient attention is given to the spiritual, moral and social aspects of pupil development. Consequently, the primary aim of collective worship is identified as, 'The opportunity for pupils to worship God' (para. 50).

Whilst noting that worship in schools is necessarily different from that of a body of believers, the Circular states that the term should be used in its ordinary meaning and 'should be concerned with reverence or veneration paid to a divine being or power' (para. 57). This is broadly echoed in the handbook of *Guidance on the Inspection of Secondary Schools* (OFSTED, 1995), which states: 'worship is generally understood to imply the recognition of a supreme being. It should be clear that the words used and/or the activities observed in worship recognise the existence of a deity' (ibid., p. 93). Passive attendance therefore will not meet the declared aims, and the act of worship 'should be capable of eliciting a response from pupils, even though on a particular occasion some of the pupils may not feel able actively to identify with the act of worship' (para. 59). Such definitive guidance is found by many schools to be in contradiction not only to the needs of pupils and the communities they represent, but also to the subsequent aims identified in the Circular which are broadly supported by schools:

> to consider spiritual and moral issues and to explore their own beliefs; to encourage participation and response; . . . to develop community spirit, promote a common ethos and shared values, and reinforce positive attitudes. (Ibid., para. 50)

Inevitably, the extent to which individual schools are able to meet the requirements for worship is dependent on a variety of factors. These include the personal philosophy and influence of the headteacher and staff and, importantly, pupil interest and community support. Difficulties are experienced by all types of school throughout the country but the situation in multicultural schools poses specific problems, and it is to these that I shall now turn.

The provision of worship in multifaith schools

As might be expected, there exists no clear agreement on an appropriate form of worship for schools whose pupils include representatives from non-Christian traditions. Here, a distinction can be observed between schools where such pupils are in a small minority and those where the majority of pupils belong to other faith traditions. Even this must be recognised as a simplified classification: there are schools where the percentage of ethnic minority pupils is not large but where in their religious commitment they nevertheless outnumber the pupils in the school who are Christian in their practice rather than by historic tradition. In addition, there are schools which are multicultural in the sense of containing pupils from several cultures but which are monofaith schools (for example, denominational schools whose pupils include members of that tradition from around the world). I do not intend in this chapter to make reference to practice in schools in the latter category, however.

In schools where pupils from non-Christian families are few in number, little attention appears to be paid to their presence. If parents have not availed themselves of the right of withdrawal, the assumption is made that their children's attendance at collective worship is acceptable to them. However, parental reluctance to take advantage of the law is often based on a strong desire for their children to be part of the school community rather than an expression of support for shared worship. Although withdrawal is described as a commonsense solution (Stewart, *Hansard*, House of Lords, 1988 vol. 498, col. 651; Redwood, 1996), moderate groups of Muslims, for example, fear the further marginalisation of their children through this practice (Halstead, 1992) and argue that such an approach would also be contrary to the educational goal of mutual understanding and cooperation (O'Connor, 1989; Thornley, 1989; Mabud, 1992). Consequently, these pupils may find themselves in situations which are less than sensitive to their presence and needs (Sonyel, 1988; Sarwar, 1988); and what many Muslims would prefer is a form of gathering which is modified to take into account the needs of their children so that they are not placed in situations where they are required to act in a manner which is in opposition to the practice of the family and faith community. The provision of facilities for Islamic forms of worship would also be welcomed (Mabud, 1992) and this is a growing practice in some areas.

Although an exemption from the requirement for broadly Christian worship can be obtained, multifaith schools where the majority of pupils belong to other religious traditions are nevertheless required to provide a form of worship which is appropriate for their pupils. In the current debate it is possible to identify a range of possible alternatives. Multifaith, broadly spiritual, non-religious, and parallel faith assemblies are all possible approaches. One further alternative, that of mono-faith worship in schools where a large percentage of pupils belongs to one tradition, such as Islam, appears to be a theoretical notion only. At least in the sample of schools which I visited, the presence of even a small minority of pupils from other traditions allied to the pluralist nature of the surrounding environment precludes this approach. In practice, schools adopt a system which they perceive best serves their principal aims and the social needs of their pupils, who are usually drawn from three or more religious traditions. This does not result, however, in the adoption of the same approach.

Approaches to worship: the arguments

Multifaith worship

Because of the diverse nature of their pupil populations, the majority of multicultural schools choose to adopt a form of worship which they describe as multifaith. Supporters of this policy claim that it enables pupils to share common understandings and values and that there is no other acceptable approach (Hull, 1990). However, strong opposition continues to be directed at this form as a trivialisation of worship. In the House of Lords, it was claimed that multifaith approaches constitute a 'meaningless contrivance' (Thorneycroft, *Hansard*, House of Lords, 1988, vol. 496, col. 1350), that they are 'dangerous' (Jakobovits, ibid., col. 419) and destructive of 'the purity of worship' (Cox, ibid., vol. 498, col. 642). Since worship can only be directed at one object, a multifaith approach cannot be conducted by believers without compromising their integrity. Any such arrangement must necessarily result in 'a bland, flavourless experience which

skirts the fundamentals of the faith' (Walker, 1990, p. 36). On the other hand, it is argued that where a form of worship can be produced which is based on interfaith dialogue between the school and local groups, this might produce an act which is more accessible and meaningful to pupils from different backgrounds (Sonyel, 1988) and might offer opportunities for a 'rich comprehensiveness' (Adie, 1990, p. 522).

Parallel monofaith worship

In the minority of schools where the multifaith approach is rejected, the main alternative in mixed communities seems to be the adoption of a policy which incorporates a number of parallel acts of worship, often known as faith assemblies. Objectors argue that this would be divisive for the school and for the local community (Horne, 1990; Goodman, *Hansard*, House of Lords, 1988, vol. 496, col. 430), and might add to racial tension. There is a fear that such an arrangement might lead to inappropriate and restrictive instruction by community leaders (Cole, 1990), and might also include forms of unrecognisable denominational bias (Horne, 1990). Furthermore, such a practice would undermine the development of an integrated and collaborative approach to living in community and is in opposition to schools' goals of mutual understanding and co-operation (Hull, 1988). However, the argument of divisiveness overlooks the fact that pupils are in fact frequently separated for a variety of purposes, and Gibbons (1989) and Chadwick (1994) remind us of precedents for parallel forms of worship found in the arrangements made in joint RC/Anglican schools. Even in the House of Lords' debates, it was argued that separate faith assemblies may have a contribution to make to the life of the school:

> Differences of worship within a community need not divide a community: but they can do so, if, on the one hand, they are over-emphasised or, on the other hand, suppressed or ignored. Sometimes the maintenance of harmony within a multi-faith school will be best achieved by expression of the differences that exist through the provision of different forms of worship. (Bishop of London, *Hansard*, House of Lords, 1988, vol. 499, col. 432)

Broadly spiritual assemblies

In the search for meaningful acts of worship in which all pupils can participate, it is suggested that an emphasis on the spiritual dimension, which might also incorporate a religious element if appropriate, could provide a valuable approach. The nature of spirituality is not readily accessible to definition, however. For some, it refers to an inner subjectivity, while for others it is related to a sensitivity to aesthetic experience or to relationships and responsibility within community. Hull (1995) argues that collective worship should be replaced by 'acts of collective spirituality', emphasising 'community through participation in the lives of others ... in solidarity with others' (ibid., pp. 131–2). This approach could explore the common ground between pupils, drawing attention to the similarities which exist and minimising differences (Alves, 1989; Bishop of London, *Hansard*, House of Lords, 1988, vol. 499, cols 431–2; Halstead, 1992; Mabud, 1992). Some groups would, however, criticise this approach as a reduction and devaluation of faith and worship. Although it appears to win support from widely differing groups (ACT, 1994; BHA, 1990), for its success this approach depends heavily on the quality, experience and interest of its leaders if compulsory acts of collective spirituality are not to become little more than moral exhortation. Nevertheless, where schools choose to pursue this approach and are able to concentrate on quality rather than quantity, it is a route which an increasing number of schools may feel happy to adopt.

Non-religious or secular assemblies

The concept of a non-religious assembly is one which is seldom articulated at any length but is an approach which is common practice, especially in secondary schools. Criticism of the secularisation and politicisation of worship continues to be levied at schools (Cox, *Hansard*, House of Lords, 1988, vol. 496, col. 1345), although the inclusion of certain types of material should not be taken to indicate an absence of the common features of worship. However, some schools find themselves in a situation where a secular assembly seems to be the only approach which they can adopt under the pressures of time, space, uninterested pupils and unwilling teachers, many of whom find the government's requirements for school worship unacceptable (NAHT, 1994). The opportunity which assembly provides for the affirmation and encouragement of shared values continues to be welcomed by schools, however, and many groups who are opposed to collective worship are anxious to retain this element of the curriculum (Cole, 1990; ATL, 1995). Non-religious assemblies may vary from 'broadly spiritual' acts only in their emphasis, and most schools combine elements from more than one approach.

Approaches to worship: the school context

My current research into the nature of school worship provides further insights into the arguments set out above, and helps to identify the difficulties and achievements which are experienced as schools attempt to conform to the legislation. The discussion which follows is based mainly on interviews with teachers and observations of assemblies in five secondary and six primary schools in a multicultural city situated in the Midlands. In what follows, I wish to concentrate on the major issues which have been identified in these interviews and which can be seen to reflect certain features of the arguments which I have discussed above. In particular, I should like to examine (a) teachers' responses to the legal requirement to provide school worship; (b) the arguments relating to the selection of multifaith assemblies; and (c) the arguments surrounding the selection of parallel acts of worship. Inevitably, these arguments reflect schools' perceptions of the aims and function of assemblies and the practical difficulties which are experienced in their attempts to comply with the legal demands.

In schools where a majority of the pupils belong to non-Christian religious traditions it is clear from teachers' responses that at least some of the major issues which are inherent in the wider debate have continuing relevance and application. These are: (a) should schools provide opportunities for worship? and (b) if so, what form of worship is appropriate in particular circumstances? Answers to the latter question appear to be dependent on each school's response to two further questions: (c) which approach to the legal requirements for collective worship will best meet the school's educational aims with respect to the encouragement of tolerance, cohesion and community? and (d) given the practical limitations of time, space and leadership, is compliance with the legislation possible?

As we shall see, the motivating factor which influences the sample schools in their organisation of assembly is the social well-being and unity of their pupils and a recognition of the pluralist nature of society. All of them have religiously diverse pupil populations, and although different groups are in the majority in particular areas, there is a clear awareness of the need to encourage cohesion and tolerance. They contain pupils from the Muslim, Sikh, Hindu, Christian, Rastafarian, Jain, Bahai and Buddhist faith traditions. Their families come from Asia, East Africa, Bosnia and Eastern Europe, the West Indies and South America, as well as from the UK. Their languages include Gujerati, Panjabi, Bengali, Cantonese, Hindi, Urdu, Greek, Italian, Spanish, Turkish, Swahili and Creole. Under these circumstances, one of the main aims of schools is to develop a sense of corporate identity, and gathering the pupils together is the most favoured approach for the pursuit of this goal. Where there is appropriate accommodation, whole-school assemblies are the preferred mode, though these are usually modified during the weekly pattern to take cognisance of pupils' age and experience. Thus primary schools adopt a sequence which includes separate assemblies for infant and junior children on one or two days each week, in addition to joint sessions which continue to be the most common approach. None of the secondary schools which I visited has sufficient space to assemble the entire school, even where the building is new, except perhaps for an inappropriate sports hall where pupils are required to sit on the floor in an environment which is not conducive to worship. Consequently, pupils meet on a regular, though not daily, basis in year or house groups consecutively throughout the week, in small halls, studios and dining rooms. Drawing large numbers of pupils together from widespread buildings is, in itself, time-consuming, and this is one reason why many schools hold their assemblies at the start of the school day. A 'thought for the day' is offered at registration times on the remaining days of the week in some schools.

Approaches to worship: school practice

It is commonly argued by teachers that an act of *collective* worship is not possible in communities where many different faiths are represented. Most schools claim to adopt a multifaith approach, but this seems to be a descriptor of the group rather than of the form of worship. What occurs is, therefore, better described as a multifaith assembly which, over a period of time, usually incorporates material which could be categorised variously as religious, broadly spiritual or non-religious. Overall, however, multifaith schools tend not to adopt a secular approach, although individual assemblies may have this emphasis. With large numbers of pupils coming from homes where the practice of religion, although diverse, is an important feature of family and community life, schools appear to combine an eclectic variety of approaches in which the values of mutual understanding and cooperation are paramount. To this end, the community's major religious festivals are celebrated at appropriate times throughout the year. These usually include Harvest, Diwali, Christmas, Chinese New Year, Holi, Ramadan and Eid-ul-Fitr, Easter, and Baisakhi. In addition, aspects of the particular faiths represented by pupils may also be shared, while other common features include the celebration of individual or group achievements, material based on current local and national affairs, work for charities, the promotion of the school ethos, and the building of school and group identity. In these respects, such schools are no different from many others around the country. Most of the schools which I visited are satisfied with the arrangements they make as being the most appropriate for their broad aims in accordance with their distinctive circumstances, and feel that they can do no other. In all respects except for the daily provision of collective worship, these schools appear to be in full compliance with the aims identified in Circular 1/94 (DfE, 1994). However, it is important to stress that the absence of worship does not indicate any rejection of support for the value of religious faith and commitment, which is shown in a variety of different ways. Nevertheless, teachers continue to wrestle with the dual demand to encourage cohesive values and attitudes in their pupils and at the same time to provide acts of collective worship for their heterogeneous communities which, they argue, must logically separate the group.

Teachers' responses to demands for the inclusion of acts of collective worship in schools

Under the circumstances in which multicultural

schools operate it is frequently claimed that worship is impossible, on grounds in which philosophical and practical perspectives are intermingled. Any attempt on my part to separate them would produce a less-than-accurate picture, and consequently in the discussion which follows perceptions and pragmatics are often combined. At this point, however, it must be stressed that all of the teachers whom I interviewed are wholly in favour of school assemblies and are happy to accept their responsibility to encourage shared moral and social values, which already feature prominently in their work in this aspect of the curriculum. Where they experience sincere difficulty is in the requirement that their pupils must participate in compulsory acts of worship which they, ultimately, have a responsibility to provide.

First, in addition to an identification of Britain as a secular society, religious practice is recognised as being a matter of private and personal concern. The argument is put forward therefore that it is not the responsibility of the school to develop religious belief in children. This is not a task which schools should undertake even if it were possible (AM). The legal requirements therefore are 'out of the territory of legitimacy' (SV), and although it might be possible to satisfy the letter of the law, this could destroy the religious tolerance and understanding which schools are attempting to develop (VJ). Formal acquiescence, therefore, would be counterproductive and although token provision could meet the legal requirements, this 'would generate wrong values in children. We would have met the letter of the law but not its spirit' (FG). The practice of a shared 'Thought for the Day' which is provided in the expectation that each form teacher will introduce this to the class group is sometimes rejected, therefore, as an unacceptable gesture. However, some schools find that this procedure works well for them and is appreciated by pupils; and other schools adopt this format but, intentionally, no check is made on its use by teachers.

Second, many teachers find themselves faced with the problem of a loss of personal integrity if they are required to conduct an act of worship against their own consciences, and fear a consequent loss of credibility with their pupils:

EC: I am going to the limits of my belief-structure to uphold, accommodate something I find personally difficult. I am not hostile, but I am stretching as far as my personality, belief structure and intellect permit me to do.

Others express a more ambivalent attitude to the provision of worship, particularly with younger pupils, but feel that religious commitment is really the responsibility of the family (SO). If parents do not fulfil their responsibility, however (and in this respect, in the multifaith schools which I visited, this criticism is levelled largely at the Christian tradition), the suggestion that schools should fill this gap is challenged:

JL: Is it our place to reinforce Christian messages when – the majority of students probably – their parents say they're C. of E. but they're not practising Christians. They don't go to church, they don't reinforce Christianity at home. Is it appropriate? Are parents expecting schools to do it? It isn't schools' place to right society's ills, by telling parents, 'Well, you're not going to do it so we will!'. . . It's not really what schools are about.

This comment was made by a senior teacher in a large secondary school whose pupil population reflects the ethnic mix of the city but where a request for a determination (for exemption from the requirement to provide worship which is 'wholly or mainly broadly Christian in character') is under consideration because the number of practising Christians in the majority group is outnumbered by committed members of other faiths.

Another concern of teachers is not only for their own belief positions but also for those of their pupils, and they question the demands placed by the legal requirements on those without belief:

AM: Where does it recognise people who have no faith? As an educationalist, I feel very strongly that we're not here to convert. To help pupils and people to understand themselves and each other . . . can be carried out in Assembly as well as in an Act of Worship.

Furthermore, it is recognised that group worship is an activity that takes place under the condition of a common and shared faith which is necessary before worship can occur. This cannot be presumed to exist in county schools in either teachers or pupils: 'A deeply personal experience with others of like mind is appropriate. In non-religious schools, the preconditions do not exist' (EC). It is argued that the imposition of religion in a secular society is a tyranny and without justification. In a school which contains pupils and teachers from several faith communities as well as those with no religious family tradition, the concept of an act of shared worship is unrealistic:

EC: What I don't think is natural, I can't think of any area where it's done outside of school and therefore it must be artificial, is to put people of entirely different beliefs, in which I would include no belief at all and ask them to collectively worship. . . . I just find the whole concept so totally flawed, totally flawed, that intellectually there isn't a justification for it.

What teachers find additionally frustrating is that it would be possible to fulfil the letter of the law by providing a superficial ritual. This would, however, be rejected by pupils, especially at secondary level, as hypocritical and irrelevant if unaccompanied by evidence of personal belief. Nevertheless, where there is evidence of sincerity, pupils often appreciate the underlying care which motivates their teachers, even where they reject the message. Furthermore, young people are very perceptive and are prepared to reflect on material which is presented to them when it demonstrates personal commitment: 'In the Thought for the Day, you really feel that the teachers practise and believe in it themselves, so they are better able to teach it to the pupils' (H, year 10).

It appears to be the case, then, that one of the features which lies at the heart of schools' difficulties in the provision of acts of collective worship is the question of sincere leadership. What teachers are able to do, however, often with structured support and with justified self-confidence, is to share insights into their own values, thoughts, reflections and experience. Where this is genuine and relevant, pupils will listen: where it is insincere and imposed on young people, it will be rejected. Like the society which they represent, most teachers are not practising members of any religious tradition.

Multifaith assemblies: schools' arguments

Under these circumstances, what are the choices which are open to schools? I have indicated above that decisions regarding their approach to the provision of worship are made in the light of schools' broader aims for the well-being of their pupils and the communities which they represent. Prospectuses show that these include the celebration of diversity, the achievement of high standards of work and behaviour, the encouragement of cooperation, respect and tolerance, and the development of responsibility for self and community in order to contribute to a harmonious and pluralist society. Schools use their assemblies to foster these aims and to transmit a range of moral, social and spiritual values. Because the underlying emphasis is invariably on the school as a family community, there is a strong desire to gather the pupils together in large groups from which no pupil feels excluded: 'We're one school' (SM); 'We meet as a whole school, because we're one community. Without it, it's difficult for pupils to see the whole community' (AM); 'it's to do with part of a family within a school, for the greater good' (SV); 'I would feel saddened if pupils felt excluded' (VJ). An additional factor which is a major influence in some decisions is the fact that in the inner cities not all schools have stable populations. One primary school reported a pupil turnover of 48 per cent during the course of the year, and the school assembly is used to contribute to an important sense of belonging.

Joint assemblies provide opportunities for pupils to share their religious and cultural traditions with their friends:

SV: Pupils recognise and support the endorsement of their own faith and opportunities to experience learning about others. The sense of valuing of pupils' religions is a significant learning process for pupils *and* teachers.

By the means of shared assemblies, it is hoped that pupils are encouraged within their own faiths and that ignorance of others is dispelled. The emphasis on the value of sharing is very important:

JL: If we're going to share, then we'll share everyone's faith for that particular morning. We have to work very hard to promote tolerance and understanding of other people. . . . You'd like to think that these messages rub off into the world outside, where attitudes and practices are different. It's the only time they see themselves as part of a team which can affect what's going on.

Communication of the school's ethos is another important feature of assembly. It is felt that this is best transmitted to pupils in large groups, leaving matters which are very personal to be addressed in tutor groups:

SM: I feel it's tremendously important . . . because there are so many things that it's important to discuss – discuss would be the wrong word because it would be unrealistic for 400 people to discuss something but children and staff need to know that everybody's been told this and I feel that is a very good context for doing it . . . Everybody is party to the same principle.

As noted above, the principles adopted by schools as part of their ethos include an emphasis on the valuing of individuals, on tolerance, respect and understanding, and on friendship, kindness and responsibility. Part of the school's ethos involves a particular approach to a range of attitudes and circumstances, which is sometimes summed up in phrases such as: 'This is the way we do it here; this is the "Woodside" Way!' (EA). Such a concept is applied to a range of features, from issues of trust and honesty to the wearing of the school uniform. It helps to build up an established and common corpus, and is introduced and sustained when pupils meet together in assembly. Other schools adopt a broader approach, as was explained to me by another teacher: 'Our ethos is very successfully transmitted. Its real focus, agenda, is "Let us celebrate each other"' (AS). This was coincidentally confirmed by two year 10 pupils:

S: Our motto is 'Be concerned'
H: . . . and treat people as you would like them to treat you. The moral is valuing each other.

Conscious of responsibility for the wider community, schools are frequently involved in money-raising for charity, and this is another means whereby they can encourage in practice the cooperation and teamwork which they understand as contributing to a sense of social cohesion. In addition, each school values achievement, and the assembly provides an opportunity to articulate expectations, to encourage commitment to high standards of work and behaviour, and to celebrate group and individual success. The distribution of certificates of merit, therefore, is a common feature. Another important feature of the school assembly is the way in which it can be used to set the tone for the day or week ahead, as well as to reinforce the work ethic. This is another reason why many schools continue to start the day with assembly, feeling that it gives a sense of purpose to all that follows. Finally, the shared assembly provides an opportunity for teachers and pupils to become acquainted: 'It's the way I get to know the children and it's certainly the way I make sure they all know who I am' (JF). Furthermore, it is a means whereby the headteacher is able to exert a measure of influence on the teachers, by setting an example of good relationships with pupils and by re-emphasising the school ethos.

These are only some of the functions served by assembly. They are perceived as integral to the life of the school; and where the principal value emphasises a shared and united community, a combined act of daily worship in the sense defined by Circular 1/94 is clearly impossible in the presence of so many faith traditions. There is only one approach whereby worship can be said truly to occur and that is through the provision of parallel faith assemblies at which each religious tradition worships in its own way. Inevitably, the choice of a multifaith approach is informed by a rejection of this alternative.

Again, philosophical and practical reasons are given for this response. First, such an approach is seen as divisive: 'We have no desire for faith assemblies. We spend all our time trying to get pupils to work together!' (RF); 'They wouldn't do anything to bring the group together at all. They would be separatist and might even reinforce some prejudices' (JL). Second, such an approach would not be a collective act of worship: 'Rather than have several different assemblies, which to me isn't collective worship, I choose to have one which broadly has the spiritual and moral framework' (FG).

Practical difficulties are also given as reasons for rejecting faith assemblies. Because they would need to occur simultaneously, many schools lack appropriate spaces to make provision for all the different traditions which are represented. The shortage of suitable leaders constitutes another problem, particularly if the legal requirements for *daily* worship are to be met. In addition, fears are expressed concerning the possibility of causing offence between religious denominations unintentionally, and of permitting the transmission of extremist views:

SM: . . . unless there's a monitoring exercise going on I wouldn't feel at all happy letting someone in from outside and lead a session not knowing what was being taught to the children. I mean, we've got to be realistic. Any religious group can have extremist people with extreme views and I feel if that happened it would take over the whole week if we talked about the planning, the monitoring, the organising and it would split the school into three immediately.

Such a response indicates teachers' wariness of the unfamiliar and fear of a loss of control, especially where a range of different languages is involved, as well as their concern not to cause offence. Anxiety about the rivalry within local faith groups was also expressed, adding to the concerns of some teachers about the involvement of community leaders in school worship.

Despite all of the arguments presented above, however, one school had chosen to develop parallel faith assemblies, although it was still not possible to conform to the legal requirements for worship on every day, because of the shortage of leaders. At this school, the multifaith approach was rejected as 'a farce' (JA). It was argued that the provision of a moral story accompanied by a suggestion that pupils, some as young as 5 years old, should pray to their own god is meaningless unless children have a strong religious family background. Such an activity does justice to nothing and results in 'a mishmash of pupil perceptions completely' (JA). Consequently, this large primary school, with over 500 pupils, provides five concurrent assemblies on two days of the week. These accommodate the four largest religious traditions (Hindu, Sikh, Muslim and Christian) while an additional group caters for all of those children whose parents have withdrawn them from these acts of worship, either because they have no religious connections or because their tradition is in a small minority, for example, Cantonese Buddhists.

This approach does not appear to have had the divisive effect predicted. Rather, it is claimed that under this system pupils identify each other and themselves more positively. Because each religion is clearly valued in its own right, pupils feel more comfortable within their own tradition. Friendship groups continue to be mixed, and children are more knowledgeable of their own faith and of their friends' traditions.

Nevertheless, shared gatherings continue to occur, thus enabling the other functions of assembly identified above to take place. With an emphasis on an ethos of respect, self-esteem and shared knowledge, pupils gather weekly for departmental meetings, when achievements are celebrated; and the whole school comes together at the start of the year and for particular occasions relating to current events as they occur. Parents are invited to the annual celebrations of religious festivals, and their significance is translated into the mother tongue in order to share with them what is often an unfamiliar culture.

Some of the teachers' concerns identified earlier surface here also. It is not possible to attract sufficient community leaders, who need also to be able to intersperse English with the mother tongue, and at the present time, worship is led by a rota of teachers and local representatives. The latter sometimes lack knowledge and training, but there is no money available to correct this situation although the school is giving consideration to ways whereby leaders from the community might receive some training. Working alongside teachers is an advantage, but there is a clear need for the provision of suitable material and activities. Encouragement is being given to leaders to meet together to share ideas, resources and issues, but obviously this adds to the demands on people who are volunteers.

Finally, the problem of unacceptable or unsuitable volunteer leaders whose manner or emphasis is inappropriate is rare but does occur. In the first instance, the school tries to discuss with the person the ways in which it would like the time to be used. Nevertheless, where difficulties continue to arise through the presence of different sects and emphases, it sometimes becomes necessary to ask individuals not to continue because they are felt to be pursuing an inappropriate line.

Conclusion

One of the points which it is important to emphasise here is the danger of making judgements about any aspect of school practice in isolation from other elements of its provision. The Education Act 1988 requires schools to provide a curriculum which supports pupils' spiritual, moral, social and cultural development and prepares them for 'the opportunities, responsibilities and experiences of adult life' (chap. 40, p. 1). In the circumstances of the schools described above, crucial to the fulfilment of such aims is the development of certain attitudes and personal values which permeate schools' provision. High on the list of priorities are the values of tolerance, respect, cooperation, dignity and integrity. Schools adopt policies and practices which encourage these values, and argue that, in respect of compulsory worship:

VJ: . . . acquiescence to the letter of the law would destroy religious tolerance and the accepted school ethos. We are aiming for a deeper acceptance of pupils as individuals, and a high profile for religious tolerance as part of the school's ethos. We support pupils' religious activities and commitments rather than put an emphasis on whole group uniformity.

Schools aim to encourage a spirituality without promoting a particular religious line and many feel confident that 'This is successful in giving everyone a feeling that their religious and cultural background is recognised *and* respected' (DA); and as a tangible means of showing this, support is available for pupils to practise their faith commitments, as, for example, in the provision of facilities for Islamic midday prayer. In some circumstances, the contribution which pupils' religious commitment makes to the ethos of the school is significant:

SV: . . . the nature of living faith and commitment – and spirituality – they have faith, and you can see the way it leads their lives, following a strict code. This doesn't apply to all people; there's a spectrum of faith and practice, but we can see here what it does for your school. The nature of faith and spirituality evident in a school like this is very strong but you can't put your finger on it.

The contribution which pupils themselves make to the quality of life in the school community is one which is seldom identified but should be an element of any debate on 'shared values', which all too often presumes a situation where the culture of the school managers controls the values agenda which is to be transmitted to pupils. Thus an opportunity for genuine sharing and of learning from the young may be missed.

At the time of writing there are renewed calls for changes to the legislation on collective worship, demanding a reduction in its frequency. This chapter has described some of the difficulties faced by multifaith schools in their implementation of the legal requirements. At the heart of their problems, two main features can be identified: one is the practical question of the availability of time, space and appropriate leadership for group worship; the other is the controversial issue of the provision of any act which might be categorised as the collective worship of a deity. In multifaith schools, this is an impossibility, although many schools make facilities available for acts of corporate worship amongst pupils who are committed members of their traditions. This is not, however, to suggest that such schools would choose to abandon the activity called school assembly. As shown above, schools value the opportunity this provides for developing the school ethos and for exploring spiritual, moral, social and cultural values and dimensions. Religious worship, however, 'might prove to be a poor substitute' (SO). Without exception, however, if the require-ments for worship are repealed, every school in this sample intends to maintain the practice of regular assembly.

References

Adie, M. (1989) Basic or marginal? *Education* 21/28. 12. 1990.

Alves, C. (1989) Religious education and collective worship in schools: the thinking behind the Act. *Head Teachers' Review*, Spring 12, 14–15.

Association of Christian Teachers (ACT) (1994) *Collective Worship and Religious Education*. St Albans, Herts.: ACT.

Association of Teachers and Lecturers (ATL) (1995) *Collective Worship: Policy and Practice*. London: ATL.

British Humanist Association (BHA) (n.d.) *Standing Together*. London: BHA.

Chadwick, P. (1994) *Schools of Reconciliation*. London: Cassell.

Cole, W.O. (1990) Religious education into the nineties. *Forum* **32**(2) 47–49.

Department for Education (DfE) (1994) *Religious Education and Collective Worship*, Circular 1/94. London: DfE.

Gibbons, J. (1989) Sacre blues. *School Governor*, March.

Halstead, J.M. (1992) Muslim perspectives on the teaching of Christianity in British schools. *British Journal of Religious Education* **15**(1) 43–54.

Horne, M. (1990) School assemblies and anti-racist education. *Forum* **32**(2) 53–54.

Hull, J.M. (1988) Religious education in the Education Reform Bill. *British Journal of Religious Education* **11**(1) 1–3.

Hull, J.M. (1990) Editorial. *British Journal of Religious Education* **12**(3) 121–123.

Hull, J.M. (1995) Collective worship and the search for the spiritual. *British Journal of Religious Education* **17**(2) 66–69.

Mabud, S.A. (1992) A Muslim response to the Education Reform Act 1988. *British Journal of Religious Education* **14**(2) 88–98.

National Association of Head Teachers (NAHT) (1994) *Survey of Members on Religious Education and Collective Worship*. Haywards Heath, Sussex: NAHT.

O'Connor, M. (1989) The Year Ahead – RE and Collective Worship, *AMMA Report* **11**(3) 6–7.

Office for Standards in Education (OFSTED) (1995) *Guidance on the Inspection of Secondary Schools*. London: Her Majesty's Stationery Office.

Redwood, J. (1996) Sermon to the bishops: stop moralising and do something. *The Sunday Times*, 29 December.

Sarwar, G. (1988) *Education Reform Act 1988: What Can Muslims Do?* London: Muslim Educational Trust.

Shephard, G. (1996) We owe it to our children to teach morals at school. *Sun*, 29 October.

Sonyel, S.R. (1988) *The Silent Minority: Turkish Muslim Children in British Schools.* Cambridge: Islamic Academy.

Thornley, N. (1989) Religious education and collective worship in schools. *Head Teachers' Review* Spring, 15, 16, 18.

Walker, J. (1990) Religious observance in secondary schools: educationally and theologically unacceptable. *Education Today* **40**(3) 35–38.

22 Beliefs and Values: the Western Australian Experience

CYNTHIA K. DIXON

This chapter traces the attempts from 1975 to 1997 to establish in the government schools of Western Australia a programme which through the study of religious beliefs and values would offer students an opportunity to explore questions of ultimate meaning, understand better their context of cultural diversity, develop sensitivity to moral responsibility and the ways that religion has contributed to the development of a personal values system.

> Doctors might be the clinical experts, but it's a shame there aren't people who can help us with our mind, with our belief system. It's the belief system that empowers or destroys you.

This was the plea of a young Australian battling severe illness.[1] Australia on the surface is a land of promise, of sunshine, energy, sport, tough-mindedness, a fair go and countless opportunities. Yet it is a land where the male suicide rate at times surpasses the death rate caused by motor vehicle accidents in the age group 16–24. It is a land where eating disorders abound, and broken families, drugs and alcohol take a dreadful toll. Social analyst Richard Eckersley (1993) bemoaned the fact that 'our young people are offered no coherent or consistent world view and no clear moral structure to help establish a sense of meaning, belonging, purpose or sense of values'.

Major religious traditions have long provided models and examples of a coherent world view, embodying morals, ethics, values and ways that countless people have made meaning of their lives in their quest for answer to such questions as 'Who am I?', 'Why am I here?', 'How should I live? and 'Why is the world the way it is?' The extent to which young people in their government school experience in Western Australia have had access to such an option over the past twenty years is the focus of this chapter. It describes the attempts to provide students with an opportunity to engage in the study of religious beliefs and values as part of their general education. The account will indicate the interaction of a range of variables which include creative curriculum, enthusiastic and dedicated teachers, community and academic support, and policy decisions on funding and resources, reflecting the powerful influence of personal values.

Western Australia

Western Australia is a vast state covering 2,527,632 square kilometres, almost one-third of the continent of Australia. The first white settlers arrived in 1825. The sparse population of 2 million, of which just over 2 per cent are indigenous, comprises about 15 per cent of the total population of Australia. Of this, 1.1 million are concentrated in the metropolitan area of Perth, and half a million are tucked into the more temperate and fertile south-west corner of the state. The school population in 1996 consisted of 251,000 students in government schools and 89,150 in non-government private schools, which represent a range of denominations, faiths and beliefs.[2] The government schools are under the jurisdiction of the Education Department of Western Australia (EDWA).[3]

History of religious education in the government schools of Western Australia

In 1893 the Elementary Education Act established a dual system of religious instruction in the government schools. One system, carried out by the class teacher, was labelled 'secular instruction'. The Act stated that:

> in all Government Schools the teaching shall be strictly non-sectarian, but the words *secular instruction* shall be held to include general religious teaching as distinguished from dogmatic or polemical theology.

The second system allowed was called special religious instruction (SRI) and consisted of faith education on a weekly basis provided by the clergy, or their representatives, to the children of their particular denomination. The Anglican church had particularly requested this provision because it comprised 50 per cent of the government school population.

A survey in 1975 revealed that only 14 per cent of primary school children received special religious instruction, and only half the primary schools taught any general religious instruction. The situation in secondary schools was even worse. This evidence, combined with the efforts of the Government School Teachers' Union, church leaders, the Churches' Commission on Education (CCE), and the WA Council of Government School Organisations convinced the Minister for Education in 1976 to establish a committee of inquiry. The outcome was the Nott Report, *Religious Education in the Government Schools of Western Australia* (1977) which outlined fourteen recommendations on religious education in the government schools of Western Australia. The major thrust was to recommend that religious studies programmes be introduced throughout all government schools, their aim being conceptualised thus:

> A general education should include the aim of initiating students into the major forms of religious thought and experience characteristic of their culture in such a way that each learner acquires an understanding of them, and sensitivity to them, sufficient to enable him [*sic*] both to make informed choices as to the part, if any, which particular religious activities and commitments will play in his personal life-style, and to be sensitively understanding of the religious commitments of other persons. (Nott Committee, 1977, p. 80)

This report reflected a general raising of consciousness about religious education throughout Australia in the 1970s, which, in turn, reflected a similar development in Britain and North America. Factors contributing to change included sociological, educational and philosophical factors.

In Britain, in 1974, the outcome of concern for the needs of its increasingly pluralistic society was the City of Birmingham Agreed Syllabus. The agreement to be sought in the 'Agreed Syllabus' was not agreement on what was held in common to be true, but what was to be held in common as worth knowing: the first attempt to cater for a changing society. Students were required to study not only five world religions (Christianity, Hinduism, Islam, Judaism and Sikhism), but also a secular alternative (Humanism or Marxism). The storm of protest at the inclusion of the secular alternatives led to legal action, resulting in the revision of the syllabus in 1975. While the syllabus itself was quite brief, it was accompanied by an encyclopaedic 'handbook' of resources, *Living Together; a Teacher's Handbook of Suggestions for Religious Education* (City of Birmingham, 1975), which in fact did not also undergo revision. The syllabus suggested that the purpose of religious education should be to

- help boys and girls to live and work together in a pluralist situation (p. 7); and
- enable them to develop skills involved in coming to a mature understanding of religion (p. 6).

Although noting difficulties surrounding the Birmingham syllabus, in particular that it rested upon one particular view in which religion should be regarded, Leslie Newbigin (1977) would acknowledge its pioneering effort thus:

> I recognise that it is a very able and courageous attempt to deal with a quite new situation, and that it is very difficult to propose anything which would be an improvement on it.

While sociological reasons were a catalyst for initiating change, new curriculum models and educational practice in religious education would draw on contemporary writings in the philosophy of education, developmental psychology and the study of religion. The influence of such curriculum innovations would travel across the world, appearing in some detail in the Nott Report of Western Australia.

The *philosophical* rationale for including religious education in a general curriculum was located in the work of R.S. Peters (1967) and P. Hirst (1970, 1974) in Britain, and Philip Phenix (1964) in the USA, in their 'forms of knowledge' argument. Each theorist argued that the fully educated person was one who had been initiated into each of the major ways of knowing, which for them included religion. Each argued for a core curriculum structured on the distinctive ways of knowing.[4]

On the *psychological* front Ronald Goldman's (1964, 1965) application of Piagetian cognitive developmental stages to children's religious understanding, although causing great controversy, had the benefit of drawing the developmental needs of children to the attention of religious educators.[5] Insights from developmental psychologists on the cognitive and emotional needs of the religious development of the child would henceforth be taken into consideration, as in other curriculum areas.

Religious Studies as an academic discipline reached centre stage through the work of Ninian Smart (1968, 1969). Adopting a phenomenological approach, Smart offered a description rather than an explanation of a religious tradition. The phenomenologist, in an attempt to understand, would suspend intellectual judgement by a process of bracketing (epoche) while seeking to clarify the phenomena of a religious tradition. Smart identified seven dimensions as characteristic of any religious tradition. These included the dimensions of ritual, myth, doctrine, ethics, social, experiential and material. Smart added the seventh dimension, the material, to allow for physical expressions such as buildings after the six dimensions had received wide publicity and already been incorporated into curriculum models.

Smart himself was a leading force in promoting the study of world religions in schools. He argued that by using the phenomenological method students would be assisted not in the truth *of* religion, but in the truth *about* religion. This approach was quickly adopted by curriculum writers, who saw in it an attempt at a value-free description of religion, which at that time was seen to be the vital factor.

Curriculum innovations

The 1970s' educational view of religious education replacing a religious view of religious education as a means of addressing pluralism became the foundation of two curriculum projects in England. These were financed by the Schools Council, a central government body, which offered suggestions for curriculum reform and encouraged research. The projects were based at Lancaster University under the direction of Ninian Smart. Rationale and theory were provided by two publications, the Schools Council Working Paper 36, *Religious Education in Secondary Schools* (1971) and the Schools Council Working Paper 44, *Religious Education in Primary Schools* (1972). The outcome in curriculum material came in 1977 with *Discovering an Approach* (the Lancaster Project: Schools Council, 1977) and *Journeys into Religion* (the Cheshire Education Committee, 1997).

The aim was to promote the view that religious education should be plural in the sense that it 'was not restricted to one tradition, but would take seriously the existence of different religions and secular alternatives', and be open, exploratory and aimed at understanding. The view was held that seeing the place of religion in society would help children understand their culture and the culture of others. Religious education would introduce children to the basic human activity of searching for some meaning in life (Schools Council, 1977, ch.1).

In 1973 Michael Grimmitt, Principal Lecturer in Religious Education at Westhill College in Birmingham, presented a model based on Smart's dimensions in *What Can I do in R.E.?* He provided a framework which included two levels: Level 1, the *Existential Approach*, and Level 2 the *Dimensional Approach*. The Existential Approach was aimed at helping children look at their own existential experiences in depth, with the appropriate introduction of religious concepts through the Dimensional Approach, based on Smart:

> through presenting selected religious concepts by way of these six dimensions and linking them with insights gained from work with the Existential approach, it seeks to enable children to build conceptual bridges between their own experiences and what they recognise to be the central concepts of religion.   (Grimmitt, 1973, p. 93)

These developments in the philosophy of educational theory, religious studies and curriculum in Britain and North America were reflected throughout a series of Australian reports on religious education which included the Overton Report of Tasmania (1971), the Gutekunst Report of Queensland (1972);[6] the Steinle Report of South Australia (1973); the Russell Report of Victoria (1974); and the Nott Report of Western Australia (1977).[7] In particular the Nott Report incorporated accounts of the Birmingham syllabus, Ninian

Smart's contribution to religious studies, and reproduced Michael Grimmitt's model.

The Nott Report

The major focus of the Nott Report's fourteen recommendations was the provision and resourcing of a religious studies programme throughout the primary and secondary government schools. Until such time as this was established, special religious instruction could continue, under certain conditions, including training of the voluntary instructors.

In accepting the Nott Report, the Minister for Education instructed the Education Department to implement it in an exploratory fashion in 1978. The Report has continued to be the definitive statement on religious education in government schools, although its implementation has been subject to a range of forces, ideological, economic and practical, which will now be outlined as an example of perseverance, with some questions to pose on the difficulties encountered.[8]

The development of curriculum, the provision of teacher training and of resources needed both to design and implement a new syllabus would require the support of three major agencies. The Education Department, the Tertiary Institutions and the Churches' Commission on Education would form a partnership to provide the infrastructure to attempt to implement the Nott Report.

The Education Department appointed a full-time religious studies curriculum officer to work in the Curriculum Branch. In mid-1979 an Advisory Committee on Religious Studies to the Minister for Education was established. The recommendation to appoint a superintendent responsible for religious studies was refused, but an existing superintendent was required to supervise religious studies as an additional portfolio. Despite the recommendation that teacher education institutions be involved, it was not until 1984 that a tertiary lecturer was invited on to the Advisory Committee.

Developing a curriculum

To develop the religious studies curriculum, the curriculum officer sought volunteers for a pilot study from classroom teachers. The curriculum model chosen by them from the options offered by the curriculum officer was an integrated thematic approach, using Grimmitt's existential/dimensional model, and therefore Smart's dimensions. Teachers worked in year groups to develop themes with the aid of resource people from the community and tertiary institutions. In primary schools the framework involved themes to be developed at appropriate times. Themes included Myself, My Home and Family, Water, Buildings, Light, Suffering, Who is my Neighbour?, Forgiveness, Truth, Rituals and Symbols, Differences, Children from Other Lands, Living Together in Community, Essentials for Living, the Supernatural, Acceptance and Rejection, Celebrating Holy Days, Some Major Religions, Easter and Christmas.

Each theme was developed into an explosion chart to show where the theme could be integrated into different topics. In Year 2, for example, the theme of water explored in science, English, health, mathematics and drama would include the religious significance, symbolism and traditions associated with water.

In the secondary programme religion was to be integrated into science, English and social studies. In science the work group's method of operation was to take the existing syllabus and to

- include a social context for each topic;
- extend selected themes in order to examine appropriate values;
- present alternative scientific interpretations for some themes.

Within English, the aim was to include personal development, and understanding and tolerance at individual and cultural levels. Social studies included belief systems and comparative political systems.

Following trials in twenty pilot schools in 1978, the materials were refined and extended, culminating in the production of a series of handbooks, *Guidelines for Teachers*, *Primary Work Programmes* and *Secondary Work Programmes*. These programmes, in draft form, comprised an extensive range of 42 themes and a comprehensive list of resources. A genuinely school-based integrated curriculum had been produced.

Religious studies in action

Social science, English and science teachers enthusiastically took up the task of integrating the religious dimension into their teaching with the aid of the resource materials they had helped to generate. However, it proved to be a daunting task. Evaluation of the secondary programme indicated that, despite the excellent range of resource materials generated by the pilot teachers' workshops, secondary teachers found the effort of preparing the material and integrating it into their regular curriculum proved such an onerous task that they withdrew from the programme. The integrated model, therefore, did not suit the subject approach of the secondary schools. By 1982 the secondary programme had failed to be implemented, and was abandoned.

The curriculum officer position was reclassified as a religious studies development officer, indicating a change of focus to implementation of the curriculum. Emphasis was now placed on the primary programme, which had been well received by teachers. They had found the integrated approach a very accessible way of introducing religion into the curriculum. Preference for continuing an integrated approach rather than a central departmental syllabus was to be achieved by including the religious dimension into the new K-10 social science curriculum, the first total curriculum in this area to be developed in Western Australia. However, the points for inclusion agreed between the religious studies Primary Working Party and the social science curriculum writer failed to appear when the social science curriculum was published in 1981, complete with glossy format, much publicity and in-service provision.[9] Nevertheless, the religious studies primary programme continued. By the end of 1983 12 per cent of primary schools, mostly in the metropolitan area, were involved to some extent in the religious studies programme.

A major change in the educational policy of Western Australia took place with the publication of the Beazley Report in 1984. The Report reorganised the school curriculum into seven curriculum components. Under a brief paragraph on religious studies, reference was made to the existence of the Nott Report, indicating that implementation of its recommendations had been a slow process because of the complex and sensitive nature of the task and the scarcity of suitable trained personnel, concluding:

> On the question of the extent to which religious awareness and practice may be part of a school programme, this will have to remain in the province of

the particular school and be dependent upon local community wishes.   (Beazley, 1984, p. 62)[10]

Thus the Beazley Report did little to encourage the implementation of the Nott Report, making no specific recommendation on the subject of religious studies, either on curriculum or on the need to encourage training and career opportunities.

An even shorter paragraph in the 459-page report referred to moral education: values and ethics. Attracted to the idea that students would benefit from a course in ethics and morals, the Committee indicated that time constraints had prevented them from examining the area, but concluded:

> Students need to have the opportunity to identify for themselves a set of criteria by which choices are made; search out and come to grips with contradictions in their own value systems; probe their own life goals deeply; and operate competently in a society which allows various sets of values. The development of moral reasoning and a capacity to discriminate and choose among values and beliefs is a crucial part of the growth of personal integrity and a social responsibility.   (Ibid., p. 64)

It was recommended that the topic of moral education should be included in the vocational and personal awareness component of the curriculum.

Because of rival claims to fund the implementation of the Beazley Report, the Minister for Education would not approve further funding for religious studies. This was particularly ironic since the religious studies programme had virtually preempted the Beazley approach by demonstrating the effectiveness of school-based programmes, through the use of adequate in-service facilities and community resources. Thus the struggle to continue the religious studies programme without resources or revision of the materials took its toll. The original draft materials remained a popular resource for teachers for many years, where they were available. In 1989 the remaining copies were shredded by the Education Department, whereupon permission to copy them for students was sought and granted to the Religious Studies Department at Edith Cowan University.[11]

Post-Beazley 1984

In the seven years since the innovative recommendations of the Nott Report an integrated religious studies curriculum had been developed, implemented and virtually lapsed in both the primary and secondary schools. Nevertheless the Advisory Committee throughout 1985 continued to promote religious studies. It recommended to the Minister that within the Beazley framework the religious dimension should be accommodated in social studies, with respect to content, and in personal and vocational education (PAVE), with respect to the existential dimension. The Minister's approval led to a fruitful meeting with the Director-General of Education. The Education Department announced that it proposed

> to appoint as soon as possible a senior officer to explore the fields of religious studies and religious awareness so that alternatives can be identified, and decisions made and implemented to put into effect the principles announced in the Nott and Beazley reports.[12]

The religious studies development officer resigned at the end of 1985 and a primary school principal was seconded to the department to act as the executive officer for religious studies. In view of the experience with the school-based integrated curriculum it was agreed that a centrally designed religious studies syllabus now be developed, and a support structure based around a superintendent and appropriate resources be established within the Education Department.[13] The syllabus proposed for adoption was that already developed by the South Australian Education Department. While this curriculum, also based on Smart's dimensions, with a rich array of teaching materials, was sufficiently compatible with the thrust of the Nott Report such that it would require only minor local modification, there was considerable pessimism expressed by some members of the Advisory Committee and the CCE. It was felt that the answer to establishing religious studies in schools was not 'just another curriculum', but a more adequate structure of support. Nevertheless, a free set of South Australian religious studies material was offered to every Western Australian primary school which wished to have it. Some guidelines for their use were developed by the executive officer. The offer was taken up by 208 schools. No in-service was available, the seconded executive officer returned to his school, and the Education Department felt it had fulfilled its obligations.

A review of 51 of these schools in 1988 by the District Councils of the CCE indicated that not one had attempted to use the materials.[14] In-depth discussion with one school indicated that the materials were regarded as social studies resources, and certainly not as a religious studies curriculum. Indeed, they hankered for the earlier integrated WA material which they had enjoyed using. It seems that the South Australian materials have since sunk without trace. Likewise the Advisory Committee faded from the scene about 1988.

The struggle to maintain a religious studies option in secondary schools would now be located in the continuing work of a religious studies sub-committee of the CCE.

The CCE, set up in 1971 as the Council for Christian Education in Schools to support a Christian presence in government schools, was given a wider brief as it had vigorously supported all efforts to encourage the opportunity for children to study the religious dimension. The CCE had considered it vital that the young be not denied exploration of this major field of human experience, and thus had been instrumental in the generation of the Nott Report. On the failure of the integrated themes in the secondary programme and the absence of religious content in the social science curriculum, the CCE took the initiative to provide what it perceived the Education Department was failing to provide in implementing the Nott Report. The executive director called on the tertiary institutions and the community to assist her in the production of a course in religious studies for Years 11 and 12 students. Contributions to the curriculum were quickly forthcoming from university lecturers and clergy. Under this energetic leadership there was little problem in generating a syllabus and teacher resource manuals, despite the absence of funding. This syllabus, *Beliefs and Values* (CCE, 1985), has continued to exist, constantly adapting and changing to the demands of the changes in educational policy, and of evaluation.

Beliefs and values

In 1985, the Religious Studies Sub-committee of the CCE published *Beliefs and Values: The Human Search for Meaning*, a religious studies curriculum for upper school students. Moving from the earlier failed integrated model, the curriculum comprised twelve modules divided into four groupings: these were an introductory module, *Searching for Meaning*; six modules on *Religion in Australia*, which included Christian Traditions, the Pop Scene,

Outside the Mainstream, Other Major Faiths, Materialism a Way of Life? and Worship and Commitment; two modules on the Bible, an overview of the Old Testament and an overview of the New Testament; and finally three modules on *Religious Problems*, Self Worth, Suffering and Social Justice. A second series, *Faiths and Lifestyles*, was started for Year 12, but not completed. Experience indicates that there was more than sufficient content in *Beliefs and Values* for the two years.

Aimed at the government school system in particular, it was hoped that independent schools would also take advantage of the programme. *Beliefs and Values* was enthusiastically received when launched by the Religious Studies Department of what is now Edith Cowan University, at a luncheon attended by 90 teachers from both government and non-government schools. Shortly afterwards, however, the Catholic school system was issued with an internal memo banning the use of the *Beliefs and Values* curriculum. This withdrawal of support (eventually to be renewed in 1993) left the viability of programme on very shaky ground. In the long run only two government schools offered *Beliefs and Values* to its students. Of these, one agreed on condition that a volunteer teacher could be found. The school principal was unwilling to offer a teacher what would be considered a soft option by other staff, in his opinion, since numbers would be low. The CCE found a volunteer for the first year. The course, though successful, was taught only once because of the condition made for a volunteer teacher.

A few non-government schools took up the programme, in particular a Uniting Church school, a Jewish school and a Seventh-Day Adventist school, and successfully and enthusiastically taught the course. Eventually in 1995 the Uniting Church school phased it out because of other curriculum demands.

In 1989 the Religious Studies Sub-committee of the CCE, which consisted of representatives of the three major agencies, appealed to the new Minister for Education to honour her predecessor's approval of a religious studies consultant. In response, a senior education officer was appointed, whose primary task was to implement the recommendations of the Nott Report. The officer's main aim, in the view of the Sub-committee, was to consist of public relations and of selling *Beliefs and Values* to schools, principals and teachers.[15] The Sub-committee also operated as a support group for the officer. In 1991, in a final report on completion of the two-year appointment, thereafter discontinued, the officer, disappointed and frustrated, identified the factors he perceived to be hampering progress. He noted that he had found the issue of religious studies to be contentious, and that misunderstandings existed both in the Education Department and the community, concluding that:

> The establishment of Religious Studies in Government Schools requires the Ministry of Education to take certain steps related to policy development, public education and implementation planning. (Mordini, 1991)

Accreditation of Beliefs and Values: Secondary Education Authority

The Beliefs and Values syllabus was accepted to be accredited for government schools by the Secondary Education Authority (SEA), an independent statutory body whose function was the certification of courses. Thursday, 10 March 1988 had seen the inaugural meeting of the Religious Studies and Beliefs and Values Syllabus Committee, to ensure that the Syllabus would conform to the requirements of accreditation, through such aspects as the assessment procedures, and grade related descriptors.

As the SEA policy stipulated that a course had to be reviewed every five years, the Syllabus Committee in January 1994 resolved that the Beliefs and Values syllabus be reorganised to fit in with the Curriculum Area Framework for Personal Development Studies.[16] The syllabus content was now grouped into the following areas:

Year 11

- Self-concept and religious belief
- Religion in Australia
- Religious claims and tradition
- Moral responsibility – public and private

Year 12

- Religion: quest and systems
- Religious problems
- Ethical responsibility

The basic philosophy, however, has remained the same, as the Rationale in the SEA Syllabus Manual for Personal Development Studies (SEA, 1997, p. 1) makes clear:

> Students should be given the opportunity to encounter and to gain some understanding of the ways in which leading religious traditions claim to satisfy the quest for personal meaning and purpose. Such a study can help them to identify religious resources on which they may draw, if they so choose, in developing their own self-concept and life-style. It can also help them, in the pluralistic society which Australia has become, to understand their choices for them, or to insist on agreement with a particular religious viewpoint. But it is not for formal education to make their choices for them, or to insist on agreement with a particular religious viewpoint. Beliefs and Values invites students to embark consciously on a quest for a view of the world, and of their moral duty, big enough to live by.

As Australian curriculum design continued to change, a major development was modelled on the British National Curriculum. In 1989 the Hobart Declaration on Schooling described ten common and agreed national goals for schooling. This National Curriculum comprised eight national learning statements and profiles for English, health and physical education, languages other than English, mathematics, science, studies of society and environment, technology and the arts. Religion appeared under the strand of culture and beliefs in the studies of society and environment. Although the vision of a national curriculum did not eventuate and control reverted to the individual states, the model was virtually reproduced by Western Australia. Curriculum was to move from being objective-based to being outcome-based. In April 1995 began the task of considering a Learning Outcome Based Curriculum Model in relation to the Beliefs and Values syllabus. A Common Assessment Framework was duly written up for the syllabus, which would be expressed in student outcomes rather than objectives. Thus everything possible had been done from a curriculum point of view to offer a well-designed, contemporary course.

The role of tertiary institutions

During the 1970s, interested lecturers in the Colleges of Advanced Education and Murdoch University offered units for religious educators, which included curriculum, theory and content.[17] In 1981 Claremont Teacher's College introduced a graduate diploma in religious education studies, and in 1984 a Department of Religious Studies was created offering a bachelor's degree. While non-government schools made very good use of these facilities, there was very little prospect of career opportunities in the government sector. Encouraged by the Nott Report, many students had opted for units in religion, but soon found that there was little prospect of a career. The Education Department continued to decline to nominate religion as a major curriculum area, so students at the undergraduate level were confined to studying religion as a minor or elective topic. Nevertheless, between 1971 and 1991 over 2000 tertiary students completed at least one unit in religious education or religious studies at either postgraduate or undergraduate level at what would eventually become Edith Cowan University. A further several hundred took the opportunity to take a religious education unit at Murdoch University. A survey in 1992 revealed that 210 of these teachers would currently have been willing to teach a religious studies programme in government schools if they were given the opportunity.[18]

By 1986 training for volunteer teachers of SRI by the Education Department, as outlined in Recommendation 12 of the Nott Report, had still not been provided, despite the fact that by 1983 there were 1949 persons registered and 40 per cent of primary schools now received SRI, an increase of 26 per cent since 1977. A submission by Claremont Teachers College of an appropriate training course in religious education was accepted both by the heads of churches and the Education Department. From 1986 all volunteer religious instructors who were not trained teachers would have to complete two semester-long units, one on basic teaching method, lesson planning and classroom management, the other on creative teaching in religious education through the dramatic arts. In 1995 there were 1220 registered instructors working in 263 schools. A total of 2293 completed the training over the nine years.[19] Thus there were two bodies of educators available for the two strands of religion programmes in the government schools of Western Australia.

Who studies *Beliefs and Values*?

Over a period of twenty years religious studies programmes for government schools have been attempted. The Years 11 and 12 courses have survived, reworked in a variety of formats: integrated; modular; objective-based; and finally, outcome-based. While this syllabus continues to wait in the wings to be chosen as an elective by government school students, there are signs that it is being taken up more widely in the non-government schools. The contribution of the Catholic Education Office to the latest revision through representation on the SEA reflects their intention to promote *Beliefs and Values* as an appropriate accredited course to round off ten years of Catholic education. The consequent overall increase in the number of schools teaching the course should increase awareness of the course in school and the community. From 1992 to 1996 the number of schools teaching *Beliefs and Values* has gone from two to eight non-government schools (Anglican, Catholic and Islamic in addition to the Jewish and Seventh-Day Adventist schools). The number of students enrolled has gone from 171 to 1036. While this is heartening, the question still has to be posed as to why it has been so extraordinarily hard to establish the programme in the government school system.

In the primary schools the religious studies integrated model was replaced by a thematic model, but this lapsed. On the other hand, the specialist religious education programme in the primary schools, SRI, has grown from strength to strength both in the metropolitan area of Perth and throughout the state. What explains the startling contrast between the success of one programme and the demise of the other? A pool of enthusiastic teachers was available for each programme. Both the programmes had the same trio of infrastructure, that is, of academics, the religious community and the education authorities. In addition the secondary syllabus *Beliefs and Values* had been accredited by the Secondary Education Authority. Which factors can be suggested as being particularly significant? Relationships, networks and a commitment to the topic are the strongest contenders.

The universities supplied the training, the Education Department monitored registration, but it was the CCE's structure that was the greatest strength. The CCE had generated a model of District Councils, where an ecumenical local group of clergy and church representatives took responsibility for their local high school and feeder primary schools through the provision and support of volunteer instructors and the employment of chaplains. A District Council would be set up only at the instigation of that district, the CCE providing some expertise and general monitoring.

In addition to its excellent community network to support the major task it valued, the CCE developed very positive relationships with the two universities, which took religious education seriously, and with the Education Department. It was the CCE who took the initiative at various low points in the whole area of religious education, rallying the other agencies, for example in lobbying for the setting up of the Nott Committee, the production of *Beliefs and Values*, the appointment and support of the senior education officer, the training of volunteer instructors, and representation on many committees.

But the programme has needed more support from the Education Department, particularly in policy. The Catholic Education Office's policy that every teacher must be equipped with at least a core of content and curriculum in religious education resulted in the provision to trainee teachers by Edith Cowan University for twenty years of agreed courses for Catholic schools. At the same time, along with Murdoch University, the option to become equipped in general religious education was also available. The Education Department's decision not to accord religious studies the status of a major teaching area has been a disincentive either for students to take the units or for any faculty of education to invest resources in training teachers for religious education. So while hundreds of Catholic students over the years enrolled in specialist courses few others enrolled in the general courses, after the first euphoria of the Nott Report. Government schools have welcomed SRI, and secondary government schools have eagerly sought chaplains, suggesting their concern to cater at least in some part for the spiritual dimension of their students.

The way forward

Beliefs and Values is available for students in Years 11 and 12 who wish to take advantage of it. This requires the motivation and commitment of educators and parents to recognise its worth and to encourage schools to offer the courses and pupils to enrol. In the meantime there is still the avenue of the extent to which a religious and values dimension can be present throughout the general curriculum of the major learning areas. Analysis of the draft curriculum revealed both a very attenuated version of beliefs and a minimum allocation of values in the outcome statements. Using Smart's dimensions as a framework, an analysis of the religious content of the Student Outcome Statements in the learning area Studies of Society and Environment found that 63 of the 144 outcomes in the statements could pertain to religion.[20] The Religious Studies Sub-committee continues to pursue the possibilities of developing resources to encourage this. Likewise, identification of a dearth of reference to values in the Student Outcome Statements of the proposed national curriculum led to a National Professional Development Project instigated by the non-government schools, which drew up an Agreed Minimum Values Framework, Values Outcome Statements and a Values Review Project.

The most significant feature throughout has surely been the forging of a strong network of interested individuals in each of the major agencies concerned with education, whose values have led them to work together to initiate projects, develop resources, provide training and chair committees. In these ways innovations have taken place, policies have changed, resistance has been overcome and resources have been allocated. Hopefully, the momentum gathered by the current promotion of *Beliefs and Values*, of Value Outcome Statements and of Religious Outcome Statements will augur well for the students of the government schools of Western Australia.[21] As this account was completed, the headline on the front page of Western Australia's leading newspaper blazoned 'Teach Students Ethics: Governor', noting:

> lessons on Christian and other religious values should become part of the School curriculum in a bid to tackle crime and youth suicide, WA Governor Major General Michael Jeffrey said yesterday. (*West Australian* 9 January 1997)

The reader response generated in letters to the editor was swift and voluminous, expressing every opinion for and against the Governor's claim and his suggestion that schools should explore the way religious traditions have tackled the major questions of life. Perhaps the time is now ripe for *Beliefs and Values* to find its niche in WA government schools.

Notes

1 *West Australian*, Saturday, 12 June 1993.

2 The majority of independent schools are Catholic, then Anglican, Uniting Church, parent-controlled Christian schools, Seventh-Day Adventist, Jewish and Islamic.

3 From 1975, the centralised state education moved from being a Department of Education to becoming a Ministry of Education under a Labour government, then back to a Department under a Liberal government. Throughout the chapter, for ease the term Education Department will be used.

4 For a critique, see Moore and Habel (1982, pp. 39–41).

5 The controversy continued for many years. Slee (1986) gives an excellent overview.

6 The Gutekunst Report was presented to the Minister, but not released to the public. In 1977 Ian Mavor, who had worked with Michael Grimmitt, headed a Queensland RE project based on Grimmitt's model.

7 For a full account of each and the associated curriculum development, see Rossiter (1981), where it is possible to trace the major theorists and their appearance in most of the state reports.

8 For a fuller account, see Dixon (1991, 1992).

9 The draft social science syllabus was presented to the Religious Studies Primary Working Party and the integration of the religious dimension was worked out in detail, written into the appropriate slots, but never reappeared.

10 The Beazley Report, being the report of the Committee of Inquiry into Education in Western Australia, under the chairmanship of Mr Kim Beazley, March 1984.

11 The syllabus continued to he made available to university students, who were bemused at the loss of such a rich resource to the schools.

12 Position statement of the Education Department on *Religious Studies and Religious Awareness*, November 1985.

13 This decision was supported not only by the Advisory Committee, but also the heads of churches and the Churches' Commission on Education.

14 Noted in list of concerns to be raised with the heads of churches by the Religious Studies Sub-committee, circulated at the meeting of 21 October 1988.

15 Notes of Religious Studies Sub-committee, 5 July 1989.

16 Record of meeting of SEA Religious Studies/Beliefs and Values Syllabus Committee, 31 January 1994.

17 In addition, students intending to seek employment in the Catholic system could attend units offered by Catholic educators on campus and available to everyone through an arrangement with the Catholic Institute for Adult and Tertiary Education.

18 For a full account of the follow-up, see Dixon (1993).

19 For further details on the quality of the programmes,

see the follow-up of students' performance in Dixon (1990).

20   See Witham (1996).

21   Professor Brian Hill, Murdoch University, has made a continuous and pioneering contribution throughout as a major author of the Nott Report, chair of the Personal and Vocational Education Curriculum Advisory Committee, member of the Religious Studies Sub-committee of the CCE, major contributor to *Beliefs and Values*, provider of religious education units, and major consultant to the Values Review Project. Associate Professor Cynthia Dixon was a member of the Primary Working Party of the Nott Report, a member of the Advisory Committee to the Minister, the initiator and author of the programme for volunteer instructors, a member of the Religious Education Sub-committee, a consultant to the Values Review Project and currently chair of the Religious Studies and Beliefs and Values Syllabus Committee of the Secondary Education Authority. Mrs Margaret Williams was the Executive Director of CCE who initiated District Councils, chaplaincy, and *Beliefs and Values*. The Reverend Dr Peter Wellock, from executive director of CCE, became the first curriculum officer, generating the school-based programme and the curriculum materials.

References

Beazley, K. (Chairman) (1984) *Report of the Committee of Inquiry into Education in Western Australia*. Perth, Western Australia: Government Printers.

Cheshire Education Committee (1977) *Journeys into Religion: Agreed Syllabus*. Chester: Cheshire Education Committee.

Churches' Commission on Education (CCE) (1985) *Beliefs and Values: The Human Search for Meaning*. Perth, Western Australia: CCE.

City of Birmingham Education Committee (1975) *Living Together: A Teacher's Handbook of Suggestions for Religious Education*. Birmingham: Education Committee.

Dixon, C. (1990) *Adult Learning: A Tertiary Programme in Christian Education for Volunteer Instructors*, Technical Report no. 21. Perth: Western Australian College of Advanced Education.

Dixon, C. (1991) The saga of religious education in Western Australia. Part I: A cautionary tale. *Journal of Christian Education* Papers 101, June, 15–27.

Dixon, C. (1992) The saga of religious education in Western Australia. Part II: An encouraging tale. *Journal of Christian Education* 35(2), 27–39.

Dixon, C. (1993) Is there an appetite for religious education in Western Australia? *Religious Education Journal of Australia* 9(2), 13–16.

Eckersley, R. (1993) Facing the Future. *West Australian* 9 January.

Education Department of South Australia (1977) *Religious Education Syllabus K-12*. Adelaide: Government Printer.

Education Department of South Australia (1980) *Me and My World. Teacher's Guide Years R-3*. Adelaide: Government Printer.

Education Department of South Australia (1980) *Exploring a Wider World. Teacher's Guide Years 4–6*. Adelaide: Government Printer.

Education Department of Western Australia (1980) *Religious Studies Pilot Project: Guidelines for Teachers*. Perth: Education Department, Curriculum Branch.

Education Department of Western Australia (1980) *Primary Work Programmes: Draft*, Perth: Education Department, Curriculum Branch.

Education Department of Western Australia (1980) *Secondary Work Programmes: Draft* (Revised 1981). Perth: Education Department, Curriculum Department.

Goldman, R. (1964) *Religious Thinking from Childhood to Adolescence*. London: Routledge & Kegan Paul.

Goldman, R. (1965) *Readiness for Religion*. London: Routledge & Kegan Paul.

Grimmitt, M. (1973) *What Can I do in R.E.?*. Great Wakering, Essex: Mayhew-McCrimmon. (2nd edn 1978).

Hirst, P. (1974) *Knowledge and the Curriculum*. London: Routledge & Kegan Paul.

Hirst, P. and Peters, R.S. (1970) *The Logic of Education*. London: Routledge & Kegan Paul.

Mavor, I. (ed.) (1977) *Religious Education. Its Aim and Nature*, Queensland Religious Education Curriculum Project, Brisbane: Government Printers.

Moore, B. and Habel, N. (1982). *When Religion Goes to School*. Adelaide: SACAE Press.

Mordini, T. (1991) *Religious Studies Report to the AGM of the Churches' Commission on Education*, Perth, Western Australia: Churches' Commission on Education.

Newbigin, L. (1977) Teaching religion in a secular plural society. *Learning for Living* 17(2), 82–6.

Nott Committee (1977) *Religious Education in the Government Schools of Western Australia*. Perth, Western Australia: Government Printer.

Overton Committee (1971) *Religious Education in State Schools*. Hobart, Tasmania: Government Printers.

Peters, R.S. (ed.) (1967) *The Concept of Education*. London: Routledge & Kegan Paul.

Phenix, P. (1964) *Realms of Meaning*. New York: McGraw Hill.

Rossiter, G. (ed.) (1981) *Religious Education in Australian Schools*. Canberra: Canberra Curriculum Centre.

Russell Committee (1974) *Religious Education in State Schools*. Melbourne: Government Printers.

Schools Council (1971) *Religious Education in Secondary Schools*, Schools Council Working Paper 36, London: Evans/Methuen.

Schools Council (1972) *Religious Education in Primary Schools*, Schools Council Working Paper 44, London: Evans/Methuen.

Schools Council (1977) *Discovering an Approach: Religious Education in Primary Schools.* London: Macmillan.

Secondary Education Authority (SEA) (1997) *Syllabus Manual, Year 11 and Year 12 Accredited Courses.* Vol. 6: *Personal Development Studies.* Perth, Western Australia: SEA.

Slee, N. (1986) 'Goldman yet again', *British Journal of Religious Education* **8**(2), 84–93.

Smart, N. (1968) *Secular Education and the Logic of Religion.* London: Faber & Faber.

Smart, N. (1969) *The Religious Experience of Mankind.* Glasgow: Collins.

Smart, N. (1974) *The Science of Religion and the Sociology of Knowledge.* Princeton, NJ: Princeton University Press.

Smart, N. (1975) What is religion? In N. Smart and D. Horder (eds), *New Movements in Religious Education.* London: Temple Smith.

Steinle Committee (1973) *Religious Education in State Schools.* Adelaide: Government Printer.

Witham, T. (1996) *Studies of Religion and Student Outcome Statements from the SOSE Learning Area*, Interim Report for the Religious Studies Sub-committee. Perth, Western Australia: Churches' Commission on Education.

Index